KANSAS POPULISM
ideas and men

KANSAS POPULISM

ideas and men

by O. Gene Clanton

THE UNIVERSITY PRESS OF KANSAS
Lawrence and London

for $\left\{\begin{array}{l} \text{\textit{Donald R. McCoy, who contributed}} \\ \text{\textit{invaluable direction and inspiration}} \\ \\ \text{\textit{Jane Ann, Spencer, and Kimberly}} \\ \text{\textit{who have made it all worthwhile}} \end{array}\right.$

PREFACE

Three decades ago there was a remarkable degree of interpretive unanimity concerning the Populist movement. Since then, especially in the last twenty years, this consensus has been shattered by a series of conflicting interpretations. Most of these revisionist studies have been critical, and some serious charges have been levied against Populism. C. Vann Woodward, an adherent of the earlier and more sympathetic view of Populism, has stated that if these charges were summed up "the Populists would be held partly responsible for Anglophobia, Negrophobia, isolationism, imperialism, jingoism, paranoidal conspiracy-hunting, anti-Constitutionalism, anti-intellectualism, and the assault upon the right of privacy."[1] This by no means exhausts the list of charges in the full indictment of Populism, nor does it reflect the depth of disagreement among historians of the movement or among the dilettantes.

Populism's first interpreters found that the Turner frontier thesis provided a rationale that explained its origin and ideology, while at the same time according it a place, rather begrudgingly, within the context of progressive political action.[2] Another, more recent, group of historians, discounting the validity of the Turner thesis, have sought to interpret the movement as an episode in the enduring tradition of American entrepreneurial radicalism. This newer rationale has emphasized the conflict inherent in a rapidly commercializing agrarian society that had allegedly retained many of the values and ideals of a preindustrial age. To these scholars, the Populists were striving for a utopia that existed in the past; hence, Populism was portrayed as retrogressive-utopianism.[3] But this removal of Populism from the ranks of progressivism has not gone unchallenged. Studies have appeared reasserting the case, in even stronger language, for Populism as a progressive response to industrial America.[4] There is, then, considerable conflict in interpretation, making the Populist movement a major problem in American historiography.

This controversy has awakened a lively interest in the Populist movement; and, since much of the revisionist work has been predicated upon research from the general to the particular, a need has arisen for studies dealing with the movement in its local setting. In addition, work by George E. Mowry, Alfred D. Chandler, Otis L. Graham, Jr., and other students of progressive leadership has served to point up the need for similar studies of the Populist leadership—especially since there now is considerable disagreement about the relationship between the two movements.[5]

Kansas was probably the center of Midwestern Populism. It therefore provides an excellent opportunity for exploring some of the questions that have been raised. Taking advantage of that opportunity, the author has attempted to research and to write a study of the Kansas Populist leadership, and to place that leadership within its proper historical context—in other words, to write a history of Kansas Populism as well as a leadership study. Actually, the two are inseparable; but they could not successfully be managed that way. The leadership analysis demanded and received separate treatment. Also, the findings of that study revealed that a significant segment of that leadership had been active reformers for some time before the Populist party was organized. The Gilded Age was their background, just as it was the background of the Populist movement, and the need for an appraisal of that controversial age became all too obvious. Briefly, then, it was this situation that dictated the particular approach employed in the following pages.

The author would also like to acknowledge a special debt in advance to two men who preceded him with path-finding works on the subject of Kansas Populism—Raymond Miller and Walter T. K. Nugent.[6] Although these two University of Chicago scholars are in no way responsible for what follows, this study was fashioned on the foundation they constructed. In particular, the author would like to state that he has not made a calculated effort to reassess the economic origins of Kansas Populism, which Miller has done in his unpublished dissertation; nor has he made a special effort to deal with the charges of anti-Semitism and nativism, which Nugent has done in his *Tolerant Populists*. Suffice it to say, Miller's work has been an invaluable aid, and the material encountered substantiated Nugent's findings precisely. Finally, the author would like to acknowledge a more indirect debt to Richard Hofstadter and Norman Pollack, who have reopened this whole subject and touched off a discussion that will culminate in a more meaningful understanding of Populism.

O. G. C.

ACKNOWLEDGMENTS

To an extraordinary degree, I am indebted to
Donald R. McCoy, who, at an earlier stage, directed this
study through to final completion as a doctoral dissertation at the University of Kansas. I doubt that any student
could have had a more patient and inspiring teacher than
it was my good fortune to have had in Professor McCoy.
Whatever merit the study may have owes much to his
skillful direction; its faults are purely my own. For certain, it would have been a better work had I been more
capable and diligent in applying his advice.

I am indebted to many other people as well. In
particular, I would like to express my gratitude to George
L. Anderson, John G. Clark, J. Eldon Fields, George M.
Beckmann, Oswald P. Backus, and Clifford S. Griffin,
University of Kansas professors, all of whom, in various
ways, contributed to the making of this book.

Others gave willingly of their time and patience
while I threshed out many of the problems encountered
along the way. It was the suggestion of a friend, Robert
F. LaForte, that gave birth to the idea of the study; to
him I am deeply indebted. David R. Woodward of Texas
A&M University, my friend and colleague, graciously

gave me the benefit of his reading of an earlier draft. Stuart Kaufman, also of Texas A&M University, read one critical chapter, and he and Robert Calvert of North Texas State University, at different stages of the writing, both allowed me to share their special historical insights. I alone, however, bear full responsibility for any flaws the book may contain.

I would also like to express my gratitude for the able assistance provided by the archivists and librarians at the University of Kansas and at the Kansas State Historical Society. I am especially thankful for the help provided by Portia Allbert, Elsie Beine, Robert Richmond, Nyle Miller, and Forrest R. Blackburn of the Historical Society. All illustrations are by courtesy of the Kansas State Historical Society, Topeka.

Finally, I would like to thank Texas A&M University and Pamela Rowe. The first named for providing financial assistance toward meeting the expense of typing the manuscript; the last named for typing the manuscript, not once but twice.   *O. Gene Clanton*
Washington State University
Pullman, Washington

CONTENTS

ILLUSTRATIONS

"NOTHING SUCCEEDS LIKE SUCCESS":
Kansas Populism's Gilded-Age Background

As the last decade of the nineteenth century opened, vast numbers of Kansans would probably have been amused to learn that they were participants in an era later to be called the "Gay Nineties." Gaiety was in short supply. But whatever else it promised to be, the new decade gave every indication of being anything but dull. Kansas was in great ferment. Disenchanted farmers and townspeople were organizing for political action throughout the state. Undeniably, the masses were agitated in an unprecedented manner. The battle cry was reform; reform, they insisted, in the interest of the working classes of farm and factory. By June, 1890, this ferment in Kansas had produced a new political organization called the People's party (soon to be known more popularly as the Populist party), which would challenge the Kansas governmental establishment as it had never been challenged before.

Naturally, individuals who were fiercely attached to this establishment were alarmed by the ominous signs of impending storm. Some, of course, launched a bitter counterattack, utilizing the formidable antireform rationale of the Gilded Age. On May 14, 1890, the Topeka *Advocate,* then emerging as the leading journalistic voice of Kansas Populism, published a letter of one of those individuals. Using the pseudonym Justicus, the correspondent minced no words in appraising the reform movement and American society. "Hayseed and manual labor," the writer averred, "has been compelled to step down and out to make room for those who by birth and education and wealth are fitted to guide this nation onward and upward. This inexorable law of the survival of the fittest is fully exemplified in the position occupied to-day by the various classes; it is a natural result, and all your labor organizations and gas cannot alter it." The writer went on to assert that the laboring man's problems were not caused by any injustice on the part of "the ruling class," but were "directly traceable to the socialists and many reformers whom no condition could satisfy, but are ever seeking to stir up the common people, who otherwise would be content in the comfortable position they now occupy." Turning to the demands of the new movement, the writer then stated: "The mad projects now talked of by these self-styled reformers would be enough to drive a Plato mad with envy; government ownership of railroads; government warehouses, for the farmers to stow away their crop of pumpkins; government loaning money to the laboring men; now that is rich. . . . these things will never be." The real punch line of the letter was: "Because you have not the brains to get rich, you raise a hue and cry that those who are rich made it at your expense, when it was the natural result of their energy and superiority."[1]

The question "If you're so damn smart, why aren't you rich?" had a special meaning for Americans who lived through that exciting and dynamic period in American history labeled the Gilded Age. The adjectives *exciting* and *dynamic* may seem inappropriate to those who recall Vernon L. Parrington's portrayal of that era of American history. To Parrington, the period between the Civil War and the Spanish-American War was openly and crassly materialistic, a colossal national feast labeled "the Great Barbecue." "With no social conscience, no concern for civilization, no heed for the future of democracy it talked so much about," he wrote, "the Gilded Age threw itself into the business of money-getting."[2] The end result was a period representing an interregnum of waste, corruption, and inefficiency.[3]

Although interpretations of the Gilded Age are still quite polarized, its analysts more and more have recognized it for what it was, an extremely complex and critical transition period in the development of American society. True, all periods in history are transitional, but the Gilded Age was influenced profoundly by an entirely unique factor—the emergence of industrial capitalism.

Most Americans interested in reviewing the period between

the inauguration of Andrew Jackson in 1829 and that of Ruther-
ford Hayes in 1877 have focused their primary attention upon the
issues relevant to the coming of the Civil War and its aftermath—
as did the participants in the drama. In doing so they have failed
to note fully the extent to which some rather fundamental social
values were being altered. One of the most significant of these
involved the role of government relative to the economic order.
The politico-economic system being challenged was that known
rather ambiguously as laissez faire.

In the United States, laissez-faire thought began to take
root in the wake of the Revolution, if not earlier, but it was not
until the age of Jackson that it became a pervasive force. After
having said this, though, it must also be emphasized, as Arthur W.
Thompson has written, that during the Jacksonian era "advocates
of economic individualism were far less concerned with *laissez
faire* than with attacking existing monopolies, real or imagined, in
their pursuit of a freer and more genuinely competitive brand of
enterprise." For some of those Jacksonian enthusiasts who joined
in the assault on "state-chartered monopolies" the objective was
the achievement of "particular economic goals." For others, the
struggle against monopolies "was part of a broader onslaught
against special privilege—corporate or otherwise—and directed toward the goal of creating a democratic society in which all individuals would be equal in the exercise of rights."[4] With a great
assist from this diverse influence, therefore, the period between
Andrew Jackson's inauguration and the Civil War provided fertile ground for two potent forces—democracy and industrialism.
In this period, however, as Thompson noted, "many small, struggling Jacksonian entrepreneurs developed into relatively large and
powerful industrial capitalists." Ironically enough, within a decade or so after the Civil War "they had contributed also to the
appearance of corporate monopoly and restricted competition, the
very evils against which they had fought." But that was not all,
for it was not just "the Jacksonian persuasion against economic
privilege" that was "undermined," "new and cynical political
spoilsmen also appeared to challenge the successful operation of
popular government."[5]

Unwittingly, the real revolutionaries at work within American society were the captains of industry who fashioned the new corporate structure, and not "the socialists and many reformers" as Justicus believed. The large corporation was the culprit. There simply was no place for this gigantic form of enterprise within the old system of American values. The institutions and values prevalent in the United States were founded upon the social and political ideal of the free individual. Essentially an inheritance from the late eighteenth century, the free individual was by birthright entitled to the natural rights of "life, liberty, and property." In a state of nature the free individual was responsible only to the law of nature or nature's God. When the individual became a member of society he did not surrender his natural rights but merely consented to certain restrictions upon his freedom for the good of society. The ideology was of course predicated upon a static conception of the cosmos that took for granted, as historian John Tipple has phrased it, the "constancy of nature in moral as well as physical operations, and the universal efficacy of its laws."[6] It was to such a conception of the cosmos that Adam Smith had attached his natural economic laws. But unlike the British setting where the growth of industrialism proceeded in advance of democratic ideas, in America the ideas of free competition and equal opportunity held a revered place within the ideology.

Within a closed system of this sort the large industrial corporation was indeed incongruous, since it was neither an individual nor accounted among the phenomena of nature. Obviously, the corporate body enjoyed considerable advantages over the individual. Relatively free of mortal limitations, the corporation was capable of growing to irresistible size and power upon "the accumulated lifetimes and earnings of many individuals." Even worse, it was generally considered to be devoid of natural reason and consequently not inherently responsive to the governance of nature. Ideologically, then, the modern corporation was, as Tipple has stated, "an outlaw to the society which spawned it."[7]

At least as early as the age of Jackson there were Americans who were ready to revamp the old ideology to accord a place to the newly emerging corporate structure.[8] Their task was formidable, since changes in the structure of social ideas seem to wait on general changes in economic and political life.[9] But then, although the old system of values provided no ready place for the large corporation, it became increasingly obvious that prevailing ideology provided no great obstacle to the consolidation of economic triumphs.[10] To many it became obvious that the ideology could in fact be put to good use in its defense. The Civil War and an English philosopher, in their own individual ways, were to make this course quite popular.

Whether the Civil War actually accelerated industrial development in terms of production figures, it did enhance, in the long run, the social and political atmosphere in which it operated, making it much easier for American entrepreneurs to apply the nation's vast resources to the best advantage to produce revolutionary results.[11] Charles Francis Adams, for one, noted the great change that had come over America when he returned from his diplomatic post in England following the Civil War. The "most noticeable" change, he pointed out in his well-known article for the *North American Review,* was "perhaps to be found in a greatly enlarged grasp of enterprise and increased facility of combination." The many-sided experiences of the war, he was sure, taught "lessons not likely to be lost on men quick to receive and to apply all new ideas."[12]

Industrial leaders were indeed "quick to receive and to apply" new ideas, but as Thomas C. Cochran and William Miller have demonstrated: "Neither secession nor Civil War had called businessmen to national leadership; both events only marked their ascension. When the southern states seceded from the Union they left with the conviction that the reign of agrarianism was over. That conviction proved correct." As is now apparent, "Businessmen had developed their plants, refined their techniques in the fifties. In 1860, aided by northwestern farmers, they had captured political power. By 1865, they had strengthened their control beyond agrarian recall."[13]

By means of political alliances, mainly but not entirely within the Republican party, industrial businessmen fortified their position. With the removal of a South unsympathetic to northern economic interests they occupied the place of "a pampered only child"; and congress, spurred on by the necessities of war, showered them with unprecedented gifts in land, protective tariffs, and favorable banking laws. Then with northern economic supremacy assured by the outcome of the Civil War in 1865, that position was fortified further by the process of radical Republican Reconstruction. Corporation lawyers persuaded the supreme court to define a corporation as a person within the meaning of the Fourteenth Amendment, thus affording the corporation the protection of the prevailing ideology of the free individual and vastly reducing the regulatory power of the states and subsequently the national government.[14]

General Ulysses S. Grant's two terms in the presidency from 1869 to 1877, backed as he was by the leaders of the emerging industrial order, served to secure politically the cause of northern business interests. Business strategy was indeed eminently successful in this period, although the effort was mainly a holding action that was aimed at retaining benefits that were secured almost fortuitously during the Civil War and Reconstruction, or to blocking legislation it did not desire.[15]

The background of the settlement of the disputed presidential election of 1876, moreover, seemed to demonstrate that southern political leaders had learned the lesson of industrial power and were ready to defend Yankee economic interests with as much alacrity as the northerner himself.[16] Within the confines of this apparent paradise, private profits were sacrosanct. In 1870 the inheritance tax had terminated. Two years later, the income tax expired. Corporate or excess profits taxes were nonexistent, and by 1890 most of the revenue of the national government came from import taxes and excises on liquor and tobacco, the burden of which fell heavily on the nation's consumers. Amid such favorable conditions, industrial capital practically doubled itself every decade.[17] Needless to say, private fortunes of colossal proportions were amassed, and the chasm separating the rich and the poor opened immensely and threateningly.

That American society between 1860 and 1900 assisted so well in the rise of industrialism, however, was hardly the result of a monumental conspiracy. This state of affairs was created by a special set of historical circumstances. The post-Civil War generation was afflicted with a kind of myopia left over from all the bitterness generated by years of sectional conflict and four years of bloody warfare, and the issues of Reconstruction intensified the condition. The Republican party emerged from the war with vast moral assets that it was quick to exploit. The party could present itself as the savior of the Union, while portraying Democrats as traitors to the flag. This fixation on war issues tended to push aside discussion of other critical issues of the period.

It should be noted, moreover, that the last twenty-five years of the nineteenth century was not a period of Republican supremacy. Nationally, the two great parties fought each other to a standstill. It was an era of stalemate and equilibrium in party politics characterized by a bitter fight for control of the government. In the presidential contests from 1876 to 1892 the Republican party failed in each to win a majority of the popular vote, even though the party did win three of the five contests. This struggle was also reflected in congress. From 1877 to 1897 the Republicans controlled the presidency and congress concurrently only four years, from 1881-83 and again from 1889-91. The Democrats, on the other hand, commanded both only two years, 1893-95.[18]

The unique circumstances created by the emergence of industrial capitalism were in themselves a problem of no small dimensions for both their apologists and their critics. As Vincent P. De Santis has observed, "The men who served in the presidency and congress in the post-Reconstruction years knew little, if anything, about the major problem of their time—the adjustment of American politics to the great economic and social changes that came to the United States with the rise of industrial capitalism and urbanism." Measured by today's standards of politico-economic relationships, wrote De Santis, "the Republican leaders of the Gilded Age were conservatives. They believed governmental interference with economic natural laws impeded progress; thus government regulation should be limited to the barest minimum." From their point of view, however, and from the point of view of many of their contemporaries, "they were not conservatives. They were not committed to lessening federal power. They did not oppose spending public money for special interests, as their support of national subsidy programs shows, especially the protective tariff."[19]

Business was dominant in this age of enterprise, but the values of the captain of industry, if not the values of the vast majority of Americans, were at least not significantly at variance with those values. The concept of the free individual lent itself well during the Gilded Age to a reformulation of the Gospel of Wealth. Andrew Carnegie's 1889 article in the *North American Review* provided the title, but, as Ralph Henry Gabriel has written, "he merely formulated a philosophy as universal in the United States as smoke in Pittsburgh."[20] "It was an elaboration of the doctrine of the free individual of the American democratic faith," wrote Gabriel, "and was a result of the discovery that this tenet had important utilities in the new industrial capitalism."[21] Having both a religious and a secular base, the Gospel of Wealth reduced to its most simple formulation was a popular faith in material success, one that equated wealth and morality. It contained within it the idea that the American economy should be controlled by a natural aristocracy brought to the top through the competitive struggle of the marketplace; the idea that the state should confine itself strictly to the role of protecting property (which had divine sanction within the gospel) and maintaining order; that poverty was a natural result of inferior abilities, or sin, or both; and that the rich were obligated to do good with the riches they accumulated.[22]

In *noblesse oblige* fashion, the Gospel of Wealth recognized the social obligations of riches, but it vied with another point of view that was devoid of altruistic pretensions. Adherents of this latter viewpoint represented what Thorstein Veblen later designated as the "hawk influence of pecuniary competition," and Ralph H. Gabriel has called their faith the "gospel of grab and hold."[23] However they are called, the adherents of both viewpoints were quite receptive to ideas that strengthened their position—especially as the conflict between rampant economic individualism and expanding political democracy became more obvious.[24] For those who were committed intellectually to laissez-faire individualism and to those who espoused an ambiguous form of laissez faire (no governmental intervention in the economy except to aid their particular interests), Herbert Spencer's special use of Charles Darwin's evolutionary hypotheses provided a splendid new rationale that appeared to harmonize magnificently with prevailing thought.

The captains of industry were indeed fortunate to have begun their great work at a time when Charles Darwin had shocked a quasi-religious age with his *Origin of Species* (1859) and Herbert Spencer had begun to popularize his rendition of the social counterpart to the biological processes in evolution (late 1860s). It may well be, as Edward C. Kirkland has written, that the Spencerian rationale did "no more for the business community than to furnish a new terminology for old ideas," for the record demonstrates that industrial leaders were eminently pragmatic and always ready to exploit the main chance without reference to ideals.[25] However that may be, Spencer's thought was, for the business community, rationalization not philosophy, and its adoption, as such, was clearly within the scope of the pragmatic business mind. Darwinism not only undermined the fixed conception of the cosmos upon which the doctrine of the free individual rested, thereby further reducing its effectiveness as a weapon for democracy, but Spencer provided a rationale that facilitated the appropriation of much of the doctrine itself to be used in defense of the shiny new order.

Later labeled social Darwinism, Herbert Spencer's synthesis presented a many-faceted picture of society, embracing the whole of man's past, present, and future history. He contended that history demonstrated evolutionary progress towards perfection, but that this progress took place only under conditions that allowed the economic struggle for existence and the survival of the fittest to work itself out within a system of unrestrained free enterprise. The "fit" had to be left utterly free to overcome the "unfit." The massing of wealth or the attainment of power and success demonstrated "fitness," while disease, poverty, and failure to improve one's status in society were evidence of "unfitness." It followed

that governmental efforts to ameliorate the condition of the weak
and to defend the poor against the rich, the unsuccessful against
the successful, were a violation of "scientific law" and detrimental
to progress. Men were born unequal, and any effort to equalize
them by governmental action was contrary to the laws of nature.[26]

The Spencerian synthesis rapidly won converts and spokesmen in America—some who accepted it as philosophical explanation and others who recognized its utilitarian values. As a
rationale, it was tailor-made for the times. As Richard Hofstadter
has written, "It offered a comprehensive world-view, uniting
under one generalization everything in nature from protozoa to
politics. . . . Moreover it was not a technical creed for professionals.
Presented in language that tyros in philosophy could understand,
it made Spencer the metaphysician of the homemade intellectual,
and the prophet of the cracker-barrel agnostic."[27]

Significantly, England gave Spencer's ideas a rather unenthusiastic hearing. The Industrial Revolution had proceeded a
considerable distance in England by the 1860s. Her industrial
leaders had already enjoyed their halcyon days, and Englishmen
were beginning to deal seriously with the problems that followed
in its wake.[28] The United States, on the other hand, had just
entered the period of its most feverish industrial activity, and
Spencer enjoyed a fantastic vogue in the United States over the
last three decades of the nineteenth century.[29]

The ideas of Herbert Spencer did not go unopposed, of
course; criticism of social Darwinism was registered continually
throughout the period by many individuals. The critics, however,
were by no means as popular as Spencer, whose ideas filled a great
intellectual vacuum.[30] The alternative to social Darwinism, moreover, developed in just that manner—as an alternative. Henry
George, Lester Frank Ward, Richard T. Ely, Thorstein Veblen,
Edward A. Ross, Henry D. Lloyd, the adherents of the Social
Gospel, and numerous unsung reformers launched a veritable gale
of criticism against social Darwinism, which would in time, along
with the extended development of an urban-industrial society,
seriously weaken its hold on the American mind; but until the

end of the nineteenth century, if not longer, the Spencerian rationale carried the day.[31]

The popularization of social Darwinism blended with, strengthened, and added new dimensions to that indigenous American doctrine Carnegie had tagged with the label Gospel of Wealth. It especially operated to make political action less desirable. Politicians, it was argued, were after all not subject to rigorous natural selection and therefore could not be trusted to the same degree as the leaders of the business world. And, for those who sought to make the democratic process more effective, it became necessary to overcome the presumption that even the peaceful implementation of majority will was contrary to science, progress, and morality.

Within this social and political atmosphere industrial development in the United States proceeded with giant strides. Production statistics fail to reveal the whole meaning of the great changes occurring in industry, but they do provide some indication of their magnitude. The growth rate was most rapid in the ante-bellum period when the more fundamental alterations in production techniques and transportation facilities occurred. In the five decades before the Civil War the output of American industry increased tenfold in value, rising from about $200 million to almost $2 billion. The rate of growth slowed after the Civil War with maturation, but absolute growth continued on a grand scale. By 1899 the value of manufactured goods had risen to $13 billion. This development was quite impressive in comparison with the growth of other countries. On the eve of the Civil War the United States trailed the United Kingdom, France, and Germany in the value of manufactures; by 1894 she came close to equaling the value of manufactures in all three combined.[32]

The distribution of industrial resources throughout the nation was just as significant as the growth of industry nationally, for it was basic to the varied response to industrialism. The manufacturing center of the nation in the ante-bellum period was clearly in the Northeast. In 1860 the value of manufactured products of the New England and the Middle Atlantic states was double that of all the other states and territories combined. This geographic pattern altered little in the post-Civil War decades, even though the Midwest and the South spawned some important industries. As the nineteenth century closed, the Northeast still reigned as the manufacturing center, producing over half of the nation's manufactured goods. Three-fourths of American industry was confined to a relatively narrow manufacturing area north of the Ohio River and the Mason-Dixon line and east of the Mississippi River.[33]

One aspect of this industrial revolution was not confined to the Northeast. The phenomenal expansion of American railroads over the last half of the nineteenth century was a development that affected the lives of Americans throughout the nation. At the end of the Civil War 35,000 miles of track were in use. Then came the era of great expansion. By 1873 over 30,000 miles of new track had been opened; by 1893 the total had reached 150,000 miles; and by 1915 the figure had climbed to 250,000 miles.[34] Progress could be, and indeed was, measured in terms of the extension of railroad facilities. The rapid extension of railroads, itself partly a result of a social and political atmosphere ripe for speculative business enterprise, encouraged speculative ventures embracing the whole of American economic life. Undeniably, the development of railroad transportation assisted immensely in the alteration of American society, creating additional opportunities and improvements of incalculable value, but the nature of the modern railroad corporation and the manner in which it had risen to prominence assisted greatly in the creation of problems that increasingly disturbed American society as this dramatic enterprise consolidated its achievements over the latter half of the nineteenth century.[35]

Improved transportation facilities, especially as represented in the railroads, in conjunction with the growth of manufacture worked an equally significant change in American agriculture. Farming became increasingly mechanized and commercialized in the post-Civil War decades. Business agriculture, of course, existed long before the Civil War. Southern planters and truck farmers near large towns, among others, had engaged in agricultural pursuits for profit, even in the colonial period, but the extension of the railroad after the Civil War made possible a vast extension of business agriculture in the older settled regions and into the new western areas. Consequently, the trend away from local self-sufficiency to specialization and distant marketing intensified significantly.[36]

In commercializing his activities and specializing in cash crops, the farmer enhanced his standard of living; at the same time he heightened his dependence upon decisions and policies originating largely from urban centers remote from his base of operation. He increased his vulnerability to fluctuations in the market and became more susceptible to the capriciousness of the weather. With an abundance of land, moreover, especially in the West, the farmer was encouraged to practice extensive agricultural methods, which provided further inducement for the use of machinery. To buy machinery and the land for its use he generally found it necessary to go into debt. At the same time, the individual farmer's position within the evolving competitive structure—never very strong—was weakening significantly. He simply lacked the market power of those with whom he was forced to deal. The system he operated in lauded competition but denied the principle by practical action. In fact, the farmer remained one of the few real competitors in a business world that was becoming less and less competitive. Ironically, the farmer's reverence for the ideal of free competition and his commercialization even assisted in the triumph of industry over agriculture—especially in the early phase of industrialization.[37]

Machinery, science, and vast new markets, then, changed American agriculture from a relatively simple operation, demanding small capital investment and a modicum of knowledge, into a complex operation, requiring increasing amounts of capital, equipment, scientific information, and closer attention to markets. "The farmer now was irrevocably entwined in the complex industrial system," writes Samuel P. Hays. "Not as a Jack-of-all-trades, but only as a calculating, alert, and informed businessman, could he survive."[38]

The drive to create wealth, which was behind these revolutionary changes in industry and in agriculture, also pervaded political institutions. Politics and government were expected to assist in the creation of wealth, and government on all levels was more than generous in performing this task. Most spectacular, of course, was the assistance given to the nation's railroads. Beginning in 1850 the federal government initiated the granting of land to railroad corporations which by 1871 amounted to more than 170,000,000 acres—roughly equivalent to the area of Texas—of which some thirty-five million acres were later declared forfeit because the roads failed to fulfill the conditions of the grants. In 1862 the federal government also voted public assistance to agriculture in the Homestead Act and the Morrill Act. Public assistance to agriculture was significant and far-reaching in its effect, but railroad construction became the major investment opportunity and the nation's economy came to be intimately related to the growth and stability of railroad enterprise.[39]

It was truly an era of rapid economic advance, and this advance occurred in an atmosphere of speculation, waste, and disorder. Seemingly convinced that America's resources were inexhaustible, those who participated in the drive for wealth gave little thought to preserving those resources, or for that matter, little thought to the great changes in American society their actions were producing. As never before, property-holders became speculators, and the promoters had a field day, while unbounded confidence as to the future prompted enterprisers everywhere to pay generously those who promised to create an economic advance.[40]

In this atmosphere, it was not surprising that economic freebooters of both small and large caliber, on the national and local scene, were able to operate on a scale previously unmatched in American history. The exploits of Jim Fisk, Jay Gould, Daniel Drew, the swindles of Crédit Mobilier, the wars between powerful bands of railroad buccaneers, the exploitation of the defenseless immigrant laborer, and countless other infamous episodes were emulated throughout American society and form a part of that history that was the Gilded Age.

But what of the voice of reform in the Gilded Age? Until the formation of the Populist party in the 1890s—and not entirely even then—social and economic critics failed to constitute a solid phalanx of consistent opinion. Prior to Populism the voice of reform was by no means mute, however, even though it was frustrated, discordant, and ostracized. It could hardly have been any other way, given the complexity of the problem reformers were up against. The unique manifestations brought about by the revolutionary changes in agriculture and industry were just as perplexing to those who styled themselves reformers as they were for the rest of society. The idea of reform itself was up for grabs.

Reform, in its more general sense, can be considered as an assertion of a determination to make the actual society, as the reformer views it, conform to the ideal, wherein the ideal is accorded a positive ethical value. Obviously, reform to the reformer is an upward movement, an effort to realize the good society. To the extent that the individual has some meaningful conception of the good society and attempts to make it a reality that person is a reformer.

Traditionally, however, within American society the ideal of the reformer has drawn heavily upon the humanistic values of the democratic faith—equality, freedom, and equal opportunity being especially high on the list. This trilogy of democratic concepts was firmly rooted in preindustrial, late eighteenth- and early nineteenth-century American society. Representing the aspirations, principally, of the American middle class of the period, the ideals of equality, freedom, and equal opportunity were closely associated with the idea of laissez-faire individualism. The methods of the reformer were of course conditioned by his belief in laissez faire. He might consider joining like-minded individuals in formal association to accomplish a particular end, but few considered government seriously as an agency through which reform could be or should be achieved in the ante-bellum period. As Arthur Bestor has written, "Individualism is commonly thought of today as a conservative doctrine. In the late eighteenth century, however, it figured rather as an attack upon than a defense of the established order in government, economics, and even religion."[41]

The reformist implications of individualism were still influential in the first half of the nineteenth century when a rather uneasy adjustment was made between the ideals of equality, freedom, and equal opportunity and an industrial system just on the verge of a great expansion. Considering the extensive opportunities available in this formative period of industry, this adjustment was not illogical nor incompatible with the furtherance of those ideals, representing and enhancing as it did the aspirations of the middle class of the period. But as industry consolidated its achievements between 1850 and 1890 the accommodation of democratic ideals with the emerging industrial order became increasingly precarious. The advance in industry, in addition to remarkable economic achievements, created a new kind of urban society, which was plagued with problems for which there were no ready solutions. The growth of industry also meant an ever-growing laboring class largely denied by circumstances a share in the aspirations that made life more endurable for the middle class. Poverty as well as progress, both in unprecedented magnitude, were a part of the industrial advance.

It must also be emphasized that the negative side of industrial growth was not as readily seen as its positive side—in time sequence the former generally followed the latter. Industry was the coming thing and there was hope that the problems that came in its wake would remedy themselves. The predominant economic theory of the period promised just such an occurrence, and laissez-faire economics were further bolstered by the popularization of social Darwinism.

As Richard Hofstadter has noted, "Acceptance of the Spencerian philosophy brought with it a paralysis of the will to reform."[42] In addition to this great obstacle, the reformer (especially those reformers who were firmly rooted in the agrarian tradition) had to reckon with two serious handicaps: he first had to make an effective and rational appraisal of what was essentially a novel development; he then had to overcome an ingrained aversion to the use of government as an agency of reform, not only in others but within himself. The great power commanded by business enterprise in its modern form, unintentionally of course, made the exercise of governmental power essential for any effort to regulate that power. Many reformers in the 1870-1890 period failed to make a rational analysis of the problem and were unable to offer effective remedies. Their failure was understandable, given the set of historical circumstances operative at that point in time.

The use of national power to control industry in its modern form (an increasingly obvious step to the agrarian reformer in the case of the railroads) was an especially troublesome issue. Not only were reform elements divided and hesitant on the desirability of such a step, but institutionally no such apparatus existed that was capable of performing the task. There was, moreover, a good deal of antipathy built into the institutional structure of the national government (particularly as evidenced in the supreme court) that stood in the way of such a development.[43]

Constitutionally, the Civil War had signified a marked centralization of authority in the national government. The party championing national sovereignty and centralized authority was of course the Republican party, the Democratic party holding to its traditional states' rights position. National governmental power during the period of Republican dominance (1861-1876) was used most effectively to promote private enterprise, but the use of that power to regulate enterprise was not seriously considered. As a matter of fact it was consciously avoided. The Democratic party was by its own antipathy to the use of national power encouraged to resist efforts by Republicans to assist industry, but it was likewise unable to entertain the idea of giving the national government regulatory powers.[44] Reformers who were able to countenance the use of federal power to regulate industry were thus confronted with the fact that the party that had demonstrated the greatest facility for the use of national power was closely allied with the very interests they wished to regulate.

To complicate the task of the reformer even more, the real change-makers in the two decades before the Populist revolt were the leaders of the industrial advance. If one were to ascribe to a definition of reform as simply "the reshaping of society," then the captains of industry were the true reformers of the period. A good many people, laboring under the influence of social Darwinism and the Gospel of Wealth, believed that to be the case. The promise of the captain of industry was no "pie in the sky"; his ideal of an industrial America was rapidly being converted into reality.

Considerable time elapsed before a significant number of Americans became alarmed by that reality and began to view the leaders of industry simply as change-makers, for the Gilded Age was an age that could readily agree that "nothing succeeds like success."

The history of Kansas during the Gilded Age was more than just a pale reflection of the frenetic activities that affected the nation at large. In a sense, the state served as a stage upon which the rest of the nation acted out its antagonisms, hopes, and frustrations. Enactment of the Kansas-Nebraska Act had focused the sectional conflict on the territory, stimulating a movement of as determined and self-righteous a group of people to the area as existed in the nation. The resultant struggle that occurred there was never merely the product of opposing views on slavery. The conflict between the two great sections was of course never that simple, and the people, representing both North and South, who rushed to that frontier territory carried with them all the divergent views motivating those on both sides of the Mason-Dixon line. As it turned out, the entrance of Kansas into the Union as a Free State was as much a victory for railroad promoters, political speculators, and land sharks as it was a victory for Free-Soilers and antislaveryites.[45]

Destined to remain an agricultural area far into the future, Kansas was ushered onto the national stage in 1861 as a junior partner of the rapidly industrializing North in her war to save the Union from the machinations of a slave-holding, agrarian South. But if ambitions provide any guidelines Kansas was never just a junior partner. The struggle from 1854 to 1865 served to identify the state solidly with the Republican party, the Union cause, and the wave of the future—business enterprise.

The key to the growth of industry and commercial agriculture in Kansas was clearly the development of railroad transportation. Kansans in all walks of life recognized this, and practically everybody became, in one way or another, railroad promoters. The need being immense and the recognition of that need being all but universal, it was hardly surprising that railroad builders found fertile ground upon which to operate. Even before the territorial period had drawn to a close, fifty-four incorporation charters had been granted by the legislature.[46] Most of these early projects never got beyond the charter stage. The dream of making Kansas the commercial hub of the nation was deferred for a time as the great energies of the state and nation were absorbed by four years of Civil War. The year the war ended Kansans could boast of only seventy-one miles of single track. This was quickly remedied. Five years later they could speak of almost 1,234 miles of track; the next ten years saw this figure more than doubled to 3,104 miles. By 1890 Kansas was ranked second in the nation with 8,797 miles of track. The pace of railroad construction actually reached its height in the late eighties, and the twenty-year period following 1890 would result in only about a hundred added miles of track within the state, while in the same period the national expansion of railroads continued at an accelerated rate.[47]

The speed with which the Kansas prairies were bedecked with rails was matched by remarkable expansion in other ways. In 1860 the population of the state was just over 100,000; by 1870 it had surpassed the 360,000 mark; by 1880, over 990,000; and by 1890 the Kansas populace had increased to more than 1,420,000. As in the case of railroad expansion, a population plateau was reached in the late eighties, as the population of Kansas remained virtually stationary through the last decade of the century. The greatest increase came in the seventies when over 630,000 people were added to the census rolls. The period from 1870 to 1890 represented an impressive increase of more than 1,060,000. The overwhelming majority of these newcomers were natives of the states carved from the Northwest Territory, although Iowa and Missouri also contributed their share to this movement of humanity between 1860 and 1890.[48]

Most of these settlers were lured out to the Kansas plains to take advantage of her highly publicized resources. For the majority this meant agricultural pursuits.[49] Those who survived the periodic droughts and grasshopper plagues and who managed to make the necessary adjustment for farming the plains soon created an abundant agriculture in Kansas. Wheat and corn were the principal crops. In 1878 the State Board of Agriculture reported that Kansas had advanced from twenty-fourth to nearly first in the production of wheat and from twenty-fifth to fourth in the production of corn since 1866.[50] Other crops were grown with some success, and stock raising flourished on an excellently suited terrain; but these could not compete with corn and wheat as Kansas farmers rushed headlong into business agriculture.

As the westward-moving migrants spread out over the prairies, preceding or following the rapid extension of the railroads, and began to farm her virgin soils, they were also faced with the task of creating all the other accessories of organized society. Riding the wave of spirited optimism characteristic of the Gilded Age, these matters were dealt with in short order. By 1870 sixty-one counties were established in Kansas. The next eighteen years saw this number swell to 106. Towns sprang up all over the state. Municipal, township, and county governments were set in motion. In short, these pioneers, with the assistance of Eastern capital, converted a barren territory into a thriving state with such rapidity that many were awed by the accomplishment.[51]

Throughout the period of great expansion from 1870-1887 there were those who continually advised circumspection and who insisted that all was not right with the world, but the great majority of Kansans who surveyed the scene, particularly in the early 1880s, were convinced that the work was good. Politically, all this "good work" was credited to the Republican party. Nationally the party may not have been as dominant as it was once thought, but in Kansas the Republican party was supreme. Kansans voted just as they had shot in the Civil War. Party regularity was a matter of great pride throughout most of the period. In the nine state elections from 1862 through 1880, Republican gubernatorial candidates carried ninety percent of the counties. The year 1882 saw the election of the first and only Democratic governor until 1912. The anomaly of the 1882 election—largely a result of a serious split in Republican ranks—was redeemed in 1884, and the next three gubernatorial contests saw the party recapture its former supremacy. The three contests from 1884 through 1888 saw Republican gubernatorial candidates carry ninety-four percent of the counties.[52]

Although the era from 1862 to 1890 was a period of Republican party dominance in Kansas politics, it should be noted that it was also an era of steady decline in Republican strength generally. This was evident in the percentage of the vote cast for Republican presidential candidates in the state from 1864 to 1888. Beginning with just over seventy-eight percent of the popular vote in 1864, the party saw its strength diminished gradually to just over fifty-five percent in 1888.[53]

The margin of victory had decreased over the years, but it was still substantial. Throughout the period Kansans were led, through the mechanism of the Republican organization, by a group of men who were by residence, occupation, and background closely associated with business enterprise. Of the eleven elected governors between 1862 and 1893, all save one were Republicans. Most had served in the Union Army. All were residents of the eastern third of the state. Eight of the eleven actually came from residences no farther west than Lawrence or Garnett, both towns less than forty miles from the eastern boundary. Occupationally, six lawyers, two editors, one merchant, one physician, and one surveyor-farmer provided the nominal leadership for this young but ambitious agrarian state. In addition, every United States senator from 1861 to 1891 was a Republican. Eight men represented Kansas in the senate during the period; six of the eight were residents of Lawrence, Leavenworth, or Atchison. All were intimately associated with the Kansas business community.[54] It had been their task to promote the economic growth of the state, and by close attention to the construction of railroad transportation, more than anything else, they had assisted in the creation of an economic boom.

Numerous Kansans, and probably the Republican leadership to a man, recognized the importance of the railroad to their state and to the West in general. Unquestionably, settlement of the West was expedited by the rapid extension of the rails, but the acceleration process was not an unmixed blessing. Civilization carried forward in great haste led quite naturally to great waste, and, as this wave of settlement into an agricultural domain was spearheaded by the railroads (the earliest and more obvious representative of the modern corporation), the ingredients were there to produce a serious reappraisal of the course American society had taken since the inauguration of the age of enterprise. Edwin L. Godkin, the famous New York editor, noted contemporaneously that devotion to material pursuits became "absorbing in a country like the West, by the richness of the prizes which are offered to shrewd speculation and successful industry. Where possible or even probable gains are so great, the whole community gives itself up to the chase of them with an eagerness which is not democratic, but human."[55] By bringing out the worst in the system, then, as well as by bringing an older agrarian world and the new industrial world into sharp relief, the West could indeed become a crucible of contention and reexamination. This reappraisal could even assume the shape of a full-scale political revolt if the forward progress of the nation, or even a segment of the nation, were seriously checked.

As long as the prospect for advancement remained real or seemed realizable, however, momentary economic setbacks, challenges to democratic institutions, and even revelations of political corruption could be overlooked or minimized. If worst were to come to worst, moreover, there was always that useful social-Darwinian rationale to supply the badly needed touch of innocence to society's bold new course.

Kansas was served a rather large portion of the problems that afflicted the era. The hustling, bustling, scheming, frantic, heartbreaking, and hopeful years from 1870 to 1890 were years of great vitality, years that were characterized more by their dynamism than by their ethics. Most of the participants were just too busy to view closely what was taking place. As one student of the era so aptly put it, "Greedy manipulators, routine politicians, conscientious Kansas leaders, and possibly a statesman or two are all found there—but one searches a long time to locate any of the latter."[56]

The great speed with which local government was fashioned throughout the state was adequate tribute to the acceleration process, although not always complimentary. The difficulties inherent in rapid state-building, demonstrated with emphasis in the first sixteen years of Kansas' experience, were reemphasized in the eighteen years following 1870 in the central and western thirds of the state as her political borders were filled in with an additional forty-five counties. Every new county went through, to a greater or lesser degree, the usual building and growing pains associated with new communities struggling to create at least a semblance of organized society. Most were successful and managed to establish viable communities; some encountered extraordinary difficulties and began under serious handicaps.

Occasionally, eager promoters of local government, at times out-and-out swindlers, took advantage of Kansas settlement to line their pockets. Officials of Barber County issued over $200,000 in warrants and bonds for the construction of a courthouse, bridges, and a railroad that were never built. In 1873 six men from Topeka concocted a scheme and netted $72,000 by traveling to what was to become Comanche County, copying names from a Missouri city directory, holding a "special election," and voting a bond issue to that amount. The state legislature, ever alert not to "scare away capital," later upheld the bond issue as having been legally issued by a *de facto* government. The purchasers of the securities subsequently sued for payment, and the legally organized county of Comanche was held accountable for the debt.[57]

Fraudulent activity of this kind was by no means the rule, but it was repeated in various parts of the state and on various levels of government. There were those, too, who managed to reap handsome profits by staying within the letter of a system of laws that quite clearly lagged behind accumulating and unprecedented opportunities for money-making.

Problems of this sort were not restricted to the local scene, for the state administration, from the beginning, had trouble maintaining an unblemished reputation. To shape a state government against a background of civil strife, civil war, and reconstruction would have been difficult enough, but the men who guided Kansas politics in the early years did so amid fierce competition generated by the rich prizes to be had in connection with the distribution of lands and the location of railroads and state institutions. It was a time when politician-promoters were in great demand, and few influential souls indeed looked with disfavor upon those who used their position or wealth to enlarge their fortune or to influence a decision.[58]

The corrupt and ambitious intrigues of Senator James H. Lane and his rivalry with Kansas' first governor, Charles Robinson, attracted greatest attention in the early years. Rancorous intraparty struggles revolving around one political leader or another continued to plague the Republican party, and charges of malfeasance—many of which were politically inspired—were standard political fare as the warring factions competed for favors, position, or monetary rewards. They accomplished much, for themselves and for the state in the process; their actions also contributed to the creation of an image of corruption and political intrigue—real and imagined—which would subsequently provide substance to the wrath of a perturbed populace.

Certainly the record of men representing Kansas in the United States senate in the early period fell short of being illustrious. Senator Lane ended his stormy career in 1866 by committing suicide. After Senator Edmund G. Ross was denied reelection in 1871 (chiefly because of his vote for President Andrew Johnson's acquittal), he was replaced in the senate by Alexander Caldwell, who had spent $60,000 to obtain the seat. Senator Caldwell resigned following an investigation by the United States senate and the Kansas legislature. Shortly thereafter Samuel C. Pomeroy, United States senator from 1861 to 1873, with a long history of questionable deals behind him, was charged with bribery and denied a third term by the Kansas legislature.[59]

The Pomeroy episode earned for itself a place in Mark Twain's and Charles Dudley Warner's *The Gilded Age,* but there were other occurrences that attracted less attention. In 1872 the state auditor stole $4,550 in addition to registering bonds for three nonexistent cities. In 1874 the state treasurer resigned in the face of impeachment proceedings. In 1876 the holder of that office, one Samuel Lappin by name, took flight to South America, after a series of actions that saw him resigning, breaking jail, and hiding in Chicago, rather than confront charges involving the issuance of bogus school bonds in four Kansas counties.[60]

Who could become alarmed over such occurrences? or why

should one be alarmed? Kansas was booming and the future appeared unlimited. Throughout the 1870s and well into the 1880s Kansas settlement and economic expansion were carried forward on an ever-growing wave of optimism. After a brief slump in the early seventies, the price of wheat rose steadily, reaching its high point for the period in 1881-1882; and just as the price of wheat began a steady decline, not to be checked until well into the next decade, increasing prices for meat products created a greater demand for corn, taking up some of the slack temporarily.[61] The population of the state was increasing at a truly remarkable rate. Railroad lines had fanned out all over the state. The majority of Kansans could appreciate the crude poetry of the editor of the Pittsburg *Kansan* when he wrote:

> Come millionaires and scholars,
>   Bring your wisdom and your dollars,
> To Pittsburg, Crawford county, State of
>   Kansas, U. S. A.
>
> Bring your money bags and learning,
>   Your translucent, deep discerning,
> And when you plant your shinners, we
>   will label U. O. K.[62]

If all that glittered was not gold, who would or could dispel the illusion? The visible signs of a marked advance were irrefutable facts. That the advance had come at a high price, and was dependent largely upon factors beyond the control of the Kansas citizen, was scarcely considered. The important thing was that the myth of the Great American Desert had been laid to rest, and in its place had been raised the vision of limitless agricultural and industrial progress.[63] Kansas, as advertised by railroad agents, Eastern moneylenders, and Kansans in all walks of life, was the land of milk and honey.

Not all Kansans were so complacent. There were those of course who refused to acquiesce, individuals who were usually identified in contemporary literature as croakers, failures, demagogues, anarchists, or communists; or at times the label Democrat by itself was deemed sufficient to cover their alleged iniquities. The course and character of Kansas growth created a number of issues that readily lent themselves to exploitation by dissatisfied elements. Such issues as currency contraction, unequal distribution of the tax burden, political corruption, distribution of public lands to the railroads, and the insecurity of settlers on the public lands, not to mention the difficulties experienced by Kansas farmers resulting from the whims of nature, the rise and fall of the market, mounting surpluses, and their utter dependence on railroad transportation, and more, virtually assured the rise of parties seeking immediate relief.

Significant reform agitation in Kansas began with the 1872 election, when a faction of reform-minded Republicans joined with Democrats to present a Liberal-Republican slate. Defeat— measured simply in terms of offices won or lost—was the fate of the 1872 Liberal Republican-Democratic effort, as was the case of the national movement of which it was a part, but reform agitation continued without cessation and with similar results. Between 1872 and 1890 Kansas had a multiplicity of reform parties. The rise and fall of these organizations was adequate testimony to the complexity of the situation confronting those who actively sought political change in the period. The Independent Reform party followed the Liberal Republican-Democratic coalition and waged two campaigns before it went out of existence, challenging the Republicans in 1874 and both major parties in 1876. The Greenback party entered the contest in 1878 to battle the Democrats and the Republicans. In the three contests between 1880 and 1884, the Greenback-Labor party carried the reform banner. In 1886 the Prohibition party continued the agitation, and it was joined by the Union-Labor party in 1888. There were, in addition, a number of splinter groups active in several of the campaigns.[64]

With few exceptions, all post-Civil War reform proposals in Kansas politics were introduced by the third parties rather than the two major parties.[65] These reforms embraced a wide variety of changes involving economic, political, and social life.[66] In fact, practically all the demands of the 1890 Populist platform had been called for by earlier third-party movements.[67] Occasionally, one of these proposals found its way into the platforms of one major party or the other, and, even more rarely, an occasional demand was enacted into law.[68] Much of the reform legislation demanded by the third parties and by the two major parties, however, required support and action by the national government, and on that level the matter was even further beyond the control of Kansas parties.

Reform politics was not the great concern of the vast majority of Kansas citizens. Actually, the advocates of reform came as close to victory in the 1874 election as they would in any contest up to 1890. Even with the support of the Democratic party in that election, the Independent Reform party was able to muster only about forty percent of the vote for its gubernatorial candidate —more than thirteen thousand votes short of victory.[69] After 1874 farmers recovered from the relatively dismal years of the first half of the decade, and the state entered into a truly spectacular period of boom settlement; in the process, political dissent became an unpatriotic profession, as the majority of Kansans busily concerned themselves with other matters. It was this trend that pulled the rug from under the Greenback party.

Like their contemporaries throughout the nation, many Kansans gambled heavily on the future. The land, they assumed, was there to be conquered, and the earlier the conquest could be completed the better. Whatever assisted in accomplishing that end was adjudged wise and good and right; whatever stood in the way was considered an obstacle to progress. Railroads received the blessing from the beginning. Kansans beckoned and they came—at times it was the railroads that did the beckoning. The roads were financed largely by grants of aid from the nation and state, and from the county, township, and municipality through which they passed. The national government gave land grants in the state which at the average sale price of $3.50 an acre gave to the railroads well over $32,000,000. Between 1870 and 1890 municipalities contributed over $16,500,000, of which over $8,500,000 were given in 1887-88.[70] The state contributed 500,000 acres of its internal-improvement lands, and underwrote the payment of mortgage bonds of over $27,000,000. Altogether, assistance to the railroads came to about $85,000,000, or approximately $10,000 per mile, which should have satisfied a significant portion of the real costs of building the rickety roads on the Kansas prairie.[71] In total acreage, including about two million acres of Indian land, the railroads came into possession of over ten million acres of Kansas soil, or about one-fifth of the total acreage of the state.[72]

Railroad expansion proceeded simultaneously with municipal, township, and county improvements of all kinds. Bond issues came in excess. At the same time, the Kansas farmer made the necessary but expensive adjustment required for the mechanized and extensive agriculture of the plains. Debts were piled on top of debts with reckless abandon.[73]

In the 1880s the public debt of all Kansas governmental units rose from $15,000,000 to $41,000,000, which was the largest increase of any state, and with the exception of four slightly populated states in the far West, was the largest per capita public debt.[74]

Private indebtedness, especially among farmers, increased markedly at the height of the boom between 1883 and 1887. By 1890 over sixty percent of the taxable acres of the state were burdened with mortgage, a figure exceeded by no other state. According to Raymond Miller, "There was one mortgage for every two adults, which means more than one for every family; and the per capita private debt, counting adults alone, was over $347, about four times that of the Union as a whole. Mortgages on lands equalled more than one-fourth of the actual value of the real estate of Kansas."[75]

Before the boom collapsed in 1887-1888, land values soared to unbelievable heights. In some cases the increase amounted to as much as four hundred percent above the original purchase price.[76] The timing of the boom and collapse was such, moreover, that the distribution of gains and losses was clearly sectional within Kansas. The older settled counties of northeastern Kansas, in particular, and to a lesser degree the counties of eastern Kansas, generally, within a zone extending west approximately sixty miles, were in the enviable position.[77] Eastern Kansans not only arrived early enough to reap some of the profits of the great expansion, they were, by early arrival, better able to survive the collapse. The majority of farms in the area had been purchased prior to the advance in price, and the subsequent decline in values affected the owners, for the most part, only to the extent it affected their plans for resale. Existing mortgages on eastern Kansas farms, moreover, having been contracted at an earlier date, were, by 1890 at least, only small remainders of the original sum.[78] Once Kansas discontent was translated into political revolt, this area became the citadel of antireform politics.

It was in the middle counties of Kansas, from Marshall to Phillips in the north, and from Chautauqua to Comanche in the south, that the boom attained its most reckless proportions. Between 1881 and 1887 more than 220,000 people settled in the area, approximately 100,000 of these between 1885 and 1887. In this area mortgages were the rule. There were counties in 1890 with three-fourths of the farms encumbered, and practically all counties had more than sixty percent of their farms mortgaged. These settlers came as land values were rising and paid higher prices for their lands than had earlier settlers. In addition, municipal improvements and railroad projects tended to soak up whatever excess capital existed locally, and many of these newcomers were therefore forced to pay more dearly for the loans they obtained.[79] These middle counties, plus several extreme southeastern Kansas counties, provided the Populist party the bulk of its rank and file.

That portion of the state lying west of the one-hundredth meridian, roughly the western third of the state, felt the tragic impact of the collapse first. This, the more arid part of the state, was the least suitable for small-scale farming. Most of the inhabitants had just arrived on the eve of the boom's abrupt end. Many were forced immediately to vacate the land, leaving the section to those who resided there before the inflation, and to those few who were able to make the difficult adjustment. Such laconic phrases as "In God We Trusted, in Kansas We Busted" were common parting words as the discontented were swept away. With the important exception of seven counties in the extreme northwest corner, which were settled at about the same time as the middle counties, the Populist party subsequently drew little support from the area.[80]

This boom-and-bust cycle that affected extensive areas of the West as well as Kansas has too often been written off, almost entirely, as the product of the shortsightedness of the people who participated in the westward movement. Westerners and Kansans shared the same hopes and aspirations of Americans generally. By the same token they shared the same limitations. What happened in Kansas in the 1880s was not unrelated to the great industrial changes that came over the United States in the period. Newspapers, railroads, local bond-assisted projects, or even the unlimited wealth of Kansas enthusiasm could not have produced the boom unassisted. Eastern capital flowed to the state in a steady stream, providing the means whereby the inflation could be maintained. The picture is not completed either by emphasizing the revolutionary changes in an agrarian way-of-life. Indeed there were changes, and few farmers were able to comprehend fully the significance these changes held for them. As a result, their reaction to hard times was occasionally irrational. It must be emphasized that the circumstances were unique. The farmer's middle-class, city cousin in the West and in the East was likewise befuddled by the great changes accompanying the industrial advance.

Kansans, like Americans generally, had placed the leadership of their state into the hands of men who viewed government primarily as an instrument of material progress, men who were effective spokesmen of business enterprise but who were unable to guide and promote Kansas growth while at the same time checking abuses and offering constructive proposals to solve the unique problems confronting an agrarian state operating within a rapidly industrializing system. These men could no more escape a share in the responsibility for the course of Kansas development than could the mass of her citizens who acquiesced as long as the future appeared bright. For years the Kansan had been taught that Kansas was the land of beauty and unexcelled opportunities, and when his world came tumbling down upon him it was difficult to swallow the argument that his woes were the *sole* result of his own stupidity or the whims of nature.

The disillusioned were more inclined to remember they had paid too much heed to Civil War-inspired oratory. The "bloody shirt" all of a sudden seemed quite moot. They recalled they had not taken a very lively interest in politics, but they did remember the regularity with which they had cast a Republican ballot. They vaguely remembered too the more sensational revelations of political corruption within and without the state. Most had quite real reminders of the high rate of interest they were required to pay on the public and private debt they had contracted. They were reminded of the taxes they were required to pay also. The tax on land seemed somewhat out of proportion. All of a sudden they were convinced railroads were evading their share of the tax load.[81] This seemed less than fair, considering the generosity that had been shown the railroads by all governmental units. They remembered too that the railroads had been rather demanding in their rates. The state had finally created a Board of Railroad Commissioners in 1883 but they now saw this as a façade, for its powers were generally advisory. After all, the representatives of railroad interests occupied seats close to the power center of the state.[82]

All the fuss that had been made over the tariff suddenly appeared quite silly, if not misleading, to many farmers who were having a difficult time making ends meet. It became clear that they bought their goods in a protected market and sold their crops in an unprotected market. At the same time, the farmer became aware as never before that the very fact of his isolation made his bargaining position frightfully impotent, and although few were clear as to why, they were convinced something was radically wrong with the credit and money system of the nation. Somehow the system needed to be more flexible.[83]

Although it was by no means the only consideration, there can be little doubt that it was mainly economic discontent that provided the decisive stimulant that agitated Kansas citizens and spurred them on to the formation of a political party that would seriously challenge the normal pattern of Kansas politics. It was the disillusionment of shattered dreams that caused them to view society as they had never viewed it before. A good many of those, perhaps even a majority, who sang "Good-Bye, My Party, Good-Bye" between 1889 and 1890 as they gathered under the banner of the People's party, were committed to the reform cause in no greater depth than the mortgage that hung over their heads. Much of their criticism of the existing system was exaggerated and unfair and occasionally irrational—especially true considering they had shared in the responsibility for what had happened to them. In spite of all that, the reappraisal of American society made possible by that wave of discontent was no less meaningful and instructive.

The superficial commitment of much of the rank and file to the reform cause was to prove a real handicap to the fortunes of the Populist party; a brighter future could deplete the ranks almost as quickly as a dismal one could fill them. The realization that the actions of many of the rank and file were not founded upon a profound understanding of what was happening to their world, however, should come as a shock to no one. When or where has this not been the case of any large political movement? It has not been recognized to the extent that it should, on the other hand, that the leadership of the Populist party in Kansas was provided by a group of individuals the majority of whom had been committed to reform long before the Kansas boom collapsed. Their reasons for dissent were varied: most were progressive, some were retrogressive, and some were contradictory, but they were seldom superficial.

On the whole, Populism in Kansas, especially as revealed in the thought and actions of the individuals who led the movement, was a constructive response to the technological achievements that had revolutionized agriculture and industry over the course of the nineteenth century, a response which was called forth prematurely by agriculture's peculiar position in the 1880s and 1890s. It was premature in the sense that prevailing American thought was not ready to accord its spokesmen a fair hearing. Rising as they did on this wave of agrarian discontent, they were all stigmatized by the association. The brave new world of the future, revolutionized or not, was industrial, not agricultural.

A DISSIDENT DIALOGUE

Kansas society in the Gilded Age produced its share of critics. Beginning in the early 1870s, dissent was registered with increasing frequency and organization. Special attention affixes, however, to the period immediately preceding the formation of the People's party and to the criticisms of those individuals who were later influential in the Populist movement, either as active leaders or as spokesmen in some capacity. The explanation these individuals presented to account for what ailed society, and the measures they proposed for their solution, are important not only in revealing the quality of dissident appraisal, they also provided—leaving aside the question of their validity—the rationale for thousands of Kansans who joined the movement for third-party action in behalf of reform in 1890.

One subject with instant appeal to a segment of the Kansas populace was the proposal for relief from money and credit problems. The collapse of the Kansas boom after 1886 would intensify interest in that issue. In February, 1886, William D. Vincent, a thirty-four-year-old hardware merchant from Clay Center, Kansas, who had the ability to express himself in forceful terms, plus a lively interest in the issues of his time, proposed that the national government loan money directly to the people. Vincent's destiny had been linked with Kansas in 1862, when as a boy he made the journey west with his parents from their home state of Tennessee. The family had been drawn into reform politics at an early date, and young William D. Vincent came to play an active role in the Greenback-Labor party, serving as one of its presidential electors in 1884. He would later figure prominently in the organization of the People's party, and during the Populist decade of influence would serve on the state board of railroad commissioners and in the United States congress from 1897 to 1899.[1]

William Vincent made his loan proposal in a speech delivered before the Clay Center Debating Club. He began with the premise that "every man has a right to the product of his own labor." As he saw it, the rule that had been followed in the past and which was still being followed resulted in the situation whereby "the man who earns the most gets the least and he who earns the least gets the most." He then stated that this process "should be reversed." Probably anticipating the thoughts his proposals might raise in the minds of some of those in his audience, he then remarked: "it is not asked that there shall be a division of property. We would not have one dollar of Shylock's ill-gotten gains taken from him. We only ask that he be restrained from further robbery." He then stated, "Communism in any form is bad, but that particular form which takes from the few and gives to all is certainly no worse than that which takes from the many and gives to the few."

Vincent then informed his Clay Center audience that he was aware that "some men will grow rich faster than other men under a perfect system of law." The more industrious man, he conceded, should receive a larger share than his "indolent neighbor," but that was not the whole problem as he viewed it. "There is another class of men," said he, "who will always grow rich faster than their neighbors—the sharp unprincipled men." Then in language remarkably devoid of social-Darwinian conclusions, he added: "But because nature has given them the advantage of their fellows is no reason why laws should step in and give them still greater advantages. These are the strong men. They need no special legislation in their behalf. The object of law is supposed to be protection of the weak against the oppressions of the strong."

Vincent reasoned that the situation would be improved if the government were to make a limited amount of money available for loan to the people at a low rate of interest. He suggested three percent as a desirable rate, with one percent going to the county where the loan was made, one percent each to the state and national governments to cover the costs of handling the program. For those who were shocked by such heresy, he argued that the national government had already been in the loan business for a quarter of a century, during which time it had "loaned out to National bankers over $300,000,000 at one per cent a year."[2]

Undoubtedly, William Vincent's Clay Center speech would have been attacked bitterly had it been circulated freely. It would subsequently seem less heretical to Kansans who were in desperate search of an answer to their money problems, and the Populist state committee would distribute the speech as campaign material. In 1886 the situation was quite different. Kansas papers were filled with much talk of "anarchists," "bomb-throwers," and "communists." The nation was afflicted with a rash of labor strikes and violence. In April Kansas experienced some violence of its own during a strike of railroad workers against the Missouri Pacific. Railroad property was destroyed at several points in the state, and a few people were killed. At the height of the turmoil, a regiment of the Kansas national guard was sent to Parsons in southeastern Kansas to restore order.[3] Then on May 4 the Chicago Haymarket Square violence made the issue of anarchism headline news. Radical causes and the champions of radical causes were clearly suspect. In September, 1886, Republican Governor John A. Martin, normally quite moderate in his rhetoric, referred to the leaders of the Greenback-Labor party as "those noisy, turbulent, and vicious demagogues and loafers who muster under the flag of the anarchist and communist."[4]

The aging editor of the Junction City *Tribune* remained undaunted in the face of the foreboding menace of anarchism. The editor in fact used the occasion to point out what he regarded as an even greater danger to society. The editor was John Davis. Reared in Illinois, where he was born in 1826, Davis had settled in Kansas in 1872. His interest in political and economic questions dated back at least to 1850. He became in that year one of the principal actors in a movement that culminated twelve years later in the passage of the Morrill Act by the United States congress. The provision for grants of land for the endowment of state colleges that would devote attention to the agricultural and mechanical arts along with the usual curriculum, made possible by that act, he regarded as the most noteworthy endeavor with which he had been associated. He had been a Republican before settling in

Kansas, but once on Kansas soil he became active in opposition to the party, which he lamented no longer bore any resemblance to the party of Lincoln.[5]

In 1873 John Davis presided over the first farmers' state convention held in Kansas and he wrote the message of the convention urging farmers to organize to promote their interests. Davis nevertheless had no great illusions about the farmer. As early as 1873 he stressed, "Farmers are just as good as, but no better than, other people. And their interests are no more to be respected than any other necessary and important interest, except that they are larger, and hence more important." Majority interests, he felt, were vitally affected and threatened by the character of state and national development. He was convinced in 1873 that the "wise and timely regulation of the whole management of railroads by the general government" was imperative for sound national growth.[6]

Always in the forefront of reform activities, Davis had presided over the convention that organized the Independent Reform party in Kansas in 1874. He helped organize the Greenback party and ran as its nominee for congress on two occasions. After 1887 he would devote his efforts to the work of the Union Labor party, and then join in the effort to organize the Populist party in Kansas. As a Populist he would serve two terms in the congress.[7]

John Davis' article on anarchy, reprinted by William A. Peffer's widely circulated *Kansas Farmer* out of Topeka in February, 1887, argued that "the more dangerous forms of anarchy come from above, from the lawless corporations, who, considering themselves above law, steal the people's lands and the people's means of travel, transportation and communication." These same corporations, he said, "usurp the control of finances, suborn the law-makers and courts, and then with their stolen prerogatives to tax, oppress and defy all men and all communities within their reach."[8]

The year 1887, apparently because of the collapse of the boom, signaled the beginning of an interesting dialogue among a wide segment of the Kansas populace concerning the formidable problems of their time, which was far more constructive than has been heretofore recognized. Peffer's *Kansas Farmer* made itself available to all shades of opinion. In March, 1887, one unidentified correspondent noted that the great changes produced in society by the creation of "labor-saving machinery" was nothing short of miraculous. "Seventy years ago," he wrote, "each community contained the nucleus of an independent empire; there was the hatter, the tailor, and more independent than any sort, the farmer, who raised his own food and manufactured most of his own clothing." At that time "there was no barrier to free exchange, for producer and consumer lived in the same community. To-day, nearly all of the above mentioned trades are concentrated in a few great factories, employing thousands of men and representing millions of capital. And between the producer and consumer is the railway, upon which both are equally dependent . . . ." He went on to write that "no one" would deny the beneficial results of machinery for mankind, especially the railroads, but "this vast accumulation of wealth and irresponsible power over the commerce of the country has produced evils which are destroying republican equality and personal independence of character."[9]

In April the *Farmer* published another unsigned letter containing the lament of what may be seen as an early progressive-type. The writer first expressed his disillusionment with the hope that all of the "labor-saving machines" that had been introduced would produce more leisure time and more of the "necessaries" and "many of the luxuries" for the masses. In his mind "the great problem of the day is to stop the evils and extend the blessings before the wronged classes rise in their strength and overturn the good with the bad . . . ." He advised that the "present age has some great questions to settle; every day we read of strikes, riots or some kind of bomb-throwing or conspiracy, and if the capable class does not interest themselves in the solution of this question the other class will be sure to do something, and it may be as bad as some of the bloody revolutions of history."[10]

The editor of the *Kansas Farmer* was by no means as appalled by existing evils as were many of his correspondents. In 1887 William Alfred Peffer was fifty-seven years old. He had had quite a varied and eventful life to that point. Born in Pennsylvania, he received his elementary education in the Pennsylvania schools. For a few years he farmed in the summers and taught school in the winters. He was, almost by birthright, a confirmed antislaveryite and a protemperance man. After his marriage, he left his home state to seek his fortune in the West. In 1853 he settled in Indiana where he engaged in farming. After four years he moved his family again, this time to Missouri. As the sectional conflict became heated, Peffer found that he would either have to suppress his antislavery sentiments or leave the state to avoid conflict with his neighbors; he left. This time he removed to Illinois, and there enlisted in an Illinois regiment to fight in the Civil War. During his enlistment he studied law in his spare hours, and when the war ended he began the practice of law in Clarksville, Tennessee. While in Tennessee he participated in a minor way in the reconstruction of that southern state.[11]

Early in 1870 Peffer made his move to Kansas, opening his law practice in the little farming community of Fredonia in southeastern Kansas. It was there he became interested in journalism and purchased the Fredonia *Journal*. He continued his law practice in conjunction with his editorial work, and as always took a keen interest in the political questions of his day. In 1874 he was elected to the state senate as a Republican, the party that had received his loyalty from its inception.[12]

In 1876 William Peffer was on the move again, this time to Coffeyville, Kansas, where he published and edited the Coffeyville *Journal* and practiced law until he left to take over the editorship of the *Kansas Farmer* in Topeka in 1881.[13]

Not long after becoming editor of the *Farmer*, Peffer wrote and published a novel in its columns entitled "Geraldine or What May Happen." In this novel Peffer obviously drew upon his own background experiences of the middle seventies as an editor, lawyer, and state senator in the rural community of Fredonia in Wilson County amidst the grave agricultural distress of those years. He saw those difficulties basically as the natural process of ebb and flow in the cycle of prosperity. He noted that lands had been mortgaged at "unconscionable rates of usury," that "extravagance and fraud" in early county governments had been common, that taxes on property ran as high as "eight and ten" percent, that towns had been built way out of proportion to the surrounding countryside in development, but he discounted this simply by stating that "when men are moving with the floodtide they do not calculate upon the ebb." More significant was his view of the reformer. "Mr. Nimbletongue" was the name he applied to the character who represented the reformer. To Peffer, the proposals of Mr. Nimbletongue signified one thing—repudiation of debts.[14] Elsewhere in his novel he ridiculed the idea that farmers should elect only farmers to represent them. "It is open to the objection," he wrote, "that if a farmer is a mean man he is as mean as anybody else." He added that some of the same men who had opposed "Mr. Lycurgus [the main political figure of the novel which may be read Mr. Peffer] on the ground of his vocation had been caught with rocks in the hay and sand in the wheat they had hauled to market . . . ."[15]

By 1887 William Peffer's position had altered little. He obviously was trying hard to steer an independent course as editor of the most important agricultural newspaper in the state. His middle position was apparent on various issues.[16] After 1887 he would gradually become more outspoken in behalf of reform; but he sincerely desired to see the demands of Kansas farmers met within the two old parties, and he would not abandon that hope until April, 1890.[17] He would then exert his full efforts in behalf of the Populist party, which would reward him in 1891 by electing him to the United States senate.

William Peffer's Topeka of the 1880s was also the Topeka of one Gaspar C. Clemens. Peffer and Clemens both added considerable color to the Topeka scene—Peffer because of a well-groomed, unusually long, and absolutely unrivaled beard that distinguished an otherwise bland appearance; Clemens because of a strong resemblance to Samuel L. Clemens. He had the keen, piercing eyes, heavy mustache, the strong, rugged features, and, in later years, the wavy, white hair that distinguished Mark Twain. It was believed by many in Topeka that he was a cousin of the famous writer. Clemens apparently made no great effort to kill the rumor, but there was in fact no close family relationship.[18]

G. C. Clemens, as he liked to be called, was in many respects an extraordinary character in his own right. His life began in Xenia, Ohio, in 1849. Quite independent from early youth, he had been compelled to earn his living for a time by working in a brick-manufacturing plant. He acquired at the same time a common-school education by studying at night, and as soon as he was qualified he taught in a rural school near his home. While teaching he studied law and was admitted to practice before the supreme court of Ohio in 1869, and subsequently before the United States supreme court.[19]

In 1870 this tall, erect, distinguished young lawyer, with heavy dark hair and mustache, decided to launch his career in Topeka. The capital was by no means short on lawyers but Clemens was determined to establish himself there. He worked hard and long, improved his mind by reading practically everything he could get his hands on, and by 1880 he had developed a reputation and a modest practice. He had the gift of expressing his thoughts in a clear, concise, and lucid manner. Other lawyers turned to him for help in preparing their cases. He became an outstanding trial lawyer and expert in keeping a record for the supreme court of the state, and his knowledge and skill in constitutional law was recognized by the legal profession.[20]

As a man, Clemens was generous, kind, and unassuming; once engaged in a cause to which he was committed, however, he could be as severe in his criticisms and as unrelenting in his attack as any man could be. He developed a reputation in Topeka as a champion of the poor and oppressed. He would represent any person—often without fee—whom he believed falsely accused or deprived of personal rights. His sympathy for the underprivileged led him quite naturally, it seems, into the public discussion of the critical issues of his time. By 1885 he was active as a lecturer in Topeka, and on occasion he could be heard in outdoor gatherings espousing the unpopular cause of the laboring man.[21] In 1886 and afterward he scandalized many of his complacent fellow-townsmen by his outspoken defense of the Haymarket anarchists, an endeavor that marked him in the minds of many thereafter as an anarchist himself. In politics, he associated with the Anti-Monopoly party in the mid-eighties.[22] When the Populist party was formed he became active in its behalf and served as legal advisor to Governor Lorenzo D. Lewelling and as reporter of the state supreme court under Populist domination. After 1897 Clemens, more than anyone else in Kansas, was responsible for organizing the Socialist party in the state; he ran as its candidate for governor in 1900.

In 1887, however, Clemens was still searching for an answer that would satisfy him in meeting society's problems. In that year he published a pamphlet entitled *The Labor Problem, Stated for the Busy and the Tired*. In it he offered no solution but merely attempted to delineate the problem and evaluate solutions previously suggested. His scope was comprehensive, including urban and rural, local and state, national and international perspectives. Clemens was especially disturbed by the magnitude of poverty amidst increasing abundance. He wrote: "In the midst of the utmost plenty of everything to make comfortable, luxurious and happy living possible to every human being in the [world] community, only a few live in comfort, fewer still have homes and the great majority live constantly in a state of poverty similar to what would be made possible by partial famine!"[23] This great abundance, he reasoned, had been made possible by the development of labor-saving machinery. He asked: "Can it be supposed that a limited few of the human race can, with safety to themselves, lock up all nature's stores and pile up human food to rot while a starving world looks on ... ?"[24] Obviously, Clemens thought not.

How, then, was the "labor problem" to be resolved? Leaving aside the answer to that question, Clemens then offered the following commentary on current remedies:

> the leading political solutions proposed are proved to be utterly futile by prominent and existing facts. Free trade has been urged, but England has long had free trade and yet "the cry of out-cast London," has been heard all over the world. A single monetary standard, bi-metallism, unlimited coinage of silver, a paper currency—all these things have been confidently suggested; yet labor troubles are equally bad in America; in England; in France, in Hol-

land, in Belgium, in Germany and in Italy; and these countries represent the actual operation of every phase of the money question. Taxes upon incomes alone, and upon land alone, are solutions with many advocates; yet in the various countries afflicted with labor troubles every species of taxation may be found in actual operation.[25]

The Clemens response, shared by a number of other significant Populist leaders, eventually would be a modified form of socialism. Clemens' 1887 discussion of the labor problem, moreover, would be included among the People's party campaign materials.

Down in the southeastern corner of the state mounting protest served as a catalyst, prompting Percy Daniels to terminate a twenty-eight-year affiliation with the Republican party. Born in Woonsocket, Rhode Island, in 1840, Daniels obtained his education in his native state, where he studied for a career in civil engineering. That career was interrupted in its civil aspects when he became a member of a Rhode Island contingent in the Civil War. His war record was impressive. Beginning with the Army of the Potomac, Daniels participated in several of its major battles and then was transferred to the southwest in time to take part in the campaigns of Burnside and Sherman. Early in 1864 he rejoined the Army of the Potomac and shared in its campaigns until the war's end. From Sergeant to Colonel, from Fredericksburg to Vicksburg to the Wilderness Campaign, Percy Daniels could justly claim to have shared in the making of the nation's Civil War history.[26]

After the war, Daniels joined the westward movement. He and his young wife settled on a farm a few miles to the northwest of Girard, Kansas, in 1867. On the eve of the political revolt of 1890 Daniels had maintained a continual residence on that farm except for a three-year period between 1878 and 1881, when he had returned to Rhode Island to work as a civil engineer. In Kansas he farmed and worked as a surveyor for his county and for the railroads. He also maintained his connection with the military and rose to the rank of Brigadier General in the Kansas Militia. Later, 1893-1894, he would hold the rank of Major General commanding the Kansas National Guard.[27] During the same period, he served as lieutenant governor as a Populist.

It was during the summer of 1888 that Percy Daniels began to reappraise his Republicanism rather critically. The local Republican organization was considering him for nomination to the state senate. On learning of this, Daniels announced through the press that he considered the prospect of election to the senate a great honor but he wanted the party to know that he could not accept the nomination unless it approved of the following proposition indorsed by himself: "THE TIME HAS COME WHEN EVERY INSTINCT OF CHARITY, JUSTICE AND PATRIOTISM DEMANDS THAT THE POWER OF CAPITAL FOR WRONG AND OPPRESSION BE CURTAILED . . . ."[28] Percy Daniels was not nominated.

Not long after nailing his protest to the party door, Daniels initiated a lively and revealing exchange of letters with John J. Ingalls, Kansas' senior Republican senator. Daniels advised Ingalls, "The public is rapidly coming up to the point of asserting that positive legislation must interfere." Daniels then emphasized, "Assertions of these wrongs in resolution, nor idle and perfunctory discussion in legislative bodies, will long suffice to satisfy this growing conviction."[29]

Senator Ingalls replied on August 7, 1888, with the following:

> I belong to the school of politicians who think that government should interfere as little as possible in the affairs of its citizens. I have no sympathy with the paternal idea, but believe that the best results are attained when the people are left to settle the great questions of society by individual effort. All that legislation can do is to give men an equal chance in the race of life. We cannot make poor men rich, or rich men poor, except by making the natural capacities of all men exactly alike. The difficulties in society arise from the fact that Providence has established unequal conditions, making some men wise and others foolish; some men provident and others thriftless; some men industrious and energetic and others idle and self indulgent.[30]

Obviously somewhat perturbed with what he considered a rather glib response, Daniels replied on August 12 by writing:

> I cannot see that the distribution of wealth is very closely allied to our individual capacities.
>
> There are men in Kansas that are barely making a living raising grain, who are as able and *unscrupulous* as any of the Wall Street financiers, or the men who divided a quarter of a billion in the various Pacific Railroad deals. Opportunity is the larger factor in most of these transactions—lack of integrity taking second place, and capacity third. You say every man should have the same chance. Will the government ever give *any one* again the same opportunity it gave those men? . . .
>
> Again: Your reasoning followed to a conclusion would make wealth dependent on capacity. Take the Senators and write down their names in the order of their Dollars. Would you concede that the man whose name headed the list, is the ablest Senator, and the second next to him? If so, Kansas would complain at being represented by one so near the foot of the list as our acting Vice President [Ingalls was then president *pro tempore* of the Senate].[31]

Percy Daniels was at that point firmly committed to reform. He began speaking and writing to promote a number of measures he thought would have an ameliorative effect, including, among other things, the Australian ballot and immigration restriction, but, for Daniels, the *sine qua non* of reform was his proposal for a graduated tax on property. All his proposals were designed, as he admitted, to reinforce "the middle classes from the two extremes."[32] In a speech delivered before the Grange of Girard in 1889 he stated, "As a nation we are rapidly growing in wealth and power, but unless this increase in wealth is distributed with some little relation to our industry and efforts our growth is not a healthy one." "Over 90 per cent. of our annual increase in wealth," he emphasized, goes ". . . into the pockets of less than 5 per cent. of our people . . . ."[33] It was to correct this situation that Daniels proposed a tax which as first formulated would require one percent on estates above one million dollars, increasing to eighteen percent on estates above one million dollars. The revenue from the tax, according to the Daniels plan, would be used first to take care of the claims of war veterans and then for the employment of "all idle American labor on extensive internal improvements in every state, in building and improving country roads and waterways, and in constructing and maintaining storage reservoirs and forest parks . . . ."[34]

Obviously, Daniels' proposals involved an expansion of governmental roles, a decided break with the idea of the negative state. That was the import, ultimately, of the whole reform agitation, and undoubtedly its most lasting influence. But positive intervention for what purpose? That was the rub. To restore an older competitive order, or to bring about some kind of collectivist society?—or, to complicate the problem even more, were there not positions somewhere between the two extremes? Beginning in 1889, these issues came to the forefront of the discussion, bringing to the surface problems that have in fact plagued American reform movements ever since.

The November 22, 1889, edition of *The Advocate,* then published in Meriden, Kansas, but soon to be moved to Topeka to claim the journalistic leadership of the Kansas Populist movement, opened the discussion that would reveal this important ideological conflict in reform thought. The paper carried the address of John F. Willits, occasioned by his election as president of the Jefferson County Farmers' Alliance earlier that month. The theme of Willits' address was the virtues of cooperation in American society. It was a theme he had long supported. Willits was a fifty-six-year-old native of Indiana who had settled in Kansas in 1864. Almost entirely self-educated, Willits had been a farmer since settling in Kansas. He had been a Republican, too, until 1873. It was during his second term in the Kansas house of representatives that he left the G.O.P. to join the reform movement. Greenbacker, Union Laborite, Granger (he was state lecturer from 1877 to 1882), and prominent worker in the Co-operative Association, these were Willits' credentials before 1889; in 1890 he would receive the gubernatorial nomination of the People's party in its first unsuccessful contest.[35]

Willits told his farmer audience in November, 1889, that the country was experiencing "a mighty social revolution." Organized and practical cooperation, he said, was the "shibboleth of every successful business enterprise that marks the progress of this enlightened age." Speaking for his fellow Alliance members, Willits emphasized that cooperation "means to us more than any other word in the English language." The message was clear: farmers needed to emulate the methods of business organization to succeed, sanctioning, if need be, the same kind of combinations among farmers as they confronted among business interests.[36]

The same issue of *The Advocate* carrying Willits' address contained a letter from William V. Marshall of Santa Fe, Kansas, extolling the virtues of competition. Marshall was a logical anti-monopolist who claimed Pennsylvania as his native state. He was forty-three years old in 1889 and had resided in Kansas since 1874, and before he left the state early in the 1890s he did considerable writing to champion his antimonopoly views.[37] His position was simple: abolish monopolies "so that competition will become the regulator of prices instead of erring law-makers whose duty it becomes in case we try to regulate the monopolies . . . ."[38] As for the cooperative movement among farmers, Marshall later wrote that

> farmers will make a mistake if they attempt to form combinations among themselves, in imitation of the present monopolists, for the purpose of limiting the supply or controlling the prices of their products. Why? Because, in the first place, they are not in a position to succeed, and in the second place, if they did succeed what would become of the mechanics, laborers and others who could not combine? Somebody must be the victim of the combinations. No [,] sir; let us come out and say: "Natural laws are good enough for us. Competition will do. The provision which God has created cannot be improved upon; neither can it be violated without injury to ourselves . . . ; consequently we will suppress that instrument of artificialism and oppression, the combine, and restore to its full function and force the natural law of competition."[39]

To restore competition, as he desired to have it, Marshall became the sponsor of a graduated tax to be applied to trusts, a proposal which he set forth in two pamphlets that were later circulated as Populist campaign material.[40]

William Marshall's letters extolling competition did not go unchallenged. On March 20, 1890, *The Advocate* published a letter from H. H. Hutcheson (otherwise unidentified) which was a direct response to Marshall. Hutcheson asked if competition ever allowed sales at "natural prices" if it could avoid it? "We claim that it does not," he wrote. Hutcheson then offered this commentary: "Yes, 'Natural laws are good enough for us' but is competition any part of Natural law? It may be the law of 'the survival of the fitest' [*sic*]; that is if the most cruel, avaricious, cunning and dishonest are the fitest [*sic*]." Industrial leaders, said Hutcheson, had recognized the futility of competition and had, "like sensible men, quit it."

> No [concluded Hutcheson]; competition is not good enough for me; it is a relic of barbarism and we will never be civilized till we get rid of it; it is every man against his brother. A scramble to get on top regardless of who is tramped to death in the struggle, a system that sets a premium on "oneryness," makes millionaires and paupers, takes the child from school, and the mother from the cradle of her sick babe, and puts them in the factory at competition wages and sends the husband away a "tramp," an "incompetent," one of the "dangerous class."[41]

Hutcheson's substitute for a society supposedly guided by the law of competition was what he called a "grand co-operative commonwealth."

How far Hutcheson was willing to go to apply the principle of the grand cooperative commonwealth was not revealed. There were those in that atmosphere of mounting discontent who were willing to carry the principle to logical conclusions.[42] More palatable to most dissidents, however, was the proposition of James D. Holden. Holden was vice-president and treasurer of the Emporia Investment Company by occupation.[43] In a work entitled *Free Freight and Government Railways,* Holden demonstrated a willingness to use collectivist methods to strengthen the competitive system. In this work, which would also become familiar as Populist campaign literature, Holden argued that "indispensable public agencies should not be 'owned' nor controlled by private corporations or individuals . . . ." He professed to be a bit perplexed, however, why the "truth" of that proposition was so slow to take "root in the minds of men." To his mind, it was "a fact so apparent that it ought not to require elucidation," for "a nation of people cannot be generally prosperous among whom it is *legal* for a few to exercise absolute control over interests or agencies that are essential to the welfare of all . . . ."[44] Holden was convinced that "No effectual *regulation* of railroads is possible—or proper—under private ownership. *They are public in character, and should be owned and operated in the public interest.*"[45]

The course of Kansas development had indeed produced some serious reflection as the 1880s came to a close. The bubble of exhilarating optimism had been punctured, giving way to widespread public malaise. The times were out of joint—at least that was the opinion of future Populist Congressman John Grant Otis in a speech delivered before a combined meeting of the Grange and Farmers' Alliance held in Topeka in January, 1890. "The farmers of Western Kansas," said Otis, "are burning corn for fuel, while coal miners and their families in another section of our land, are famishing for food." Throughout the nation "farm products are selling below cost of production; and in our large cities men are out of employment and asking for bread." What were they going to do about it?[46]

Dissident answers to that question offered before 1890 were decidely a mélange, but they had one thing in common—government intervention. In the long run, the exact purpose of government intervention would continue to be a divisive issue; the important question immediately to be dealt with was how or by what means was the desired intervention to be achieved? Could the desired reformation be accomplished through either of the two old parties or was third-party action demanded by the circumstances?

GOODBYE, MY PARTY, GOODBYE

The decision as to whether Kansas discontent would be expressed through the old parties or through some new political organization depended largely on farmer organizations, for significant third-party action was not possible without the support of the great mass of Kansas farmers. Given the scope of the agricultural depression, the chances for extraordinary political activity were good, for in Kansas, as elsewhere, the strength of organizations among farmers, as well as their affinity for political actions, was proportionally related to the magnitude of economic and social discontent prominent at any given point.

Since the 1870s the nation's farmers had demonstrated a tendency toward organization as a means of bettering their positions in society. For a short time the Patrons of Husbandry, or the Grange, was the most popular farm organization, and its main political issue was the malpractices of the railroads. This Granger movement fell short of its major objectives, although it did manage to establish the right in several of the states to regulate to an extent the business of common carriers.[1]

The Grange had been introduced in Kansas in 1872, and once implanted on Kansas soil it grew by leaps and bounds, reaching its peak in the state in 1874, when Granger lodges, on a weekly basis, were being chartered by the score. This agrarian agitation had contributed heavily to the creation of the Independent-Reform party in Kansas, and made the party a force to be reckoned with in the 1874 election. The reform effort of that campaign, although significant, failed to unseat the entrenched Republicans, and within a few years the plight of Kansas farmers began to ease; this was accompanied by a decline in zeal in agricultural organizations. Indeed, as hard times passed into memory the disposition for political action became less intense, establishing a trend not to be reversed in Kansas until the boom of the 1880s collapsed.[2]

The fervor of farm organizations declined but the tendency toward organization continued. During the late 1870s and early 1880s, an assortment of farm organizations came into being. In the former Granger strongholds of the Northwest and Middle West, the National Farmers' Alliance and the Farmers' Mutual Benefit Association joined the Patrons of Husbandry in competing for the support of farmers; in the Northwest there was the Farmers' League; in the South there evolved the National Farmers' Alliance and Industrial Union, the Colored Farmers' Alliance, and the Agricultural Wheel.[3]

Among these organizations, the National Farmers' Alliance and Industrial Union (Southern Alliance) and the National Farmers' Alliance (Northern Alliance) were most important. Both orders got their effective starts at about the same time in the years 1879-1880.[4] The Northern Alliance, which began in Illinois, was from the beginning a much more loosely knit organization than the Texas-born Southern Alliance. It was a nonsecret organization, which, until 1887, required no fees or dues from its members; Negroes were eligible to membership, and it held that any person raised on a farm could join, thus opening the way for the recruitment of members from the nonagricultural classes. The Southern Alliance, on the other hand, was a highly centralized organization for "white" farmers, which specifically excluded from membership attorneys and all residents of incorporated cities.[5] It was bound together by ties of secrecy, dramatized by secret meetings, ritual, dues, grips, and passwords.[6] Membership in both organizations soared in the late 1880s. By 1890 the Southern Alliance claimed anywhere from one to three million members, with another million and a half in a Negro affiliate, while the Northern Alliance claimed to have over a million.[7]

In Kansas the Northern Alliance at first figured to be the chief agency through which farmers were to advance their interests. The first local group, or suballiance, was established about 1881, but the new order grew quite slowly until 1888. By the latter year, Northern affiliated suballiances had been founded in a number of counties, and on August 2, 1888, the first state meeting was held at Lyons in Rice County.[8] The same organization met in Topeka on February 6, 1889, and elected I. M. Morris as its president.[9] Six months later, however, the Northern Alliance had been all but supplanted in Kansas by the National Farmers' Alliance and Industrial Union, or the Southern Alliance.

The record is not clear as to how this conversion came about in so short a time. William F. Rightmire, a prominent leader of the Kansas Populists, later insisted that it was promoted by means of the State Reform Association, of which he was president.[10] However it was done, the two farm orders were consolidated in Newton, Kansas, on August 14, 1889.[11] Benjamin H. Clover, from Cowley County, who had been president of the Southern affiliated Alliance in Kansas from its inception early in 1889, was selected as president of the newly consolidated state Alliance.[12]

While this consolidation movement was underway in Kansas, a similar effort was being made on the national level. This resulted in the meeting of the Northern and Southern Alliances in St. Louis in December, 1889. The St. Louis Convention failed to produce a consolidation of the national organizations, but the Kansas order, already having merged the Northern and Southern affiliates, accepted the invitation for consolidation, as did the North Dakota and South Dakota Alliances. In St. Louis, also, both national Alliances adopted a set of reform demands, and in these there was a unity of purpose that pointed the way to a real political change. Abolition of the national banking system and "the substitution of legal tender treasury notes," prohibition of the alien ownership of land, a graduated income tax, adoption of the Australian ballot, and government ownership of the means of communication and transportation highlighted these two forward-looking platforms.[13] As John D. Hicks has written, "there was on the three fundamental issues of land, transportation, and finance virtually no North and no South."[14]

The St. Louis demands were not intended to be a platform for a new political party. Obviously the Alliance fully expected to translate these demands into specific governmental actions, but for most Alliancemen the means anticipated still included working within the existing parties.

In Kansas, while the Alliance movement had undergone this significant transformation, the debate as to how best to obtain desired reforms intensified as the plight of her citizens became more serious. Throughout the summer of 1889 Peffer and the *Farmer* advised against hasty political moves. Peffer thought there was little chance a successful third party could be formed. As he saw it, "it is better for farmers and workers in general to form associations for the purpose of discussing principles, leaving details alone for the present . . . ." "The masses want reform in directions other than those in which the great parties are going . . . ," he wrote, "but certain leading questions have controlled the elections, as they always will, and these special reforms which the people want are kept in the background, and will be until the people in non-partisan associations bring them forward and demand their consideration by legislative bodies."[15]

Farther south, in Wichita, "Murdock's Rebellion" was the topic of conversation. In May, 1889, Marshall Murdock, editor of the influential Wichita *Daily Eagle* and a prominent Republican, had blasted the 1889 Kansas legislature. Murdock wanted his readers to know that he was no anarchist but he believed "Kansas has grown too much one-sided and revolution is demanded for the well being of the state."[16] Murdock kept up his attack on through the summer. In August the editor of the Fort Scott *Monitor* took the position that reform had to come through the Kansas legislature. Murdock reacted to this by writing:

> Bah! It would be more sensible to go to the devil for pointers necessary to a circumspect life. That legislature is in and of itself one of the most prominent causes for the Rebellion. For years it has not only proved a disgrace but rottenness itself. . . . The Rebellion is on, and complete revolution must follow. The only power to which to look, the only power from which there can come any relief, is from the people, and not from a Kansas legislature or from any of its creatures.[17]

Marshall Murdock himself stayed with the Republican party during the "Rebellion," but many of his fellow Kansans were willing to follow his reasoning to logical conclusions. One of those was Stephen McLallin, editor of the Meriden *Advocate* in Jefferson County. A native of Pennsylvania, where he was born in 1837, McLallin had removed to Kansas about 1869. Civil War service, graduation from New York's Albany Medical School, and some seventeen years as a practicing physician preceded his association with journalism in the mid-1880s. A "compound of a Greek philosopher, of the austere, undemonstrative Scotchman, and the modern socialist"—or so his associate editor and fellow Populist Annie Diggs later described him—Dr. Stephen McLallin was above all a genuine humanist.[18]

Dr. McLallin's paper led the way in the call for third-party action. On September 21, 1889, he wrote: "It is urged that we should go into the primaries and by energetic and persistent efforts work out a reformation in the existing parties. We have tried this for the last twenty years without success. We have the same class of party leaders that have stood at the head during all these years and they are still as hungry as though they had never fed at the public crib . . . ." "Nothing short of civil revolution," he wrote, "seems capable of effecting a change in the interest of the people." The old parties could not be used successfully, for the bitter memory of past political struggles would not allow their former opponents to join. What was needed, he suggested, was a chance for the adherents of reform "to cut loose from their old moorings without a formal surrender of the colors under which they have so gallantly struggled heretofore . . . ." This he felt would enable men of all parties "to unite upon the issues that are now supreme, and insure their . . . triumph by overwhelming majorities."[19] McLallin reasoned that a strictly nonpartisan approach to reform, such as was then being advised by William Peffer, was self-defeating. In his mind it meant that the Alliance would continue to be divided on the "old lines, precisely as they have been divided before they became members of the Order." A truly nonpartisan effort, to his way of thinking, meant cooperation with neither old party.[20]

As the year 1889 came to a close the sentiment for third-party action intensified; the new disposition of the Alliance, in fact, pointed logically and persistently in that direction. One of Ben Clover's first official acts as president of the reorganized Alliance was to issue a circular letter in November, 1889, directing all suballiances to submit, by resolution, the platform of the state Alliance to their congressmen, asking for their indorsement of the Alliance demands. This was done, and every Kansas representative and Senator John J. Ingalls avoided an answer or responded evasively; only Senator Preston B. Plumb gave unqualified support to the Alliance platform.[21]

Soon thereafter, state Alliance leaders directed the suballiances to submit their demands to Peffer's *Farmer*. The deluge that followed nudged Peffer out of the middle of the road. Beginning in December, he began publishing through the columns of the *Farmer* his analysis of contemporary problems, entitled "The Way Out," and began to lecture, as well, in behalf of the Alliance platform.[22]

"The air is full of lightning," or so a Franklin County Republican leader named William Kibbe had observed a few months earlier.[23] Storm warnings were even more obvious as the new year and the new decade approached. On the surface, at least, the official Republican newspaper of the state, the Topeka *Daily Capital,* appeared oblivious to the existence of any great ferment. The readers of the *Capital* were told that prohibition enforcement was the primary issue of Kansas politics and that the Republican party alone stood between them and the menacing reign of John Barleycorn.[24] If any farmers perused the pages of the *Capital,* they were informed that "Hard work" was their "Salvation."[25] Cold words, indeed. Farmers could find little solace and less support in the chief Republican organ.

The Alliance cause was not without a voice in Topeka, however; there was William Peffer's *Farmer,* of course, and on January 9, 1890, Dr. Stephen McLallin published the first edition of *The Advocate* from its new location in the capital. He announced his paper as one which was "devoted to the Interests of the Farmers' Alliance and Industrial Union and other Kindred

Organizations." McLallin favored third-party action but was careful to appear as though he were being led rather than leading; Peffer had not yet abandoned the hope that Alliance demands could be met within the two old parties.[26]

On February 10, 1890, Peffer wrote a letter to Senator Ingalls, which he published in the *Farmer* on February 26. He called upon Ingalls to state his views for publication on the following issues: Ingalls' suggestions, if any, for farm relief; expansion of the volume of circulating money; the national banking system; and the free and unlimited coinage of silver. Senator Ingalls wrote Peffer that his views on the issues would appear in "a few weeks" but through some other channel than the *Farmer*.[27]

Whatever else may be said of the Senator's response, it was not politic. For years John J. Ingalls had been Mr. Republican in Kansas politics. He had made some bitter enemies for himself during that period of time. The Union-Labor party in the state had even singled out Senator Ingalls for special attention in its 1888 platform, calling him "a traitor unfit to represent the State of Kansas . . . ."[28] By ignoring the demands of the Alliance, and by ignoring Peffer's request, Ingalls assisted the cause of his opponents immensely. Senator Ingalls was indeed becoming a major issue himself. His adversaries were firmly in control of the Alliance movement, and therefore capable of turning the wrath of that great movement squarely upon him.

On March 3, 1890, Ben Clover made a crucial move in that direction. Apparently following the advice of the State Reform Association,[29] Clover, as president of the state Alliance, issued a call for a meeting of the county presidents in Topeka on March 25. The expressed purpose was for "consulting about matters of vital importance to our order and farmers and laborers in general." Actually, as Dr. McLallin later revealed, the object "was to take preliminary steps for the organization of a new party . . . ." The county presidents, according to McLallin, knew that to be the purpose of the meeting, although a number of them opposed that action and believed Clover had exceeded his authority in calling the meeting.[30]

However that may be, on March 25, 1890, sixty-eight county

presidents assembled in Topeka.[31] At this meeting, several resolutions were adopted: among them, one denying support to Senator Ingalls for reelection; another which declared, "the speedy
control of the legislative and executive departments of our state
and national government by the industrial classes uniting their
strength at the ballot box is an imperative necessity; and to secure
this result, we most earnestly invite the Knights of Labor, trades
unions, and trades assemblies of all incorporated cities of the state
to unite with us . . . ."[32] Another resolution stated that the Alliance would "no longer divide on party lines, and will only cast
our votes for candidates of the people, for the people, and by the
people."[33] The meeting also directed that the president appoint a
member of the Alliance from each congressional district to be
known as "the People's state central committee."[34]

The Rubicon was crossed. This March 25 meeting of the
county presidents of the Alliance was the decisive turning point in
the move to create a new party; there was no turning back. On
April 5 Clover asked the members of the Alliance, through *The
Advocate,* to select members from their districts whom they
wanted to represent them on the central committee. The following
month, on May 14, Clover published the official call for a meeting
of this committee in Topeka on the second Tuesday in June.
Included in this call was a suggestion by Clover that the Alliance
send three members from each district; he also suggested that "the
Grange, Farmers' Mutual Benefit Association, Knights of Labor,
and all labor organizations having for their object the betterment
of the laboring classes, send at least one or two delegates in order
that all interests and orders may confer together for the best good
of all."[35]

In the meantime some rather significant developments continued to influence the course of Kansas politics. Senator Ingalls
entered into public discussion in a controversial way with an interview published in the New York *World* on April 13 and reprinted
throughout Kansas by all papers sympathetic to the Alliance cause
toward the end of April. Ingalls, reportedly asked by the New
York reporter if "political ends justify the means?" replied:

The purification of politics is an irridescent dream.
Government is force. Politics is a battle for supremacy.
Parties are the armies. The decalogue and the golden rule
have no place in a political campaign. The object is success. To defeat the antagonist and expel the party in power
is the purpose. The republicans and democrats are as ir-
reconcilably opposed to each other as were Grant and Lee
in the Wilderness. They use ballots instead of guns, but the
struggle is as unrelenting and desperate, and the result
sought for the same. In war it is lawful to deceive the ad-
versary, to hire hessians, to purchase mercenaries, to muti-
late, to destroy. The commander who lost a battle through
the activity of his moral nature would be the derision and
jest of history. This modern cant about the corruption of
politics is fatiguing in the extreme. It proceeds from the
tea-custard and syllabub dilettantism, the frivolous and desultory sentimentalism of epicenes like . . . .[36]

Ingalls later attempted to explain away this statement by saying
that he was describing how politics was, not how it ought to be,
but to no avail.[37] It rhymed too well with many of his earlier
statements, and it fitted perfectly his opponent's conception of him.
As far as the proponents of reform were concerned, Ingalls' statement was a precise summary of Republican philosophy.

Significantly, on April 30 Peffer announced that he and the
Kansas Farmer "put the Alliance before party, and we advise
friends that in all cases wherein this new party question arises,
they consider what is best for the Alliance . . . ."[38] On May 14
Peffer made this announcement: "Senator Ingalls having declined
to answer our questions, the KANSAS FARMER will not support his claims for re-election, but, on the contrary, will support
the claims of any other competent man upon whom the opposition
shall unite."[39]

Abandon Senator Ingalls? but what of the grand old party
and the grand old issues? Ben Clover caught the mood of many
Kansans fairly well when he declared in May that "Kansas farmers have learned by sad experience that kinks twisted off the
British lion's tail will not pay mortgages, even though the mortgage may be held in England." True, he admitted, Ingalls was

the greatest "Democrat skinner" of them all, but Kansas farmers had learned as well that " 'brigadier' skins are the thinnest clothing a shivering family was ever wrapped up in."[40]

Ben Clover spoke from experience. The fifty-three-year-old farmer was loaded down with the kind of problems that afflicted a broad segment of the Kansas population with increasing severity at that point. This native Ohioan had moved out to Kansas in the year 1870 and began farming in Cowley County. For a time he had done rather well for himself, especially in 1874, but by 1890 the farm was encumbered with an $18,000 mortgage, on top of which was stacked another $1,800 in accrued interest on notes and renewals.[41]

Most farmers probably were not in as deeply as Clover, but indebtedness, as indicated earlier, was widespread and formidable. As these debts came due in a period of economic contraction, intensified by the collapse of the boom and the fall in farm income, the time was indeed ripe for a political revolt. Beginning in April and May, 1890, county Alliances in various parts of the state, following the example of Jefferson and Cowley Counties in the local elections of 1889, began to organize for political action. On June 12, in response to Clover's call of the preceding month, forty-one members of the Alliance, twenty-eight Knights of Labor, ten members of the Farmers' Mutual Benefit Association, seven Patrons of Husbandry, and four representatives from Single-Tax Clubs, ninety in all, gathered in Representative Hall in Topeka to further those political aspirations. Clover was elected to preside over the meeting, which by resolution voted unanimously to present a full slate of candidates in the upcoming election under the name People's party. A committee was then organized with John F. Willits of Jefferson County as chairman, and the responsibility for summoning a state convention was then assigned to this committee. The committee, in turn, then issued a call for a delegate state convention to meet in Topeka on August 13.[42]

As might be expected, considering the timing of this political move, the convention that gathered in Topeka that August was primarily facilitated by means of the existing Farmers' Alliance structure. Locally, a People's party apparatus was in varying stages of formation. Where party organizations did exist, however, they were virtually inseparable from the local Farmers' Alliance.[43]

At the convention John F. Willits was nominated for governor. Although chairman of the state committee, Willits was little known beyond the boundaries of Jefferson County where he was president of his County Alliance. Ben Clover, more widely known because of his Alliance position, had eliminated his name from consideration. The nomination for chief justice went to William Franklin Rightmire, who on the preceding day had also become secretary of the newly organized State Citizens' Alliance. This organization was to play an important role in the reform movement thereafter. The first local organization of its kind was created in Olathe, Kansas, a few months earlier by a former Greenbacker and Union Laborite named D. C. Zercher, who was named as president of the State Citizens' Alliance. As a state organization the Citizens' Alliance was apparently promoted by the State Reform Association in order to enlist residents of cities and towns in the reform cause who were ineligible to membership in the Farmers' Alliance. The State Reform Association, according to Rightmire, dissolved with the formation of the State Citizens' Alliance, and the latter organization provided the mechanism whereby non-farmer, urban-oriented reform proponents were able to make their influence felt within the new third party.[44]

If only a fraction of his own claims were admitted, W. F. Rightmire would qualify as one of the most influential figures in the creation of the People's party. Rightmire later stated the matter this way in a rough autobiographical sketch: "Was nominated by Union Labor party of Kansas, as Candidate for Attorney General of Kansas in 1888. Was president from 1888 of State Reform Association of Kansas, (that succeeded Union Labor party in December 1888) that organized the Farmers' Alliance Movement in Kansas, and then organized the Peoples Party of Kansas in 1890...."[45] Until or unless more material is turned up, however, the whole story concerning the role of Rightmire and that of the State Reform Association must remain an enigma of sorts. This much is clear: the forty-one-year-old lawyer was intimately involved in the endeavors that culminated in the creation of the People's party, even though he had resided in Kansas only since 1887. His pre-Kansas background included an academy and seminary education in New York; experience as a teacher, coal miner, and union organizer in Pennsylvania from 1869 to 1874; teaching and the practice of law in Iowa from 1874 to 1887. Politically, Rightmire had been a Republican until the late 1870s, when he left the party to become a Greenbacker while in Iowa. In Kansas he had helped organize the Union Labor party, and he was that party's candidate for attorney general in 1888. His nomination for chief justice by the 1890 Populist convention was therefore adequate testimony to the success of his reform activities.[46]

The remainder of the ticket was composed of decidedly obscure personalities. John N. Ives, the only former Democrat on the ticket and a resident of the state for only two years, was nominated for attorney general. The nominee for auditor was a Negro minister from Topeka by the name of B. F. Foster. Women were represented by Mrs. Fanny McCormick from Barton County, who was nominated for state superintendent of public instruction. For lieutenant governor the convention named Albert C. Shinn, a forty-eight-year-old stock raiser from Franklin County. Russell Scott Osborn, a Congregational minister and farmer from Osborne County, was nominated for secretary of state.[47]

The nominees of the new party undoubtedly reflected its immaturity, as well as the influence of the idea, prominent in reform circles, that the office should seek the man. About principles, however, there was more maturity and unanimity. The platform was simply constructed; it reiterated the 1889 St. Louis demands, calling for the "abolition of national banks and the substitution of legal tender treasury notes"; "the free and unlimited coinage of silver"; congressional "laws as shall effectually prevent the dealing in futures in all agricultural and mechanical productions"; "laws prohibiting alien ownership of land," to repossess "land now owned by aliens and foreign syndicates," and to reclaim land then "held by railroads and other corporations, in excess of such as are actually used and needed by them," to be "held for actual settlers";

and government ownership of "the means of communication and transportation."

The platform emphasized that its spokesmen would "waste no time discussing minor matters. The past is gone, the present is with us, and the future is before us. Old issues are dead. We come to you with new ones." It then set forth five separate resolutions in regard to railroads that were requested by the Knights of Labor. The five had to do with safety devices on railroads, arbitration of labor disputes, the use of Pinkerton detectives to coerce employees, and an existing state law that made railroad workers liable to conspiracy.[48]

In this unspectacular manner the stage was set for a decidedly spectacular campaign, which would seriously alter the conventional pattern of Kansas politics. At the time of its formation, however, there was little reason to believe the new party posed a serious threat to Republican supremacy. The G.O.P. had faced this situation on numerous occasions in the past; the People's party, faithful Republicans believed, would experience the same fate as had the other third parties which preceded it. There was about the attitude of its opponents an air of certainty and derision. The tendency was, in fact, to employ the same rhetoric that had been used successfully in the past. For the leaders of the new party there was nothing but contempt. While the party was still in the making, an opponent, whose letter was published in *The Advocate,* expressed the attitude precisely when he wrote: "let me say to the farmers, beware of the reformer. He is either a crank, a disgruntled democrat or republican, or a demagogue in some other shape. His modus operandi is to berate all who have sense enough to see that no profitable action can be had outside the two great parties." Obviously, "These chronic professional kickers and croakers are . . . aiming to get your support in some form of new party, not for your benefit, but for their's [sic]."[49]

The mood of self-assurance within the Republican party would soon be shattered but the attitude of derision would, if anything, be intensified. Undaunted by the repetitious cry that the party was led by a group of "professional kickers and croakers," thousands of Kansans joined in singing "Goodbye, My Party, Goodbye," as they moved to eradicate the "evils" which they believed responsible for their misfortunes.

KANSAS POPULIST LEADERSHIP:
Clodhoppers or Agrarian Iconoclasts?

The Kansas Republican press throughout the 1890s constantly labeled the leaders of the Populist party as "anarchists," "communists," "misfits," "loafers," "cranks," and "demagogues." In its efforts to down the party, this opposition repeatedly invoked the rags-to-riches or self-made-man myth, at times even the opposing yet parallel myth of rural virtue.[1] Invariably, Populist leaders were caricatured, verbally and pictorially, in a manner suggesting that they represented the missing link in the evolutionary chain. All the intellectual equipment of social Darwinism was brought to bear in the assault on the party. The usual caricature that emerged in the period—especially in Eastern papers —pictured a weather-beaten old man with distorted features; a dilapidated hat perched atop a head that was ornamented with a long but mangy-looking beard; between a set of irregular teeth dangled a stalk of straw; and a bony frame, after a fashion, was covered with a tattered set of bib overalls, from which emerged inevitably a pair of oversized boots recognizable as "clodhoppers."

The facts of the case have been as obscure as the picture was distorted. In order to clarify the matter, biographical material was obtained on eighty-nine individuals who made up the major leadership of the party in Kansas. Included here were all elected administrative officials, congressmen, prominent leaders in the state legislature, party officials, prominent lecturers and party workers, and writers and editors of leading Populist papers.[2] The composite picture that resulted from this analysis revealed that the Kansas Populist leader was forty-six years old in 1890; he was most likely born in Ohio, New York, Pennsylvania, Illinois, or Iowa, and moved to Kansas in 1871; he was, more often than not, a lawyer, but a number combined the occupation of farming or stock raising with that of teacher or editor. Only one in five was engaged strictly in agricultural pursuits, and many of those had been lawyers, or teachers, or merchants before becoming farmers.

It should be noted that forty-six was the median age for seventy-six out of eighty-nine for whom ages could be determined. The average age was just over forty-four (44.3) and forty-one was the age of greatest frequency, seven individuals having fallen in that category. Twenty-five of these Populist leaders (33.8 percent) were fifty or older, and eight (10.5 percent) were thirty or less. Actually, forty-one out of seventy-three (56.1 percent) were natives of Ohio, New York, Pennsylvania, Illinois, or Iowa. The states of Indiana, Kentucky, Virginia, West Virginia, and Wisconsin accounted for another fifteen (20.5 percent), and the remainder were divided among nine other states and Canada. Information as to when these individuals came to Kansas was obtained in seventy-two of eighty-nine cases. Twenty-eight (38.8 percent) came before 1870 and only fourteen (19.4 percent) came in 1880 or later. Occupational analysis, based on findings in seventy-nine of eighty-nine cases, revealed that thirty-one (39.2 percent) had been admitted to the practice of law; twenty-three (26.4 percent) were teachers by profession or had taught school at some point in their lives; and seventeen (21.5 percent) were engaged exclusively in farming.

This leadership was, in other words, a middle-class leadership—rural middle class, perhaps, but middle class nonetheless. More than half had graduated from one or more colleges, and counting those who had some college education, one arrives at the impressive discovery that almost two out of three had had some contact with the college environment. Actually, information revealing the educational background of this leadership group was available in sixty out of the eighty-nine cases. Thirty-one of these leaders (51.6 percent) had graduated from one or more colleges; another eight (13.3 percent) had attended college for varying periods of time; another seven (11.6 percent) had an academy or high school education, and fourteen (23.3 percent) were the recipients of only a common-school education. Even if the twenty-seven for whom no information was found were all placed in the common-school category, the percentage of college graduates would remain unusually high for the nineteenth century—thirty-one of eighty-nine, or 34.8 percent. As might be expected, the college environment that these people came out of was primarily that of the Middle West; but Eastern colleges were well represented, and three of the group were graduates of Harvard, Stanford, and Oxford universities.[3]

The composite Kansas Populist leader had also been active in reform for some time before 1890. The information pertaining to previous party affiliation, available for fifty-four of the group, revealed that thirty-two (59.4 percent) of these Populist leaders were active in the third-party reform movement before 1890. The usual route traveled had carried them from the Republican party to the Greenback party, then to the Prohibition party or the Union-Labor party, and then into the Populist party.

The rhetoric of Kansas Populist leaders was highly moral. Indeed their approach to reform was such that moral and political considerations were virtually one and the same. Christian ethics underlay their appraisal of society, and they were often ready with an apt Biblical allusion in appropriate situations. But contrary to what might be supposed, they were not religious fundamentalists. Of the twenty-two Populists out of eighty-nine whose biographies indicated a religious affiliation, five were Methodists, three were Unitarians, three were Quakers, and three were Congregationalists. The Baptist, Lutheran, Presbyterian, and Christian Churches contributed one each. Included among these were two Spiritualists and two Agnostics.

There was, among these leaders, general agreement and recognition of the social derivation of evil, a conviction that the conditions of their world had pitted brother against brother and man against immoral society in a contest with the cards stacked devastatingly against society's disadvantaged legions. For this reason, in religious matters a good many Populist leaders could agree with Samuel Wood, one of their number, when he wrote that "God should be spelled with two o's (Good); devil without a d(evil). In fact, I reject all the dogmas of the church. My religion is a sincere desire to do right—to do the most possible good in this world. I believe sincerely in the 'Fatherhood of God and the brotherhood of man.' "[4] Or with Mary Elizabeth Lease when she informed religious-minded defenders of the status quo that "it was not christianity but churchanity that she assailed . . . ."[5] Or with Kansas Populist Congressman John Grant Otis when he declared, "Our civilization demands the recognition of the fatherhood of God and the brotherhood of man, not upon Sunday only, but upon seven days in the week, and fifty-two weeks in the year."[6] Some no doubt would have agreed with the message of John M. Dunsmore, speaker of the Populist house of representatives in 1893, which he left to be read at his funeral. Dunsmore's "Message of Love," as he called it, stated that he "came into being with a mind so constituted that blind faith in any creed or dogma could never satisfy . . . [his] desire for knowledge concerning the mysteries of life and being." He followed this with the statement: "I have never been able to accept as true the dogmas and creeds of the so-called Christian system." Religion was to him, quoting an authority with whom he was familiar, " 'The outcome of our ideas about the universe, our response to all that we know, consciously or unconsciously, of cosmic law.' " If any hint of a fundamentalist strain still remained, Dunsmore took care of that by stating: "As an evolutionist, I looked upon the story of the fall of man as a myth handed down from dead and forgotton ages, and consequently, the dogma of the atonement to be both illogical and unnecessary." But an atheist John Dunsmore was not, and he demonstrated this by quoting another authority, with whom he also agreed, who had written that " 'while sin remains in the universe, God is defeated: and that everlasting punishment involves an everlasting failure; that sin never injured God, except through man. That it is the God within who is injured, rather than the God without.' "[7]

Apparently, quite a few of these leaders were alienated from the churches, but Christian precepts maintained a strong hold on their minds. The safest and perhaps the most accurate generalization that can be made about them is this: if the Populist leadership shared a common theological outlook it would have to

Some expressions of opposition press reaction

Undated cartoon from *Judge,* "The Foolish Appeals of the Political Tramps"

Cartoon dated April 25, 1891, *Judge,*
"A Mighty Poor Exchange"

Cartoon dated June 6, 1891, *Judge,*
"A Party of Patches"

Cartoon dated May 20, 1894, New York
World, "Hard Mowing for Uncle Sam"

A reformer's view of the Spanish-American War

Cartoon dated August 14, 1898, Topeka
Advocate and News, "Now for a War for
Humanity at Home"

Annie L. Diggs
about 1900

G. C. Clemens
Topeka's Mark Twain

Mary Elizabeth Lease
about 1890

be ethical humanitarianism which served as a yardstick by which they judged their world.

Undoubtedly this element of humanism conditioned their reaction to the problems they recognized were being created by an industrialized society—or was it the other way around? Either way, it is certain that both were an influence in making these leaders of Kansas Populism critical of the Gospel of Wealth. To their way of thinking the popularity of the Gospel of Wealth was merely a measure of the perversion of Christian doctrine to a selfish and ruthless industrial system. At one point Senator William Peffer stated the leadership's attitude toward the doctrine rather well: in responding to the attack of a minister who considered the Populists anarchists Peffer stated that the minister "is not crazy, nor is he ignorant, nor do I believe he is a bad man. On the other hand, I believe he averages high with the modern Christian, that he will average well with the modern preacher, whose philosophy comes to him from the Middle Ages, and whose ideas of finance come to him through the newspapers which are edited in the business offices."[8]

A number of the Kansas Populists, moreover, like the popular lady-orator and editor Annie Diggs, were in complete harmony with the Social-Gospel movement; and some, like Kansas Congressman Jerry Botkin, boldly and defiantly proclaimed themselves Christian socialists.[9]

By implication of argument or by direct refutation, Kansas Populist leaders rejected, as well, the so-called philosophy of social Darwinism. The evidence demonstrating their rejection of the social-Darwinian point of view is overwhelming, although it has been largely ignored in the past. Dr. Stephen McLallin, by means of *The Advocate*, repeatedly assailed Herbert Spencer's doctrine. In 1891 McLallin published a letter that fairly represented the attitude of the leadership on this matter which stated: "There never was, nor can there be, a more brutal, utterly selfish and despicable doctrine than the Darwinian 'struggle for existence,' when applied to the social relations of man. It justifies oppression, the aggregation of wealth in the hands of those able to grasp it, the occupation of everything the 'fittest' are able to gain and keep."

The letter then pointed up, by inference, the tie between the Gospel of Wealth and social Darwinism by indicating that religion had until recently mitigated the influence of the Spencerian rationale, but "Now this sacred ground is invaded. The pulpit is infected with the theories of material science, infected with the crude matter of materialism, which stops short of the halfway boundary between matter and spirit, and sees in man only an objectless animal."[10]

Kansas Populists were among the first to admit that abilities among men were not equally distributed. They were willing to concede, as did future Populist Congressman William D. Vincent on the eve of the party's formation, "that some men will grow rich faster than other men under a perfect system of law." The more industrious man, said Vincent, should receive a larger share than his "indolent neighbor." But what about "the sharp unprincipled men?" he asked. To Vincent and fellow Populists, it was clear that strong men needed no special assistance to augment their natural advantages. "They need no special legislation in their behalf," said Vincent. "The object of law is supposed to be protection of the weak against the oppressions of the strong."[11]

Over and over again Populist leaders stressed this view. To accomplish this purpose they unequivocally supported positive action by state and national government. In taking this position they were ridiculed repeatedly as paternalists, but they were scarcely bothered by the argument. In fact they countered with the argument that the country had had paternalistic government for years. As one unidentified Populist put it, "paternalism for the benefit of the few and powerful at the expense of the masses." Said he, "Every trust and combine, and every corporation is paternalism for the benefit of a class."[12] Another, also unidentified, declared that those who were horrified by the paternalistic spector of government ownership of railroads, telegraph, and telephones had "no fears of the centralization of power in the hands of a few irresponsible men resulting from corporate control of the same franchises, and the absorption of more than one half of the aggregate wealth of the entire country by less than 50,000 people."

Which was more dangerous to American liberty, he asked, "this latter paternalism or the paternalism of all the people?"[13]

As a group, Kansas Populists gloried in attacking the conventional wisdom—probably because it was employed with such devastating effect against them. Judge Frank Doster, who was the intellectual giant of Kansas Populism, more than any other figure delighted in shocking his more complacent contemporaries. This character trait earned for Doster quite a reputation in Kansas politics by 1896, and in that year his fame crossed over state boundaries, as he was the man the Populists had nominated for chief justice, the "shabby, wild-eyed, rattle-brained fanatic" of William Allen White's nationally-acclaimed editorial entitled "What's the Matter with Kansas?" Doster won that race, and many a conservative reporter clamored at his heels, attempting, by rather pointed questioning, to gauge the reign of terror they were sure was close at hand. The reign of terror was not forthcoming, but Doster gave some brash young reporters some pungent copy. In 1897, shortly after assuming office, the judge stated that he did not "believe in hell fire, nor human slavery, nor high tariff, nor the gold standard, nor in millionaires, nor in the wage system." Just as quickly he added: "I do believe in the Ten Commandments and in the Golden Rule, in the initiative and referendum, and evolution and woman suffrage, and I am edging toward theosophy and Christian science, and open to conviction in favor of any vagrant fad that nobody will admit believing in until enough do to make it respectable."[14] On another occasion Doster told a reporter: "I have been an adherent of socialism all my life. Socialism is coming about through the socialization of what we call the public utilities . . . ." It was his contention that as quickly as matters "become of sufficient public concern, either nationally or locally, they will pass into the hands of the general or local public, and some fine morning, if you live to a good old age, you will wake up to find yourself living in an almost communistic society, having gotten there by transitions so easy and natural you didn't realize their occurrence until the job was done."[15]

G. C. Clemens exceeded Frank Doster in the severity of his attack on the folklore of his times. In 1894 Clemens wrote that government, as viewed by those who controlled it, was "an ancient hand-organ, into which its ante-diluvian manufacturers put certain tunes which must never be changed. It ceaselessly grinds out the Tariff schottische, the Gold-Silver-and-Parity Waltz, the Revenue polka, the exhilerating [sic] gallop—'Our Foreign Relations,' and the soothing measures of 'After Us the Deluge.'" Prior to the Populist movement, continued Clemens, political campaigns had been fought over one all-important issue, "'Who shall turn the crank?'" At any time in the past when the people had grown weary of the "endless monotony" and had "demanded a change of program," the disenchanted "have been assured the trouble was with the unskilled or negligent wretch who was grinding the machine; but no matter how often the operator has been changed, suffering humanity's ears have still been greeted with the same old tunes which were doubtless popular with their progenitors some centuries before the flood." Finally, wrote Clemens,

> a party has arisen to demand a more radical change; which says to the people, "Let us remodel the old organ somewhat, so as to adapt it to modern music, and put into it an entirely new set of tunes. Let us substitute for this antiquated noise the beautiful strains of "The Earth was Made for All," and "All Men are Brothers Now," and . . . "Poverty is No More." But the champions of prehistoric melody exclaim in horror, "The impious innovators are going to change our consecrated tunes and even overhaul the sacred machine! Let us redeem the holy noise-box from the blasphemous wretches."[16]

G. C. Clemens, as previously indicated, was later carried by the logic of his reasoning into the socialist camp. A number of the leaders of Kansas Populism identified themselves as advocates of a moderate or evolutionary socialism, and a portion of that group chose the same course as Clemens after 1898, but they were not all convinced that governmental machinery needed as drastic an overhaul as Clemens desired. Piecemeal change was unquestionably the design of the great majority.

The *dominant* segment of the Populist leadership in Kansas reasoned, as did Dr. Stephen McLallin, that "Competition, except in the ranks of labor, in the production of farm products, and in the retail of certain lines of merchandise," was a thing of the past.[17] This element readily admitted the efficacy of cooperation and combination. They were willing to accept the organization of industry on a large and systematic scale. They agreed that measures were necessary so that large-scale enterprise could be made to better serve the public interest. They differed on how this was to be accomplished. One element of this group which felt that competition was no longer a practical regulator of industrial enterprise reasoned that the solution was public ownership of those enterprises that were national in scope and clearly affected with the public interest. For many of these individuals, however, as Chester M. Destler has noted, collectivist methods were simply a legitimate means of restoring free enterprise and small competitive capitalism; in particular, they felt government owned and operated railroads would contribute to that end.[18]

Another element of that dominant segment was reluctant to support the solution of government ownership from the beginning —or in certain cases came to that position because of pragmatic politics—and placed their faith in government regulation of large-scale enterprise. The response of this latter group would later be seen more clearly in Theodore Roosevelt's New Nationalism and in the second phase of Woodrow Wilson's New Freedom.[19]

Another faction, whose ideas represented a minority view among the leaders but may have appealed to a significant portion of the rank and file, reasoned that large-scale enterprise in the form of monopolies should be abolished so that competition would serve as an effective regulator. Those who took this position would not admit, as many of their colleagues did, that the trust was the logical product of the principle of competition in industry. The conventional wisdom was not easily evaded. Kansas Populist William Marshall must have struck some responsive chords when he pleaded with his fellow reformers to declare: "Natural laws are good enough for us. Competition will do. The provision which God has created cannot be improved upon;

neither can it be violated without injury to ourselves . . .; consequently we will suppress that instrument of artificialism and oppression, the combine, and restore to its full function and force the natural law of competition."[20] The approach of this faction would subsequently find an influential representation in the first phase of Woodrow Wilson's New Freedom.[21]

Besides these fundamental differences, party leaders were to be plagued and torn by numerous problems that can only be understood by studying the history of the party itself in its logical context—from that first whirligig campaign of 1890 to the denouement of the 1896 silver crusade and after. For the moment, suffice it to say that the leaders of Kansas Populism were by no means clodhoppers in the usual sense of that word; they were, on the whole, an extraordinary group of individuals, iconoclastic in their appraisal of society, bold and at times radical in their solutions. Their great problem derived from the fact that they were critics of an emerging industrial order whose strength and opportunity for criticism were largely the result of a wave of discontent made possible by the frustrations and misfortunes of an agrarian order functioning within a rapidly industrializing society that paid little heed to the farmer's plight.

"A TURNIP CRUSADE, AS IT WERE"

Words fail to describe the ferment that came over Kansas in the summer of 1890. The campaign was on. As Elizabeth N. Barr has written so well, "The upheaval that took place . . . can hardly be diagnosed as a political campaign. It was a religious revival, a crusade, a pentecost of politics in which a tongue of flame set upon every man, and each spake as the spirit gave him utterance." The ground had been well prepared by the Alliance. Literally hundreds of lecturers throughout the state, men and women, addressed themselves to topics that agitated their audiences. But it was not just the recognized leaders who sounded the call for action; in the words of Barr, "The farmers, the country merchants, the cattle-herders, they of the long chin-whiskers, and they of the broad-brimmed hats and heavy boots, had also heard the word and could preach the gospel of Populism." Preach they did; never before had the ordinary citizen been so engrossed in political matters. From August to November, 1890, political ferment consumed the state like a prairie fire, as tens of thousands of Kansans flocked to the banner of the People's party intent on demonstrating, apparently, that the purification of politics was not an iridescent dream.[1]

The discontented did not have to look far for spokesmen: numerous third-party campaigners eagerly threw themselves into the fray; and skill in political criticism and analysis, in some cases developed over a twenty-year period, immediately and logically catapulted them to positions of leadership. The Alliance movement, moreover, provided the forum whereby many new personalities burst upon the political scene.

By far the most spectacular of the relative newcomers was Mrs. Mary Elizabeth Lease.[2] The future stem-winding prophetess of Kansas Populism was born in 1853 in Pennsylvania, not Ireland as she occasionally claimed in the Populist era, and her maiden name was Mary Elizabeth Clyens. She received an academy education in New York and moved to Kansas in about 1873. Settling in Neosho County, she became a teacher in the parochial school at Osage Mission. It was there she met and married a druggist named Charles Lease. Shortly after their marriage they moved to a farm in Kingman County. After a brief and unsuccessful effort at farming, they moved to Denison, Texas, and then back to Kansas again. In the meantime ten years had intervened. During this period Mrs. Lease bore four children, managed the household, and in her spare time studied law. Her study of law was done entirely at home; at times, so it was said, this required "pinning sheets of notes above her wash tub to study while she scrubbed the washings she 'took in' at 50¢ a day." However it was done, she was admitted to the bar in 1885 and became one of a small number of Kansas women lawyers.

Between 1885 and 1887, Mrs. Lease began to build a reputation as a lecturer on various subjects. She gave several lectures in behalf of the Irish National League, and championed woman suffrage and temperance. Until 1888 she was a Republican. In that year, however, she left the G.O.P. to work in behalf of the newly organized Union-Labor party. She made a political debut of sorts that year also by speaking before the Union-Labor party's state convention.

Mrs. Lease gained considerable experience from her activities in the 1888 contest and a certain amount of notoriety in the middle counties of Kansas, and from there she moved quite logically and wholeheartedly into the reform agitation that led to the creation of the Populist party. Her natural talents then catapulted her to prominence among the orators of the time.[3]

Mrs. Lease obviously had a truly remarkable voice, for it was widely noted. Annie Diggs, who rivaled Mrs. Lease for the affection of Kansas Populists, considered it her greatest "distinguishing gift." William Allen White stated that he had "never heard a lovelier voice than Mrs. Lease's." He described it as "a golden voice—a deep, rich contralto, a singing voice that had hypnotic qualities." Concerning her persuasive powers, White wrote, "She put into her oratory something which the printed copies did not reveal. They were dull enough often, but she could recite the multiplication table and set a crowd hooting or hurrahing at her will." The pudgy little Republican editor supplied the following image of her appearance: "She stood nearly six feet tall, with no figure, a thick torso, and long legs. To me, she often looked like a kangaroo pyramided up from the hips to a comparatively small head. . . . She wore her hair in a Psyche knot, always neatly combed and topped by the most ungodly hats I ever saw a woman wear. She had no sex appeal—none!"[4]

Mrs. Lease, nevertheless, had that special something that made her a magnetic orator. Early in 1891 she was interviewed by a reporter who was indeed quite fair in his treatment of that interview. In summing up, he stated that she impressed him "as one of those radical, strong, warm natures which feels and has impulses rather than thoughts. She can see a wrong and feel an injury quickly, but would be slow and far from sure in her remedies. Her mind is untrained, and while displaying plenty of a certain sort of power, is illogical, lacks sequence and scatters like a 10-gauge gun."[5]

It would seem that a good deal of Mrs. Lease's success was due to her ability to feel and express what was agitating many people at the time. She was in this sense more a barometer of discontent than an originator and leader of reform activity. Years later, Mrs. Lease herself noted this fact but gave it a mystical twist. A reporter asked her how she became an orator; she replied: "Brother, I don't say that I ever did. I was untrained in the arts of the public debater, unschooled in the methods of the political exhorter. If I succeeded in swaying my audiences I did not deserve the credit. That belongs to a hidden power that worked within me. I was merely a voice, an instrument in the hands of a Great Force."[6] Reform pursued in this fashion may perhaps have been effective as long as the impulse was strong and its meaning reasonably clear, but it could be disastrous in opposite circumstances. This observation may hold the key to understanding why the subsequent careers of Mrs. Lease and several other Populist leaders, in Kansas and elsewhere, were quite erratic.

For the moment, however, the Lease style of oratory was just the thing. Unquestionably, she played a mighty role in that first whirligig campaign. She moved about the state, her reputation growing by leaps and bounds, roasting the opposition in a manner that most men would dare not use for fear of physical reprisal. A measure of the effectiveness of her attack may be seen in the following remarks of a Republican editor in Wellington, Kansas, after a Lease visit: "At the opera house last Monday night, a miserable caricature upon womanhood, hideously ugly in feature and foul of tongue, made an ostensible political speech, but which consisted mainly of the rankest kind of personal abuse of people in this city, among which [sic] the editor of this paper understands that he came in for the principal share." He went on to write that he did not know exactly what were the "old hag's reasons" for the attack. "All we know about her is that she is hired to travel around the country by this great reform People's party, which seems to find a female blackguard a necessity in its business, spouting foulmouthed vulgarity at $10 a night." He was certain "the petticoated smut-mill earns her money, but few women want to make their living that way." He capped off this bit of vitriol by noting, sardonically, "We thought at first we would write her up in something after her own style of expression, but upon reflection concluded that the space could better be devoted to something else. Her venomous tongue is the only thing marketable about the old harpy, and we suppose she is justified in selling it where it commands the highest price." Besides, "In about a month the lantern-jawed, goggleeyed nightmare will be put out of a job, and nobody will be the worse for the mud with which she has tried to bespatter them."[7]

A summary example of Mrs. Lease's oratory in the 1890 campaign was distilled in a speech she delivered in Kansas City late in March, 1891. Speaking with little attention to notes (her usual style), her speech, as noted by a Kansas City *Star* reporter, was presented in "a fragmentary, desultory way which showed it to be a crazy-patch of perhaps a dozen different speeches." Considering her importance in that campaign and the paucity of extant material, it merits special attention. She said:

Wall street owns the country. It is no longer a government of the people, for the people, by the people, but a government of Wall street, for Wall street, and by Wall street. The great common people of the country are slaves, and monopoly is the master. The West and South are bound and prostrate before the manufacturing East. Money rules and our Vice President is a London banker. . . . [Our legislation] is the output of a system which clothes rascals in robes and honesty in rags. The parties lie to us and the political speakers mislead us. We were told two years ago in Kansas to go to work, raise a big crop—that's all we needed. We went to work and plowed and planted; the rains fell, the sun shown, nature smiled and we raised a big crop they told us to; and what came of it? Eight-cent corn and ten-cent oats and two-cent beef and no price at all for butter and eggs; that's what came of it. Then the politicians said we suffered from over production, when 10,000 little children . . . starve to death every year in the United States and over 100,000 shop girls in New York City are forced to sell their virtue for the bread their niggard wages deny them. . . . John J. Ingalls never smelled gunpowder in all his cowardly life. His war record is confined to court marshalling a chicken thief. . . . Kansas suffers from two great robbers; the Santa Fe railroad and the loan companies. The common people are robbed to enrich their masters. . . . There are thirty men in the United States whose aggregate wealth is over one and one-half billions of dollars. There are one-half million tramps; that is men looking for work . . . . What the Alliance wants are money, land and transportation. We want the abolition of national banks and we want the power to make loans direct from the government. We want either the amendment or the wiping out of the accursed foreclosure system in the state of Kansas. Land equal to a tract thirty miles wide and ninety miles long in Kansas has been foreclosed on and bought in by the loan companies in a year. We will stand by our homes and stay by our firesides by force, if necessary, and we will not pay our debts to the shark loan companies until the government pays its debts to us. The people are at bay; let the blood hounds of money who have dogged them so far beware.[8]

"Raise less corn and more hell!" was the advice she allegedly gave to Kansas farmers;[9] it was the kind of advice they could well understand.

Decidedly inferior to Mrs. Lease in spectacular crowd-pleasing attributes but by far superior in intellectual attainments and abilities was Mrs. Annie L. Diggs—or "Little Annie" as she was affectionately identified by her fellow Populists. Almost a decade after this campaign, a journalist gave the following description of Mrs. Diggs:

> Imagine a little woman, slender, almost to fraility, barely five feet tall and weighing only ninety-three pounds. Picture . . . a face on which shines the light of zealous endeavor and enthusiastic championship of a beloved cause; rather thin lips, an intellectual forehead from which the hair, now fairly sprinkled with gray threads, is brushed back pompadour like; twinkling eyes which alternately squint almost shut, then open wide as she expounds her favorite doctrines of socialism; a trifle nervous, a soft voice and an occasional musical little laugh as she talks, and you have a fair photograph of [Annie Diggs] . . . .[10]

Born in Canada in 1853 to an American mother and French father, Annie La Porte had moved with her parents to New Jersey at age two. She was not a college graduate (a fact that she "regretted"), although she had a better than average education, having studied with a private tutor, in the public schools, and, for a time, in a convent school. An adventurous soul by nature, eager to confront new challenges, the young and attractive Miss La Porte had gone to Washington, D.C., to take up a career in journalism soon after the termination of her education. After working at that for a time, she decided to go out West. The year was 1873; she was nineteen; and the destination was Lawrence, Kansas. She had arranged for a position in a Lawrence music store, where she would demonstrate the quality of the store's pianos. Within a short time, she met and married A. S. Diggs, an employee in the

Lawrence post office, and the Diggs family was soon enlivened by the addition of a son and two daughters.[11]

Much too talented and energetic a woman to be content solely with the cares of homemaker, Mrs. Diggs worked enthusiastically for the Woman's Christian Temperance Union and for woman suffrage; she also became actively involved in the activities of the Unitarian Church and in the Social Science Club of Kansas and Western Missouri.[12] In the early 1880s she returned to the East on several occasions to lecture before Unitarian conferences. Then came an opportunity to resume her journalistic career, in Boston, as a representative of several Kansas papers. Back East, she maintained her interest in reform; in fact, her thinking was affected significantly by the conditions she encountered there. About this experience, she later stated: "While I studied conditions in the East I became all the more convinced that the reforms which we sought were after all economical rather than moral questions. There was little hope in the East because the wage earners were afraid to say their souls were their own. But if the farmers could become interested there was, I thought, some promise of success. You cannot evict a farmer whose farm is his own. He is a sovereign."[13]

Returning to Lawrence just as the Farmers' Alliance was becoming a force to be reckoned with, Mrs. Diggs turned her persuasive charms on Colonel O. E. Learnard, who was editor of the Lawrence *Journal,* the leading Republican newspaper in the town, and won his consent for an Alliance column written by herself. The day following her first article an editorial appeared disclaiming any responsibility for the views that appeared in her column; she was allowed to continue, nevertheless, and her articles were widely copied. Her work came to the attention of Dr. Stephen McLallin and he persuaded her, without much difficulty, to join the staff of *The Advocate* in Topeka as associate editor in March, 1890. Together they created, in *The Advocate,* a newspaper which was indeed worthy of the reputation that it soon acquired as the leading reform weekly in the state. At its peak in the mid-nineties the paper would attain a circulation of around 80,000.[14]

In spite of her numerous public activities before 1890, Mrs. Diggs was apprehensive about campaigning actively; once enlisted in the cause, however, she proved herself a highly effective campaigner.[15] In her speeches she drew upon her acquaintance with conditions in the East and in the West, added a large dose of factual argument, and in her reasoned, soft-spoken, and pleading oratorical style won over her audiences completely.[16]

Mary Elizabeth Lease, Annie Diggs, and many other Kansas women added considerable color to the campaign, but all the excitement was not generated by the ladies. The party's congressional nominees managed to create considerable enthusiasm. Ben Clover led the fight in the third congressional district, encompassing nine counties in the southeastern corner of the state. Big, insipid, malleable, superficial but determined would be a fair description of the state Alliance leader. Clover used that determination to hammer home the arguments he had perfected since leaving the Republican party in 1888.[17]

Out in the north-central portion of the state, in the fifth congressional district, John Davis drew effectively upon his twenty-year association with reform to carry the message to the people. One of Davis' favorite themes was the "new slavery." He asked: " 'Have we abolished slavery?' " Go "Ask the factory girls, the sewing women, the coal miners, the iron workers, the farmers and all the men and women of toil who form the great public which the Vanderbilts would damn to perpetual servitude!" The ante-bellum slave system, he said, "rested on three millions of blacks, whom it pauperized, but fed and clothed." But "The masters never became millionaires. They were brutal and overbearing, but they had not the means to purchase great lines of railroads and telegraphs, and through them to levy tribute on whole states." The new slavery, he insisted, was much worse, "it rests on sixty millions of people. It makes paupers which society must feed; and it has created thousands of millionaire slave masters . . . ."[18]

The "new slavery" motif was prominent also in the campaign of John Grant Otis in the fourth congressional district. A native of Vermont, where he was born on a farm in 1838, Otis was perhaps as intense and sober a personality as Kansas Populism counted among its leaders. Reform was a deadly serious matter to him, and perhaps no one took Mr. Otis quite as seriously as he did himself. He operated a dairy farm to the southeast of Topeka, but his interests and his abilities had always roamed far beyond the barnyard. His educational qualifications were considerable: he had attended Burr Seminary in Vermont, Williams College in Massachusetts, and Harvard Law School. In 1859 Otis moved to Topeka where he practiced law for about five years before giving up his practice for the dairy business. In politics, he was a Republican of "abolitionist vintage," and during the Civil War he had organized and commanded a contingent of Negro troops in an effort to turn back the Confederate forces of General Sterling Price. In the mid-seventies, however, he had left the Republican party to work for reform as a Granger, Greenbacker, and Prohibitionist.[19]

Early in 1890 Otis had informed Ben Clover by public letter that he earnestly believed that "When the American people shall introduce co-operation into the field of PRODUCTION as well as into the field of DISTRIBUTION, and shall organize for 'work' as we organize for 'war'! then will we behold PROSPERITY such as the world has never witnessed." A communitarian socialist of sorts by 1890, Otis was ready to apply that principle to American society.[20] He had also played an active part within the Grange, and when the People's-Alliance forces of the fourth congressional district looked about for a leader, Otis was ready to assume a leading role.

The John Otis message in the 1890 campaign was stated best at a Grange picnic in Olathe. Reflecting, perhaps, his familiarity with Edward Bellamy's *Looking Backward, 2000-1887*, he told his audience, "This great industrial movement, over our land to-day, is but another advancing step in the forward march of human society. We are emerging from an age of intense individualism, supreme selfishness, and ungodly greed to a period of co-operative effort. Competition is giving way to unite[d] action." It seems that we are "waking out of the mesmeric sleep of a selfish age, to find ourselves closely related to the whole human family and to discover whatever effects the interest of one, in a greater or less degree effects the interests of all." All the old issues were dead, he declared. The people were arraying themselves on one side or the other of a "portentous contest." On the one side were the forces of capital, on the other was labor. Events, he believed, indicated the struggle was about to be won by the strength of the combined forces of labor, which would herald the establishment of a society founded on "mutual co-operative effort."[21]

Out West in the sixth congressional district, an area encompassing twenty-two counties in the northwestern corner of the state, the Alliance had nominated its district lecturer, a fifty-nine-year-old rancher and former Republican from Lincoln County named William Baker, who was destined to be the only Populist elected to three consecutive terms in congress. Although Baker had been engaged exclusively in ranching since his arrival in Kansas in 1878, his background was diverse: before coming to Kansas and following his graduation from Waynesburg College in his native state of Pennsylvania in 1856, he had worked in the public school system as teacher and principal, studied law and qualified for admission to the bar, as well as engaging in the mercantile business for sixteen years. The William Baker style of oratory was hardly spectacular but it was convincing. He spoke primarily from experience, emphasizing the particular difficulties that confronted farmers, ranchers, and small businessmen; it was the kind of approach that many people of the northwestern counties could well understand. In William Baker the Alliance had found a formidable and level-headed spokesman.[22]

The southwest quarter of the state, thirty-six counties in all, made up what was generally referred to as the "Big Seventh." Like the sixth congressional district, it had become a hotbed of Alliance activities after 1888; political revolt was a foregone conclusion. In late July there emanated a cry of horror and anguish from Holton that the seventh district would nominate "a rabid fiat greenbacker with communistic tendencies."[23] That political monstrosity was one Jeremiah Simpson, or the "Sockless" Jerry of political legend.

William D. Vincent
Congressman, 1897-1899

William A. Harris
Senator, 1897-1903

John W. Leedy
Governor, 1897-1899

John W. Breidenthal
State Chairman and
Bank Commissioner

Frank Doster
Chief Justice of the State
Supreme Court, 1897-1903

John M. Dunsmore
Speaker of the House, 1893

Percy Daniels
Lt. Governor, 1983-1895

L. D. Lewelling
Governor, 1893-1895

P. P. Elder
Speaker of the House, 1891

William A. Peffer
Senator, 1891-1897

John Davis
Congressman, 1891-1895

Jerry Simpson
Congressman
1891-1895, 1897-1899

The man destined to become one of the most popular and renowned of all Populist leaders was born March 31, 1842, in the province of New Brunswick, Canada. Moving with his parents to New York at age six, he received a rather limited elementary education before he left home at fourteen to follow a seafaring life. For more than twenty years (excluding a short period during the Civil War when he had served with an Illinois regiment until incapacitated by illness) he had sailed the Great Lakes as cook, sailor, mate, and captain. Marriage in 1870, and family responsibilities that followed, greatly altered the pattern of Simpson's life, however, and he soon left the sea for the land. After a brief period on a farm in Indiana, where he was introduced to an agricultural depression and the Grange, he moved his family to Kansas, purchasing a small farm and a sawmill near Holton in Jackson County in the northeastern part of the state in 1878.

Years later, when asked by Victor Murdock what had prompted his move to the West, Simpson would answer: "The magic of a kernel, the witchcraft in a seed; the desire to put something into the ground and see it grow and reproduce its kind. That's why I came to Kansas."[24] Undoubtedly, he also had hopes of bettering his station in life, but the going was tough. Not long after their small daughter was killed in a tragic logging accident, the Simpsons moved out to a ranch in the southwestern part of the state near Medicine Lodge. With all of their savings invested in land and cattle, Jerry Simpson soon became acquainted with all the special problems confronting those who were endeavoring to earn their living as farmers and ranchers. Somewhere along the way he left the Republican party to work actively in support of the Greenback party, and in 1886 he ran as a candidate on the Independent ticket for the legislature. Then came the severe winter of 1886-87, and the savings of a lifetime were swept away with his winterkilled herd. Already a reformer by temperament and affiliation, Jerry Simpson was all the more committed to third-party politics.[25]

Simpson's education had not prepared him satisfactorily for writing; he was a terrible speller, and apparently he made no great effort to overcome the handicap, but he was an omnivorous reader and his many years aboard ship had given him the opportunity to do much reading.[26] William Allen White later recalled: "He was smart. He had read more widely than I, and often quoted Carlyle in our conversations, and the poets and essayists of the 17th century. His talk . . . was full of Dickensian allusions, and he persuaded me to try Thackeray, whom I had rejected until them."[27] One of his favorite works was Henry George's *Progress and Poverty,* and his reading of George had made him a devout Single-Taxer.[28]

Above all else, though, Jerry Simpson was a reformer with an unrivaled sense of humor. It was a rare quality that could be ascribed to few of the era's politicians. It affected his whole presence, adding the one simple touch that elevated him above his fellows. Hamlin Garland met him in Washington in 1891 and wrote a vivid description which is not likely to be improved upon:

> He is about fifty years of age, of slender but powerful figure, whose apparent youthfulness is heightened by the double-breasted short sack coat he wears. His hair is very black and abundant, but his close-clipped moustache is touched with gray, and he wears old-fashioned glasses, through which his eyes gleam with ever-present humor. The wrinkles about his mouth show that he faces the world smilingly. His voice is crisp and deep and pleasant to the ear. He speaks with the Western accent mainly; and when he is making a humorous point or telling a story, he drops into dialect, and speaks in a peculiar slow fashion that makes every word tell. He is full of odd turns of thought, and quaint expressions that make me think of Whitcomb Riley. He is a clear thinker, a remarkable speaker, and has a naturally philosophical mind which carries his reasoning down to the most fundamental facts of organic law and human rights.[29]

In 1888 Jerry Simpson had again campaigned for a seat in the legislature, running on the unsuccessful Union-Labor ticket. By this date also Simpson had been forced by economic circumstances to supplement his income as best he could. As happened with so many other third-party leaders, the Alliance movement claimed him and he claimed it. But this time the stakes were larger; the city marshal of Medicine Lodge—for that was the position he held at the time of his nomination—was a candidate for congress.

In the campaign Jerry Simpson was subjected to extremely bitter abuse by the opposition press. He was accused of being an "infidel," an "anarchist," an "atheist," a "swindler," as well as being "unpatriotic," and having "simian" characteristics.[30] But Jerry Simpson stood up well under the attack; in fact, with his humor, he usually managed to turn the abuse to his advantage. An example of this was seen in his speech at Harper on August 30. He began by stating: "You may be surprised to see me in the form of a man, after the descriptions of a partisan press, but I'm no zoological specimen—not even a monkey or an orangutan." There followed a great roar of laughter, and Jerry Simpson had attuned his audience for the remainder of the speech.

Just as in this Harper speech, he liked to stress that in spite of "improvements in wealth producing machinery" the farmer was worse off than twenty years before. What was the problem? The "People are without a medium—less than $10 per capita in circulation." The railroads also shared in the responsibility for the people's plight, he said. "We have all the machinery for the finest government on the face of the earth, but we are fast becoming entangled in the web of the giant spider which controls our commerce and transportation. We must own the railroads or enough of them to do the necessary carrying. 'Tis idle talk to say we have not the authority. The government is the *people* and *we* are the people." Land was another subject dear to his heart. The existing land system, he said, was "robbery." "Man must have access to the earth or he becomes a slave." And so he spoke, here and there interjecting a pertinent and usually humorous story to emphasize a point and to retain the interest of his audience.[31]

The Republicans of the seventh district had nominated Colonel James R. Hallowell, a rather sedate gentleman who carried the appellation "Prince Hal."[32] Much was made of the contrast between Hallowell and Simpson. "The opposing candidates are opposites in every way," said the Topeka *Capital*. "Colonel

Hallowell is a brilliant, experienced and competent man who would add strength to the Kansas delegation; Jerry Simpson is an ignorant, inexperienced lunkhead . . . ." Said the *Capital,* "Jerry would disgrace the state in congress; scarcely able to read and write, unacquainted with public affairs, without experience as a legislator, raw, boorish, fanatical with the fanaticism of sheer ignorance, he would render Kansas a laughing stock . . . ."[33]

Republican leaders hit upon the idea of bringing the two candidates together for a debate. The obscure city marshal of Medicine Lodge would be vanquished by the polished and dignified personage of "Prince Hal." The debate was arranged to take place toward the end of the campaign, and Hallowell, as agreed, was assigned the opening and closing speeches. Jerry Simpson later recalled the event as follows:

> He was a handsome fellow, a good dresser, and his followers had dubbed him "Prince Hal." He was a splendid talker, and long before he had finished his speech I knew he had the crowd with him and that I would have to do something drastic to jar them loose. He poked considerable fun at me. The idea of sending a man to Washington who had no public experience, other than being city marshal of Medicine Lodge, was really funny. He, Hallowell, on the other hand had had legislative experience. He knew how laws were made, etc.
>
> When my turn came I tried to get hold of the crowd. I referred to the fact that my opponent was known as a "Prince." Princes, I said, wear silk socks. I dont [*sic*] wear any. The crowd laughed at this but it was not enough and I had to try again. Now, I said, Hal tells you that he is a law maker. That he has been to Topeka and that he has made laws. I am going to show you the kind of laws that Hal makes. Reaching over on the table and picking up a book I opened it and, tapping on the page with my finger, I said, here is one of Hals [*sic*] laws. I find that it is a law to tax dogs, but I see that Hal proposes to charge two dollars for a bitch and only one dollar for a son of a bitch. Now the party I belong to believes in equal and exact justice to all.[34]

As one might imagine, "the crowd roared" and Jerry Simpson had his audience right where he wanted them. Having miscalculated in bringing Simpson and Hallowell together in the first place, the opposition press compounded the error by providing Simpson with an invaluable sobriquet—from that day forth it was "Sockless" Jerry Simpson.[35]

As the story of Jerry Simpson demonstrated, the Republican organization was slightly out of touch with the people. "Abuse and vituperation" of People's party candidates—or so one Republican editor admitted—was the major strategy of the G.O.P.[36] The Topeka *Capital* waged a somewhat more inclusive campaign, which amounted to one part personal abuse, one part bloody shirt, and one part prohibition. J. K. Hudson of the *Capital* repeatedly informed his readers that the only thing at stake was prohibition— whisky was the issue.[37] Speaking of the leaders of the new party, Hudson stated: "They are unworthy of citizenship and belong in the penitentiary."[38] The October 12 edition offered this commentary: "Members of the people's party: Your man Polk appears to be an unscrupulous trickster; your man Clover an unprincipled demagogue; your man Willits a low-lived perjurer; your man Rightmire an indicted swindler, and your man Ives a creature of the rum-soaked democracy." The same issue ran an article entitled "The People's Party is the Scheme of Ex-Rebels."[39]

The editor of the *Capital,* and Republican leaders throughout the state, were indeed shocked by the effrontery of Kansas voters who went to the polls early that November and administered a stunning blow to the Republican party. Said Hudson, "The people's party managers trusted for victory to the ignorance of the people, and to the shame of Kansas their confidence was not misplaced."[40] Republican Governor Lyman Humphrey was re-elected by a small plurality, as was the rest of the ticket, with the exception of the attorney general, but the People's party elected Clover, Otis, Baker, and Simpson to congress and 96 of 125 members to the lower house of the legislature. All this in a state where the G.O.P. had grown accustomed to a comfortable majority approximating that of 1888 when the party had elected 120 of 125 members of the lower house and 39 of 40 members to the state senate for four-year terms.[41]

Comparing the returns for 1888 (vote for presidential electors) and 1890 (vote for secretary of state), the vote had shifted as follows:[42]

Party	1888	1890	Loss	Gain
Republican	182,800	120,969	61,831	
Democratic	102,600	55,873	46,727	
Union-Labor	37,600		37,600	
Prohibition	6,700	1,316	5,384	
People's		115,933		115,933
Total	329,700	294,091		

The vote of 1890 showed a decline of about eleven percent since 1888, caused both by the exodus of people from the state and by the normal reduction of an off-year election. By reducing the vote of each party by that amount its natural loss may be seen; further reduction may be attributed to defection to the People's party. On that basis, then, the rank and file of the People's party included roughly 41,000 former Republicans, 35,000 former Democrats, 33,000 former Union Laborites, and 4,500 former Prohibitionists.

Populists were of course jubilant; Republicans were shaken. The latter could console themselves, however, as did J. K. Hudson of the Topeka *Capital,* by noting that "While the people's party controls the house by a very large majority, the senate is still republican by 38 to 1, and a governor's veto also stands in the way of radical legislation of which businessmen and capitalists might have stood in dread. There is no danger of the passage of any measures which would render capital unsafe . . . ."[43] There was, on the other hand, a real possibility that Senator John J. Ingalls would be defeated for reelection by the new legislature.

The legislature that convened in January, 1891, presented an interesting contrast in membership. Compositely, the Populist representative was a forty-six-year-old farmer or stock raiser, who was most often a native of Ohio, Indiana, New York, Illinois, Virginia, or Kentucky, and had moved to Kansas in 1878. About one in nine, however, was foreign born; one in three had been active in third-party politics for years; one in five was a college graduate. Only eleven had had previous legislative experience, while one in three had held local office only.[44] The Republican representative, on the other hand, was a forty-five-year-old native of Pennsylvania, Ohio, Indiana, or New York, and a business or professional man who had moved to Kansas in 1877. One out of four had had previous legislative experience; one in five was a college graduate, and only one of the group was foreign born.[45]

The holdover Republican senate offered a sharper contrast with the Populist house. The Republican senator was, compositely, forty-five years old (forty-three at the time of his election), a lawyer, a proprietor of some business, or a banker, who was a native of Ohio, Pennsylvania, or New York, and had lived in Kansas since 1868. Only four of the thirty-eight were farmers. One out of two had had previous legislative experience. Six of the group were college educated.[46]

In short, the most meaningful and distinct contrast between Republicans of the house and senate and Populists of the house was not one of age or education but of occupation. To use the terminology of Lee Benson, it was a case of the agrarian-minded versus the commercial-minded. But it was not the agrarian mind of the eighteenth century; these men were not unaffected by the considerable changes that had occurred over the course of the nineteenth century, even though their place in society predisposed them to be most concerned with what might be termed agrarian-interest politics. One should note, moreover, the rather significant contrast revealed in the major leadership's middle-class orientation as compared to the legislator's farmer background.

The most pressing assignment facing these legislators once the house was organized was the selection of a United States senator. The leading candidates for the position among the Populists were John Willits and William Peffer. Between the two, Peffer was regarded as the conservative candidate. Nearly all the former third-party leaders opposed the editor of the *Farmer*. As one of them later wrote, "they lacked faith in his loyalty to the principles on which the campaign had been fought, and believed that he would really act with the Republicans after going to

Washington."⁴⁷ The People's party caucus, nevertheless, chose Peffer, and his election was assured as long as there was no bolt from the caucus decision. To prevent this occurrence, as much as anything, a meeting of all those members who had opposed Peffer (nearly all former third-party men) was held at the Copeland Hotel in Topeka. Its participants reconciled themselves to the support of Peffer rather than elect a Republican by working for his defeat.⁴⁸

The ranks held. Senator Ingalls was defeated, and the new party had a United States senator to go with five congressmen. The defeat of Ingalls, in a sense, marked the real close of the 1890 campaign. Senator Ingalls, never at a loss for words, described himself as "the innocent victim of a bloodless revolution—a sort of turnip crusade, as it were."⁴⁹ What had occurred in Kansas did indeed represent a sharp turnabout; it remained to be seen just how revolutionary the results would be.

Following the election tri-
umph of 1890, Populist State Chairman S. W. Chase announced
that the party could be "justly proud" of its victory but they
should "not forget that the war is not yet at an end. We have still
a great work to accomplish. We must maintain and strengthen
our organization for the great conflict of 1892."[1] The agenda of
unfinished business included the work of the 1891 legislature, the
perfection of a national party organization, and the education of
the public in support of their principles.

Controlling only the lower house, there was little hope the
new party would be able to translate much of its program into
legislation. Legislative experience was stacked heavily in favor of
the opposition, as represented by the Republican senate; and there
was also the threat of executive veto. But Republican legislators
were not nearly as intractable as Populists believed, and considerable legislation was enacted. From the standpoint of reform, the
record demonstrates that when important legislation was passed it
usually required the initiation of Republicans in the senate.
Populist-sponsored measures found the going tough in the upper
house. Among the more important measures to survive this alignment was a law prohibiting alien ownership of land in Kansas,
which the new party had indorsed in its 1890 platform; an act
providing an eight-hour day for all workers engaged in work
associated with state, county, city, or township governments; an
act providing for the regulation of warehouses and the inspection,
grading, weighing, and handling of grain; an act prohibiting
combinations designed to prevent competition among persons engaged in buying or selling livestock, and to provide penalties for
the same; and an act regulating and controlling all state banking
institutions, which created the office of Bank Commissioner with

power to put an end to the era of "wildcat" or unregulated bank-ing.[2] The Bank Commissioner bill was introduced by a Populist in the house, but the Republican convention of 1890 had made that one of its primary demands.[3]

Just as important, however, were the measures defeated by the senate. The lower house drafted a bill to regulate and establish "reasonable maximum" rates for railroad freight within the state, which included a provision prohibiting discrimination in short-haul, long-haul charges and providing for the popular election of railroad commissioners who would have "full power and authority to control, fix and regulate the charges and rates"; the senate com-mittee on railroads, ignoring their party platform of 1890, rejected the bill in no uncertain terms as calculated to open "an almost limitless field of legal and business absurdities."[4] The house also passed a bill, which, according to Populist spokesmen, "would have driven unscrupulous Shylocks who are robbing the people by a usurious interest of from 25 to 100 per cent. per annum out of the state or forced them to become honest, law abiding citizens, by loaning their money at a legal rate of 10 per cent." The meas-ure required the "forfeiture of both principal and interest in case of usury," and was, as stated by Populist spokesmen, "nearly a copy of the New York laws on this subject."[5] The senate judiciary committee rejected this bill as "a declaration of animus," which they contended would at that moment unduly discourage capital investment in the state.[6] A bill providing for the Australian ballot expired on the senate calendar, and a number of important meas-ures were defeated more directly by the senate. Among the latter were bills providing penalties for accepting bribes, outlawing child labor, for prohibiting the corrupt use of money in elections, one prohibiting the use of private-detective forces in disputes between the management of railroads and their employees, and one giving women the right to vote.[7]

The most divisive issue to come before the Populists of that 1891 legislature was woman suffrage. Early in the session a Populist representative had introduced a bill to give women the unrestricted right to vote and hold office.[8] This was to be accom-plished by legislative enactment: its sponsors contended that a constitutional amendment was not required to confer the right, but they conceded one would eventually be needed to prevent a future legislature from repealing the statute.[9] Accordingly, the bill was brought to a vote and defeated on February 17, when it failed, by three votes, to receive a constitutional majority.[10] Then, by special order, the measure was brought before the house again the following day and was passed by a vote of sixty-nine to thirty-two; in the process, Populist ranks were badly shaken.[11]

The issue had drawn some of the party's leading spokesmen into conflicting positions. *The Advocate,* as edited by Dr. Mc-Lallin and Annie Diggs, was strongly in favor of woman suffrage. Just as the issue came to a head in the house the paper ran an article which declared that there was "no measure of greater importance before the Kansas legislature than the bill giving full suffrage to women."[12] The measure's chief opponent was none other than the speaker of that Populist house, Peter Percival Elder. P. P. Elder—as he identified himself—had fought woman suffrage for more than twenty years.[13] He was a formidable opponent; the more so since few men could claim to have played a more active role than he in Kansas politics during the state's brief history. After removal to Kansas from his native state of Maine in 1857, he had participated in the organization of Franklin County, the Republican party, and the first state government. He had been active in Kansas politics as a Republican for over twenty years when he left the G.O.P. in 1878 to fight for the Greenbackers. While a Republican he had served in the legislature on a number of occasions, and had been, as member of that party, house speaker, as well as lieutenant governor. In addition, he had been the Union-Labor party's nominee for governor in 1888. This big, heavy-set, sixty-eight-year-old farmer-banker-editor-politician, with rough features and an uncomfortable-looking beard, was indeed a worthy opponent.[14]

During the house debate, Speaker Elder entered a special protest into the record setting forth his reasons for opposing the bill. The measure, he argued, was "wholly unconstitutional," contrary to public sentiment, and, besides, women already enjoyed rights in Kansas "far in advance of any other state in the Union."

Then came the basic reasons that undoubtedly determined his position:

> This privilege conferred will bring to every primary, caucus and election—to our jury rooms, the bench, and the legislature—the ambitious and designing women only, to engage in all the tricks, intrigues and cunning incident to corrupt political campaigns, only to lower the moral standing of their sex; invites and creates jealousies and scandals, and jeopardizes their high moral standing; hurls women out from their central orb fixed by their Creator to an external place in the order of things.

Elder also contended, "The demand for female suffrage is largely confined to the ambitious, office-seeking class; possessing an insatiable desire for the forum, and when allowed, will unfit this class for all the duties of domestic life and transfer them into politicians, and dangerous ones at that." He ended his protest by stating: "When the laws of nature shall so change the female organization as to make it possible for them to sing 'bass,' I shall then be quite willing for such a bill to become a law." In the meantime, it would be "a grave mistake, an injury to both sexes and the party," he warned, "to add another 'ism' to our political creed."[15]

Four Republicans, four Democrats, and seven Populists in the house joined P. P. Elder in this protest, which Annie Diggs designated in *The Advocate* on February 25 as "A Relic of the Dark Ages." Mrs. Diggs evaluated the protest as "coarse, boorish, ungentlemanly and entirely devoid of that dignity that should characterize the utterances of a representative of the people and especially of the speaker of the House." She wanted to know "who authorized Speaker Elder and his compatriots to define the particular 'central orb, fixed by their Creator' as the limit in which woman shall move?" She concluded her critique by notifying Elder that if he had "any future political aspirations he may as well abandon them. In a state where woman's influence in politics is as potent as it is in Kansas, it will be useless for any man who has so little respect for that influence, and whose allusions to the fair sex are characterized by the coarseness of this protest, to ever again become a candidate for office."[16]

Although the measure passed in the house to be defeated in the senate, the struggle had revealed a point of fundamental difference in reform ranks that could well become an obstacle to Populist aspirations.[17] Another issue, not as divisive as woman suffrage but likewise fraught with danger for the party, was prohibition. A resolution was introduced in the house by a Republican to resubmit the state's prohibitory amendment to the voters; the resolution was defeated rather decisively by a vote of seventy-two to twenty-six, but eighteen Populist representatives had voted for resubmission.[18] Prohibition and woman suffrage were both anathema to the state's Democrats, and these two issues could become even more troublesome if the new party deemed it necessary to hold and enlarge upon its support from Democratic ranks.

For the moment, however, there was little thought of such matters. Early in 1891 most Kansas Populists were convinced that they were part of a great irresistible movement that was destined to move straight forward to victory, although they would concede that this could not be done without some organizational groundwork ahead of time.

Long-time third-party leaders who had been content to work quietly and inconspicuously within and behind Alliance lines before the 1890 election began soon thereafter to work diligently in behalf of a national organization of the party. The Alliance had elected candidates for governor in South Carolina, Georgia, and Tennessee. The man it had indorsed won in Texas. Eight southern legislatures were successfully captured by the Alliance. In Nebraska the Independents won a majority in both houses of the legislature. In South Dakota and in Minnesota the Alliance held the balance of power. Nationally, "Perhaps as many as forty-four" congressmen and "two or three" senators were to be counted in the Alliance camp.[19] These successes had of course greatly stimulated the hope that a third party along national lines could be formed. Nowhere was this hope more vigorously acted upon than in Kansas.[20]

W. F. Rightmire, recently defeated People's party candidate for chief justice and secretary of the State Citizens' Alliance, was perhaps as active as anyone in promoting the national organization. Following the election, he took it upon himself to contact reformers in various states to urge upon them the calling of a convention in 1891 for the purpose of forming a national party, and, according to him, "the signatures of every prominent Northern reformer were secured to a call for this purpose." "Southern men," he added, "did not join this movement."[21] The Alliance in the southern states had of course the special problem of whether to break with a one-party system that had been used so successfully to maintain white supremacy; there was, in addition, some reason to believe that the Alliance in the South could work successfully within the Democratic party.[22]

This conflict was revealed at the national meeting of the Southern Alliance held at Ocala, Florida, early in December, 1890. The Kansas delegation went to the meeting determined to commit the Alliance to third-party action. They there encountered the opposition of hesitant southern delegations. Seeing that they could not move the national organization on this point, a number of the more radical Kansas delegates,[23] working with other northern delegates, particularly Captain C. A. Power of Indiana, issued a call for a national conference to meet in Cincinnati on February 23, 1891, "for the purpose of forming A NATIONAL UNION PARTY." The call was obviously the work of men who were convinced that the movement was bigger than the Alliance; bigger even than farmer organizations; it summoned delegates from the Independent party, People's party, Union-Labor party, Farmers' Alliance, the Farmers' Mutual Benefit Association, the Citizens' Alliance, the Knights of Labor, and the Colored Farmers' Alliance. Southern delegates, however, were unmoved by this maneuver.[24] The record is conflicting and rather vague at this point, but it does appear that third-party advocates at Ocala, who were primarily Kansans, agreed to postpone the call for a national convention, and in return Ben Clover and John Willits were named as national officers of the Southern Alliance.[25]

In the meantime, some of the more radical leaders of Kansas Populism—in this case individuals of an urban orientation, who regarded the movement as a good deal more than just a farmers' movement, and who in fact were determined to unite farmers and laborers in a fight against what they termed the country's plutocratic class—met in Manspeaker's Hall in Topeka on January 13, 1891 (by design, the same day the Kansas legislature convened), to fashion a national organization designated as the National Citizens' Industrial Alliance.[26] The group formulated a radical statement of principles and elected a full set of national officers.[27] W. F. Rightmire, secretary of the State Citizens' Alliance formed five months earlier, was elected national secretary. The activities of the organization were kept secret, but it obviously became the chief agency through which the national organization was to be effected. Rightmire later stated that he was "instructed" by a resolution adopted at the Topeka meeting "to issue a call for a conference to meet in Cincinnati to organize a national third party" whenever he considered it "advisable."[28]

In January, 1891, also, the Northern Alliance, which was no longer operative in Kansas, held its annual meeting in Omaha. Although the northern Alliancemen represented at this meeting adhered to their radical platform demands earlier expressed, the general sentiment favored a cautious, go-slow approach to the third-party idea.[29]

This was not the case in Kansas. On February 7, 1891, Rightmire, by means of the press, reactivated the call for the Cincinnati conference to meet on May 19, 1891.[30] No arrangements were specified as to size of delegations, and no special provisions were made for the selection of delegates; there was only the call for delegates from various farmer and labor organizations interested in reform. This meant that the delegations would be largely self-appointed and highly motivated—or to put it another way, composed of numerous individuals who had fought the third-party reform battle for years.[31] Kansas certainly contributed her share; as the day for the convention approached, an enthusiastic delegation of 483 persons assembled in Kansas City and boarded a special train for Cincinnati. At the convention, 407 of these individuals were accredited as delegates—407 out of 1,417. More than one out of every four delegates, then, were Kansans. Ohio supplied a delegation almost as large as Kansas; Illinois and Nebraska accounted for another large portion. The rest of the convention was composed mainly of a scattering of delegates from other northwestern states; the South was represented by relatively few delegates.[32]

There was still at that time considerable hostility among Southern Alliance leaders to the third-party idea; these leaders at the convention were intent on forestalling any such action, and they were assisted in this effort, at least tacitly, by a more conservative segment of northern delegates.[33] Advocates of the third-party idea had anticipated this, of course, and were ready for all contingencies.[34] The leading figures among the third-party advocates got together soon after their arrival in Cincinnati and agreed that the first course of action, once the convention opened, would be to work together to gain control of its resolutions committee and its committee on permanent organization. Obviously, with these two committees under their domination they would be in a position to influence significantly the convention's actions.[35]

Thus armed, the National Union Conference—its official title—was called to order on the afternoon of May 19 in Music Hall by W. F. Rightmire. A temporary chairman was then selected and the committee assignments were made.[36] Avid third-party advocates, apparently according to prearrangement, gained control of the committees on resolutions and organization; the convention then recessed until the following morning.[37] In the interval, with Ignatius Donnelly of Minnesota (chairman of the resolutions committee),[38] Rightmire, a Colonel Norton of Illinois, and Morris L. Wheat of Iowa in the lead, strategy was perfected in an effort to overcome anticipated opposition to the creation of a national third party. The committee on permanent organization was persuaded to add a clause to its report advising " 'That the delegates from each state select three members of the executive committee of the new party.' " These leaders then set out to contact as many of the old third-party men as they could to get their support in moving the previous question on the committee's report as soon as it was presented to the conference. Rightmire stated that the task was handled so well that, "when the report was submitted to the conference in the morning, those opposed to the organization of a party were taken by surprise, and the previous question was moved. More than 500 delegates arose to second the previous question, and it and the adoption of the report of the committee were carried by the unanimous standing votes of the delegates assembled."[39]

Whether it knew it or not, the convention had taken the decisive step in forming a national third party. The various state delegations then caucused to select their representatives on the national committee,[40] and the resolutions committee was instructed to select a name for the new party. It in turn announced the "National People's Party" as its choice. Even Senator Peffer, who was selected to serve as permanent chairman, would seem to have cast off all reservations. In his address to the convention, Peffer stated: "Now, gentlemen and ladies, permit me to give you a word of encouragement and a word of caution. We have started and there is no such thing as stopping us [a voice: That's it], and the right thing to do is keep in the middle of the road [a voice: That's right], and to go ahead [applause]."[41]

The party's forward progress was assured, for the executive committee was instructed to attend the proposed St. Louis conference, which had already been scheduled for February, 1892, and if possible join with it. Should no "satisfactory arrangement" be devised, however, the committee was "to call a national convention not later than June 1, 1892, to name a presidential ticket."[42] As a national organization, then, the People's party came into being at this conference.[43]

The Cincinnati platform contained little that had not been stated earlier in the demands made at St. Louis (December, 1889), Ocala (December, 1890), and Omaha (January, 1891). The subtreasury plan calling for government loans at two percent per annum on farm products and real estate, first introduced nationally at Ocala, was included. For the first time woman suffragists could claim a small victory: although not an integral part of the platform, the convention had favorably recommended the adop-

tion of universal suffrage. Avid Prohibitionists were also represented in the convention; their efforts were fruitless. Former
Kansas Republican Governor John P. St. John, one-time Prohibition candidate for president, fought the prohibition fight. He left
before the affair ended, in disgust, declaring that "all meritorious
reforms were neglected" and that the convention simply had given
birth to a "third whisky party."[44]

On her return from Cincinnati, Mrs. Diggs was, in her
words, "besieged by questioners" who wanted her reaction to "the
new party in view of its refusal to incorporate a prohibition plank
in its platform." Particularly, "have I been asked," she wrote,
"concerning the reported assertion of ex-governor St. John that
'there was simply another whisky party born.'" As to the inclusion of a prohibition plank, she stated: "I have merely to say that
I did not expect it, and hence was neither surprised nor disappointed by its omission. No person who is conversant with the
cause and the purpose of our political revolution could for a moment expect that any other than the industrial and economic issues
would be made vital or prominent." The young temperance
worker of the late 1870s had indeed broadened considerably in her
thinking by 1891. She now believed that poverty was "the large
underlying cause of intemperance . . . [and] that monopoly, the
concentration of wealth and power in the hands of a few, and the
increasing poverty, degradation and helplessness of the many are
the near evils which threaten the life of the republic . . . ."[45]

Not all those Populists who were also prohibitionists were
as willing to subordinate the fight against John Barleycorn to the
fight against the system managed by Mr. Shylock or Mr. Capital-
ist; in fact, prohibition (among Populists and among Republicans) and woman suffrage (among Democrats) in Kansas fulfilled to a lesser degree, perhaps, the same role for Populism's
opponents as did Negrophobia in the South. In 1892 Tom Watson
of Georgia wrote:

> You might beseech a Southern white tenant to listen to you
> upon questions of finance, taxation, and transportation;
> you might demonstrate with mathematical precision that

herein lay his way out of poverty into comfort; you might
have him "almost persuaded" to the truth, but if the merchant who furnished his farm supplies (at tremendous
usury) or the town politician (who never spoke to him excepting at election times) came along and cried "Negro
rule!" the entire fabric of reason and common sense which
you had patiently constructed would fall, and the poor
tenant would joyously hug the chains of an actual wretch-
edness rather than do any experimenting on a question of
mere sentiment.[46]

In Kansas the witching words were "whisky" and "female suffrage."

Kansans were quite vulnerable to emotional issues and
emotional appeals—this was equally as true whether exploited by
Populists, Democrats, or Republicans. The chief beneficiary of
this condition in the 1890 campaign, however, was the People's
party, for the electioneering success of many Populist leaders owed
considerably to their skills in exploiting the widespread public
malaise. But just how loyal were those converts who had been
driven to the support of the new party by an aroused discontent?
Here was a question the more thoughtful leaders were concerned
about. The former Greenbacker and Union Laborite elected by
Dickinson County to the Kansas legislature, Michael Senn by
name,[47] advised his party, "We must not forget that a large proportion of the people are ignorant, as well as biased by prejudice.
The man who does not personally understand ... economic questions, who has not been able to emancipate himself from party
prejudice is an uncertain factor in a political campaign." Displaying extraordinary insight, Senn emphasized that this individual
"may have voted with us the last election on the principle that a
change would be desirable, or because he was inspired by the enthusiasm of the move; but in order to insure the permanent
support of this class, we must educate until they personally see the
evils and injustice of the present monopoly system, as well as the
justice, fairness and beneficent results of our proposed remedies."[48]

This was a commonly shared observation among the leaders, and the party set out after 1890 to "educate" Kansas voters on

the issues. Their task was not easy. As third-party advocates put it, the Farmers' Alliance had "graduated" when it moved into the political arena to fight the third-party battle. In one sense they were correct, for the decision for political action very largely transferred the power and energy of the Alliance to the party. In the process, the more radical Farmers' Alliance leaders moved over to party work in cooperation with their Citizens' Alliance brethren, and the now comparatively impotent Farmers' Alliance was left in the hands of more conservative leaders—among whom were some who did not particularly care about "graduating."[49] As it turned out, Frank McGrath, who had replaced Ben Clover as president of the state Alliance in October, 1890, was unsympathetic to the idea of taking the Alliance bodily into a third party. He apparently thought of the revolt almost exclusively as a farmers' movement. The best way, in his viewpoint, for the Alliance to achieve its ends was for it to operate as an independent and non-partisan interest block; this, in his mind, was the most feasible method for uniting the Alliance of the South and Northwest. Perhaps it was because of this belief that he had not indorsed the call for a national third party issued from Ocala.[50] However that may have been, his position won him the distrust of avid third-party advocates. There may or may not be any connection, but at the time the Kansas legislature was to elect a United States senator it was charged that McGrath had made a deal to work for the election of "his friend," Republican Congressman E. J. Turner. Some of the more radical leaders pushed the charge, an investigation was held by the Alliance, and McGrath was, according to it, "fully exonerated and commended to the confidence of good Alliancemen everywhere."[51]

McGrath's opponents were no less convinced that he meant to derail the reform movement. Then, in April, 1891, as plans for the Cincinnati conference were being perfected, McGrath heightened the controversy by stating that he believed he expressed the feeling of northwestern Alliancemen by saying that they would "either be in union with the South, 'in the middle of the road in 1892,' or the northwestern states will return their old time majorities for the old party . . . ."[52] Since it appeared likely at that time that the South would not join the Northwest in the middle of the road, McGrath's statement was considered by party officials as a mere subterfuge. Populist State Chairman Levi Dumbauld[53] responded immediately by saying that he was "authoritatively informed" that McGrath's statement was without "instruction or authority of the Kansas Alliance, and without the approval of his fellow officers." Nor does he have "any authority to speak for the People's party of Kansas or for Alliance voters on the subject. I therefore feel called upon to state that the People's party of Kansas is in the field to stay, and has no intention under any circumstances of abandoning the third party movement and returning to old party lines."[54]

The position of Dumbauld and not McGrath definitely represented the dominant attitude of the Alliance. McGrath subsequently announced that he would not be a candidate for reelection, and at the October meeting of the state Alliance third-party advocates elected their man in his place.[55]

The efficacy of the McGrath versus the third-party approach to Alliance goals may well be debated; it could be the former offered the better hope of success for the farmer. The revolt that had come over Kansas, however, was not just a farmers' revolt—at least not in its leadership and in its appeal for support from the combined forces of labor and urbanites generally. Unquestionably, it was the party's nonfarmer leadership that pointed the way to political action. Had the movement been exclusively a farmers' revolt, it seems likely that it would have made a much smaller ripple on the political waters. As James C. Malin has written, "the outcome of the election of 1890 was a popular not a Populist uprising—so far as organized political parties were concerned, it was a non-partisan discontent demanding reform, the exact nature of which was not clearly understood nor sharply defined."[56]

After 1890, however, Populist leaders did not cease in their efforts to understand and define the meaning of the reform effort (despite the confining approach of historical analysis which would have one believe the issues were formulated definitively by 1890), and when they spoke of educating the public they included themselves as well. Their overriding concern was with the promotion of a multiplicity of reforms bearing upon the issues of land, transportation, and finance. As might be expected, there were differences in emphasis among Populist leaders on the priority of issues, and in Kansas financial reforms probably loomed larger, but railroad regulation ran a close second.

In spite of the differences in emphasis, there was no exclusiveness in reforms advocated, and the emphasis upon finance by no means meant that the Populist party came into existence as a silver party. The concern in Kansas was for monetary reform that would provide a more flexible system than that afforded in the national banking system, which Populists, of course, proposed to abolish. Free silver was demanded, but the discussion of it usually carried a note of indifference, or at times even hostility. In 1890 Ben Clover and William Peffer, both of whom believed finance to be the most important issue, had ridiculed the idea of free silver as a relief measure.[57] *The Advocate* persistently added its voice in opposition to any suggestion that free silver would have any appreciable effect for the better.[58] Indeed, most Populist spokesmen could agree with William Rightmire's contention in 1891 that "Free coinage of silver will not bring sufficient relief, for if every ounce of our annual United States output was coined it would increase currency not over $1 per capita annually, and at that rate most of us would be dead and gone before that happy standard of 1865-66 is again reached."[59] Free silver, moreover, was Republican policy in Kansas, and the party's leaders, including Senator Preston B. Plumb and Senator John J. Ingalls, declared themselves on the issue at every opportunity.[60]

Kansas Populists were determined to have a more fundamental change than that represented in free silver, and in that 1891 "educational campaign" they made a massive effort on all fronts to win the voters to their program. The literature of that effort was overwhelming. Annie Diggs, as Washington correspondent for the Topeka *Advocate,* Jerry Simpson, Ben Clover, John Davis, James D. Holden, Sam Wood, Dr. Stephen McLallin, John Grant Otis, James Lathrop, Mary Elizabeth Lease, and scores of others, in speeches, articles, and pamphlets, interpreted the movement to the people.[61] Perhaps in all that mass of material a letter by Congressman Otis, published in *The Advocate,* stated as succinctly as possible what Populism stood for in the minds of its supporters at that triumphant stage. Populism, wrote Otis,

> is a spontaneous production, born of the necessities of the people and the demands of the period. . . . It is a party that will know no north, no south, no east, no west, but one common country . . . ; a party that will aim to secure liberty, equality and justice to all and will recognize the universal brotherhood of men. It will acknowledge unbounded faith in the ability of the common people of this republic for self government, and recognize as the supreme law of the land, the will of majorities legally and honestly expressed at the ballot box. It is a party that takes for its guide the golden rule and not the rule of gold. It is a party whose chief cornerstone is labor and the inalienable rights of humanity; and whose chief object is to rightfully protect this prime factor in production, and so organize human society as to secure general prosperity and happiness to all classes. We recognize money as a creation of law, a simple representative of value, an instrument of exchange and not in any true sense a commodity; that railroads are in the nature of public highways, which should be controlled and operated at a minimum rate. A party that holds the earth to be the common heritage of the people and every person born into the world is entitled equally with all others, to a place to live and an opportunity to earn a living. It is a party that earnestly desires the greatest good to the greatest number. In short, a government of the people, by the people, and for the people.[62]

There was nothing especially original about Otis' statement, and the same may be said of the party's position in general. Its spokesmen drew upon the past to apply the unfulfilled ideals of a democratic tradition to contemporary circumstances. Perhaps what distinguished the movement in its early stage, more than anything else, was the extent of its identity with labor, represented in the following words of Abraham Lincoln, quoted by Otis: " 'Labor is prior to and independent of capital. Labor is the parent of capital. Capital could not have existed if labor had not first existed. Labor is superior to capital and entitled to much the higher consideration.' "[63] The intensity of Populist attachment to this labor theory of value would serve as a barometer of Populist radicalism.

Republican leaders were not insensible to the threat implicit in any real cooperation between farmers and laborers; they were also not insensible to the vulnerability of that partnership. Those who were not engaged wholly in vituperation followed the lead of Senator Preston B. Plumb early in 1891 in working on that weak link in the reform chain. Senator Plumb argued that the economic interests of farmers and laborers were incompatible. "There will be sympathy to a degree," he concluded, "but no co-operation except between the destructive elements."[64] Populist spokesmen denied this, of course, but their denials lacked conviction.[65]

Shortly thereafter, on May 14, 1891, a speech by a district judge from Marion, Kansas, caught the attention of the entire state. Friend and foe alike dwelt upon his contention that "the rights of the user are paramount to the rights of the owner of capital." Quoted out of context, as they invariably were, these words immediately made their author, Frank Doster, a central figure in the reform movement, and Populism, in the state and in the nation, gained the support of a man who was one of its most brilliant intellectual leaders.

In 1891 Frank Doster was forty-four years old and recognized as one of the outstanding lawyers in the state. A native Virginian who had moved with his parents to Indiana and then Illinois, during which time he had attended Indiana University and Illinois College, fought for the Union in the Civil War, and graduated from Benton Law Institute in Illinois. It was early in 1871, not long after his admission to the bar in Illinois, that Doster had moved with his young wife to set up practice in Marion Center, Kansas. The ambitious young Republican lawyer had soon become active in politics and won a seat for himself in the 1872 state legislature. Defeated in 1874, he had remained with the G.O.P. at least until 1876. By 1878, however, he had become a Greenbacker, and he ran that year as the Greenback candidate for state attorney general and for congress in the third district. Apparently Doster retreated, politically, to a more orthodox position in the 1880s, for Republican Governor John A. Martin had appointed him in March, 1887, to serve out the remaining months of the vacant district judgeship in the twenty-fifth district. He subsequently had become a candidate for a full four-year term, and was elected in November, 1887, on a nonpartisan ticket.

As the Farmers' and Citizens' Alliance movement grew and was converted into the People's party and revolt swept over the state, Judge Doster no longer felt bound by the nonpartisan tradition of the district, for he had become actively involved in the work of the Citizens' Alliance and the People's party by 1891. Intellectual, iconoclastic, widely read, extraordinarily informed on a wide range of economic, social, and political questions, it was little wonder Judge Doster had devoted considerable thought to the meaning of the great revolt; his speech in Marion on May 14 was the product of that reflection.[66]

The judge began his speech with a commentary on why the revolt had occurred. He stated: "If these expressions of discontent were confined to the members of a particular trade or occupation in life, or to the people of a particular country we might conclude that they arose from no general cause, but were excited by the hardness of some untoward or unusual fate, bearing for the time being upon the fortunes of the impatient and over complaining." And so he continued, concluding the line of thought by stating:

> But when paralysis has seized upon every limb and member of the industrial and commercial world, and all classes except those engaged in the purely speculative lottery [and] gambling pursuits of life, and many even of such class, voice the cry of complaint at existing conditions, and stories of strikes, and lock-outs, and failures, and foreclosures, and money panics are poured out upon us daily, like a never-to-be-emptied Pandora's box of evils, and distrust and unrest and despair seize the mind of every individual awake to the situation, we must conclude that some unusual causes are operating to produce this abnormal and unhappy condition.

Turning then to the critics of the reform agitation, the judge stated:

> It is the habit of a class of dull observers and superficial thinkers to speak in terms half derisive and half slanderous of those who express dissatisfaction with existing conditions as calamity shriekers, apostles of woe, political lunatics; to class them with the vagrant and vicious, possessing no instinct beyond that of rebellion against the inexorable laws of nature and the settled and orderly methods of social life, but the fact is that the popular unrest and complaint is voiced and controlled by the most intellectual elements of society.

He emphasized this line of thought by saying that, although it was not generally known,

> every college in the land is a hot-bed for the sprouting of treason against our economic theories and our social organization. Socialism is boldly taught by professors in every school of note in both Europe and America. I think I have sufficient acquaintance with the literature of the subjects to warrant me in saying that there are now but four writers of recognized merit in this country who adhere to old time theories of economic science . . . .[67]

After some commentary on the growing influence of the new economic and social gospel, Doster then told Farmers' Alliance enthusiasts that if they thought they had "led off in a great and beneficent movement of reform" they were "mistaken." They were "simply followers," and were the "very last to fall into line among the forces of industrial revolution." Their leaders were merely "drill sergeants and minor officers in the army of labor." Their real mentors were the great thinkers of the age. Men like "Ruskin and Mill and Maurice in England, Rousseau and Louis Blanc in France, and Karl Marx and a score of others in Germany, and Emerson and Mulford and many others in this country . . . ."

Doster then hurriedly reviewed a number of the suggested theories as to the causes of the era's dislocation, and concluded that none got "at the root of the evil," or to put it another way, they were "but palliatives and stimulants, temporary and spasmodic in their effect." Then he came to his own explanation: "the cause of all industrial derangement is a misconception of the just relations between labor and capital." "Radical and unpopular as it may be," he said, "I deny the existence of that mutuality between labor and capital which we hear so constantly asserted . . . ."

Doster then approached his proposition from several different angles, attempting to clarify his point in the simplest terms. Later in the speech he said: "I do not deny that ownership has rights. I do not deny that capitalists have rights. My contention is that labor and capital, or more accurately speaking, ownership and use, or still more accurately speaking, creator and created are not mutual and equal. Ownership is a trustee for use, and the owner is a trustee for the user, and entitled to consideration as a trustee, and as nothing else." Doster recognized that there were cases where "mutuality does exist between labor and capital, or between laborers and capitalists, because the qualities of ownership and use are combined in one person . . . ." His major proposition was that when "the man who possesses a thing not for the purposes of his own use, but for purposes of somebody else's use, and whose interest in it is limited to the compensation which he can extort from others for the privilege of using it occupies an entirely different position, and must be viewed from an entirely different standpoint."

The judge also demonstrated how the demands of the Farmers' and Citizens' Alliances rested on the validity of the proposition he had just stated. And to make his speech more meaningful to his less-sophisticated audience, he then drew an interesting and knowledgeable picture of the changes that had come over agriculture during the century, demonstrating how changed industrial methods had altered the pattern of agrarian life. He made a point of emphasizing, however, that he was

> not now characterizing these as "the good old times," and lamenting their decadence. So do not misunderstand me. I speak of them only to bring into clearer view the conditions of dependence under which we now live as compared with the conditions of independence obtaining then, and to

enforce the idea of the superiority of right, because of these changed conditions, in the user of capital as against the mere owner of the same. Within this century changes of industrial method have occurred compared with which all past improvements are as nothing. We have begun a new life. We are living in a new world, as it were, so radical and complete has been the revolution in our ways of working.[68]

The reaction to Doster's speech among Populism's opponents was hysterically bitter; immediately the judge became the worst devil of them all. Republicans and Democrats subsequently summoned a "nonpartisan" antisocialist convention and nominated a Resubmission Democrat named Lucien Earle to oppose Doster in the November election. This combination proved too much for the judge and he was defeated.[69]

The polarization of politics, which occurred in Doster's district in exaggerated form, occurred in various parts of the state in 1891. Populists could flatter themselves that their opponents really considered them a formidable threat, for more than anything else this was what that particular trend demonstrated. Republican leaders, on the whole, adopted a strategy of abuse and ridicule, and, if anything, were driven to a more conservative position than was normally the case in Kansas. A few voices were heard in behalf of a radical program; for instance, ex-Senator Ingalls was expounding views by April, 1891, that could hardly be distinguished from those of the Populists, but he was attacked quite generally by the Republican press for his efforts.[70] Republican chieftain Sol Miller, in a moment of pessimism, could write: "If we do not want Alliances and anarchists, and all that sort of thing, wouldn't it be advisable to give something a chance besides capital?" Generally, though, the major opposition strategy was that old standby vituperation.[71]

The Lawrence *Journal* could write, "There is not one man in the [Populist] movement who has the necessary ability to lead any political movement, local or national," and there were echoes in the East that resounded with emphasis.[72] The New York *Sun* noted that Kansas Populists had elected to congress "four obscure men of no known fitness for political life, and one man whose qualification consists in a very red and volcanic mouth, and in the legend that he refused to wear stockings until the duty on wool is knocked off." Also, read the *Sun,* the party had chosen "a tangle-witted fanatic with a beard that reaches to his waistband" to succeed a senator and "a statesman of national distinction." They had elected, as well, a state house of representatives "whose chief pleasure and business is to threaten invested capital" and the bigger part of its economic views were "crazier than Bedlam." Said the *Sun,* "It is as intolerant as it is silly, and it seeks by many means, mostly not intelligent, the prosperity of a class at the expense of the nation." Mainly, "it is composed . . . of honest but wrong-headed men, who are doubtless at home at the plow tail, but who are as helpless and clumsy as a stranded whale when they take to political economy and financial reform and the regulation of transportation."[73]

Ex-Governor George T. Anthony delivered a major Republican address in Kansas City on October 16 which sustained the attack. Alluding to Populist leaders as "robbers," "highway-men," "dastardly villains," and "infamous wretches," he made the following confession: "I will say to republican and democratic friends, the fault is ours, for we *allowed* these fellows to collect and read the Bellamy books and such trash, and pour it into listening ears behind closed doors."[74]

In its conspiratorial attitude, its bitter, emotional, and merciless attack against the opposition, the Republican effort in this odd-year election resembled the Populist effort of the previous year—and there were other similarities.[75] The radical appeal of Populists, plus a heightened disposition to go it alone without Democratic support, assisted in driving Democrats and Republicans closer together. Populists made a special effort during the summer and fall of 1891 to win support for the subtreasury plan, which especially helped promote Democratic-Republican cooperation because Democratic hostility to this land-crop loan proposal matched or exceeded that of Republicans. For these and other reasons, then, the Republican party paid the People's party the compliment of utilizing its strategy of the previous year by cooperating with the Democratic party in hopes of defeating Populist candidates in a number of the local elections.[76]

Republican strategy was eminently successful, and the election of 1891 was a jolt to Populist aspirations. *The Advocate* quoted the Topeka *Capital* without argument that Republicans had carried 277 local offices as compared with 127 by Populists. In the previous election Republicans had elected 71 and Populists 324.[77] The effect of Republican-Democratic cooperation was attested to by the fact that in its defeat the People's party vote actually increased some eleven percent over 1890.[78]

The campaign and election of 1891 had a rather sobering impact on many Populists. What was to be learned by the defeat? J. B. Coons, Populist state representative from Miami County, concluded that the results indicated that there were two possibilities open to the party: they could proceed with "straightout missionary work as in the past" to win the voters to their program, or they could form a "coalition with one of the other parties." By coalition, he wanted it understood that he did not mean "a coalition of platforms or principles but the formation of a fighting league for campaign purposes." As to the first possibility, Coons did not believe anyone was "sanguine enough" for it at the moment. The best way of achieving victory, he said, was by working with one of the other parties. "The Republican party," he hastened to add, "has no desire or need of assistance from us in any shape. Besides, modern Republicanism is just what we are fighting." The answer, then, was coalition with the Democratic party.[79]

Whether to forge ahead in the middle of the road or to form a coalition with Democrats? that was the question confronting the party as it headed into the important election year of 1892; it was a potentially disastrous question.

"RATS, RATS, AND PICKLED CATS
ARE GOOD ENOUGH
FOR POPS AND DEMOCRATS"

Kansas Populists retained their enthusiasm in spite of the rather dismal showing at the polls in 1891. Plans for the February, 1892, St. Louis conference proceeded without interruption, and third-party sentiment dominated the delegations that assembled on Washington's birthday in Exposition Music Hall in St. Louis. Since the movement to create a national third party now appeared inexorable, the conference's primary attention focused on the platform. The most remarkable thing about the document it produced was its radical preamble, which bore the stamp of Ignatius Donnelly's passionate and lucid prose style. The platform itself simply restated earlier demands: only its return to the position of government ownership of railway, telegraph, and telephone systems instead of regulation, moderated after the 1889 St. Louis conference, set it apart significantly.[1]

But to the delegates assembled there in Exposition Hall it was not all that matter-of-fact. The press reported that when Donnelly and Hugh Kavanaugh had finished reading the preamble and platform everyone, "as if by magic, . . . was upon his feet in an instant and thundering cheers from 10,000 throats greeted these demands as the road to liberty." "For fully ten minutes," wrote this reporter, "the cheering continued, reminding one of the lashing of the ocean against a rocky beach during a hurricane . . . ."[2]

The most important work of the conference came after it was formally adjourned but with the majority of the delegates still participating. The rump action produced a committee to confer with the People's party central committee to work out plans for a national nominating convention. July 4, 1892, and Omaha were the time and place of decision.[3]

Before Omaha, however, Kansas Populists first had to deal with the important task of nominating their candidates for leadership in the state. In February, 1892, Dr. McLallin announced a significant new approach in Populist politics: whereas in 1890 he had discouraged discussion of candidates for state offices on the principle that the office should seek the man, he now was convinced he had pursued "a mistaken policy." "It will never do," he wrote, "for delegates from all parts of the state to assemble in state convention, having no knowledge of the men whose names will be presented for the several offices, and permit the slate makers to spring such names as *they* have selected and secure their nomination . . . ." He invited an open and thorough discussion of candidates for all positions.[4] The following month W. F. Rightmire assisted this effort by taking himself out of the running by suggesting that the entire ticket of 1890 should step aside. "Each of us has had a demonstration," he said; ". . . we are not wanted by the people of this state for their state officers, and . . . it is our duty for the good of the party to get out of the race . . . and let our party select new men . . . ."[5]

McLallin's concern about the manipulation of the slate-makers was prompted no doubt by the talk of fusion with Democrats then being heard in some Populist circles. The editor of *The Advocate* was a staunch foe of fusion. In McLallin's mind fusion meant "a sacrifice of principle and an ultimate sacrifice of strength"; he even went so far as to declare, "Better defeat than victory at such a sacrifice."[6] He was not willing to concede, however, that Populism would not continue to augment its strength without the assistance of Democrats. A number of other prominent Populist leaders were outspoken critics of fusion. In April, 1892, Mrs. Lease added her voice to the antifusion element by declaring: "there can be *no fusion*. We take warning by the past. The history of every fusion party has been destruction. Let us utterly and absolutely refuse to 'compromise with evil,' and go forth with the . . . hope of complete victory."[7]

But the idea of some kind of cooperation with Democrats in the upcoming election could not be stilled that easily. Democrats were anxious to work out some kind of arrangement. The year 1892 was, after all, a presidential election year and the desire to remove Kansas' electoral votes from the Republican column was irresistible. A number of Populist leaders were also aware that their party, on the basis of all indications to that point, constituted a minority of the voters; victory, they believed, required the cooperation of Kansas Democrats.

As the state and district conventions drew nearer, apparently fusion exponents among the Democratic and Populist leadership did get together to devise a plan which they hoped to have the nominating conventions accept. At least this was the contention of David Overmeyer, who was a prominent Kansas Democratic leader and allegedly one of the men who participated in a conference at the Midland Hotel on June 6, 1892, in Cottonwood Falls to concert Populist-Democratic strategy.[8] According to Overmeyer, he and some other unnamed Populist and Democratic leaders of the fourth congressional district agreed that the Democrats would, in addition to their unstated hope of removing Kansas electoral votes from the Republican column, be allowed to name congressional nominees in the first, second, and fourth districts, plus two places on the state ticket. Assuming Overmeyer's revelations were true, Populists had conceded little in the plan. The first and second congressional districts were held by Republican incumbents, and the fourth, that of John Otis, which included the Republican strongholds of Emporia and Topeka, was considered a questionable prospect—especially since Otis had made himself repugnant to Democrats by his radical views and his uncompromising antifusion position.[9]

It was one thing to make the arrangements, quite another to convince a Populist convention to go along with the plan. The agreement apparently worked well in the fourth congressional district where it had been concocted. Democrats and Populists held their conventions in Emporia on June 14, and by arrangement both conventions nominated a Democrat named W. V. Wharton. In the first and second districts, however, the plan miscarried.

Populist leader William A. Harris,[10] an ex-Confederate and an ex-Democrat who had many friends among Populists because of his Alliance activities, was known to be acceptable to the Democrats of the first district, but the Populist convention chose Fred J. Close,[11] a Union veteran and a third-party man, rather than appear to be dictated to by Democrats. First district Democrats then placed their man Ed Carroll, state senator and banker from Leavenworth, in the running. In the second district, Democrats held their convention first and nominated a banker from Lawrence by the name of H. L. Moore; fusionists in both parties then urged second district Populists to indorse Moore. At the convention, antifusionists, led by John Willits, blocked the indorsement of Moore by a slight margin and nominated the Populist leader S. S. King.[12]

By 1892 Ben Clover had adequately demonstrated his incompetence for the role of congressman; he was also embroiled in marriage difficulties by that date.[13] The third district convention therefore passed him by to name a lawyer and former Democratic leader from Fredonia by the name of Thomas Jefferson Hudson;[14] Democrats of the third district subsequently indorsed the candidacy of Hudson. Out in the seventh district, Populists and Democrats had no trouble getting together on the renomination of Jerry Simpson. William Baker in the sixth district, like Simpson in the seventh, had been unopposed by a Democrat in 1890, but unlike Simpson in 1892 Baker was renominated to oppose a Republican, a Democrat (stalwart variety), and a Prohibitionist. John Davis in the fifth district, who had won in 1890 against a Republican and a Democrat, was renominated to take on the same trio of opponents as Baker in the sixth.[15] The fifth and sixth were strong Populist districts, however, and there was little anxiety among Populists about their chances there. The real concern as Populists prepared for the state convention centered on the strong Republican districts of the first and second where Populists and Democrats had failed to get together.

The issue of Democratic-Populist cooperation carried over into the People's party state convention. Wichita, inhabitated by about as many Democrats as could be found in any one spot in

Kansas, was selected as the site of the affair, which in itself may well have been the reflection of a willingness to have Democratic support. On the morning of June 15, State Chairman S. W. Chase called the convention to order and introduced Mayor Carey of Wichita, who briefly extended a welcome on behalf of the city. Carey was then followed by another Wichita resident, L. D. Lewelling, who was a produce merchant and chairman of Sedgwick County's Populist organization.[16] Because of his reputation as an eloquent speaker the local county chairman was given an opportunity to make a formal and extended speech of welcome, which would serve as a keynote address; it was an opportunity of which Lewelling was well qualified to take advantage.

Lewelling was an impressive man physically, six feet in height and weighing just over two hundred pounds, with thinning dark hair and rather heavy dark mustache, but the convention quickly became aware of an even more impressive aspect of Lewelling's presence—his ability to give the spoken word a rather dynamic delivery. In a series of short and explosive paragraphs, which was his style, he captivated those Populist delegates completely, every one of whom had been inundated by a torrent of oratory over the course of the preceding two years. "We are met today," he said, "to direct the movement of a greater and grander army than ever before went forward to victory." Be it known, "Our battle is not for supremacy, but for equality. We demand no paternalism at the hands of the government, but we do demand protection from corporate vultures and legalized beasts of prey. We ask in God's name that the government shall be so administered that the humblest citizen shall have an equal chance." How can government expect to "command the respect of the people when so large a portion are abandoned to become victims of superior cunning and insatiate greed?" The People's party, he went on to say, would right the situation, but our "contest with plutocracy will demand the most persistent effort." "It will demand the most unswerving fidelity. It will demand the most dauntless courage. It will demand the most sublime devotion of the citizens of our commonwealth."

Populist principles, it had been said, were "but the ground work of anarchy, a sort of basement story of the edifice of destruction. But we don't believe it." No, "the farmers and laborers of this country are not anarchists. They are earnestly seeking to avert the experiences of the old world and to subdue the spirit of anarchy with the milk of human kindness." But "God only knows what another generation of misrule may bring!"

Toward the end of the speech he offered some significant advice to the convention: "While we are brave let us also be wise. Let us welcome honorable allies and we shall go forth to victory."[17] At the finish, he was given a wildly enthusiastic burst of applause, and the local county chairman left the stage a prime prospect for the gubernatorial nomination.

Up to the time of the convention, Lewelling had not been mentioned seriously for any state office. The discussion of possible nominees for governor in the Topeka *Advocate* included fourteen names. William D. Vincent, S. M. Scott, John Willits, P. P. Elder, Frank Doster, and John W. Breidenthal were among the better-known men suggested.[18] Dr. McLallin personally favored the nomination of William Vincent.[19] Six men were actually placed in candidacy—the candidates for governor and lieutenant governor in 1890, Willits and A. C. Shinn, Vincent, Elder, John S. Doolittle of Chase County, and Lewelling. John Willits withdrew his name before the first ballot, and that vote subsequently narrowed the contest down to Vincent and Lewelling. Lewelling then won on the second ballot by a vote of 339 to 217.[20]

According to tradition, Lewelling won solely because of his speech. Undoubtedly, his rousing address was important in bringing his name to the attention of the delegates, but this interpretation minimizes the desire to obtain the indorsement of the Democratic party. In a close contest, fusion sentiment, although in the minority, could have been a decisive factor. William Vincent was not opposed to having the support of Democrats, but he was a well-known third-party leader; Lewelling, on the other hand, had resided in the state only six years (liability or asset?) and was as new to Kansas politics as Populism, had emphasized in his welcoming address the necessity of working with "honorable allies," and was the resident of a city with a sizable Democratic vote. Availability, as well as oratorical abilities, must be considered in accounting for Lewelling's nomination.

The influence of fusion leaders in the convention was not great enough to follow through on the arrangements of the Midland Hotel conference. John Martin (not to be confused with the former Republican governor by the same name) and David Overmeyer, the two leading Democrats in the state, were slated for the two places on the ticket. Reportedly, Overmeyer would not accept the nomination as a Populist, insisting on the Democratic label; his name was not presented to the convention. Had Overmeyer been nominated, it appears unlikely he would have received the indorsement of the convention. John Martin was far more acceptable to Populists than Overmeyer. Martin was there. He was nominated for associate justice, and he lost, receiving only 199 of 556 votes, which was an indication of the strength of the fusion block.[21]

The convention chose General Percy Daniels for second place on the ticket. Stephen H. Allen of Linn County won out in the contest for associate justice. Russell S. Osborn, state Alliance lecturer from Rooks County, and W. H. Biddle, president of the state Alliance from Butler County, the party's nominees, respectively, for secretary of state and treasurer in 1890, were renominated. John T. Little, a forty-seven-year-old lawyer from Olathe and a former Greenbacker, was the choice for attorney general.[22] Forty-two-year-old Van B. Prather, one of the founders of the National Citizens' Alliance and Industrial Union, an ex-Democrat and a college-educated, former teacher turned rancher from Cherokee County, was selected as the candidate for auditor. For superintendent of public instruction, the party selected a thirty-two-year-old educator and Populist orator from Linn County by the name of Henry Newton ("Newt") Gaines.[23]

Kansas was allowed another congressman as a result of the 1890 census to be elected at large, and the selection of the man for that position became one of the highlights of the 1892 Populist convention. William A. Harris, the party's popular ex-Confederate and ex-Democrat from Linwood in Leavenworth County who had lost to Fred J. Close in the first district convention, was the man to beat for the nomination. Harris had been proposed for the office through the columns of the Topeka *Advocate*, and, if anything, the Harris bandwagon had gained speed all the way to the convention.[24] When it came time for nominations, Fred J. Close himself rose to place Harris' name before the delegates. The memories of the Civil War were still much alive for many of those assembled in the convention, and this gesture by Close, the one-armed Union veteran of Chattanooga, Missionary Ridge, and Lookout Mountain, was, however melodramatic it may seem in the telling from this point in time, deeply moving to the convention. A McPherson delegate recalled that Close rose "and pointed to his empty-sleeve, then to the American flag, and said he had sacrificed an arm for the preservation of those stars and stripes, God knew that he no longer harbored in his heart any ill feeling for the boys who wore the gray . . . ." There was no question in his mind that "Mr. Harris would shoulder his musket now as quickly as any Federal soldier to defend the stars and stripes and to keep this one united country."

As soon as Fred Close sat down, a Captain Evans, another Union veteran, was on his feet to second the nomination. Evans then appealed to the delegates to demonstrate their willingness "to shake hands across the bloody chasm." For far too long, he said, "have evil designing men stood between the blue and the gray. We have been taught to look through distorted mediums, held up by those men for the sole purpose of dividing public opinion, that they might, like Judas, satisfy their thirst for gold."

Mixed metaphor notwithstanding, in response to a request by Evans that all ex-Union soldiers stand to second Colonel Harris' nomination, several hundred "gray haired veterans" were said to have been counted. Needless to say, William Harris was the party's candidate for congressman-at-large, and more than a few delegates were rather naïvely convinced, as was the McPherson man, "that on the night of June 16, the great rebellion closed . . . . The war started in Kansas in '56 and ended in the People's party convention at Wichita in '92. The bloody shirt was buried there, never to be resurrected again by men who are lovers of liberty."[25]

In its platform, the state convention reaffirmed the 1892 St. Louis "preamble and platform" and made a point of stressing that they indorsed "every sentence and line of the same . . . ." The platform singled out a number of issues, however, which were of special interest to the convention. Included were resolutions in support of government-owned telephone and telegraph lines, a free mail delivery system, and the direct election of United States senators. A number of other resolutions applauded the work of the Populist house and condemned the Republican senate. It concluded with the statement that even though the Populist party was composed mainly of farmers "we sympathize with all classes of laborers and will aid them in their contest for a better system and a more equitable division of the profits of their toil, and we invite their cooperation in our warfare against a common enemy."[26]

The convention took one other action, quite unheralded at the time but of great consequence for the party; it elected John W. Breidenthal state chairman. Breidenthal was a thirty-five-year-old organizational genius of sorts. Although young of age and youthful in appearance, his leadership credentials were impressive. The new chairman was a native of Minnesota who had removed to Kansas in 1877 from Indiana, then in his twentieth year. After residing on a farm in Labette County for several years, he moved to Chetopa (Labette County) to work as a clerk in a real estate office. By 1882 he was a partner in the business; by 1884 the business had grown with Breidenthal's assistance into a much more ambitious venture organized as the Neosho Valley Investment Company. With Breidenthal as secretary, this company then grew to comprise "nearly four hundred companies" in Kansas, but only seven of these were said to have survived the financial difficulties of the late 1880s, one of the seven being the original company. Breidenthal was bold, daring, occasionally reckless in his ventures; in 1890, for example, he became involved as secretary and chief promotor of an unsuccessful cooperative colonization project at Topolobampo, Mexico.[27]

Politically, Breidenthal was just as unconventional. He had been a third-party man from the time he was old enough to shave, if not earlier. In 1876, at age nineteen, he had attended the Greenback convention that had nominated Peter Cooper for president and had campaigned actively in behalf of the ticket in Indiana. His politics had not changed in Kansas, nor had his interest in economic questions. In 1884—he was then twenty-seven—Breidenthal had been the Greenback-Labor party's candidate for lieutenant governor. With the demise of the Greenback party, Breidenthal had then become one of the principal organizers of the Union-Labor party and had served as its state chairman until it gave way to the People's party.[28]

The new chairman assumed his duties at a crucial point, for Republicans were more determined than ever to vanquish the Populist enemy. The Republican convention that met toward the end of June, however, was badly divided on the best approach to Populist defeat. On the one hand were the conservative regulars led by Cy Leland and Sol Miller who favored E. N. Morrill, a banker, and on the other the radical or reform faction led by George L. Douglass and other young Republicans who supported A. W. "Farmer" Smith.[29] The we're-as-radical-as-you approach to defeating Populists controlled the convention. Smith was nominated, and the convention adopted a platform that was every bit as radical as that adopted at Wichita. The Republican problem was that of convincing the voters that their rather sudden conversion to reform was any more than political subterfuge.[30]

The radical stand of Republicans, especially their indorsement of a plank favoring the submission of a woman-suffrage amendment, made the way of fusion easy. Democrats met in convention, and John Martin, despite the aborted Midland Hotel deal, made a speech asking that the party indorse the Wichita nominees man for man; the convention did just that, and one large obstacle in the road to Populist victory was cleared away.[31]

Only the existence of Democratic and Populist candidates in both the first and second congressional districts prevented there being only one major opponent for the Republican nominee in each contest.[32] The adroit management of John Breidenthal was soon at work to solve that problem. In a letter dated July 5, 1892, S. S. King notified Breidenthal that he was willing to withdraw in favor of the Democratic candidate, H. L. Moore. Then by letter to the second district chairman on August 15, King withdrew from the race officially; as he put it, in order to "greatly strengthen our ticket all over the state . . . ."[33] Later, only a few days before the election, Ed Carroll, the Democrat, withdrew in favor of Fred Close in the first district to make the united front complete.[34] If all went well, Populists were now in a position to poll the bigger part of the 55,000 votes that had gone to the Democratic party in 1890.

Having assured themselves of "honorable allies," Kansas Populists set out for Omaha on the first day in July to help select their party's national ticket. The convention opened on Saturday, July 2. Between thirteen and fourteen hundred accredited delegates, and many more observers, were on hand to see that the great affair would have few dull moments. With a flair of dramatics, it was arranged so that the platform and the nominations would be consummated on the third day—Independence Day. The platform was no great problem: the finished product was an extraordinary document as national party platforms had gone, but it was not a new statement by any means; it was the St. Louis demands of the preceding February with only slight alterations. The Omaha platform, however, was the official statement and rallying cry of a party waging its first national campaign, and as such it assumed immediately a far more reverential aura than all the reform statements which had preceded it.[35]

The selection of candidates was a more trying assignment. Who in the movement had the national stature desirable in presidential candidates? Colonel L. L. Polk, the main southern contender, had died a few months earlier; Senator Leland Stanford of California was mentioned but rejected since he was unacceptable even to fellow Californians in the party. Ignatius Donnelly was a willing prospect, but he was too radical, too controversial, and too little known to inspire any general move in his direction. There was General James B. Weaver of Iowa, of course, but the Greenback party's presidential candidate of 1880 had his liabilities. Too conservative for some and too closely associated with third-party politics for others, the general nevertheless was willing, and he did have as great a claim to national stature as could be found in the Populist camp.

But how about going outside the party for a candidate? It was rumored that Judge Walter Q. Gresham was willing to accept the nomination. The Indiana Republican was a tried and tested national leader, and the judge was at the moment on the outs with his party over its tariff policy.[36] The Indiana, Illinois, and Iowa delegations were determined to have the judge, and they dispatched a committee to get his consent for the use of his name. So determined were they that one of the Indiana delegates caused quite a stir on the third day of the convention by reading a telegram which said: "Have just seen Gresham. If unanimously nominated he will accept." The message was greeted with applause, and in the heat of the moment it appeared that the convention might be stampeded into nominating a man who, in addition to being a Republican, might not even want the nomination. Several leaders immediately saw through the whole thing and gained the floor in an attempt to take the steam out of the demonstration, but with little success. At this critical moment, Mrs. Lease obtained the floor. Her presence was enough to command the attention of the delegates where others had failed. Then in her "most sepulchral tone," she announced that "she had a message in her hand which read that if unanimously tendered Benjamin Harrison would accept the nomination."[37] This facetious announcement had the desired effect, and the Gresham boom was punctured with the adjournment that followed. It was subsequently learned that the judge had refused the use of his name "unconditionally."[38]

In the aftermath, there was little else the convention could do but nominate General Weaver. Second place on the ticket went to General James G. Field of Virginia. Although the ticket was not the kind to generate great enthusiasm, the delegates may have derived some satisfaction from their obvious ridicule of the bloody shirt by having nominated an ex-Union general and an ex-Confederate general on the same ticket.[39]

On the national level the new party may have suffered from disorganization, stemming mainly from the very fact of its newness, but in Kansas the activities of the party were now as coordinated as they had ever been. Soon after the Omaha convention, John Breidenthal established a lecture bureau under his direction so that all speaking in the campaign could be coordinated by the central committee, and hundreds of Populist speakers were readily available to blanket the state in that crucial campaign.[40]

Quite unintentionally it seems, the campaign got a premature start on July 30. Lewelling attended an Alliance picnic in Windom (McPherson County, Kansas) on that date which was supposed to be a nonpartisan affair. But Windom was the home of the Republican nominee, A. W. Smith. Naturally, the appearance of the two candidates at the picnic immediately converted the gathering into a partisan rally. Both men delivered speeches. An observer reported, "Mr. Lewelling presented in a forcible manner the trend of the present public policy of the Republican party, and the inevitable ruin that is daily entailed thereby upon the country." The Populist candidate was followed by A. W. Smith who praised "the thrift" of Kansas farmers which had in two decades "transformed a desert into a blooming garden," and he deprecated "the fact that there should be, in view of the blessings that we do enjoy, . . . people that will belittle the grandeur of our achievements, and raise the wail of a calamity howl."[41] The reporter was probably a Populist but the report was accurate enough, for it was the Republicans and not the Populists who invoked the "myth of the garden." The report contained, as well, what Republicans made the major issue of the campaign—the "calamity howl."

At about the same time, John Martin was under heavy attack for having "turned the Democratic party over to the calamity howlers." The chiding of a Republican friend prompted Martin to respond in an open letter by writing: "These 'calamity howlers' to whom you refer are the farmers, the laborers and the general workmen of the country . . . ." It was they who produced "the products and commodities that you and I and other nonproducers have no lot or part in contributing to the world's mass of wealth." The intimation that the Populists, "100,000 or 125,000 citizens of Kansas," were "engaged in a conspiracy against the honor, the credit and the welfare of the state" was in Martin's mind an "insult" to any "intelligent man."[42]

Moderation was in short supply. Republicans and Populists were inclined to think the worst of their opponents, and both sides went all out in their political battle. Populists hammered away at the system; Republicans, generally, ridiculed Populist leaders.[43] The G.O.P.'s defenders did not allow even trivial opportunities for ridicule to escape. It began when Sol Miller's newspaper and other Republican sheets supplied their own name for the initials of Lewelling's name—L. D. Lewelling became "Lorraine D. Lewelling." Sol Miller, for one, refused to use the name Populist, used the name People's party as little as possible, but preferred the name "Calamity party."[44]

J. K. Hudson of the Topeka *Capital* told his readers that there were two things at stake in the election (the crisis was obviously mounting, for Hudson had argued that there was only one thing at stake two years earlier—"whisky"). First of all, wrote Hudson, "Let the majority of the people of Kansas vote for the party of irredeemable money and paternalistic hobbies of the most preposterous stamp and we cannot blame the rest of the country for distrusting us in the future as a community of wild-eyed socialists and cranks. Kansas can ill-afford to bear such a reputation." Without question, "It is better to get the credit of having obliterated this party of humbug and political insanity by a majority that will establish the good name of the state and assure all observers that fiat and communism were a mere ephemeral fad in Kansas . . . ." The second thing at stake was "property," said Hudson. "Give them the power, encourage them with a sense that the people are with them, and it will be a long farewell to the hope of business revival and property improvement in Kansas."[45]

In this atmosphere it was little wonder the sudden conversion of Republicans to radical reform was not taken seriously; or that Populist candidates were rotten-egged,[46] and children of Republican parents were heard chanting little rhymes like: "Rats, rats, and pickled cats, / Are good enough for Pops and Democrats."[47] Nor was it surprising that an attempt to discredit State Chairman Breidenthal resulted in his arrest midway through the campaign for allegedly having violated the state banking laws in connection with his Topolobampo project.[48] Small wonder, too, that the slaughter of the Dalton boys at Coffeyville that October would be injected into the contest when Jerry Simpson was quoted as saying that "the Dalton boys were no worse than the national bankers and thousands of others in Kansas who are engaged in pretended lawful pursuits, while they are really robbing the people."[49] Or, for that matter, it was no less unexpected that the Topeka *Capital* would refer to Congressman Simpson as a "Freak," "Buffoon," "Anarchist," "the Political Mountebank," "Sockless monstrosity," and the "Clown of Kansas Politics."[50]

As the campaign came to a close the same paper stated rather succinctly what the election signified from the Republican standpoint. Said Hudson, the issue facing Kansans was "whether to vote that the state has been a failure, that we can't pay our debts out of our own resources, that Uncle Sam must come to our assistance and satisfy our creditors, that our business is not a success and we are a state of bankrupts; or to vote that Kansas is the most beautiful, the most progressive, the most prosperous and the most promising state between the Allegheny mountains and the Pacific ocean."[51] Populists of course looked upon the contest a bit differently, and apparently, with Democratic support, so did a majority of the voters.

The day after the election the Topeka *Capital* announced in bold type, "KANSAS REDEEMED," "Jerry Simpson Slaughtered by the Voters"; the Topeka *Advocate* announced in comparable fashion, "CALAMITY OVERTAKES THE APOSTLES OF PLUTOCRACY."[52] Both sides were a little premature in their rejoicing. The victory belonged to Populists and their Democratic allies but it was not as complete as was first thought. The state's electoral votes went to Weaver by a margin of 5,900 votes. Lewelling and the entire Populist state ticket was elected. Harris, Simpson, Davis, Baker, Hudson, and the Democrat Moore were elected to congress by a combined Democratic-Populist vote—six of eight congressional seats, then, were denied Republicans.[53] The picture was not quite so bright on further analysis. The Republican vote for governor since 1890 was revealed to have increased 43,000, going from 115,000 to 158,000. The combined vote of Democrats and Populists, on the other hand, was shown to have decreased from 178,000 to 163,000, which left Lewelling with a 4,432 vote (1.3 percent) margin of victory. The fourth district congressional race, which Otis had carried in 1890 by a 5,000 vote (11.2 percent) margin, was lost by the Democrat Wharton to Charles Curtis by almost 3,000 votes (5.6 percent), and Populist margins of victory in the third, fifth, sixth, and seventh were all smaller than they had been in 1890. In the first and second districts, the Democratic-Populist vote had dropped considerably. In 1890 the combined votes of separate Democratic and Populist tickets had exceeded the Republican vote by 5,000 to 6,000 votes in each district, but in 1892 Fred J. Close lost to the incumbent Case Broderick in the first and Moore won by a mere 83 votes in the second.[54]

Worse yet for Populists, it was uncertain whether they had gained control of the legislature. The senate was safely in the hands of the party with twenty-four Populists, fifteen Republicans, and one Democrat having been elected to the upper house, but the situation in the lower house was badly confused. On the face of the returns certified by the Republican-dominated state board of canvassers, Republicans had elected sixty-five members, Populists fifty-eight, and Democrats two.[55] A number of irregularities had occurred, however, and both sides were crying "steal." And as Kansas awaited the installation of the Lewelling administration it appeared that an explosive situation was building.

"THE FIRST PEOPLE'S PARTY GOVERNMENT ON EARTH"

January 9, 1893, was Populism's triumphant moment in Kansas, for on that day Populist leaders and supporters from all over the state gathered in Topeka to celebrate the inauguration of the "first People's party government on earth." A procession down Kansas Avenue and the ribbons, flags, and flowers adorning the Capitol's Representative Hall bore witness to the jubilant mood of party faithfuls, but through it all there was a note of sobriety, an awareness that their party was on trial, and a realization that they had an important mission to fulfill.

More than others, perhaps, Governor Lewelling felt the responsibilities of the moment. The forty-six-year-old Wichita resident was indeed about to embark on a difficult and demanding assignment. But Lorenzo D. Lewelling was better prepared for the task than most people realized at the time. The designation "Wholesale Butter Merchant" of the Wichita directory belied quite a diversified and capable background. The Salem, Iowa, native was articulate, well educated, acquainted by occupational experience with the problems of labor and management, as well as an experienced administrator of demonstrated liberal persuasion.[1]

Governor Lewelling was also a man with literary training and literary aspirations; he long had prided himself on his ability to use the spoken and written language. His grand opportunity came with his inaugural address, and he presented Kansans an incomparable message. He asked that they put aside partisan differences to see that

> political parties shall exist by reason of progressive principles rather than subsist upon the spoils of office. The "sur-

vival of the fittest" (or strongest) is the government of
brutes and reptiles, and such philosophy must give place to
a government which recognizes human brotherhood. It is
the province of government to protect the weak, but the
governments of to-day are resolved into a struggle of
masses with classes for supremacy and bread, until business, home and personal integrity are trembling in the face
of possible want in the family.

In this situation, said the governor, "I appeal to the people of this
great commonwealth to array themselves on the side of humanity
and justice."

Later in the speech, he declared:

The problem of to-day is how to make the State subservient to the individual rather than to become his master.
Government is a voluntary union for the common good. It
guarantees to the individual life, liberty, and the pursuit of
happiness. If the Government fails of these things, it fails
in its mission. It ceases to be of advantage to the citizen;
he is absolved from his allegiance, and is no longer held by
the civil compact.

The governor then injected a bit of poetry: "Talk to the
winds, and reason with despair, / But tell not misery's sons that
life is fair." Then came a discussion of the conditions confronting
farmers, laborers, and businessmen, which the governor concluded
by asking if government were powerless to deal with these conditions. His answer was:

Government is not a failure, and the State has not been
constructed in vain. This is the generation which has come
to the rescue. . . . Conscience is in the saddle; we have
leaped the bloody chasm, and entered a contest for the protection of home, humanity, and the dignity of labor. The
grandeur of civilization shall be emphasized by the dawn
of a new era, in which the people shall reign; and, if found
necessary, they will "expand the powers of government to
solve the enigmas of the times."[2]

No mealy-mouthed words these. For Populists they were
at once an inspiration and a call to action. For Republicans, and

not a few Democrats, they were the worst kind of heresy. J. K. Hudson of the *Capital* referred to the speech as "his incendiary Haymarket inaugural" and an "old fashioned calamity howl," which was "well enough for the stump, but not so becoming in the executive of one of the most prosperous states on earth."[3] The editor of the Topeka *Journal,* the other major Republican daily in the capital, on comparing the inaugural with the governor's innocuous message to the legislature, later concluded that there was "a Doctor Jekyl[l] and a Mr. Hyde in the executive office . . . . Doctor Jekyl[l] wrote the governor's first message to the legislature; Hyde delivered the inaugural address."[4]

The worst fears and exaggerations of Populism's opponents appeared to be confirmed the day after the governor's inaugural when the opening of the legislative session became at once an *opéra bouffe.* Things went well enough in the senate where the Populist majority managed to organize in routine fashion. But in the house chaos was the order of the day. Populist representatives were determined to prevent Republican organization of the house. Leaving aside the Populist claim that their party "had a majority of the *legally elected* representatives,"[5] the fact remained that Republicans held sixty-five certificates of election, Populists fifty-eight, and Democrats two. One of these Republican certificates was clearly in error,[6] and Republicans and Populists had challenged each other in a number of other cases.[7] After the state supreme court had refused to intervene on the ground that the legislature was the sole judge of its own elections, Populists took the position that all those representatives who had contests filed against them should not be allowed to participate in the organization of the house—a sure way to insure a Populist majority, since ten Republicans had been challenged. But precedent was all on the Republican side in their contention that certificates of election were *prima facie* evidence of election, entitling them to organize the house before an investigation was conducted into the contested seats—a sure way of maintaining a Republican majority.[8]

Both parties had sized up the situation and had mapped out their strategy before Secretary of State Russell Osborn called the session to order on the afternoon of January 10. It was the secretary's duty to read the official list of members-elect. Populist strategists apparently hoped to have the secretary installed as temporary chairman so that he could assist in organizing the house for the Populists—presumedly by helping to enforce the Populist position that all contested members-elect be omitted from the original organization. Whether Osborn was in complete accord with this plan is not known, but he did announce that he recognized that he had no legal right to serve as temporary chairman and would not do so unless he had the unanimous consent of the house. Immediately, Republicans voiced their opposition to this proposition; Secretary Osborn, in turn, refused to read the names of the members-elect and left the hall with the official list. As soon as he had departed, both sides scrambled to elect a temporary chairman. Sixty-four Republicans on one side and sixty-eight Populists (fifty-eight with certificates and ten contestants) on the other then proceeded, amidst utter pandemonium, to elect a dual set of officers. When they had completed this riotous maneuver, both sides notified the senate and the governor that the house was organized for action.[9]

Adjournment was then in order; but the Douglass house (Republican) and the Dunsmore house (Populist), as they were immediately identified according to their speakers, were both afraid to vacate the hall for fear the other might bar their reentry; so both sides remained in the hall throughout a long, cold, and uncomfortable night. Midway through the next day a truce was arranged, according to which each would occupy the hall at alternate periods without attempting to prevent the other's reentry.[10]

The following day, the Populist cause suffered a damaging blow when the three Democrats joined the Douglass house, bringing its membership up to sixty-seven. Perhaps it was to counteract this move that the governor and senate—in one of those we'll-be-damed-if-we-do and we'll-be-damned if-we-don't situations—accorded their recognition to the Dunsmore house.[11]

For the next thirty-one days the situation in the house remained unchanged: Populists and Republicans used the hall alternately, passing bills and making speeches, attempting to be as oblivious as possible to the existence of each other. The world outside, thanks to an unusually partisan press, was anything but oblivious to what was going on. Newsmen were having a field day with what was soon publicized throughout the nation as the "Kansas legislative war." From the opening blast, the battle of the press was won by Populism's opponents; without a daily paper in the capital, the shaky Populist position was riddled through and through and little could be done to offset the devastating attack. All kinds of advice and advisors descended on Topeka. Populists were of course waging their fight on a Republican sea, and in the heat of the moment the city of Topeka was first of all the citadel of Republicanism and secondly the state's capital city. Before long, the local Republican county sheriff had sworn in around "sixty Republican deputies," and Populists had recruited their own force of partisan "deputy adjutant generals," as both sides prepared for the worst.[12]

In the meantime, both houses and the senate met in joint session, with Lieutenant Governor Daniels presiding, to elect a United States senator to fill the vacancy created by the death of Senator Preston Plumb the previous year. Republicans were out-maneuvered in this contest. Populists, reluctantly and not without causing irreparable damage within the party, supported John Martin, the Democratic leader who had promoted his party's in-dorsement of the Populist ticket.[13] The refusal of Republicans to respond to the call of the clerk of the Dunsmore house allowed Daniels, with the aid of parliamentary legerdemain, to muster a majority vote of duly elected members for Martin. Republicans protested but the Democratic majority in the United States senate subsequently honored Martin's certificate of election.[14]

The senatorial election took place on January 26, and the legislative session was obviously being frittered away with no im-mediate prospect for solution. Feelings on both sides were also becoming more inflamed with each passing day. The leaders of the two factions professed their willingness to resolve the conflict, but the terms of each were completely unacceptable to the other.[15] Then on February 14 Republicans decided to break the no-conflict agreement in hopes of precipitating a solution favorable to them-selves. On that date the Douglass house adopted a resolution stating that if the duly elected representatives of the Dunsmore house did not join the Douglass house by February 21 their seats would be declared vacant, and to expedite the matter even further they ordered the arrest of the clerk of the Dunsmore house on charges of having "continuously interrupted the regular proceedings of the House by loud and boisterous language and unlawful noises . . . ."[16] With these fatal steps out of the way, the Douglass house then adjourned until 9:00 o'clock the next morning.

The Republican desire to force the situation to a conclusion was fulfilled; the Douglass house was called to order the next morning in the Copeland Hotel. In the interval, Populists had "rescued" their clerk, taken possession of Representative Hall, and posted armed guards intent on admitting only those members of the Douglass house whom they deemed eligible to membership. Republicans countered by marching in a body from the Copeland Hotel to Representative Hall; whereupon they diverted the guards and took possession of the hall by battering down the door with a sledge hammer, which Populists claimed bore rather appropriately the label of the Atchison, Topeka, and Santa Fe Railroad. Populists then retired from the hall to regroup and to plan their next move; Republicans resumed business and issued an appeal to the outside for support in their battle to save "constitutional government" from the "forces of anarchy and revolution."[17]

By afternoon the situation was critical. Republicans had recruited over six hundred assistant sergeants-at-arms, and the sheriff now had about four hundred deputies as well. With this force at their disposal, the refusal of the Republicans to allow the Populist house to take possession of the hall at its usual time that day appeared to indicate that a bloody battle was close at hand. Governor Lewelling at this point alerted the state militia; later that evening he appeared before the Douglass house and pleaded with the Republicans to vacate the hall and wait for a decision through the courts. "As the matter now stands," said the Governor, "it becomes my duty to use some method which I almost shrink from naming, to secure possession of this hall."[18]

Republicans did not vacate the hall, they merely made preparations for additional barricades; and Governor Lewelling did not have to worry about using the militia, for the ill-equipped, undermanned, and outnumbered force that responded to his call was under the command of a Republican colonel by the name of Hughes. It was no secret that Hughes had made up his mind not to use the troops to oust fellow Republicans from Representative Hall. The next day, Thursday, February 16, Colonel Hughes was ordered to clear the hall, and he refused to carry out the order. In disobeying the governor's direct order, Colonel Hughes got himself relieved of command, and earned for himself, ultimately, a court-martial and dismissal from the militia; he may also have given both sides a little more time to work out a peaceful solution. The militia, under new command, took up its post around the Capitol but no order was issued to clear the hall.[19]

At this point in the dispute Populism's journalistic opponents were taking full advantage of the situation to prove that all they had ever written about Populism was true. The Kansas City *Mail* told its story under a banner headline that read "ANARCHY!"; the Wichita *Daily Eagle* preferred "ANARCHISTIC"; the Marion (Kansas) *Times* employed the headline "The JACOBINS"; and the Kansas City *Gazette* asked its readers the headline question: "Is the Kansas Trouble the Incipiency of a National Anarchist Uprising?"[20] Similar headlines and articles flooded Kansas and the nation, delivering, no doubt, a devastating blow to whatever little good will the party may have accumulated since 1890.

The Populist leadership was guilty of having made some terrible errors of judgment in their determination to control the house, but one would have to search long and hard to find any anarchists among them and even harder to find any Jacobins. Little wonder, then, that on the snowy winter night of February 16-17, an overture by Governor Lewelling prompted a communication between the two sides that ended the conflict. The concessions were Populist concessions. The militia, assistant sergeants-at-arms, and deputy sheriffs were to be dismissed or discharged; and, while both sides awaited the verdict of the courts as to which was the legal house, Republicans were to retain possession of the hall and Populists were to meet in other quarters. The agreement to resolve the issue in the state supreme court was crucial, for the decision of that Republican-dominated tribunal was a foregone conclusion.[21]

On February 28, after the court had made the anticipated decision, all those Populists who had the Republican stamp of approval (fifty-four to be exact) pocketed their pride and claimed their seats in the Douglass house.[22] Animosity generated by the dispute was not easily dispelled, however, and any real hope for cooperation between Populists and reform-minded Republicans had vanished. It was the situation of 1891 all over again, with the senate and house working at cross-purposes, and with only eleven legislative days left on the calendar. At the session's close, Republican and Populist legislators—all of whom ran on a reform platform it will be recalled—had little to show for their effort. Only two major pieces of reform legislation (an Australian ballot law and an act prohibiting corrupt practices in elections) and three minor reform laws were added to the statutes.[23]

The most important measure of the session was the railroad bill, and it was beyond all doubt a casualty of reciprocal party animosity. Republicans in the house, with the aid of quite a few Populists, passed the so-called Greenlee railroad bill late in the session which would have made the board of railroad commissioners an elective board with the necessary powers to carry into effect most of the regulations then desired. But Republicans had specified that the "present commissioners" (meaning Republicans) would serve until January, 1894; in addition, the new commissioners were to be elected in the 1893, off-year, election. Populists objected to the first provision for obvious reasons, and to the second because they believed their strength was diminished in the off-year contests. The senate therefore amended the bill rather drastically before passing it with only three days left in the session; house Republicans refused to reconsider the bill as amended.[24] Thus ended the work of the 1893 legislature.

Their record was bleak, but what manner of men were these veterans of the "legislative war"? In background, the men of the 1893 house differed little from those of 1891. As a matter of fact, thirty-two of these men (twenty-one Populists and eleven

Republicans) had served in the 1891 house.[25] As for the typical Populist representative, he was a forty-five-year-old farmer or stock raiser who was in most cases a native of Ohio, Illinois, Pennsylvania, or Indiana, and a resident of Kansas since 1878. Twenty-three of the group were experienced legislators; two out of four had attended or graduated from college; most of the remainder had only a common-school education. Roughly three out of ten were former third-party men, while four out of ten had come to the Populist party from the Republican party and three out of ten from the Democratic party.[26] The Republican representative, on the other hand, was a forty-six-year-old business or professional man, a native of Indiana, Pennsylvania, Ohio, New York, or Iowa, and a resident of Kansas since 1871. Slightly more than two out of four had attended or graduated from college; the rest in approximately equal numbers were recipients of only an academy or common-school education.[27]

Like their colleagues in the house, the most significant contrast between the Populist and Republican senator was that of occupation. The Populist senator was in more than three of four cases a farmer or stock raiser, and the Republican senator was in almost as high a ratio a business or professional man. At forty-four, the Populist senator was four years younger than his Republican counterpart, but both were natives in greatest frequency of states like Illinois, Indiana, New York, or Pennsylvania, and both had come to Kansas in about the same year—the Populist in 1871 and the Republican in 1872. Republicans had more college-educated men in their ranks and more experienced legislators, but the majority on both sides had only a common-school education and only three of the entire group had served in the previous senate.[28]

These senators and representatives could claim some special legislative experiences that were not likely to be repeated; they were the veterans of the Kansas legislative war. But the short biennial session made no allowances for the kind of campaign they had waged, nor were they likely to be decorated for their services. They had failed in their purpose. In particular, Populist representatives had failed, for they had lost the war, and fate was not kind to losers—especially the kind who were portrayed by opponents as determined and desperate men, and who by their own admission were fighting for a righteous cause, but who nevertheless submitted to the enemy at the height of battle. It made no difference that their opponents had created a distorted and exaggerated image of them, or that they were well within the pattern of American democratic radicalism which had long been more radical in rhetoric than deed. Times had changed, and the cross-fertilization of urban and agrarian radicalism in the new industrial age had culminated in a literal-mindedness fatal to reasoned reform.

The Populist legislative defeat was also the Lewelling administration's defeat; but unlike the house, Governor Lewelling had time to soften his image in the public mind. Due to a combination of factors, however, the governor failed in this endeavor. His troubles began with some unfortunate appointments. The most troublesome of these was the appointment of a lawyer named H. H. Artz as adjutant general. In the case of Artz, the spontaneity and newness of Populist politics appear to have worked to the governor's disadvantage. Artz was the man who had presented Lewelling's name to the Wichita convention, and his appointment as adjutant general, a rather innocuous administrative position with respect to the Kansas militia, was not an unreasonable political reward. Soon after his appointment, however, it was publicized throughout the state by the Republican press that Artz had earlier been arrested in Colorado for bribing a witness in the district court, had been fined, ordered to appear before the court on perjury charges, and subsequently disbarred by the Colorado supreme court because he had "skipped out" of the state. The merits of the charge were not demonstrated one way or the other, but considerable confusion in Populist ranks was created by the Artz controversy.[29] The adjutant general was not removed until a year later, and then because an investigation of his accounts revealed minor irregularities in his office.[30]

The legislative war also had far-reaching effects on the administration not directly related to the controversy itself. After the 1893 session the worst that could possibly be said about the

Lewelling administration was not too bad to print nor too difficult to believe as far as the Republican press was concerned. Populism's Republican opponents were especially eager to exploit those issues that would hasten the demise of Democratic-Populist coalition. The appointment of police commissioners was most conducive to this end, for it involved the highly emotional issues of prohibition enforcement and gambling. J. K. Hudson of the *Capital,* even before the legislative session had ended, charged that the administration had accepted "boodle" from Kansas City gamblers in return for the selection of favored men as police commissioners. James F. Legate, an erstwhile Republican lobbyist who had joined the Populists the year before, admitted receiving $4,500, which he maintained was his to use without strings attached, and stated that Hudson's charge that Governor Lewelling or any other administration official was involved in the "transaction" was "an absolute *lie.*" Legate told Hudson he welcomed an investigation but he desired that it "be broad enough to cover [all] expenditures of money upon the legislature. Then I think you will have bitten off more than you can 'chaw.' "[31]

The investigation was held by the senate, and before it had ended testimony had been offered stating that Republican party "boss" Cy Leland had attempted to buy votes in the senatorial contest, that J. K. Hudson had done the same in attempting to get the state printer's job; but there was no evidence that Legate's story was false, and the bipartisan committee reported unanimously that the charges were not sustained by the evidence. The revelations of the investigations, however, failed to silence the boodle cry.[32]

Governor Lewelling and State Chairman Breidenthal were guilty of attempting to maintain an effective Populist-Democratic coalition. Both men were realistic enough to know that Democratic support was crucial if the party were to maintain itself in power. As part of that strategy, the administration and the Populist organization under Breidenthal's leadership tried to steer clear of the prohibition and woman suffrage issues, while at the same time attempting to strengthen the coalition by rewarding their Democratic supporters in the distribution of political offices.

This could not be done without increasing their vulnerability to Republican attack, nor could it be done without creating dissension within the Populist party itself. Quite a few Populist leaders believed that the reform cause would flounder on the rock of fusion, and after the Democrats had abandoned them in the legislative war, and the Democratic Cleveland administration was saddled with the panic and depression of 1893 and had made itself extremely unpopular by the repeal of the Silver Purchase Act, antifusion sentiment intensified. Most of those who held that opinion, however, were not willing to destroy the Populist party to drive the Democrats out; but some were.

Throughout 1893 the extreme antifusion view was aired in Topeka through the columns of two weekly newspapers, one edited by Cyrus Corning and the other by A. J. R. Smith.[33] Both men claimed to be "true Populists," but neither had ever been a key figure within the party; their Populist antagonists were convinced they were working for Republican pay. Of the two, Corning was most vehement in his attack. The latter had earned for himself a reputation that followed him to Topeka. On learning that Corning had set up shop in the capital, the editor of Wichita's Populist paper commented: "If Cyrus will try to use just a little bit of discretion, be content to stick his knife in without twisting it, he may be useful. He has the ability, is zealous, and we believe honest, but Cyrus ought to learn that aqua fortis, lunar caustic, nitric acid and cayenne pepper mixed and applied with a red-hot poker may be a vigorous treatment but not calculated to be at all convincing."[34]

Corning's first Topeka edition of *The People*, later called the *New Era*, came out shortly after the legislative session ended, and it struck an immoderate note from the beginning. He stated that he had "little hope for relief to the people through political methods," and believed reform could best be obtained by the idea of voluntary cooperation as embodied in the Labor Exchange idea, which was a plan for superseding money with labor checks.[35] The paper was, of course, intensely antifusion; Democrats were boodlers per se; and Corning wanted it understood that "fighting fusion is not fighting the People's party any more than fighting prostitution is opposing virtue."[36] After all, said Corning, in another edition, "Christ was no fusionist."[37] As for the legislative war, Corning's position was that it had been "a disgraceful row between republicans and FUSIONISTS, and that is all there is to it. The People's party had nothing to do with it . . . ."[38]

At the same time, A. J. R. Smith's *Populist* was promoting an identical antifusion line and attacking Lewelling as "a tool in the hand of the Rock Island railroad," a "traitor" to the party, and "an unprincipled adventurer."[39] Republican papers, of course, picked up every choice passage of the Corning-Smith *ad hominem* attack and distributed it appreciatively throughout the state.

Governor Lewelling refused to dignify the Corning-Smith barrage with a reply, but Chairman Breidenthal stated that Corning had turned on the administration because he had demanded ten dollars a speech for himself and a daughter in the 1892 campaign and had been refused, and also because "he was not given an office." "Smith," said Breidenthal, "is a man whose hand is against everybody." Secretary Osborn seconded Breidenthal's appraisal of Corning with the humor of an ex-Congregational minister: Corning "was like the old maid," said Osborn, "who, when she prayed to the Lord for a husband, said, 'O Lord anything, anything, so it is a man.' We did not give him anything, and now he is firing a popgun at us thinking it is a cannon."[40] And Dr. McLallin of the Topeka *Advocate,* an antifusionist himself, later commented that "Corning's record in nearly a dozen counties of Kansas prove[d] him to be a swindler, a sneak, a common confidence man and an all around dead beat." If he were not "guilty" of more than that, said McLallin, it was because he was "a miserable coward; and it is probably this latter qualification that has kept him out of the penitentiary."[41]

If Smith and Corning were not receiving Republican pay for their hatchet job, they should have been; their papers could hardly have been improved from the Republican standpoint even if they had been written by the Republican central committee. Both papers reserved their whole attack for Governor Lewelling. But perhaps the extremity of the Corning-Smith assault rendered it more of an annoyance than a serious threat; besides, the influence of both papers was practically nonexistent outside Topeka (excepting, of course, many happy Republican editors), and the checkered reputation of both editors was generally recognized. It would probably have remained no more than an annoyance had it not had a sequel of more dramatic proportions.

On November 10, 1893, that episode began to unfold in Topeka. Mrs. Lease made the front page with an interview reported in the Topeka *Capital*. The Populist party had just suffered some reverses in the 1893 local elections, and the reporter asked Mrs. Lease how she accounted for the losses. In no uncertain terms she attributed them to the Lewelling administration. Said Mrs. Lease, "the present administration is enough to damn any party." She described Lewelling as a "weak man" without "backbone," and stated that she had been the only delegate from the Sedgwick County delegation who had voted against him in the 1892 convention. The defeat, as she saw it, was "a loud and effective protest against corrupt men and their measures and fusion with the democrats."[42]

Several days after the Topeka interview Mrs. Lease was interviewed again, this time at home by the Wichita *Beacon*. She promptly denied everything she reportedly had said in the Topeka interview. She said that she had "never spoken unkindly of Governor Lewelling." She considered him a "brave, noble man," who was doing a fine job under difficult circumstances. He was, moreover, her first choice for governor in 1894.[43]

The Topeka *Capital* was not above fabricating stories, but it would appear that the first interview reflected her true feelings at the moment and that the second was an attempt to smooth over the whole affair. A break between Mrs. Lease and the administration had been building for some time. Lewelling had appointed her to the state board of charities. As chairman of that board she was in a position to determine appointments that came under its jurisdiction. Governor Lewelling on several occasions attempted to obtain positions for favored individuals, some of whom were Democrats. Mrs. Lease resented Lewelling's efforts to dictate the allocation of jobs, and she especially detested the idea of appointing Democrats.[44]

Mrs. Lease was in fact psychologically incapable of cooperating with Democrats. In spite of all the talk about leaping the "bloody chasm," not a few Populists failed to make it across the sanguinary abyss; Mrs. Lease was a prominent example. One of her brothers had been killed at Fredericksburg, another at Lookout Mountain, and her father had died under ghastly circumstances in Andersonville prison.[45] She insisted that her "whole life" had "been a struggle with poverty because of that cruel war," and she harbored a deep resentment against the Democratic party, which to her mind was solely responsible for bringing it about.[46]

On December 28, 1893, the whole thing came to a head when Governor Lewelling notified Mrs. Lease she had been removed from the board of charities. She refused to consider the removal final and immediately countered with a bitter tirade against the administration. On January 2, 1894, the Kansas City *Star* published Mrs. Lease's version of the dispute. She argued that Lewelling wanted to get rid of her not because she had "interfered with his office trading" but because she intended to fight for the inclusion of a woman-suffrage plank at the upcoming state convention. Governor Lewelling, she said, knows that with that plank in the platform "every hope of fusion is gone." She added: "Let me say now that the woman's suffrage plank will go in and that there will be three tickets in the field. As to fusion the people won't stand it." And when asked if she would support Lewelling if he were renominated, she answered that he would not be renominated, but if he were she could not support him and be true to her conscience.[47]

Shortly after this it was common knowledge that Mrs. Lease was working closely with the "Corning crowd." She admitted contributing money to support the *New Era*. It was also reported that she met with George R. Peck and W. H. Rossington, attorneys for the Santa Fe Railroad, on January 9, 1894, in St. Louis, and there was speculation that the Republican party had to be tied in somehow. Curiously, about two months later it was revealed in the Kansas City *Gazette* that she was one of the heirs of a five-thousand-dollar estate of a relative in Ireland.[48]

Before that, however, on January 26, 1894, the Pleasanton

Herald published a letter from Mrs. Lease that topped anything she had written to that point. She wrote:

> It is necessary to "kill me politically" ere they can succeed, and to destroy me they say I am working for Republican pay. . . . Not only that, but they paid $500 to obtain affidavits that General J. B. Weaver and I slept together at many of the leading hotels during the campaign. . . . The governor said to two of the state officers: "If Mrs. Lease makes any fight on me I will spring those affidavits on her!"[49]

Governor Lewelling avoided a newspaper debate with Mrs. Lease, but the press did manage to get a reaction from Secretary Osborn to the Pleasanton letter. Asked what he thought of her latest charges, Osborn replied: "I am no longer surprised at anything she says. The woman is crazy. Her reference to the supposed story about J. B. Weaver and herself is new to me and new to everybody in the state house. I have nothing to say about it. If she wants to advertise her own shame that's her business, not ours. The story I have heard about Mrs. Lease does not drag in the name of Weaver."[50]

By the end of January Mrs. Lease had made three major accusations: she claimed that the administration was in partnership with Kansas City gamblers; that bribes had been taken from three railroad companies; and that they had paid for false affidavits purporting to prove improper relations between her and General James B. Weaver. She offered no proof to substantiate these charges. At one point she indicated in a speech that the time was not yet right for revealing the evidence; apparently that was as far as she ever got.[51]

The administration claim that Mrs. Lease was working hand-in-glove with the Republican party would not seem worthy of consideration were it not for the existence of a long-overlooked manuscript contained in the Kansas State Historical Society. The manuscript in question was a handwritten biography of Mrs. Lease by James Arnold, with a note attached by the author to a Mr. McCray. The biography was not dated, but internal evidence indicates that it was probably written in January, 1894. James Arnold was unquestionably Mary Elizabeth Lease.[52] Mr. McCray, to whom the "biography" was sent, was by all indications David Owen McCray. McCray was prominent in the Republican organization. From 1887 to 1889 he was managing editor of the Topeka *Capital;* from 1889 to 1893 he was executive clerk to Governor Lyman Humphrey; and, in the period in question, he was working in Topeka as a representative of various Eastern newspapers as Kansas correspondent.[53]

Mrs. Lease obviously wrote this autobiographical sketch for McCray's assistance in preparing a formal treatment of Populism.[54] In her note to McCray she instructed that he be sure to give her "sole credit" for the defeat of Senator John J. Ingalls. She advised that he "say nothing" about her "political views *now*." From the standpoint of implication, the most damaging part of the note read as follows: "get the Capital to slobber over Breidenthal, [sic] and McLallin they are going to use against me that the Republican papers are friendly to me and have said nice things about me. . . . I have obtained the promise of the Wyandotte reps [representatives or republicans?] . . . . Get the Capital to make fun of my radical views and abuse me a little."

Mrs. Lease's autobiographical sketch was also quite revealing as to her state of mind at that point. Writing under the pseudonym James Arnold, she described herself as "Thoroughly genial and unemotional . . . ." Mrs. Lease, she wrote, was a woman who "moves in close touch with the people. The lower strata of laborers [,] rough-handed begrimy fellows love her, and she bears among her loyal subjects the title of 'Queen Mary.'" She then wrote, "Success and popularity make no difference in her demeanor and warm praise and cutting sarcasm are alike unheeded." At another point she decribed herself as "original in thought, prompt and decisive in action, forcible and eloquent with tongue or pen," a woman who "possesses in a marked degree the traits of leadership." Concerning her work in the party, she wrote that it was due to Mrs. Lease's "efforts more than to any other factor" that the "People's party owes its inception, and upbuilding." Then with obvious reference to her dispute with the Lewelling administration, she wrote that Mrs. Lease "has made it possible for men who would never have been heard of to boil up and scramble for office. And in their greedy haste they would ever mete out to her the fate of her protoype Joan of Arc, but calm and dignified Mrs. Lease forges ahead, winning triumphs and cheering success in all she undertakes."[55]

In February, 1894, the state supreme court ruled that Mrs. Lease could not be removed from the board of charities "without cause and without notice." It then became a question of preferring charges against her, and the administration wisely elected to drop the whole matter.[56]

The controversy had ended Mrs. Lease's effective association with the Populist party, but irreparable damage had been done in the process. Just how great the damage was would be impossible to determine; it undoubtedly contributed heavily to the 1894 Populist defeat. As for Mary Elizabeth Lease, the key to understanding the actions of that famous lady would appear to revolve largely around three facets of her personality: an exaggerated sense of her own importance, which made her a formidable spokesman but allowed her to be used by the opposition; an intense hatred of Democrats, which made fusion unthinkable; and a shallow understanding of the problems of her time, which gave her little to hold to once the going became rough and the impulse for reform less intense.[57]

Undoubtedly the Lease revolt gave an immense assist to antifusionists (both irrational and rational types), but an important assist also came from that combination of circumstances that had burdened a Democratic president with a depression, and by the policies adopted by President Grover Cleveland in combating that calamity. As the depression deepened, furthermore, Kansas Populism, at least in its urban leadership, became bolder, more radical in its rhetorical position. This combination of developments virtually assured the termination of any effective coalition between Populists and Democrats.

Indeed, it was in 1893 that Populist leaders began to discuss and indorse socialism with any degree of frequency. After the legislative war Republicans had launched a concerted attack on the Populist party as a foreign product led by socialists or worse;[58] Populists, in turn, initiated a discussion of socialism in defense.[59] Perhaps "Gas-and-Water," or Fabian, would be an appropriate prefix for the brand of socialism espoused by most Populists; but whatever prefix is applied, socialism received a sympathetic hearing among Kansas Populist leaders. Quite a few of them reasoned, as did Dr. Stephen McLallin of the Topeka *Advocate,* that

> The best features of our government to-day, national, state, and municipal, are those which are purely socialistic. We would refer especially to our public school system and our postal system. There is not a feature of either that is not an exemplification of pure socialism; and these meet with universal approval. Municipal ownership of waterworks, gas works, electric light plants, and other public utilities by which the people receive the maximum of service for a minimum of cost afford other examples of pure socialism, by which serious abuses are corrected and great benefits secured to the public.[60]

Such talk merely confirmed the worst fears and exaggerations of Republican leaders and evoked more extreme attacks like that of Republican leader J. G. Waters in the 1893 campaign, when he told his audience in Newton that it was "the duty of every Kansan to give this party a black eye, it is a foreign product, it has none of the sunlight of the state about it. It has the taint of steerage bilge-water that imported anarchists have brought ashore in their clothes. It is a bold pander to every bad element in society."[61]

Having convinced themselves that the Populist party was led by men who hated "our competitive system of government" (or so Republican chieftain Ed Hoch maintained)[62] and were openly critical of capitalism, Republicans began to employ all the weapons of the success myth and the folklore of capitalism in their continuing war upon Populism. None were more brilliant in that attack than a young Republican leader named James H. Troutman.[63] At the annual Republican banquet in January, 1894, Troutman stated the Republican case against the Populists in a clever combination of vitriol and exaggeration that may have won him his party's nomination for lieutenant governor, which he received a few months later. A party like the Populist party, he said, which was "conceived in iniquity, born in sin, rocked in the cradle of superstition and perfidy and nurtured in ignorance and hypocrisy must be of few days and full of trouble." In addition to "its contempt for the constitution and laws of the state, it has lived a life of duplicity and falsehood." The party had announced itself as the party of the laboring classes, said Troutman, but

> it has crucified upon the altar of personal ambition and aggrandizement the distinctive claims of every form of industrial toil, and elevated to exalted places a class of nondescripts having no visible means of support. This party, organized as it maintains, to subserve the interest of the toiling masses, is dominated by lawyers without clients, by doctors without patients, by preachers without pulpits, by teachers without schools, by soldiers without courage, by editors without papers, by bankers without money, by financiers without credit, by moralists without morals, by farmers without farms, by women without husbands, and by statesmen out of a job.

The people had been fooled for a time by a Populist "elixir of moonshine," he continued, but they were now demanding "a more substantial diet" since they realized that the "entire creed" of the Populist party, "when reduced to its simplest form, is the sublimated quintessence of flapdoodle."[64]

Troutman's assessment of the Populist party was severe, and understandably so since the new party had challenged the conventional wisdom as it had never been challenged before. Perhaps this was best illustrated by the reception accorded one of Governor Lewelling's executive orders. Early in December, 1893, the governor appealed to local law enforcement officers to exercise restraint in applying the vagrancy law passed by the legislature of 1889. Governor Lewelling predicated his action on the belief that

> the monopoly of labor saving machinery and its devotion to selfish instead of social use, have rendered more and more human beings superfluous, until we have a standing army of the unemployed numbering even in the most prosperous times not less than one million able bodied men; yet,

until recently it was the prevailing notion, as it is yet the
notion of all but the work-people themselves and those of
other classes given to thinking, that whosoever, being able
bodied and willing to work can always find work to do....

Under the vagrancy law and similar city ordinances, said the governor, "thousands of men, guilty of no crime but that of seeking
employment, have languished in the city prisons of Kansas or
performed unrequited toil on 'rock piles' as municipal slaves, because ignorance of economic conditions had made us cruel."[65]

Populism's opponents professed to be shocked that a message of this kind would be released by a Kansas governor; immediately the order was dubbed Lewelling's "Tramp Circular,"
and the opposition press rushed into print to heap abuse on the
"disgraceful" message. The Cawker City *Record* wrote: "Bums,
tramps, thugs, and wharf-rats, come to Kansas. The right hand of
fellowship is extended to you by our governor. Fear not the 'rock
pile' or the 'bull pen,' they are banished. Walk right into the
governor's office and occupy his chair; you are better qualified to
fill it than the present incumbent." The Dighton *Herald* declared:
"According to the suggestions of the Governor's letter, the safe-
guard of society has been torn down, idleness has been raised to
the plain of pleasure and a premium placed on vagrancy.... This
is some more of Lewelling's socialism and is an insult to society
and civilization." And the Salina *Republican* told its readers:

Governor Lewelling has issued another semi-social-
istic manifesto declaring that the social conditions under
which we now live are responsible for tramps and intimates
that the individual is not in any way responsible for his
financial condition and that if he chose to be a lazy shiftless
tramp he has a right to do so and that the people ought still
to keep him in plenty of food and clothing. Lewelling is a
disgrace to Anglo-Saxon civilization. A cowardly repulsive
demagogue.

Similar press comments were made by Republican newspapers
throughout the state.[66]

As governor, Lewelling was of course by no means as
unconventional as Populist rhetoric and attacks upon his admin-

istration might lead one to believe. There were limits to what he could do to act upon his beliefs, and he was also determined that whatever was done violence was to be avoided.[67] Within these limitations, there was little he could do, as he put it, but utilize the powers of moral suasion in behalf of "suffering humanity"; and in the heated political atmosphere of 1893-94, that particular course was calculated to inspire Populism's opponents all the more in their campaign to see that the first People's party government on earth was also the last.[68]

NOTHING FAILS LIKE FAILURE:
1894 and the Redeemers

O n the eve of the nominating conventions of 1894, it was quite obvious the Lewelling administration was in trouble. Most Populists and quite a few Democrats were in no mood to listen to talk of a Democratic-Populist coalition, an end toward which Republican party managers had been working since the humiliating defeat at the hands of the coalition of 1892. Regulars were back in command of the G.O.P. again, and Republican strategy was being molded, rather adroitly, to accomplish one supreme objective—Populist defeat. As one Republican regular put it, "In Kansas politics I am a firm believer in the doctrine of the survival of the fittest."[1] There was of course no question in his mind which party was fit and which was unfit; nor was there any question that the concept of survival included a large dose of political cunning. With the wealthy Troy merchant and wily political boss Cy Leland calling the shots again, Republicans were assured an ample supply of the latter.[2]

By the time the Republican state convention assembled in Topeka the first week in June, the party's conservative wing had the upper hand. This faction, with Leland's careful direction, then proceeded to draw up a platform and to nominate a slate of candidates which not only suited their conservative temper but which also was designed so as not to assist in patching up the rift between Populists and Democrats. The latter maneuver was achieved by avoiding statements on woman suffrage and prohibition enforcement, despite a rather vocal demand from within and without the convention that the party declare itself on those two issues as it had done in 1892. The gubernatorial nomination went to Leland's man, Edmund Morrill, a banker and a former congressman from Hiawatha.[3]

Republicans had done all they could do to divide the opposition, but the final decision on whether Populists and Democrats would make a joint effort depended on the actions of the Populist convention which was to follow. If the convention could avoid committing itself on the proposed woman-suffrage amendment, as Governor Lewelling and State Chairman Breidenthal apparently hoped, there was still a chance that the Democrats, for whom there was no more abhorrent reform, would indorse the Populist ticket. But Populist conventions were noted for making their own decisions.

On June 12 the Populist state convention was called to order in the same hall the Republicans had used less than a week before. Close to three thousand enthusiastic delegates and observers were on hand. According to one sympathetic observer, the contrast between the delegates of the two conventions was most striking. Said he, "untanned faces, spotless shirt fronts, and new clothes" had been "the rule in the Republican convention"; most of the Populist delegates had the mark of "the sturdy sons of toil" upon them. To this observer there was an unmistakable message in this contrast. He was sure this great representation of the state's working classes, "the very men from whom in years gone by the Republicans used to roll up their overwhelming majorities," met, as they were, to oppose that "once grand old party," would be "a lesson to this fanatical, hidebound Republican town of Topeka . . . ."[4]

The Populist organization had not been content to rely on the subjective powers of observation to convey their sentiments. The hall was decorated in gala colors. Flowers and bunting were used liberally throughout. The most striking decor, however, adorned the south wall of the hall. Under a large banner which read "REPUBLICAN REDEEMERS" (the theme of the Republican state convention and campaign), a number of placards were on display which expressed quite aptly the Populist feeling about the would-be redeemers. Former Republican Governor George T. Anthony appeared in one which pictured him getting away with a sack of money from a safe designated as the "New York school fund." Edmund Morrill was portrayed over the words

"Three per cent. a month redeemer." J. K. Hudson, editor of the Topeka *Capital,* champion of prohibition, and arch foe of the Populists, was caricatured in one showing him drinking a bottle of beer. Another placard pictured a bloody shirt, and under it were the words: "This is a real live issue, and we mean what we say." Beneath a cartoon of John J. Ingalls, Populists had applied the words of Kansas poet Eugene Ware: "Up was he stuck, but in the upness of his stuckitude he fell."

Of the several banners which also appeared on that south wall, two in particular caught the eye. One read "DEATH TO POPULISM," with the words "Republican State Convention, June 6, '94" attached. Directly beneath this hung another reading: "DEATH TO POPULISM MEANS DEATH TO THE COMMON PEOPLE."[5]

If the banners and placards were there to evoke enthusiasm, they were not needed. The delegates and observers all knew that the convention would have to deal with the issue of the woman-suffrage amendment placed on the ballot by the 1893 legislature, and, whether they opposed or favored the commitment of that Populist convention to woman suffrage, both sides were convinced that the decision was critical for the future of the party. No simple explanation would suffice to explain why the convention was split on the issue. Among the opponents of a supporting resolution were some who opposed woman suffrage on principle and others who believed an indorsement unnecessary and unwise, who may or may not have supported the right of women to vote, but who were certain an indorsement would cost the party badly needed Democratic support. The motives of those who favored a support-ing resolution were more complex. For extreme antifusionists the woman-suffrage issue had become a test of the party's purity. Prohibition was involved as well. It was a commonly shared opinion that if women were given the vote the state's prohibitory amendment would be that much safer from repeal. For those Populists then who were also prohibitionists and antifusionists, woman suffrage was a means of striking a double blow at the Democratic party, to which of course both prohibition and woman suffrage were anathema. There were many Populists, however, who nevertheless supported woman suffrage on principle and wanted the convention to indorse the pending amendment.

Even before the convention opened, both sides had settled on a man for temporary chairman—W. F. "Ironjaw" Brown of Kingman for the anti's and Ben S. Henderson of Winfield for the pro's. In that first test of strength, Henderson was the choice of the convention for temporary chairman, and in his acceptance speech the Cowley County lawyer wasted no time in getting to the crucial issue. He told the convention he was proud to have been selected to preside over a party that had as "its mission the destruction of both the Republican and Democratic parties, both of which were responsible for the legislation that had doubled the mortgage indebtedness of the United States, and cut the price of wheat down from two dollars to fifty cents a bushel [a voice in the crowd rang out: 'thirty-five cents a bushel']," and for the legislation that "had made four million . . . tramps." He then told the convention that it must not emulate the cowardice of the Republican convention on the issue of woman suffrage. "The women," he said, "were in this convention, just as they were in that, asking for nothing but their God-given right, and this Populist convention ought to give it to them." This statement evoked a loud cheer, especially from the galleries where the Equal Suffrage Association was present in force.[6]

The rest of the morning passed rather quickly and without incident. When it came time to close for the noon meal, Henderson requested that the convention stand while a minister from Pawnee County offered a prayer. That prayer became one of the highlights of the morning session. The Populist reporter representing the Ottawa *Journal and Triumph* recorded that the

> prayer was of rather a small-sized kind, injected into a large-sized political speech. It was full of timely and telling hits, and pleased the audience immensely. When the reverend gentleman, after praying for Governor Lewelling, the state administration, and the success of the people's cause, got to that point where he called upon "God to bless the President of these United States—*after he has repented of his sins,*" the audience, running over before, could contain

itself no longer, but broke loose in a storm of appreciative
laughter and applause.[7]

The reporter could have added that the minister also made a direct
plea for action in support of woman suffrage.

By afternoon the crowded hall grew quite warm. The delegates and observers, many in shirt sleeves by this time, sat and
sweltered and fanned themselves while listening to speeches and
awaiting anxiously the reports of the various committees. Most of
the time on the floor during the afternoon was consumed by
speeches for and against a formal indorsement of the woman-
suffrage amendment. Woman-suffrage interests were well represented in the personages of Mrs. Carrie Lane Chapman Catt, Miss
Susan B. Anthony, Reverend Anna Shaw, and Frank Doster.
These speeches, plus the selection of the officers of the ill-fated
Dunsmore house as the convention's permanent officers, rounded
out quite an eventful first day's activity.

Chairman John Dunsmore's call to order the next morning,
however, signaled the beginning of a session that made pale in
comparison the events of the previous day. The majority report
of the resolutions committee was presented to the convention
minus a resolution in support of the woman-suffrage amendment.
The convention was clearly agitated by this development. At this
tense moment E. R. Ridgely of Crawford County was presented
to the convention in order to make a minority report on resolutions. With this announcement the hall fairly exploded with applause and cheering. Women in the audience were especially
demonstrative, as it was now obvious that this Populist convention
was not about to be gagged as had been the Republican convention.[8]

In his remarks before reading the minority report, Ridgely
announced with obvious satisfaction that the antisuffrage men on
the committee had served notice that they would file a minority
report if the suffrage plank was inserted; consequently, when the
suffrage advocates found themselves in the minority they felt no
qualms about pursuing the same course. Great applause accompanied this announcement. It was plain to everyone now that this

divisive issue would have to be fought out on the floor of the convention. The committee had divided fourteen to eight on the question. Peter P. Elder and W. L. Brown were the only members on the committee who had distinguished themselves as leaders of state Populism up to that point, and they were the leading opponents of the plank. This by no means, however, should be taken as an indication of the position of the major leadership on this question; loyalties were clearly divided, although the party organization, as it had managed to represent itself on the resolutions committee, preferred to avoid the issue.[9] Ridgely's appearance on the stage smashed that preference.

Ridgely stated the minority position rather succinctly: "*Whereas,* The People's party came into existence and won its glorious victories on the fundamental principle of equal rights to all and special privileges to none: therefore, be it *Resolved,* That we favor the pending constitutional amendment." Pandemonium then broke loose in the hall. Delegates were on their feet in an instant, standing on chairs, yelling, seeking recognition from Chairman Dunsmore. The chairman at the same time began pounding and screaming for order, which, as one might expect, seemed a long time in coming. As soon as a semblance of order had been restored to the hall, the chairman was deluged with motions and amendments on the critical issue. Finally, W. H. Wilson, delegate from Miami County, obtained the floor and presented the following compromise amendment: "Whereas, The initiative and referendum is one of the cardinal principles of the Populist party, we indorse the action of the people's legislature of 1893 in submitting the question of female suffrage to the voters of the state of Kansas." W. L. Brown was then recognized, and he stated that the woman suffragists who had appeared before the committee would accept nothing but an unequivocal indorsement of the pending amendment. Brown turned to Annie Diggs who was on the stage with him at the time and asked that she verify his statement. Mrs. Diggs, who since the disaffection of Mary Elizabeth Lease wore undisputedly the laurels of the most outstanding woman in Populist ranks, declined to do so but stated emphatically that her co-workers in the cause of woman suffrage "did not like the milk and water amendment" presented by delegate Wilson.[10]

An animated discussion then ensued, initiated by Wilson in behalf of his compromise proposal. He was followed by another delegate, advocating the defeat of the Wilson amendment and an immediate vote on the minority report. Then Ben Henderson, the convention's temporary chairman, obtained the floor and spoke quite strongly in opposition to the compromise measure. He told the convention he regarded the Wilson amendment as a "subterfuge." As for him, he wanted "the noble men of the People's party to declare where they stood upon the question." His next statement revealed the prohibitionist-antifusionist side of the woman-suffrage question: "God Almighty hated a coward," he said. The People's party was "not making platforms for Republicans or Democrats or whiskyites." The party "stood for right and law, and the opponents of suffrage for the beer classes."

The argument that the opponents of the suffrage plank were either "whiskyites" or were afraid to alienate the "beer classes" had been circulating freely about the convention; Henderson's statement therefore stirred W. J. Costigan from Franklin County to the attack. After obtaining the floor this opponent of the suffrage plank declared:

> I have been in this reform fight for sixteen years, and the charge of cowardice does not apply. I was in it when it was so small and weak that the gentleman who has just spoken went back on us, after being state secretary of the party, and fought us from the ranks of the Republican party. The charge of cowardice comes with poor grace from him. I received my education at the knee of a Christian mother, who taught me to hate whisky, and I protest against being called a whiskyite by a graduate of the Keeley cure.

A mixed response of cheers, hisses, and cries of "Shame!" "Shame!" prevented Costigan from going any further. Henderson then regained the floor on a point of personal privilege and stated: "I have listened with considerable contempt to the sarcastic words of the gentleman who preceded me. I will admit to you that I have been one of those unfortunates, and I stand here now and say . . . , God being my judge, I propose to stand for the women."

It now seemed that everyone had something to say on the matter. Hence it was suggested that speakers be limited to five minutes with debate coming to a close at the noon hour. The last ten minutes, it was proposed, would be reserved for Annie Diggs and P. P. Elder to make closing statements for their particular sides.

This agreed, the debate continued in earnest. There is no count of how many delegates spoke during this period. Undoubtedly more wanted to speak than did. Most used less than the allotted five minutes. Speakers followed each other in rapid succession and engaged in a heated dialogue, the arguments of one speaker generally rousing another in response. T. J. Thompson from Miami County pleaded the case of the compromise measure and warned, without specifying how, that the suffrage plank was "detrimental to the party and to the cause of women." G. E. Miller, delegate from Republic County, declared that "cowardice was always contemptible" and admonished the convention to "stand for what they believed to be right, and cease following the will-o'-the-wisp-policy." A Negro delegate from Pottawatomie County, identified only as Beck, declared that "the Republican party had been buried by isms," and in his opinion "it was very foolish for the Populist party to get down on all fours and play horse and allow these isms to be unloaded upon it." He then spoke out in no uncertain terms in opposition to woman suffrage. His effort accentuated feeling on the issue.

At this point, Frank Doster, who was a leading proponent of woman suffrage, managed to gain recognition from the chair. He stated with as much feeling as he could muster that

> The Populist party *is* a party of isms, and without desiring to say anything which will bring back unpleasant memories to the gentleman who has just sat down, I will remind him that if it had not been a party of isms, he would have not had a chance to speak before this convention.

What does this substitute for all these other resolutions signify? Does it signify that the Populist party is about to take any progressive step? I stand against regarding this as a question of expediency, and ask that the Populist party take a step forward and adopt the minority report.

John Otis, elected to congress in 1890 but sacrificed in 1892 for the fusion nominee in the fourth district, obtained the floor several times during the debate to speak for the suffrage plank; he did so again a short time after Doster's effort. Otis was a prohibitionist and an extreme antifusionist—he was in fact president of the recently organized "Anti-Fusion People's Party League of Kansas," which featured Cyrus Corning as secretary.[11] This time up, Otis stated that the issue was simply a question of whether "the people of the People's party control its policy or the politicians?" As he saw it, the opponents of the plank "simply wanted to bid for the ignorant foreign vote, the Democratic vote, and the whisky vote." Beck from Pottawatomie then rose to a point of order and requested that Otis be silenced. Said Beck, "He has been talking all morning. He has talked himself to death, and now he is talking the party to death."

Mrs. Eliza Hudson, the only woman delegate in the convention, gained the floor a short time later, spoke a full five minutes in support of the plank, and then sat down dejectedly when time was called. A delegate from Marshall County, Andrew Shearer by name, identified himself as a Scotchman and as a spokesman for the foreign-born. He stated that those who had arrived more recently on American shores were "catching on to the spirit of American institutions as rapidly as possible." Conceding that the adjustment was difficult, Shearer indorsed the suffrage plank, advising: "Don't turn back for us!"

Of the many speeches in opposition, that of an unidentified farmer must have struck a responsive chord. Speaking in a manner that communicated at once the honesty and conviction of his position, he informed the convention, the Ottawa *Journal and Triumph* reported, that it was not so much a question with him or his wife whether she should have the right to vote, but the question was whether they would be able to retain their home. The People's party had been organized and educated on the line of the paramount importance of the financial question, and he believed that it was only by a reformation of this system that the people could find relief. He thought it unwise to incorporate planks in the platform to which a large number of the delegates were opposed . . . .

Amidst all these lively happenings, the time had slipped away almost unnoticed. Shortly before the noon hour Chairman Dunsmore brought the floor debate to a close and called Annie Diggs and Peter Elder to the rostrum for their closing statements.

It was no accident, of course, that Mrs. Diggs and P. P. Elder were selected to represent each side in the finale; they had clashed three years before when the same question was before the 1891 house, and if the passage of the woman-suffrage bill by that Populist house was any indication, Mrs. Diggs had won the first encounter.

Mrs. Diggs spoke first. Woman-suffrage proponents were indeed fortunate to have "Little Annie" on their side. Now forty-one and as attractive as ever, no other woman within Populist ranks could have won as readily as she an instant hearing for the cause of woman suffrage. Since that first rough-and-tumble Populist campaign of 1890, through thick and thin she had maintained her equilibrium, demonstrating by word of mouth and by pen that she was eminently qualified to play a leading role in the male world of politics. All this she had done without destroying her image of femininity—no small accomplishment in the last decade of the nineteenth century.

Mrs. Diggs first tried to allay the suspicion entertained by some that the women who had appeared before the convention in behalf of the plank were enemies of the party. "Does any man here doubt my loyalty to the Populist party?" she asked. "I stand here to say that these women are simply here in the interest of suffrage, as I was on the Republican platform in the interest of suffrage." She then stressed that the issue being debated was of vital concern to men as well as women. "It is to your interests," she said, "to get this amendment in your state constitution, and I believe that the vast majority of this convention means to stand by their own Populist women and give us their votes for the amendment." This statement brought cheers from the audience. She then pointed out that it would be broadcast that the Populists were going to vote for the amendment, so it would be used against them just as strongly whether in or out of their platform.

"The Republicans met in convention the other day," she continued. "They had not the courage to declare in the presence of the people that they were going to vote for the amendment, but their candidates promised the women, on the sly, that they would vote for it on the sly." She then assured the delegates that the amendment would be approved and asked:

> Don't you want to have the leverage of having the gratitude of the women of this state? Don't you want to be able to say, to the Populist party belongs the honor of not only submitting this amendment, but also of supporting it at the polls? If you take a noble, manly and courageous stand, as I am sure you will, then every cowardly Republican candidate will be forced to go upon the rostrum and plead the record of his party in its defense. My good friends, the thing for you to do now, from a People's party standpoint, is to have the courage of your convictions.

She had used her five minutes, and her talk ended with the great applause of the convention resounding about the hall.

The mood of the convention being what it was, Peter Elder had an unenviable assignment ahead of him as he rose to address the delegates. Elder's long experience in public life, his enduring commitment in opposition to woman suffrage, should have enabled him to present an effective case against the minority report. But the situation was delicate, and the Ottawa *Journal and Triumph* reporter recorded that the old reform campaigner "proved himself wholly inadequate" to deal with the arguments of Mrs. Diggs. In the words of that reporter, "his rambling speech was no match for her downright reasoning." Elder simply took second place to Mrs. Diggs when it came to extemporaneous speaking.

The essence of his plea came toward the end of his talk. With much feeling, he remarked: "In the name of the great Jehovah and the Continental Congress, we have been struggling for fifteen years against Republicanism. Don't, for God's sake, ladies, don't drag us down this time so we cannot whip them. You will not gain anything. This question has been submitted as an independent proposition." He then assumed a more confidential tone of voice and stated: "I confess to you, gentlemen of the convention, that I did not dare to have a vote taken in the presence of the ladies in the committee room." This remark prompted some loud jeers. As the noises began to subside, Chairman Dunsmore signaled to Elder that his time was up. Elder turned and remarked: "My God, is my time up?" Granted more time to make a brief closing remark, Elder then made one very large *faux pas*. "I want to say just one word," he remarked. "Now I say let us have a clean repub—" At this point the convention broke loose in a demonstration of continuous and uncontrollable cheering. In the meantime Elder returned to his seat; perhaps, as the reporter of the Ottawa *Journal and Triumph* observed, to "meditate upon the mutability of human affairs." He made no effort to clarify the remark that had ended his talk.

What followed was anticlimax. The compromise amendment was defeated by a decisive 528 to 82 vote. The vote was then taken on the minority report. The ayes and nays remained close throughout most of the count. At the end, the vote stood 337 for and 269 against, and John Breidenthal's announcement that the minority report had carried touched off the most enthusiastic demonstration of the convention.

To whom did the victory belong? To a small segment of extreme antifusionists like Corning, Henderson, Otis, and Lease who were psychoneurotically prohibitionist, at times nativistic,[12] and above all anti-Democratic? Or did it belong to that greater number who supported woman suffrage simply because it was a progressive measure, without relating it to any particular prejudice, who may or may not have been antifusionists but, if so, were such primarily because they believed the Democratic party much too backward in its economic policies for fusion to be of any benefit? The answer to that question is that both groups shared in the victory; Populist-Democratic coalition was the immediate loser, and both elements were satisfied principle had triumphed over political expediency. It remained to be seen whether woman suffrage or fusion would be the ultimate loser.

Compared to the struggle over the suffrage plank, the remainder of the convention was anticlimactic. Before the convention several Populist leaders had spoken out in opposition to the renomination of Governor Lewelling (Noah Allen and W. F. Rightmire had even attempted to resuscitate the Citizens' Alliance to oppose the administration), but this opposition failed to materialize in any significant form in the convention, and Governor Lewelling was renominated without difficulty.[13] Secretary of State Russell Osborn declined to run again, and Lieutenant Governor Percy Daniels was not renominated because he had conditioned his candidacy on the convention's adoption of his graduated tax reform; the rest of the ticket was renamed.

The symbolic woman-suffrage struggle held center stage, even to the closing moments when the noted writer Hamlin Garland addressed the convention and said, in part: "If you had not put that suffrage plank in your platform I would not have been here this afternoon, because it would have taken all the heart out of me. I want the people of this great party in Kansas to stand by their great principle of equal rights to all." He assured the convention "that every humanity loving man in the East expects you to support that principle. It does not matter what the Eastern papers say of you. I know that the thinking people of the East look to Kansas as the great battleground of all these great reforms."[14]

Kansas had indeed become a battleground of reform, and the stage was set for one of the most vitriolic campaigns the state had yet experienced. The principal combatants, of course, were Republicans and Populists, but there was to be a third party. As expected, the state's Democrats, represented rather heavily by the patronage element, met three weeks after the Populist convention and nominated their own slate of candidates and adopted a strict-constructionist platform that praised President Grover Cleveland, called for re-submission of the prohibitory amendment, and opposed woman suffrage.[15]

There was no waiting to commence the campaign; each faction was engaged in a holy war that would brook no delay. On the Populist side, Governor Lewelling delivered a major address in Kansas City on July 26 which served notice that the administration was not backing away from the major issues it had already emphasized. Among other things, the governor said:

> It is my opinion that if you are an honest and industrious citizen; if you are frugal, if you are careful of what you earn, that you have a right to enough to eat and drink, and clothe yourself and family, and if you do not have it, it is because somebody else has got more than his share. Now, that is anarchy—Talking treason now. But, if that is anarchy my Republican fellow citizens, put it in your pipe and smoke it. . . .
>
> If that be treason, when I state a citizen is entitled to enough to eat and decently clothe himself— If that is treason, my Republican fellow citizen, "Make the most of it." What is government to me if it do not [sic] make it possible for me to live! and provide for my family! The trouble has been, we have so much regard for the rights of property that we have forgotten the liberties of the individual. . . . I claim it is the business of the Government to make it possible for me to live and sustain the life of my family. If the Government don't [sic] do that, what better is the Government to me than a state of barbarism . . . . That my fellow citizens is the law of natural selection [,] the servival [sic] of the fittest—Not the survival of the fittest, but the survival of the strongest. It is time that man should rise abive [above] it.

The governor concluded his address by stating that there was no "greater crime breeder in the world than poverty." His purpose in coming to Kansas City, he said, was to ask if its citizens would join him in "the organization of a great anti-poverty society."[16]

The governor's speech was no isolated phenomenon; it contained a message that a number of Populist leaders attempted to put across to the Kansas electorate during that campaign. None were more effective in that endeavor than Frank Doster. In a Labor Day speech delivered in Topeka, Doster declared, "There is a fatal mental inability in both Democratic and Republican parties to comprehend the new and strange conditions of our modern industrial and social life, an utter inability to cope with the new and vexing problems which have arisen out of the vacillation of this latter day." After commenting on the magnitude of "the revolution in our ways of working," Doster stated:

> The failure to adapt the legislation of the country to the strange conditions which this new life has forced upon us is the cause in greater part of our industrial ills. A recognition of this fact I make the supreme test of intelligence in the discernment of causes and cures. . . . The Populist party proposes as the only means to the desired end to utilize the power of the social mass to bear upon the rebellious individuals who thus menace the peace and safety of the state. It says that the subjects of those monopolies and trusts are public in their nature, and that the powers exercised through them are in reality the functions and agencies of government itself.

He went on to say that Populists would have the government, which was, after all, only the people in their organized capacity, "assert their rightful dominion" in this new situation. And as a basis for such action, they advanced two political propositions: first of all, "it is the business of the government to do that for the individual which he cannot successfully do for himself, and which other individuals will not do for him upon just or equitable terms; the other, that the industrial system of a nation, like its political system, should be a government of and for and by the people alone."[17]

Other Populist leaders battled to make a discussion of society's problems the major topic of the campaign, but with little success. Republicans were convinced that what ailed society was the Populist party; they therefore made the charge of corruption and immorality in the Lewelling administration the major point of their attack. They were aided in that task by several widely publicized desertions from the Populist camp. Early in August

Ben Clover released a letter to the press charging that the party had "FALLEN INTO THE HANDS OF A DICTATOR...." Then, after listing numerous ways in which he believed the party had been corrupted, the former Populist congressman announced his return to the Republican party by emphasizing: "We don't want anarchy; we don't want socialism."[18] A few weeks later, Ben Henderson, who as temporary chairman of the Populist convention had made such a fuss to help get the woman-suffrage plank included in the platform, announced that he could not support the Lewelling administration because of its alleged corruption.[19]

Needless to say, Republicans were pleased with developments. The Clover-Henderson disclosures dovetailed exactly with the party line, stated rather succinctly in the Topeka *Capital* as follows: "The administration is the friend of tramps, saloon keepers, lottery gamblers, anarchists, defiers of law and order and government. Its record is a festering conglomeration of crimes and blunders."[20]

Republicans were also assisted by Corning's *New Era,* which had immediately pronounced the Populist convention a "fusion convention" and called for the defeat of the party.[21] The Corning line, repeated continuously until after the election, was that "Kansas Populism stands for unrestricted operation of saloons," "gambling dens and policy shops," "more bawdy houses and more prostitution," and for "moral, financial and material ruin."[22]

Most Populist leaders had at first written Corning off as a spiteful crank intent upon putting an end to any kind of Democratic-Populist cooperation; but when he intensified his attack upon the administration, despite the obvious rebuke of fusion at the convention, they began to wonder if there were not more to his attack than met the eye. By late August they were all the more convinced when it was discovered that the Republican state central committee was distributing Corning's *New Era* to Republican candidates to use as campaign material.[23] Then, on October 4, midway through the campaign, Cy Corning and other so-called "middle-of-the-road" Populists filed a separate "Populist State

Ticket" headed by Corning himself. If the scheme had not been concocted by Republican manager Cy Leland, it certainly had his support, and Leland, at the very least, was prepared to provide the Corning group with railroad passes during the remainder of the campaign.[24] That was the clincher; Populists generally were ready to agree with one of their major papers when it declared about "the Corning gang":

> We always knew they were not Populists but a lot of rotten boodlers, but were unable to prove it until now, when we are able to hold them up to the light and prove to the world that they are not Populists at all, but a lot of sneaking cowardly Republicans [sic] character assassins, working in the interests of the Santa Fe railroad corporation, under the . . . direction of the Republican state central committee, for boodle.[25]

Populist State Chairman Breidenthal wasted no time in filing a protest against the Corning ticket as an obvious attempt to mislead and to divide the Populist vote. Later, less than three weeks before the November election, a hearing was held on the matter with Secretary of State Russell Osborn and Attorney General John Little serving as the board of certification; the Corning slate would not appear on the ballot.[26]

After the Corning diversion was foiled, the thoroughly vicious campaign—the tone of which was largely determined by Cy Leland's direction—came to an inglorious conclusion with charges and countercharges being fabricated almost entirely out of whole cloth.[27] Only the most partisan voter could have avoided being utterly bewildered as he headed to the polls that November. There was no mistaking the outcome though—Kansas was "redeemed."

The entire Republican state ticket was elected by a substantial margin; the lower house of the legislature was taken by the Republicans by an overwhelming majority; in the congressional races, only William Baker out in the sixth district managed to survive the Republican landslide, and he only by less than two hundred votes; Jerry Simpson, John Davis, William Harris, and

Jeremiah Botkin[28] were defeated. Woman suffrage, too, since it
had become a partisan issue, was turned down in referendum by
a decisive 130,139 to 95,302 vote.[29] The outcome, it would appear,
demonstrated that Populism, on its own resources, had gone just
about as far as it could go; the party had started with roughly
108,000 (36.8 percent) of 290,000 votes for its gubernatorial candidate in 1890 and had climbed to just over 118,000 (39.4 percent) of
300,000 votes in 1894.[30] Populism had begun with only a minority
of the voters behind it, and it was still a minority party four
years later.

Governor Lewelling ran four to five thousand votes ahead
of the rest of the ticket, so his renomination appears not to have
hurt the party. Populist support for woman suffrage, on the other
hand, may have been a decisive factor. Lewelling carried twenty-
nine counties; fourteen of these also voted favorably for woman
suffrage—all fourteen were overwhelmingly rural, agricultural
counties. Only three of the twenty-nine could even be said to have
had any significant urban industry—Crawford, Cherokee, and
Osage. These three were strong Populist counties which contained
important mining industries as well as a large farm vote. Because
of the mines, these three counties also contained a significant
foreign-born vote. In Crawford County, Lewelling defeated Morrill by a vote of 3,388 to 3,250; woman suffrage was defeated there
by a 2,797 to 2,722 vote. Osage County voted for Lewelling 2,846
to 2,640; woman suffrage failed by a vote of 2,443 to 2,121. In
Cherokee County, the vote was 2,982 for Lewelling and 2,864 for
Morrill; woman suffrage lost by 2,508 to 2,124. In the urban areas
throughout the state, where the foreign-born, Democratic vote
was concentrated, woman suffrage was rejected rather soundly. It
would of course be impossible to measure the effect of the Populist
suffrage stand with precision, but the issue unquestionably had
cost the party badly needed votes.[31]

The defeat was devastating, and as its full impact began to
work its effect upon the reform camp, Populism's foes gloated
over their redeeming triumph. Cy Corning dashed off an editorial
line that expressed his mood with characteristic style: "Pimps,
thugs and prostitutes will not be permitted to longer administer

the government of the people," said Corning.[32] The *New Era* then became a semimonthly and shortly thereafter ceased publication; Corning's parting words advised, "The republican party of Kansas has the opportunity of a life time. Will it be wise enough to use it?"[33] Republicans were perhaps less slanderous than Corning in their triumph but certainly more ostentatious. On the night of November 13, they held an elaborate public funeral in Topeka to celebrate the death of Populism.[34] It was a devastating gesture, for only the most impractical Populist could fail to see that Populism in its original form was indeed dead; it might rise again to fight another day but never again in the same form.

METAMORPHOSIS

As their Populist opponents retreated to reexamine their position, Republican redeemers, obviously invigorated by their triumph, set about putting the ship of state back on its accustomed course. In his inaugural address on January 14, 1895, Governor Edmund Morrill struck a Republican keynote in this undertaking: "We have had withering droughts and devastating insects; 'booms' of prosperity and phenomenal speculation, followed by 'boomerangs' of adversity and stagnation." Admittedly, Kansas had suffered some great afflictions, "But from the worst, or all of these, we have suffered far less than from the virus of unrest, discontent, and disloyalty, injected into our blood by the hand of an evil genius to poison manly courage and self-reliant energy at the fountain of its source." In recent years, "We have been tempted to despise the methods and look with contempt upon the legitimate fruits of honest industry and individual enterprise; to lean upon the Government and demand from it that which can alone be obtained through personal industry and rigid economy." It would seem that "The lesson taught in the framing of our non-paternal government, that 'A people governed least is governed best,' remains yet to be learned."[1]

The following day in his message to the legislature, Governor Morrill served notice that he was "not aware" that there was "any demand from the people for a radical change in the law." And as for legislation he advised the legislature that there were "laws of trade which will control business and which cannot be repealed by any statute of any legislative body." The role of the legislature, according to the governor, was to assist this invisible hand in its work of promoting "industry and economy"; while they should avoid legislation that "may disturb and restrict trade."[2]

Numerous statements by fellow Republicans were forth-coming which praised and seconded the governor's appraisal of the situation.[3] From the vantage point of their decisive triumph, Republicans were also prone to deal with their opponents in the past tense, as they attempted to demonstrate why the Populists had been subjected to defeat—revealing, by the way, much of their own political philosophy in the process. A prime example was the work of B. B. M'Call, a Republican chieftain from Lawrence. In a speech before the Kansas Day Club, not long after the inaugura-tion, M'Call told his audience of prominent Republicans that the Populist party had come into existence "upon false theories of government." It was a party founded upon two primary corner-stones—"Class prejudice and the intensified misfortunes of man-kind." Populists had forgotten that "a great political party must possess well-defined and fundamental principles of government, broad enough in their conception for the grouping of all classes, regardless of social conditions or professions . . . ." In recent years, Populists have "told" us that "the theory of all government in the past has been wrong, and a new dispensation is preached unto us . . . ." They have said that "the great competitive system is an evil, and that monopolies and all branches of public industry must be absorbed by the General Government; that paternalism is the only safety to the future Republic." They are wrong; if one at-tempts to get at an explanation for "past progress," it will be clearly seen "that nations have become great by the exertion of the individual citizen." By all means, "I am not yet ready nor willing to sink all identity and individuality in the common cesspool of paternalism, and thus allow all society to fall from its present high pinnacle to one low level of common mediocrity."[4]

Not all Republicans would have subscribed to M'Call's theory of government, nor would all Republicans have agreed with the governor's contention that there was no demand from the people for "a radical change in the laws." But the outcome of the 1894 election was generally translated into a holding action with the Republican party calling the shots.

The twists and turns of Kansas politics had again created a situation with a built-in deadlock. The holdover senate was still

controlled by a Populist majority; the house was recaptured by the
G.O.P. Republican representation in the house was in fact increased to eighty-nine. The redeemer Republicans varied only
slightly from their colleagues of the previous legislatures. The re-
surgence of regular party leaders, however, may have been reflected in their number. Less than one-half (twenty-nine) of the
Republican veterans of the legislative imbroglio of 1893 were
returned to the legislature. All but twenty-two had been active for
years within the party organization. Compositely, the Republican
representative was forty-five years old (slightly more than one out
of three were fifty or older). He was a business or professional
man (sixty-two out of eighty-seven) who was most likely born in
Ohio, Indiana, Illinois, Pennsylvania, or New York, and had lived
in Kansas since 1874 or 1875 (eleven had arrived prior to 1861).
The majority had only a common-school education, although one
in three was college educated. One in four was also a Union
veteran.[5]

Thirty-four Populist representatives claimed seats in the
house. These men were five years younger at forty, and, compositely, farmers or stock raisers, who had moved out to Kansas
three or four years later in 1878 or 1879 from the same native
states. Only eight of the thirty-four were veterans of the legislative
war, although one out of three had previous legislative experience.
More than one out of four were college graduates, but the majority
had only a common-school education. In their previous political
affiliations, Republicans, Democrats, and third-party men were
represented by the ratio of five, three, and two respectively.[6]

With the important exception of the Populist representative's comparative youthfulness, the most significant contrast between the two parties was still one of occupation. The line was
clearly drawn between the political and economic interests of business and agriculture, town and country, factory and farm, professional men and farmers, entrepreneurship and husbandry.[7]

This cleavage was even sharper in the holdover, Populist-
controlled senate.[8] Considering, then, the depth of this cleavage
in the legislature, the governor's interpretation of the role of gov-

ernment,[9] and the intensity of partisan rancor, it was not surprising that the 1895 legislature enacted few reform laws.

While the new house had been occupied with the business of organization and the selection of a United States senator and a state printer, the senate had concerned itself with legislation. By the time the house turned its attention to legislation the senate had already passed a number of bills for house consideration. The Republican majority of the house, jealous of its power and at odds with the Populist senate majority, gave scant consideration to measures that originated in the upper house. As one contemporary legislative analyst put it, "A bill, no matter how meritorious, that passed the senate, when messaged to the house was scarcely considered worthy of notice, and usually died in the hands of the committee to whom it was referred . . . ."[10] Among these bills passed by the senate were measures designed to increase the duties of the board of railroad commissioners, to regulate and establish "reasonable maximum charges" for railroad freight, to fix passenger rates on railroads and to prevent rebates and passes (except under certain prescribed conditions), and another to regulate telegraph charges (passed by a vote of thirty to nothing), but all were turned down in the house.[11] A house-sponsored railroad bill was not even brought to a vote in the house of origin.[12]

Four measures originating in the house were passed and subsequently enacted into law which received the indorsement of reformers. One provided for the health and safety of persons employed in the mines, another provided for the purchase of seed grain to be distributed "to the needy farmers of Western Kansas," and a similar measure appropriated $2000 to be used by the Board of Railroad Commissioners to purchase coal for distribution to "the needy people of Western Kansas." The most important legislative enactment, however, was that which created a board of irrigation with powers to conduct experiments and to coordinate efforts in promoting irrigation projects.[13]

Populists could find little solace in these few enactments. The performance of the 1895 legislature, in fact, simply emphasized all the more the necessity of gaining full control of the state government. But how were they to accomplish that task? Their resounding defeat of 1894 had complicated the problem to a seemingly hopeless degree. Perhaps the answer was contained in M'Call's vituperative speech before the Kansas Day Club. Populists, said M'Call, had forgotten that "a great political party" must champion principles "broad enough in their conception for the grouping of all classes . . . ." To put it another way, a party should not challenge the consensus so directly; it should narrow its platform, deal less with particulars and more with generalities or issues that find support among a wider segment of the voters. Perhaps the fervor then being generated in behalf of "free silver" pointed the way to an issue that could command the needed support?

As a political issue, free coinage of silver had formidable roots, going back at least twenty-two years, when congress, as silver partisans liked to say, perpetrated the dastardly "crime of '73" and demonetized silver. The issue began to assume greater importance, however, when President Cleveland, in an effort to deal with the panic and depression that began in 1893, summoned a special session of congress to repeal the Sherman Silver Purchase Act of 1890. The measure was repealed, but the effort accentuated feeling on the issue, contributed immensely to the division of Democratic and Republican parties along sectional lines, and gave an importance to the issue of silver vastly out of proportion to its true merits.[14]

Kansas Populists in congress figured prominently in the fight against repeal. But they did not allow their opposition to distort their analysis of the causes of the depression, nor were they inclined to indorse free silver as a panacea. For example, as part of his effort against repeal Jerry Simpson stated:

> To my mind, Mr. Speaker, the causes of the condition of our people to-day are numerous; and they did not begin yesterday or the day before, or last year or the year before. This condition had its rise in the bad institutions of government with which we started out. We began wrong. We have failed to secure to human society and to individuals the rights that belong to them. This great nation in the course of its progress has created enormous

powers, and instead of fortifying the rights of the people, has granted these vast powers to a privileged class. . . .

To my mind, Mr. Speaker, while the money question is a great question, and one that demands immediate attention and settlement, one that calls for the best efforts of the statesmanship of this country to give this nation a permanent system of finance, yet the lack of this is not the only evil that has produced the present lamentable condition of the country.[15]

As an antidepression measure the repeal of the Sherman Act was a monumental failure. Repeal failed even to save the monetary system, for the House of Morgan was called upon to manage that feat.[16] The net effect of it all was to exacerbate the money question; and, especially in the West and in the South where bimetallism had long enjoyed wide support, the cause of silver engendered the kind of accord not available on other issues.

Prominent Populist leaders exerted every effort to prevent the silver issue from pushing aside other Populist reforms. In November, 1893, Dr. Stephen McLallin had faced the problem in *The Advocate* by writing: "While the demand for free coinage of silver is one of the planks of the Omaha platform, it is the one of least importance among them all." Events, he noted, had brought it into prominence "recently," thereby creating "an excellent opportunity for a general discussion of the whole subject of American finance; but it can never be permitted to sidetrack the more important questions expressed and implied in the new declaration of independence adopted at Omaha on July 4, 1892." McLallin warned, in that same article, "Free coinage of silver if accomplished and other things left as they are would do the people no good."[17]

Interestingly enough, it was at this time, when the issue of silver was coming to the front, that Dr. McLallin and other radical Populists took up the subject of socialism, not only to defend themselves against the onslaught of their opponents but also to obtain support for more fundamental reforms. To the extent, then, that the "cow-bird" label conveys the idea of reform taking on an importance not held in the beginning of the movement, silver and the "socialistic" measures of the Populist program both qualify as "cow-bird" issues in Kansas Populism.[18] But it was silver that finally qualified as the "cow-bird" in the full sense of the phrase as coined by Henry Demarest Lloyd, for it was the issue of free silver that relegated other Populist reforms in Kansas to a secondary position.

On February 6, 1894, the president of the state Alliance told that organization's annual meeting, "We have had much advice of late looking towards reducing the number of our demands to one. I am utterly opposed to the elimination of a single demand. To make a contest on the one plank of 'free coinage of silver' would be entirely too narrow for a progressive organization."[19] Dr. McLallin kept up his opposition to the same trend on through that election year. The party generally, in its platform of 1894 and through its spokesman during the campaign that year, in no measurable sense retreated from its broad program of reform in favor of the single issue of free silver.[20] After all, even that conservative Republican platform of 1894 had demanded "the use of both gold and silver as standard money."[21] Then came that decisive and shattering defeat of 1894. Antifusionists, rational and irrational types, were greatly discredited. To win control of the machinery of government the party needed to win a majority of the people to its support. It was reasoned that this could be accomplished by narrowing the platform. The national committee soon after the election, as represented in the expressions of Chairman H. E. Taubeneck, pointed up this new thinking.[22] It found an expression in Kansas Populist circles as well. On December 12, *The Advocate* published an article by state Senator Michael Senn which emphasized the need for broadening Populist support. Senator Senn advised that this should be attempted by dealing with only one reform at a time, and as a beginning he suggested the single issue of free silver.[23]

Dr. Stephen McLallin considered Senn's suggestion "the height of absurdity."[24] On into 1895 *The Advocate* continued to oppose the tendency to make silver the primary issue.[25] It was a losing battle. Gradually, McLallin gave in to the demand. On May 29, 1895, he wrote: "If free coinage of silver will relieve the industrial people of the country until they learn more about the science of money, let's have free coinage."

It was at this time that W. H. Harvey's *Coin's Financial School,* the great silver classic, and Kansas treatises, as well, were taken up by the reform press for publication.[26] Irrepressibly, it seemed, the subject monopolized the field. But not all Populist leaders were willing to concede all to the issue—not even for the sake of expediency; it was a terribly divisive issue.

With fusion lurking in the background, Republicans were quick to sense an opportunity to divide the enemy by driving a wedge between the crack thus opened in Populist ranks. Early in June, 1895, the new, young, Republican editor of the Emporia *Gazette,* William Allen White by name, demonstrated his sagacity on this point. White singled out for special abuse those Populists who were attempting to rally Republican opposition around the issue of free silver. "There is nothing of the old alliance Puritan cry for reform in these men," wrote White. "Has not the whole fabric of the reform party," he asked, "its heroes, its aspirations, its ambitions, its lofty desires fallen among thieves on the Jericho road?" "Where is the Alliance man with the courage to deny that his party that was going to reform the world has made a 'deal' that would have been hissed out of the first farmers convention in the year of our Lord 1890."[27] In a July issue of the *Gazette,* White took the occasion of a meeting of the Populist state committee as the opportunity to heap more ridicule upon the opposition. Just a "handful of schemers sitting around a box full of saw dust," he wrote, was all that was left of a movement that "was to reform the world, make life run smoothly on the grooves of change, and give every man a living in comfort and idleness." Here it was now,

> a fizzle,—and not even a glorious fizzle, just a dreary [,] soggy, fagged out, limber-kneed, red-eyed fizzle. The party that was going to pay off all the debts of the people by legislation, that was going to even up the inequalities of life that come from inequalities of brain, the party that was going to stop the smart man from getting the best of the stupid chump, the party that was going to do what God

himself couldn't do—make men equal .... And all that is
left of this great nightmare is a roomful of sad visages,
seedy citizens and a terrible past.[28]

With or without Republican abuse on the point, the emphasis on free silver was bound to create dissension. The state
Alliance was firmly in the hands of representatives of the party's
antifusion wing, men who would "compromise nothing with
evil," and who would oppose all concession or retreat from their
original program.[29] Late in September, 1895, moreover, the antifusionist Kansas Populist League met in Topeka and adopted a
resolution stating that they were "unalterably opposed to making
the free-silver plank the dominant issue in the coming campaign,"
for them it was "the Omaha platform in its entirety" and nothing
less.[30] Antifusion sentiment had a good deal more going for it
than it had in 1894; the turn towards free silver undeniably represented a moderation of the party's stand, and on this account
antifusionist ranks were bound to grow.

The situation was decidedly altered. Early in October, 1895,
The Advocate announced that Senator Peffer had obtained a controlling interest in the paper, and that thereafter its editorial policies would be under his "general direction." McLallin remained
on the staff four months longer, retiring officially on February 3,
1896.[31] Under the senator's direction, the paper again took issue
with the emphasis on free silver; it also took a stand against the
amalgamation of all reform elements in the upcoming campaign.[32]
Both positions were of course interwoven; both were contrary to
the drift of Kansas politics.

The same issue of *The Advocate* announcing Dr. Stephen
McLallin's retirement (a significant event in itself) published another letter from state Senator Michael Senn which took issue
with the paper's position. "Why a single issue—free coinage?"
asked Senn. "Not because it is the most important question; not
because it would benefit the people more than any other reform
measure, but because it is the only question that the great majority
of the people are really interested in."[33] It was difficult to deny the
logic of Senn's answer, but there was another haunting question

facing the party. Late in April, 1896, *The Advocate* asked it in an article entitled: "If the Democrat National Convention Declares for Free Silver Coinage, Then What of the People's Party?"[34]

Most Populists gave little thought to this possibility, or if they did they convinced themselves the Grover Cleveland, gold-standard wing of the party would maintain its control. The unifying qualities of the free-silver issue overshadowed other considerations; in it there was hope of rejuvenating a weakening and badly discordant reform cause. The turn towards free silver, moreover, was not just dictated by circumstances and the undeniable predicament of the party as a state and national organization; on the county level five years of vigorous discussion and sustained organization, success and failure, had wrought some significant changes at the base.

These changes were well illustrated in the case of Osage County. Situated about midway across the state from north to south and about fifty miles from its eastern boundary, Osage had become one of Populism's greatest strongholds. First organized in 1859, the county's growth and development after that date was typical of her sister counties in the Kansas mid-section. Only her standing as one of the state's leading coal producers set her apart significantly from the vast majority of Kansas counties, but agriculture was her primary source of wealth.[35]

After 1887, when the boom and bust cycle had completed its work, Osage was among the first to join in the Alliance movement in its rural and urban forms, and the county was in the forefront of the move which led to the creation of the People's party. Following the leadership of a group of men drawn almost without exception from the ranks of farmers, teachers, and lawyers (many of whom had been active in third-party reform politics for years), discontented Osage County citizens were channelled into a political organization which made its appeal on the basis of a dualistic interpretation of social struggles—"productive labor" (farm, factory, and mine) against the "non-producers" (capitalists). The party's leaders unquestionably identified the cause of the farmer with labor; whether the laborer identified his cause with the farmer was another question.[36]

The election results in Osage County soon provided the answer—the labor vote was not drawn en masse to the People's party; in fact, the backbone of party strength in the county readily revealed itself to be dependent on an alliance between farmers and their middle-class cousins of the towns (the very groups that had been organized in the Farmers' and Citizens' Alliance).[37] This was best illustrated in the voting patterns of Osage City, which was the county's largest town (population 4,243 in 1895). The town was the center of the coal-mining industry, and the labor vote enjoyed a sizable majority. This majority cast its vote with a high degree of consistency for the Republican party throughout the 1890s, rather than for the Populist party or the Democratic party. For voting purposes the city was divided into four wards. Two of these were overwhelmingly labor wards; the other two contained a significant, although numerically smaller, segment of business or professional elements who voted along with their laboring-class neighbors. Significantly, when the Populist ticket was successful in Osage City, it was successful in the two wards that contained the middle-class vote and not in the two predominantly labor wards.[38]

Recognition that the party had failed to win significant support from the ranks of labor could not help but effect a significant change in Populist attitudes, for its middle-class orientation was all the more emphasized. Add to this a natural tendency toward moderation encouraged by the passage of time, the responsibility of political office, and the bitter attack of opponents upon the party leadership as a group of misfits, who not only had committed the unpardonable sin of attacking the success myth but who were adjudged to be the failures of society, it was not surprising that the movement had altered considerably by 1895.

Within a few months of the 1894 election, Populist leadership in Osage County had undergone noticeable change. Although control had shifted to new hands, the change was more one of tone and emphasis than a shift to men of a different background; throughout the decade the party's leadership came largely from farmer-teacher-lawyer circles (in the balance it could be said that the urban wing outweighed the rural after 1894). The men of

1895 were more compromising and decidedly less class-conscious than the party's original leaders had been. This transition was well illustrated by the kind of campaign that was launched early in 1895. The official Populist paper of the county was *The Peoples Herald,* which was published in Lyndon. From 1890 to 1898 the paper's editorial management changed hands frequently; usually, the editor of the paper also held the position of county chairman. Such was the case when S. H. Gill took over as editor in February, 1895. On assuming editorship, Gill announced that he had not taken over the paper "to set the world on fire," and he immediately shifted the emphasis of the paper.[39] "The financial question is the fundamental issue," he wrote.[40] All other issues in his view were of "minor consideration."[41] By April, he contended that it was "acknowledged on all hands that financial reform [would] . . . be the main issue in the next campaign."[42] This contention was vigorously challenged, however, by the Farmers' Alliance of Osage County, which insisted that their "trinity of principles" (land, finance, and transportation) was indivisible.[43]

Gill continued nonetheless to use *The Peoples Herald* to popularize the silver issue. Beginning in May he began to run a column on *Coin's Financial School.* By August, the emphasis on silver had produced results. The county convention was held that month to select candidates for six county offices. The delegates reaffirmed their allegiance to the Omaha Platform, but in their resolutions they stressed their demand for the coinage of silver with that of gold at a ratio of sixteen to one without restating their demands pertaining to land and transportation.[44]

The manner in which *The Peoples Herald* presented Populist candidates to the voters that fall also revealed much about the movement. The county convention selected four farmers, a doctor, and the proprietor of a brick-manufacturing firm to represent the party. Charles F. Mitchell, the party's candidate for county commissioner, was introduced to the voters by Gill as a man who had "as tidy and neat a home and as good a farm as there is in Arvonia township, and all without a cent of debt whatever." J. I. Sweezey, their candidate for coroner, was presented as a young doctor who "is now enjoying a lucrative practice at Lyndon . . . ." Thomas Cain, the nominee for county treasurer, was portrayed as a "successful and well-to-do farmer of Burlingame township." The candidate for sheriff, Woolford Wyatt, was said to be "a man of shrewd, keen and splendid business ability . . . ."[45] Times certainly had changed since the party's candidates were first presented to the voters in 1890.[46] A keen business sense and affluence, instead of a working man's perspective and a mortgaged farm, apparently had become the hallmark of suitable candidacy.[47]

As a county organization, the election that November saw the Osage County Populists suffer their first defeat since they had taken the field in 1890 (actually the party lost only three of the six contests).[48] All the more reason, it was felt, for the party to endeavor to broaden its support by emphasizing its stand on free silver.

Certainly, that was the position of *The Peoples Herald* following the 1895 election. The editor of the paper was much disturbed to learn at about the same time that the Topeka *Advocate* under Senator Peffer's direction was opposing fusion and writing that "If Populism means nothing more than free coinage of silver, there is no excuse for the existence of such a party."[49] The editor of *The Peoples Herald* responded in time by insisting that "if Senator Peffer will come home and talk with the people he will find them heartily in favor of union of all forces on the money question."[50]

To fuse or not to fuse? free silver or a more fundamental reform of American society? these were the vital questions agitating reform ranks as the crucial election of 1896 approached. Perhaps there was a logical dilemma underlying it all. Could it be that Populists were doomed to defeat with or without fusion, with or without a union of forces on the silver issue?

SILVER, FUSION, AND SUCCESS?

If they dare to come out in the open field and defend the gold standard as a good thing, we will fight them to the uttermost. Having behind us the producing masses of this nation and the world, supported by the commercial interests, the laboring interests and the toilers everywhere, we will answer their demand for a gold standard by saying to them: You shall not press down upon the brow of labor this crown of thorns, you shall not crucify mankind upon a cross of gold.

Width these words William Jennings Bryan concluded his speech before the 1896 Democratic national convention held in Chicago early in July. The young Nebraska Democrat became at once the man of the hour, the champion of the silverites, and in due course the presidential nominee of his party. The convention also did what more cautious Populists had feared most: it had embraced the cause of free silver. Populist strategy was at that point completely bankrupt. The national committee had purposely delayed its convention until both major parties had committed themselves. The hope was that the Republican and Democratic conventions would both be controlled by the "gold-bugs," thus enabling the Populists to gather in their bolting silverites. At St. Louis in June, Republicans obliged with William McKinley and a gold platform; but Populists obviously had reckoned without William Jennings Bryan and the great appeal of silver within Democracy.[1]

Needless to say, Bryan's nomination seriously complicated Populist politics. In Kansas, the immediate reaction to the Democracy's Chicago conversion was quite favorable. Abe Steinberger, Populist editor of the Girard *World* and president of the Kansas Reform Press Association, registered his dissent, however, by raising some pertinent questions: "Is the Populist party ready to be dumped into the lap of Democracy? Are the men who have been fighting the battle of humanity in this country for twenty years willing to acknowledge all they wanted was a change in basic money? Are we ready to sacrifice all the demands of the Omaha platform on the cross of silver?"[2]

What choice did they have? Kansas Populists were vulnerable to the appeal, duly fostered by the Democrats, that there should be only one silver leader in the campaign. Even the Topeka *Advocate,* which until then had advised caution, was moved by the nomination of the Nebraska silverite, and within a short time it became clear that the Populist press of the state was all but unanimously behind Bryan's nomination at the party's upcoming national convention.[3]

But could Populists support Bryan and still maintain party integrity? To a small segment of ultra-antifusionists the answer was an unqualified no; to another, larger segment of antifusionists there were doubts but recognition that the party had little choice; to the fusionists of the party, and to those who had conceded everything to the silver issue, the question was of no particular importance.

Ex-Governor Lewelling and Frank Doster advised that the party indorse rather than nominate Bryan. Said Doster, "If we nominate Bryan . . . we must trim our platform. We must pitch our tune to suit his voice. I am not in favor of this. Let us make our own platform a Populist platform and then indorse the candidacy of Mr. Bryan. That would obviate the danger which surely will come if we adopt any other course."[4]

The position of Lewelling and Doster required of course that the Populists desist from naming men to head their national ticket. This proposition was opposed by two significant stumbling blocks: first, there was the determination of extreme antifusionists to carry on without paying the slightest heed to other considerations; secondly, there was the Democratic party's vice-presidential nominee, Arthur Sewall. As a shipbuilder, national banker, and railway director, Sewall had nothing in common with Populists, except free silver, and was a bit more than most Populists could swallow. As Ignatius Donnelly so aptly put it, Populists were "willing to swallow Democracy gilded with the genius of a Bryan" but were quite unwilling to "stomach plutocracy in the body of Sewall."[5]

Given this situation, the decision of the St. Louis convention was understandable although not especially logical. After much maneuvering and excitement, the delegates first nominated Tom Watson of Georgia, as fervid a mid-road Populist as existed in their camp, for vice-president, and then they nominated Bryan for president.[6]

It was the kind of arrangement that few Populists were entirely satisfied with; it in fact created new problems that would have to be dealt with to manage a successful campaign. But most Kansas Populists easily reconciled themselves to the outcome, sensing a real possibility of raising the banner of silver over the White House that November. With the Topeka *Advocate* they could agree that Populists should go all out in their support of Bryan while maintaining their independence and principles.[7]

It was a difficult, if not impossible, assignment; fusion was the order of the day, and fusion, rather than coalition as it had been before 1896, was a proper word for what occurred in that campaign. On August 4, Kansas Democrats assembled in convention at Hutchinson, and the Populist convention met in Abilene the following day. Communication between the two conventions resulted in an arrangement whereby the Democrats, who were given two places on the ticket, agreed to name man for man the same candidates the Populists selected for state officers. Populists, in turn, agreed to name the same presidential electors as the Democrats selected, although it was understood that the Populist ticket would be headed by Bryan-Watson and the Democratic ticket by Bryan-Sewall. The decision as to whom these electors would support for vice-president was, according to the Populist state central committee, to depend upon which candidate—Watson or Sewall—received the larger number of electoral votes outside of Kansas.[8]

In the Populist convention, fusion and antifusion sentiment was not sharply drawn but it existed. It was in fact reflected in the selection of a gubernatorial candidate. The principal contenders were William A. Harris, ex-Governor Lewelling, and State Senator John W. Leedy. Harris represented the hope of fusionists and Lewelling the antifusionists. Leedy was comparatively a non-entity, and therefore the man both sides could turn to as least objectionable. State Chairman Breidenthal apparently favored Harris. The state chairman certainly objected to Lewelling's renomination and had worked against the former governor before the convention.[9] On the first ballot Harris received the larger number of votes, followed by Lewelling and Leedy. Finally, on the fourth ballot the nomination went to John W. Leedy.[10]

Senator Leedy's background was as ordinary as his personality was mediocre. The forty-six-year-old farmer from Le Roy in Coffey County had distinguished himself chiefly as a staunch advocate of a maximum freight bill in the senate. He was a native Ohioan who had settled on a farm in Kansas in 1881. He had only a rudimentary common-school education, but that had not proved too great a handicap to many a successful farmer and businessman. Apparently things went along reasonably well for the Leedy family for the first few years. Then the picture altered drastically; before long Leedy was forced to turn over his properties to his creditors. His politics changed as well. He entered the state a Republican. In 1884, however, he threw in his lot with the Democrats. He left that party in 1890 to join the Populists, and in the contest of 1892 he was elected to the state senate. His nomination for governor at Abilene, as indicated, was due mainly to the party's inability to unite on any one outstanding leader. Leedy's nomination was a way out of the deadlock, but he was not the kind of individual who could unite the party under his personal leadership.[11]

Actually, Senator Leedy was among the lesser qualified men on the Populist ticket. At the top of the list was Frank Doster, nominated for chief justice of the state supreme court. Doster's nomination was considered a "bitter pill" for the Democrats and the worst kind of perfidy by Republicans. The remainder of the ticket consisted of relatively unknown but capable nominees. For lieutenant governor the convention selected Alexander

M. Harvey from Topeka, a thirty-year-old lawyer and teacher who had won distinction as one of the party's youngest county chairmen; for attorney general, Louis C. Boyle from Fort Scott, a thirty-year-old law graduate from the University of Michigan who had served as county attorney for two terms in Bourbon County as a Democrat; for secretary of state, W. E. Bush, a long-time third-party man and editor of the *Western Advocate* in Jewell County; for state treasurer, David Heflebower, a rather well-to-do farmer (he was said to own "2,400 acres of well-improved, well-stocked land") and long-time third-party worker from Miami County; for superintendent of public instruction, William Stryker, a thirty-year-old educator and college president who had been with the party since 1890; and for state auditor, W. H. Morris, a lawyer and former Democratic county attorney from Pittsburg.[12]

For Republicans, the performances at Hutchinson and Abilene were quite disheartening. The G.O.P. was confronted with a difficult situation. Fusion of its opponents was not its only problem, but fusion was the most formidable and the most exasperating of all. Some Republican leaders like Sol Miller were prone to spew out pure vitriol in the face of the forces that were lining up against them. In reporting the outcome of the Populist national convention, Miller had dashed off these lines:

> The Calamity Convention at St. Louis last week, pretending to represent a great national party, was the most disgraceful aggregation that ever got together in America. Anarchists, howlers, tramps, highwaymen, burglars, crazy men, wild-eyed men, men with unkempt and matted hair, men with long beards matted together with filth from their noses, men reeking with lice, men whose feet stank, and the odor from under whose arms would have knocked down a bull, brazen women, women with beards, women with voices like a gong, women with scrawny necks and dirty fingernails, women with their stockings out at the heels, women with snaggle-teeth, strumpets, rips, and women possessed of devils, gathered there, and sweltered and stank for a whole week, making speeches, quarrelling, and fighting like cats in a back yard. Gray-haired, scrawny, yellow-skinned women appeared

upon the stage, dressed in hideous or indecent costumes, and gave performances that disgusted the most hardened Calamityites, until even Jerry Simpson gagged, and protested that the Convention was too much of a circus . . . . The gathering was so outlandish that each delegate imagined that the others were burlesquing him. To wind up the whole thing, delegates were bought up like the hogs they were.[13]

Trapped by the gold plank of the Republican national platform and painfully aware that free silver appealed as strongly to a broad segment of Kansas Republicans as it did to Populists or Democrats, ridicule was just about all Republicans had left in their armory. As James Malin has written, "Many if not most Republicans in Kansas, who had remained with the party through Populist days, had accepted the silver philosophy with a pentacostal fervor that admitted of little compromise. . . . For most Kansas Republicans the necessity of accepting the gold plank was a shattering experience."[14] In addition to this, Governor Morrill, like Governor Lewelling before him, had bogged down in the administration of the metropolitan police law and in his handling of the liquor question so as to alienate both the liquor and prohibition interests. By 1896 Governor Morrill, in his bid for renomination, had even lost the support of party boss Cy Leland.[15] The Republican malaise was therefore no mystery.

On August 12, Governor Morrill won his renomination nonetheless, and Republicans set out to make the best of a bad situation. It was the Republican party against the fusion forces of Populists, Democrats, and Silver Republicans.

Down in Emporia, young Bill White sensed the hopelessness of developments. A month before McKinley's nomination White wrote an editorial stating that as the next president William McKinley had "a great opportunity before him." The question confronting the next president, wrote White, is "Shall we have a new deal, or lose the deck one of these days?" Earlier in the editorial, White wrote: "The West has lots of labor; the East has lots of capital. . . . Heretofore the capital end of the bargain has been given the best of it by the courts. It is time for the West to get a cinch. The farmer and his friends have paid the fiddler long enough to have a right to dance some."[16]

That editorial was not at all typical of the kind of campaign White waged in his Emporia *Gazette* that year. In fact, he waged precisely the same kind of battle against the Populists that Republicans had been waging for years. The usual bill of fare was ridicule, the cry of "anarchy," and a social-Darwinian framework designed to depict Populist leaders, or farmers generally by inference, as the misfits of society. On August 6, White declared: "The man who supports the Populists in this election whether for road overseer or for President, is lending his vote and his influence to the cause of anarchy."[17] A week later White wrote: " 'Every man for himself and the devil take the hindermost,' is a fair statement of the idea of American government as it exists today. But during recent years, there has grown up in the West the un-American doctrine of state pateranilism [*sic*]." Obviously, he said, "These two theories are violently antagonistic—one is American, Democratic, Saxon; the other is European, Socialistic; Celtic."[18] On October 29, he wrote: "From time to time during this campaign the *Gazette* has charged that, while the rank and file of the Populists were honest, sincere but deluded men and women, the leaders are the failures, the incompetent, the riffraff, the ragtag and bobtail of the community—in short the scum of the earth."[19]

With editorials like these, small wonder the pudgy little editor was jostled about by aroused Populists on the streets of Emporia, prompting the young editor to compose a more extensive, although not especially new, attack on the Populist party that he entitled "What's the Matter with Kansas?" His answer:

> We all know; yet here we are at it again. We have an old mossback Jacksonian who snorts and howls because there is a bathtub in the state house; we are running that old jay for Governor. We have another, shabby, wild-eyed, rattle-brained fanatic who has said openly in a dozen speeches that "the rights of the user are paramount to the rights of the owner"; we are running him for Chief Justice, so that capital will come tumbling over itself to get into the state. We have raked the old ash heap of failure in the

state and found an old human hoop-skirt who has failed as
a preacher, and we are going to run him for Congressman-
at-Large. . . . Then we have discovered a kid without a
law practice and have decided to run him for Attorney
General. Then, for fear some hint that the state had become respectable might percolate through the civilized por-
tions of the nation, we have decided to send three or four
harpies out lecturing, telling the people that Kansas is raising hell and letting the corn go to weeds.

There was more of the same. The article's only claim to orig-
inality was its pertinence to that political campaign and the clever
manner in which White had written it. The same kind of arguments had been used over and over since 1890. White's satirical
prose imperatives ("Whoop it up for the ragged trousers; put the
lazy, greasy fizzle, who can't pay his debts, on an altar and bow
down and worship him. Let the state ideal be high. What we
need is not the respect of our fellow men, but the chance to get
something for nothing . . . .") had been worked countless times
before.[20] Why then was the article picked up and copied by nearly
every Republican paper in Kansas and by nearly every Republican
paper in cities of more than 50,000 population outside of Kansas,
and why was the article used as campaign material by the Republican national committee? Indeed, why? Because it aptly represented the feelings of Republicans in their campaign (not to
mention the railroad companies which apparently distributed
numerous reprints) against Bryan and his allies? Indeed, that was
the case. Beyond that, however, White's was a view that struck a
sympathetic or nagging chord at that precise moment throughout
American society, a response that was all the more devastating
because Populism—in its move towards free silver and fusion—
had been stripped of much of its protective ideological shield. The
Populists of 1890-1894 had not been greatly disturbed by their
opponents' use of the success myth and social Darwinism against
them; many, perhaps most, of the Populists of 1896 were sensitive
to that attack.

A few Populist spokesmen sensed the party's weakness on
this account and pointed up the futility of waging a campaign

that treated the silver issue as a panacea. G. C. Clemens, for one, hit out at the fusion managers by writing:

> These traitors to the holy cause of the people would have us abandon, as they have already abandoned, every aim of our party, in order that we may secure the accession of old-party politicians, who, we are cooly informed, are too ignorant or too capitalistic to endure even the mention of postal savings banks, the public ownership of public utilities, a national currency issued directly to the people without the intervention of banks, the extinction of the monopoly of the earth, or the paring of the rather dangerous claws of the federal courts.

In that protest, Clemens emphasized: "We can put silver back where it was in 1873, but we cannot put the world back there. And, in the world of to-day, with its gigantic trusts and combinations—none of which will our proposed allies permit us to touch—would free silver restore the conditions of twenty-three years ago? What folly to even dream!" "The whole trouble is and has been," wrote Clemens, "our national chairman has lacked a whole Napoleon of being a great leader or any leader at all." If he had "not deliberately stifled all agitation of everything but the money question, other parts of our platform would be just as popular as free silver to-day; and under capable leadership we can rally for our most radical demand a greater host than any 'single-issue,' free silver party can hope to inspire." Make no mistake about it, "Not a Populist in the land is hostile to free silver. Our objection is to preaching that free silver alone can work any great economic change."[21]

G. C. Clemens' contention that the "radical" demands of the Populist program would have been just as popular as free silver if party managers had not pushed the silver issue to the exclusion of all else was probably just wishful thinking on his part. There was much merit to his protest nevertheless, and it must be conceded that the emphasis on free silver tended to undermine other Populist reforms.

Although Clemens (and undoubtedly many other Populists) felt this way, he chose not to support the movement then under way to create a "middle-of-the-road" Populist electoral ticket in Kansas.[22] The middle-of-the-road effort was led by Abe Steinberger, John F. Willits, Cy Corning, W. F. Rightmire, and W. H. Bennington. Claiming to be interested only in real reform and in securing the election of Tom Watson, these men set up a party headquarters, obtained a place on the ballot for middle-of-the-road electors in behalf of Bryan-Watson,[23] and launched an attack on the fusion leaders. The mid-roaders declared that "the only people willing to follow the commands of these treacherous leaders are the hungry leaders of the People's party who are so anxious for office that they would follow a garbage cart." All producers of Kansas, they said, desired relief from "corporate greed and the oppressions of the gold standard," but could that relief be obtained by working with "putrid Democracy, the co-worker with the Republican machine under the dictates of the money gamblers and corruption boodlers of the Hanna stripe?" Obviously these men thought not, and they warned:

> Honest farmer, while you are toiling by day and puzzling your brain by night, assembled in the capital city of Kansas is a coterie of political manipulators, headed by Chairman McLove of the Democratic party, Chairman Breidenthal, Cy Leland, Chairman Webb McNall of the Free Silver Republicans, assisted and in consultation with other proteges of the Hanna-Sewall-Cleveland conspirators, planning, through the assistance of a plutocratic Supreme Court, to deceive you and secure your vote for their schemes, under the deception that you are supporting Watson . . . .[24]

In spite of all the attention they attracted, the mid-road element consisted of a mere handful of intransigents who were assisted all too openly by the Republicans.[25] The regular Populist organization insisted that "Hanna's money" and support from the Republican state central committee was all that kept the mid-roaders afloat. This, it was charged, explained their gaining control of the *Weekly Co-Operator and Topeka Press* to air their views.[26]

Midway through the campaign *The Advocate,* which until then had been skeptical about the charges of collaboration between mid-roaders and Republicans, wrote that it seemed a little "peculiar" that such a weak organization without any visible means of financial support could obtain a headquarters banner that exceeded anything ever before displayed in Topeka. It was even more peculiar, said *The Advocate,* that "this banner should be anchored to the building owned and occupied by the leading State bank of the city, which bank is largely owned by the owner of the goldbug *Capital.*" *The Advocate* also professed to be somewhat perplexed by the fact that the mid-roaders had secured "almost unlimited free transportation," as well as the encouragement and assistance of Republican papers.[27]

The most troublesome problem for the fusion managers, however, was not the indigenous mid-road attack but the appearance of Tom Watson. The Georgian carried his campaign to Kansas early in September, much to the dismay of Chairman Breidenthal, who above all wanted to avoid any dispute that might upset the "arrangement" concerning the Watson-Sewall electors. Breidenthal met with Watson behind closed doors and pleaded with him to avoid conflict on that issue for the sake of the Populist party. Watson refused; and, in one of several speeches, he declared: "Somebody else must be asked to kill that Party; I will not. I sat by its cradle; I have fought its battles; I have supported its principles since organization . . . and don't ask me after all my service with the People's party to kill it now. I am going to stand by it till it dies . . . ." Sewall must be cast off, said Watson. Kansas Populists, he pleaded, ought to realize "I took my political life in my hands when I extended the hand of fellowship to your Simpsons, your Peffers, and your Davises in Georgia. The Georgia Democrats murdered me politically for that act. I stood by your men in Congress when others failed. I have some rights at the hands of Kansas. I have counted on your support. Can I get it?"[28]

The middle-of-the-road, Bryan-Watson electoral ticket was devised after Watson's visit, and Watson undeniably won the sympathy of many rank-and-file Populists momentarily; but the regular Populist organization was not about to alter its fusion course. Abe Steinberger, the leader of the mid-roaders, subsequently arranged a second Kansas tour for Watson, but the trip never came off.[29] Watson wrote Steinberger that an "ulcerated throat" would force him to cancel his previous commitment. Added Watson: "I greatly regret this. The middle-of-the-road Populists all over the Union have my sympathy and admiration. They have been sold out and their party made a foot mat for Democratic politicians to wipe their feet on . . . . The fusionists have abandoned principle and gone into a mad scramble at the pie counter."[30] Needless to say, Watson's decision relieved the regular Populist organization of a potentially disruptive and embarrassing situation.

For the rest, the campaign went forward with a great hurrah. Kansas had seen nothing like it since that incomparable campaign of 1890. Few eligible Kansas voters, indeed, failed to go to the polls that November; whether they backed gold or silver, McKinley or Bryan, all were equally convinced that the election was crucial.

In Kansas, the Populist-Democratic-Silver Republican combination emerged victorious. The state's electoral votes belonged to Bryan, six of eight congressional seats were captured, and for the first time in the state's history Republicans lost control of all three branches of the state government. The victory was marred nationally, however, by the decisive defeat of Bryan and an impressive victory for the Republican party.

It was a time for political assessment. William Allen White summed up what he believed the election had settled: "The fight came squarely," he wrote. "Mr. Bryan arrayed class against class. He appealed to the misery of the poor; he indexed the luxurious appointments of the rich. He attempted to draw to his side all of those of the debet [sic] side of the ledger." Republicans, on the other hand, "fought out their fight on the principle of individual responsibility for individual failure or success." The G.O.P. position was that of "laissez faire" or "hands off." They "stood squarely for 'vested rights.' They said, in effect, you cannot cut off the rich man's wealth without curtailing the poor man's income." Free silver was just a "dummy" issue, wrote White. "The issue went deeper. It permeated the political structure of the

Nation. A change was a resolution—a resolution to a mild yet dangerous form of socialism." White believed the issue had been "settled for this generation."[31]

Nationally, White's assessment was not too far off target. On the state level, at least as far as Kansas was concerned, the issue was yet to be decided. The allies of 1896 were defeated in the nation but victorious in the state. They thus took themselves to Topeka eager to do the will of the people who had supported them. But what was their will? The silver issue had served as a catalyst, bringing Populists, Democrats, and Silver Republicans together; it was the only issue upon which they were in total agreement. But free silver was totally beyond the power of the state. What then would the allies of 1896 do with the power they possessed? Much depended, of course, on how the administration and the legislature translated a rather vague directive into political action.

The installation of the Leedy administration was a festive occasion. According to the Topeka *Capital,* a "larger crowd" had "probably" never before "witnessed the induction of new state officers in Kansas . . . ." The mood of the participants, however, was strikingly different from that of 1893. In a few words, the sense of mission and righteous determination, which had characterized Governor Lewelling's inauguration, was conspicuously absent. Populists, it was reported, even "interrupted" Governor Morrill's departing address "with hearty applause" when he spoke of the state's "great prosperity and marvelous progress" and castigated those who would besiege her with "calumnies."[32]

The word for Governor John Leedy's inaugural address was bland.[33] Republican editor Harold Chase of the *Capital* made the inevitable comparison: "The contrast between the inauguration of Gov. Leedy . . . and the scenes four years ago [,] when Gov. Lewelling made his famous stump speech . . . , could not fail to be noticed by all witnesses . . . . The address of the new Governor was well chosen in words and sentiment, and met the approval of his audience without regard to political affiliation." Editor Chase was especially pleased to report that the speech was devoid of that "sickly balderdash" of old.[34]

In spite of the uninspiring note sounded by their leader, the legislators of 1897 had reason for giving encouragement to their own expectations; nominally, at least, the legislature was in reform hands. Senate membership counted twenty-seven Populists, eleven Republicans, and two Democrat-Populists (Popocrats). The house counted sixty-two Populists, forty-eight Republicans, eight Popocrats, four Democrats, and three Silver Republicans.

Perhaps the only significant change in the kinds of men the parties elected to office was reflected in a slight increase in the number of nonfarmer, middle-class personalities in reformer ranks—especially in the Popocrat category. Compositely, the Populist senator was a forty-eight-year-old farmer or stock raiser; eight of the group, however, were engaged in some other business occupation along with farming, or to the exclusion of farming altogether. The Republican senator was four years younger, at forty-four, and a business or professional man by occupation. Populists and Republicans in the senate were both natives, in greater numbers, of states like Ohio, New York, Illinois, or Pennsylvania, and the average senator of both parties had moved to Kansas in 1872. The Republicans were better educated, but both Populists and Republicans could claim about half their number as experienced legislators.[35]

In the house, the Populist representative was a forty-four-year-old farmer or stock raiser, who claimed Ohio, Illinois, Pennsylvania, Tennessee, Iowa, or Missouri as his native state, and Kansas as his residence since 1877. Roughly one of three Populists, however, were not farmers. Thirty-eight of fifty-six (67.8 percent) Populist representatives, for whom the information was available, were engaged strictly in farming; compare this with the 1891 legislature which claimed seventy of eighty-eight (79 percent). Taking the percentage of representatives who were associated with farming in some capacity, the figures were eighty-four of eighty-eight (95 percent) for 1891; forty-four of fifty-six (78 percent) for 1897. The Populist representative's Popocrat and Silver Republican allies, moreover, were business or professional men. The Republican representative, in contrast, was four years older, at forty-eight, and a business or professional man (only eight of forty-two, for whom the information was available, were engaged exclusively in farming) who had moved out to Kansas in 1878 from essentially the same native states as his Populist counterpart. As was the case in the senate, the house Republican was better educated—one of every two Republican representatives were college graduates as compared to less than one of every five Populists. In the case of the house, however, legislative experience was not a saving factor; the representatives of the 1897 house, in both parties, were unusually inexperienced.[36]

One of the first tasks facing this legislature was the selection of a United States senator to fill the vacancy soon to be created by the expiration of Senator William Peffer's term. This assignment really agitated the legislative ranks, for it was a political plum long coveted by a number of Populist leaders. Senator Peffer was in the running; five months earlier he had announced that he would accept another term if it were offered.[37] There was talk that the senator was too old and that the party needed to send a younger man up in his place. *The Advocate,* which was then under Peffer's general direction, was quick to demonstrate that the average age of the senators was sixty-five—exactly the age of Senator William Peffer.[38] The senator was misrepresented on various positions he had taken, especially on the tariff, and *The Advocate* worked to set the record straight.[39] It made no difference; the senator had no determined support. On January 6, 1897, *The Advocate* quoted an anti-Peffer article from the Le Roy *Reporter,* which was replete with contradiction, and which, incidentally, revealed much about the state of the reform party at that point. It read: "Peffer is rather antiquated in his ideas and not in full sympathy with the vigorous and progressive element of his party. He did very well for a figure-head when the party was new and its members comparative strangers to one another." But the situation had changed. "Strong men have come to the front. Weak men have dropped to the rear. Black sheep have been weeded out. Crazy and impracticable notions have been dropped out of the profession and faith. Victory and a sense of responsibility have made the party more conservative and imbued its leaders with broader and deeper ideas of statesmanship." Little wonder, the editorial concluded, that men like Peffer had "gradually" lost "their grip and young, vigorous men come to the front."

William Peffer's major failing, however, had been his cool disposition regarding fusion and his nonsupport of the Leedy faction at the Abilene convention. Certainly, few Populists had championed Populist principles more consistently or more persistently than had he. His performance may have been unspectacular and excessively loaded with a cargo of facts, but there was no denying the effort. His first resolution in the senate had called for an inquiry into the business of loaning money; his last resolution, almost six years later, called for the establishment of a national monetary commission. The first important bill he introduced in the senate aimed at creating a national bureau of loans, and his last provided for a system of public banking.[40] There was indeed a certain irony in the fact that opposition to Peffer in 1891 had been based primarily on the fear that he would fuse with Republicans once he went to the senate, and that he was opposed in 1897 primarily because he had resisted fusion with Democrats.

When the legislature voted that January, not a single vote was cast for William Peffer in the final count. William A. Harris, the party's fusionist *par excellence,* won the legislature's vote of confidence on the thirty-third ballot.[41] But Peffer had not remained untouched by the considerable changes that had come over his party. On assuming active editorship of *The Advocate,* March 17, 1897, the ex-senator stated that the paper would remain a Populist paper and it would continue to support the party's principles as enunciated in its national platforms, but he emphasized that he saw the need for "applying them along conservative lines." "This world is too big," he said, "for men to recreate it. Too many things are now established to make it possible or even desirable that all needed changes should be immediately and at once completely wrought."[42]

The same sentiment, no doubt, was shared by many of the party's new legislators, but there was a variety of other sentiment as well. Certainly the degree of unity and zeal that had characterized the party's legislators in earlier sessions was gone; it had been replaced, in the main, by contention and indecision, aided and abetted by lobbying pressures unknown to the Populists of earlier legislatures. Until 1897 interested and powerful groups had had at their disposal a check against undesirable Populist legislation, inherent in the fact that Populism's antagonists had always controlled at least one element of the legislative process. Because of this, the champions of reform, whose voices, incidentally, were even less harmonious than in the past, were about to be tested in their fidelity to the reform creed as they had never been tested before.

The legislature managed to pass a number of reform measures nonetheless. It placed in the statutes a law forbidding the blacklisting of workingmen by employers, it provided for the regulation of stockyards, it passed another measure "defining and prohibiting trusts," and it added additional laws to the books pertaining to the health and safety of miners and to the regulation of banking. It also created a department for the inspection and weighing of grain, as well as a school-textbook commission.[43] Notable accomplishments all; but the party's supporters had a right to expect greater things.

Legislation to reduce the legal maximum rate of interest in the state had long been a favored Populist measure. A bill introduced in the senate to reduce the legal and contract rate from six and ten percent to five and eight percent failed to gain the support of enough Populist senators for passage. Every Republican senator opposed the interest bill, to no one's surprise, but it was the Populist majority's nonfarmer, middle-class element that defeated the bill. Talk of betrayal to Populist principles and purchased votes was soon forthcoming.[44]

An initiative and referendum amendment passed the senate but was defeated in the house, primarily because Republican opposition made it impossible to obtain the needed two-thirds vote. A few Populists, however, were counted among the opposition. Representative U. T. Tapscott, a Popocratic lawyer from Coolidge, called the measure, strangely enough, a "Populist whisky measure," which he insisted was "wrong" because it favored "the bum element of our state," and because it was "contrary to democratic principle."[45] Republican opposition to the measure was more severe, but that there was any Populist opposition was decidedly the most inconsistent.[46] It was the vote on this measure and on others like the interest bill that prompted *The Advocate* to state that "Populists of certain districts in Kansas have sent men to the legislature who are more nearly Republicans than Populists."[47]

The most important measure to get caught up in the legislative snarl was the perennial railroad bill. It was the measure nearest to Governor John Leedy's heart. In his message to the legislature the governor had recommended a maximum-freight law that would vest the railroad commission "with the judicial powers of a court." He also had recommended that the commission be "given the power to adjust fares and freights within the state" as it deemed just within the limits of a maximum rate. The powers of this body, said the governor, should "be made definite and certain, but subject to appeal" to the state supreme court.[48]

A variety of railroad bills were introduced in the legislature. The final decision on the matter, however, came to rest within the senate railroad committee. Two different plans found support among committee members: one, sponsored by Senator Moses Householder from Cherokee, who apparently was Governor Leedy's man on the committee, included the maximum-rate feature; the other, drafted by Senator William A. Harris, chairman of the committee, proposed to assign the rate-fixing task to a strengthened railroad commission. After reaching an impasse over the two bills, the committee voted out a compromise measure, which was essentially a weakened version of Senator Harris' bill with Householder's maximum-rate feature tacked on. This brought the struggle out into the open. The night before the bill was to be acted upon by the senate, Populist-Democratic senators met in caucus to decide whether to support the measure as reported or to strike out the section containing the maximum-rate schedule. Senators Harris, H. G. Jumper, and George Hanna led in the move to strike out the rate schedule; Senator Householder led in the effort to retain it. The opponents of a maximum-rate schedule won by a vote of fifteen to ten.[49]

The next day, when the measure came up for full senate

consideration, the struggle was renewed. Senators Harris and Jumper again figured prominently in the effort to strike out the maximum-rate schedule. In his remarks before the senate, Harris stated: "I have always been opposed to a maximum rate, because I do not think it practicable. The commissioners have all the data necessary to fix a rate and I do not believe that any committee or Legislative body can fix a rate and arrive at a result as well as the commissioners." He went on to say that the maximum-rate feature enacted "would entail endless litigation, that would last for years, and we would never be able to give the people the relief they are demanding." Senator Householder pleaded with the senate to give "the people a maximum rate, give them relief at present, and lay the burden of proof on the railroads and let them go into the courts and show that the rate is unjust, instead of compelling the shippers to go into the courts and fight against the large corporations, as at present." After defeating several attempts to amend and to substitute, however, the maximum-rate section was eliminated from the bill by a vote of twenty-four to fourteen.[50] The bill, minus its maximum-rate provisions, then passed the senate by a surprisingly unanimous vote.[51]

With sentiment running strongly in favor of a maximum rate in the house, many observers predicted that the legislature had lost its chance at railroad reform. But the house passed the measure by an equally remarkable vote of 121 to 1; however, the legislative surface was not nearly as placid as the votes indicated. In the house, forty-four Populists signed a formal protest against the bill because, as they put it, "it is not the measure we have promised the people." These men also stated that they opposed the bill because it "met with the full approval of the railroad lobby, and because we believe it was drawn at the suggestion of the railroad attorneys of this state, and despite the fact that this bill has met the sanction and approval of men high in the councils of our party, we feel it is a makeshift and an evasion, a compromise, and we are convinced . . . that a compromise is nothing more nor less than a defeat." One Populist representative even suggested that the simple fact that Republicans had supported the bill was enough reason for Populists to oppose it. Another Populist, a friend of the bill, told his colleagues that they had best learn that "a half loaf is better than none" or their constituents would send someone up in their place who understood that proposition. Obviously, the protesters were not eager to assume responsibility for killing the bill, for they voted aye in spite of themselves.[52]

Governor John Leedy had no such reservations; he vetoed the measure. He gave as his main reason his contention the bill provided "no way by which an aggrieved shipper can secure relief." "The penalties named," he stated, "are so hedged about that they will neither compel obedience to the terms of the law, nor enforce subjection to the order of the commission." Most important, "the bill makes of the railroad commission a mere justice of the peace court from which litigants pass to the district courts to begin anew the trial of their cause, but fails to give to this tribunal even the power to compel attendance and to enforce its decrees with which that less august functionary is gifted."[53] But Governor Leedy was not being completely candid, for it was the lack of a maximum-rate schedule that decided his position.

Perhaps Governor Leedy did not see the measure as "half a loaf," or perhaps he did not sympathize with that proposition at all when it came to railroad legislation, but whatever the reason the measure was vetoed. The whole affair was then subjected to a wide range of subjective interpretation that did the party no good. Walter J. Costigan, the Populist leader from Ottawa, maintained that the "veto is simply one feature of a game of politics between Mr. Leedy and several other ambitious Populist statesmen." The problem was that these gentlemen were fighting over the "exclusive glory" to come from passing "such a law." Costigan stated, "There has been and is now no end of rivalry and jealousy on this matter. No man in the party has this weakness more than Leedy. I regard it the sole cause of his veto . . . . No matter what bill would have passed, I feel certain it was his intention to veto it, and to say it was not good."[54] Other Populists felt that whatever else he may have been guilty of Governor Leedy had blundered badly in vetoing the railroad bill without making any effort to secure a substitute measure while the legislature still had time to act upon it.[55] Partly because he failed to do this, the legislature adjourned that March discredited and confused to a degree that was neither necessary nor deserved, and many a Kansas reformer had cause to wonder whether their victory of 1896 had not been a Pyrrhic victory.

Not long after the legislature adjourned, the Populist cause was dealt another blow as a result of actions initiated by the Populist-dominated board of regents of Kansas State Agricultural College in Manhattan, actions that ultimately resulted in the disruption or termination of the tenure of the entire faculty and staff. George T. Fairchild, president of the college and an outspoken conservative-Republican opponent of Populism, resigned in the face of the board's determination to alter the curriculum and faculty for the purpose of infusing the college with liberal ideas. President Fairchild was replaced by Thomas E. Will, an independent in politics but an advocate of economic policies quite acceptable to the Populist board members, who had been appointed to the chair of political economy during Governor Lewelling's administration at the insistence of the Populist members of that earlier board. Following Fairchild's resignation, three professors resigned and ten others (professors and assistants) were notified that they would not be reemployed. Fourteen other faculty members, twelve of whom were known to be Republicans, as well as ten of sixteen staff members, were reemployed.[56]

Apparently the crucial test of whether individual faculty members were to be retained hinged not on political affiliation so much as on indorsement or at least tolerance of the "new political economy," which in the polarized atmosphere of the mid-nineties was practically tantamount to political affiliation.[57] In any case, the board had not demonstrated adequate cause for its actions, and the anti-Populist press of the state seized upon the affair to heap abuse upon the perpetrators of the deed. The Newton *Kansan* stated that Thomas Will, the new president, "knows nothing of managing a college, but he is a ranting alarmist and will be much better able to teach the young men attending the college how 'to raise less corn and more hell' . . . ."[58] The Iola *News* concluded that the board had "shown themselves to be the most industrious, ambitious, picturesque, and variegated sort of idiots that the 'Agrarian uprising' has produced."[59]

In point of fact, however, the actions of the board of regents did infuse new life into the college. Constructive changes were introduced into the curriculum, some outstanding academicians were appointed to the faculty, and the institution, with its Populist board of regents and new faculty, fared better financially at the hands of the Populist state administration than would probably have been the case had no alterations taken place. But the politics of the affair was not without its price, for several years later, with the board of regents back in Republican hands, the college underwent another changeover in personnel similar to that of 1897. As if to prove that it was Populist means and not ends that were objectionable, the continuity of the course of instruction introduced by Populist influence was maintained in the less frenzied political atmosphere of the post-1900 period.[60]

For the time being, controversy deriving from the reconstitution of the state agricultural college and the performance of the Populist-Democratic legislature sufficed to launch the Leedy administration on a stormy course that gave little promise of future tranquility. The ship of reform, fashioned in 1896, was, after all, a flimsy structure put together with incompatible materials, and it was destined to be torn to pieces by the rocks of adversity and the capricious currents of political change.

THE DETERMINED AND THE DISGRUNTLED

opulist dissension during John Leedy's administration was perhaps not as sensational as that under Governor Lewelling, but it was decidedly more widespread and persistent. Criticism came almost at the outset, when Governor Leedy began administrating patronage according to the political alignment that had elected him. Disillusioned Populists immediately raised the cry of bribery and sellout. One such attack on Leedy prompted Wesley Bennington, one of the extreme antifusionists, to write a rather cavalier defense of the governor. Said Bennington, "Governor Leedy may be wrong in many things, but he is consistent. In matters of 'patronage' and 'policy,' so far as we are able to discover, he is simply trying to maintain and perpetuate that fusion which you 'marble hearts' . . . persisted in making in the face of . . . all our protests and admonitions." Bennington's advice for the disenchanted was "go behind the barn and kick yourself into Missouri for not having intelligence enough to know the legitimate and inevitable consequences of political prostitution . . . ."[1]

The critical eye seemed to turn upon itself with full force. Attention focused primarily upon a special investigating committee organized by the legislature, apparently at the instigation of Governor Leedy, to look into the charges of corruption that were raised in the wake of the legislative session. Thanks to this committee, which continued its work, on and off, from April to June, 1897, the opposition press feasted on sensational copy provided by the quarrelling partisans of reform.[2]

State Senator Andrew Jackson Titus, Populist from Anthony, became the principal figure in the exposé attempt. Senator Titus, allied with two other prominent seventh congressional district Populists, George Washington McKay and Harry S.

Landis, was already at war with a wing of the state organization —that which was controlled by Jerry Simpson in the seventh congressional district.[3] Peevish personality issues played an important part in creating the dissension, especially in the case of the long-standing Barber County feud between Simpson and McKay, but it had its political side. Titus and Landis were both former Republicans who were thoroughly dismayed with Simpson's pragmatic fusion performance.[4]

The affair began to unfold early in the legislative session. D. O. McCray, the same Republican newspaper correspondent who was, unknown to everyone, implicated in Mary Elizabeth Lease's war against the Lewelling administration in 1894, wrote an article for the Leavenworth *Times,* published on January 17, which hinted that three senators on the educational committee had been "fixed" and therefore no legislation contrary to the interests of the book trusts would be passed. Apparently McCray wrote the article out of spite, after having been refused a position as lobbyist for the American Book Company. Senator Titus, chairman of the committee, responded by attempting to get the senate to pass a resolution denying McCray access to the floor of the senate until he retracted his "libelous" story.[5] The matter was then dropped. Later, in his testimony before the investigating committee, Senator Titus stated that former-Governor Lewelling had "taken him to a room" in a Topeka hotel for the purpose of persuading him "to introduce a substitute for the text book bill . . . ." By doing so, alleged Titus, it was intimated that he would be "financially rewarded."[6] Senator Lewelling quickly denied the charge. He said that Senator Titus was a "stupendous liar, and a dense, stupid and ambitious puppet who has not sense enough to know that a few conspirators are making a tool of him in their own interest." It was all a "conspiracy," said Lewelling, concocted by Harry Landis, Senator Titus, and "others," for the purpose of destroying him politically.[7]

Several days before Senator Titus made his statement about Lewelling's alleged bribery attempt, the Topeka *Capital* stated that Jerry Simpson, during the legislative session, had been "the busiest lobbyist on the floor, bringing every influence to bear to defeat maximum railroad bills, mortgage taxation bills and every other hold-up Populistic scheme against corporations and people who loan money . . . ." The *Capital* asked: "Which is the real Simpson, the sockless ranter in Congress, or the conservative lobbyist in Topeka?"[8] Senator Titus did not mention the name of Jerry Simpson in his testimony before the committee, but several months later he also charged that Simpson had lobbied against the stockyards bill. Other Simpson opponents in his district linked his name with lobbying efforts made against the maximum-rate railroad bill.[9]

Jerry Simpson denied the charges, and nothing credible came out of the investigation.[10] It is, of course, conceivable that a number of Populists succumbed to the lure of the lobbyists, but there is no real evidence to place before the bar of history. In the absence of such, the whole episode must be credited to lack of cohesion in the reform camp. The struggle over the railroad bill proved most conducive to the creation of discord. An honest difference of opinion concerning whether it was desirable to enact a maximum-rate schedule or to leave the matter in the hands of a railroad commission became a test of whether one had sold himself to corporate interests.[11] Rumors fed on rumors, and persisted despite the facts, noted unexpectedly by the Topeka *Capital* itself, which indicated that "With all the testimony in the boodle investigation there has not been a syllable of evidence to show that any man or corporation attempted to bribe any member of the Legislature for any purpose."[12] An editorial remark by the *Capital* also provided an apt partisan conclusion for the whole episode: "There is a homely old adage to the effect that when a certain class of people fall out, honest men get their dues, and it applies to parties as well as individuals."[13] To paraphrase the statement differently, it might be said that when a group of reformers become aware of their incompatibility and part company, honest and dishonest men, alike, are likely to be tarred with the same brush.

The discord certainly did not augur well for the future of the fusion forces. All indications pointed to a waning cause. The party's influential state paper in the capital was itself a good example. In April, 1897, *The Advocate,* under William Peffer's direction, was designated "the official state paper"; it nevertheless became increasingly less partisan. In November, 1897, the paper came under new ownership and new editorial management. Peffer stayed on the staff for a time, and by mid-December the "official state paper," which was now called *The Advocate and News,* had disassociated itself completely from the Populist party.[14]

Governor Leedy, like Lewelling and Morrill before him, also came under attack in his handling of the metropolitan police law and prohibition enforcement. Ben S. Henderson made the headlines early in 1898 with an attack on the governor on this account. Henderson, then living in Kansas City, Kansas, charged that Governor Leedy had made a deal with the liquor interests.[15] The governor, neither a prohibitionist nor a resubmissionist,[16] minced no words in telling his critics that he had not joined the Populist party "to hunt joints nor to fight resubmission." "If there are violations of the prohibitory law," he said, "citizens who know the facts should complain to the [local] magistrates and have the violators prosecuted."[17] However realistic, such a stand failed to endear the administration to the extreme fringe of prohibition-minded Populists. By 1897 prohibition was just about the only ideological commitment that some of these people had left, which as much as anything revealed the vulnerable side of the progressive mind in its efforts to affix blame for the ills of a society increasingly perplexed by the onward march of industrialism.[18]

This prohibition-minded element was strongly represented within the antifusion wing which had maintained its state committee after the contest of 1896; and in the aftermath of William Jennings Bryan's defeat and the eclipse of free silver as an effective issue, the mid-roaders grew bolder, more extreme in their attack on Governor Leedy's fusion administration. On January 1, 1898, as their barrage reached a certain crescendo, the mid-road chairman, Wesley Bennington, addressed an open letter to Taylor Riddle, who had been chairman of the regular Populist organization since the preceding August.[19] Chairman Riddle was working diligently to assure the continuation of the combination that had won in 1896. Bennington decried that effort, of course, and reminded Riddle that both of them had participated in the 1894 national convention which had assigned to both old parties the blame for the nation's plight. He asked, "Who lied? When did the ballot box stuffing nigger killing Democrats of the south get good enough to become a fit associate for you? When did the Tammany ring boodlers of New York and the east become your brothers, and by what process?"[20]

For Governor John Leedy, the explosion that sank the American battleship *Maine* in Havana harbor on February 15, 1898, was rather a mixed blessing. The diversion thus created took the administration out of the spotlight of public attack, yet the war enthusiasm and subsequent mobilization also resuscitated the Republican party, monopolized the energies of the administration, and, with an important assist from returning prosperity, relegated reform issues even further to the background.[21]

American intervention against Spain in Cuba was a popular outcry among all manner of Kansans. The initial reaction of Kansas Populist leaders to the "crisis" in Cuba was mixed, though far from unfavorable to intervention. Annie Diggs, state librarian at the time, indicated that she "would not have the United States stand imposition, but before going into actual bloody war, the awful results should be carefully [considered] from the standpoint of humanity."[22] G. C. Clemens cautioned, "It is quite possible that somebody on the insurgent side blew up the *Maine* for the very purpose of compelling this country to intervene." Caution aside, Clemens stated, "The Cubans would not be a great deal better off under a sugar king, with a federal court attachment, than an heriditary baby monarch; but Spain is an excrescence and should be mopped off the map in order to give civilization a chance to spread." The Spanish "government belongs to the middle ages and ought to be kicked back into harmony with history."[23]

In congress, Jerry Simpson, after having earlier supported the demand for war, courageously raised his voice against intervention, but the rest of the Kansas Populist delegation clamored for quick retaliation.[24] On April 12, Jeremiah Botkin stated, "Every consideration of humanity requires the United States to issue, without an hour's delay, an imperative command to the oppressors to quit at once and forever the Western Hemisphere . . . ."[25] Congressman Botkin's sentiments represented Kansas Populist feeling precisely. A war for humanity was enjoined. "The Benedict Arnolds of this period," said Botkin, "are those who . . . would sacrifice national honor, the cause of freedom, and humanity itself upon the altar of a heartless commercialism."[26]

No politician was more naïve in his demand for war than Jeremiah Botkin, but it seemed to be a national affliction. Americans, generally, had committed themselves to the Cuban crusade without giving due consideration to the long-run consequences. Governor John Leedy was no exception. He was an avid supporter of intervention almost from the moment the news of the *Maine* disaster was spread across the nation; and when the decision for war came on April 25, he was more than ready to direct the Kansas effort.[27]

As a war governor, John Leedy pleasantly surprised Republicans when he selected Colonel Frederick Funston to command the first of three volunteer regiments to be organized. Funston, the young son of a prominent Republican family, was without question the best possible choice; he had just returned to Kansas shortly before the *Maine* disaster, after a well-publicized period of service as an officer in the Cuban insurgent army.[28]

In the first few weeks of the war, rumors circulated to the effect that Governor Leedy would resign to assume command of one of the volunteer regiments; however, if he had visions of himself at the head of a charging column, which seems probable, he suppressed them. On the other hand, the young lieutenant governor, A. M. Harvey, had no reservations about relinquishing his thankless duties for the visions of laurels to be won as a major of the volunteers. Quite likely, though, given the state of disorganization and delay that was soon to be the fate of the Kansas units, Major Harvey found occasion to relish his former position.[29]

Criticism of the governor, abated by the war enthusiasm and the appointment of Colonel Funston, was soon renewed by Republicans. The governor's decision to fill Kansas' troop commitment by volunteer units, while ignoring the state's three national guard regiments, was seen as a bungling political move, especially when the outfitting and training of these volunteers literally and figuratively bogged down in the mud. Criticism of John Leedy's performance as a war governor in that election year was to be expected, but the many new appointments opened to the governor by the organization of three regiments was a political blessing too great to be disguised. And from all indications, Governor Leedy used this opportunity rather effectively to heal some of the wounds in his strife-ridden party.[30]

Although the war may have solved some of the party's problems, it just as quickly created new ones. There was no denying at the outset that most Kansas Populists joined hands with Republicans and Democrats in supporting the objective of throwing Spain out of the Western Hemisphere and freeing Cuba. They were not long in discovering, however, that the undertaking was far more complicated than they could possibly have dreamed.

Populist state Representative Isom Wright would win no prizes for writing, but in a letter of August 11, 1898, he put into words exactly what was troubling many Populists at that stage in the *Cuba Libre* movement: the war, he wrote, was leading to "some complications that were but little thought of at the begining [*sic*] . . . ." "I am opposed to our Government extending her Sovereign power over any colonial possession in the high seas [.] I was opposed to the annexation of the Hawaii [*sic*] Islands. While I do not wish the Phillipine [*sic*] Island returned to Spain I have no desire for them to become a part of our possessions. I do not even wish Cuba or Portorico [*sic*]." He went on to write, "This expansion policy means that we are to unnessarily [*sic*] convert ourselves into a strong military nation which never savors of any good for the masses of the people." Moreover, it was "not in safekeeping with a Republic and our free institutions but means a grinding taxation which under the pernicious policy of the Republican party will fall on the class of people who are the least able to bear it."[31]

There were among Kansas Populists leading advocates of expansion and the "big policy."[32] The most characteristic position, however, was anti-imperialism. In a speech before the house on

January 30, 1899, Congressman Jeremiah Botkin deprecated the argument that "The Stars and Stripes must forever float over every land wet with the blood of an American soldier." It was criminal aggression, he maintained, for the United States to annex either the Philippines or Cuba. Botkin, as a former minister, had also listened intently to the argument of retaining the Philippines in order to "civilize, christianize, and uplift" the natives. His answer was: "American soldiers must not be used to forcibly establish any religion or any church anywhere in this world. . . . You can not shoot the religion of Jesus into the Filipinos with 13-inch guns, nor punch it into them with American bayonets."[33]

While Americans had engaged in the "splendid little war" and the debate over American policy had begun to take shape, the parties held their state conventions that June and prepared for the campaign of 1898. Republicans, it was plain to see, were greatly invigorated by the post-1896 developments and confident their party would return to power in the state. Their optimism was explained in their platform where they "heartily" approved the war effort and insisted that with the national government in Republican hands "every promise has been kept and every prediction has been verified."[34]

At the Populist convention there were a few leading figures who preferred to dump Governor Leedy, but there was no other leader among them whose appeal was great enough to overcome the political stigma of a no-confidence maneuver of that kind.[35] Leedy was therefore renominated, as were all the other incumbents, to run on a platform that was as radical as any before constructed by the party. The convention's demands included initiative and referendum, "the public ownership and operation of stockyards," and "insurance protection against fire, lightning and tornadoes as a state function, at cost." The convention also went on record in favor of proportional representation and "the public ownership of all public utilities." Far down the list was the waning issue of free silver.[36]

From the point of view of the opposition, it was a platform devised simply to catch votes; extravagant promises the People's party had no intention of fulfilling, or, better yet, promises it would never have a chance to fulfill. Several Populist leaders, well in advance of the election, prominent among whom were former-Governor Lewelling and former-Lieutenant Governor Daniels, even conceded that the reform cause was lost.[37]

So it was. Even though fusion did not break down that year as it had in previous off-year contests, the combined Populist-Democratic ticket was soundly defeated. Republicans won seven of eight congressional seats, the lower house of the state legislature by a commanding margin of ninety-three to twenty-eight,[38] and their state ticket, headed by William E. Stanley, an attorney from Wichita, defeated the Leedy slate by just over 15,000 votes.[39]

Despite his and his party's repudiation, however, Governor Leedy summoned a special legislative session to enact reform. The session, which ran from December 21 to January 9, managed to carry out two of the party's 1898 pledges: it repealed the Railroad Commission Act and substituted in its place a court of visitation with ample power to perform the tasks that its proponents deemed necessary; the legislature also did away with the troublesome metropolitan police law.[40] The merits of this undertaking were highly questionable. It had the mark of desperation and defiance stamped all too plainly upon it. In doing away with the police law the legislature performed a service that practically all factions were willing to recognize at that point, but the repeal of the Railroad Commission Act turned out to be a rather futile gesture. The court of visitation was shortly thereafter invalidated by the state supreme court, which had been restored to Republican domination, and the state was left without any regulatory body.[41]

Populism's denouement obviously was at hand. The cement of economic discontent had crumbled. Ideological conflicts that had existed within reform ranks from the very beginning in more or less subdued tones were now magnified to fatal proportions. Actually, the failure of the great silver crusade had signaled the beginning of the end; with Bryan's defeat the partisans of reform had reached the parting of the ways, and the parting created an even more interesting dialogue than that which had characterized their union.

One significant part of that dialogue involved the relation-

ship between Populism and "Bryanism." In September, 1897,
A. C. Shinn insisted in a letter to William Peffer in *The Advocate*
that the two were "synonymous terms" that had grown "out of
the same cause" and which aimed "at the same object." A. C.
Shinn had been the party's unsuccessful candidate for lieutenant
governor in 1890; he had been president of the state Bi-Metallic
League for some time; and in 1895-96 he had been the acknowledged leader of the Silver Republicans. Though back in the party,
he could hardly be classified as a radical Populist; silver was his
obsession. In his letter, Shinn challenged a speech Peffer had delivered expounding undiluted Populist doctrine.[42] According to
Shinn, it showed that Peffer had "wandered far from the fold."
The discrepancy, wrote Shinn, between the ex-senator's and his
own interpretation of the meaning of Populism was "fundamental. It appears that your version of Populism means the
nationalization of all the essentials of existence—land, labor, transportation and money, while my idea of Populism is that we demand a return to just laws, or 'equal rights to all and special
privileges to none,' so that *as in the early days of the republic* the
individual . . . may go on enjoying his . . . right to life, liberty and
the pursuit of happiness [italics added]."[43] Shortly thereafter,
Shinn's views occasioned a reply by former-Speaker John M.
Dunsmore, which perhaps came as close to capturing the essence
of Kansas Populism as anything that had been written. Dunsmore wrote:

> It cannot be affirmed with truth that Bryan stands for any-
> thing more than the free coinage of silver and the ascend-
> ancy of the Democratic party . . . . Populism, however,
> stands for something more. It demands the enactment of
> new laws based on the natural rights of men, and not
> limited by precedents and accepted theories in relation to
> property, when such precedents and theories do not meet
> the requirements of modern life. Populism does not neces-
> sarily mean "to nationalize all the essentials of existence,
> land, labor, transportation and money." It does mean,
> however, that the power of law shall control and prohibit
> the centralization of land titles. That labor shall be pro-

vided with all necessary legal machinery to protect itself against the unjust demands of aggregated wealth. That not only the means of transportation, but all public utilities, shall be subject to public control, and when necessary, public ownership. That money of all kinds shall be issued direct by the government, and its legal tender value regulated by law, and not by foreign bankers and money-lenders.[44]

The gulf between Shinn and Dunsmore had existed all along; it was now simply more apparent and more imposing. Dunsmore represented the party's progressive side; Shinn, the retrogressive. Fusion having complicated the picture, it would be difficult to say with certainty which side was dominant in 1897; but the Populist-Democratic platform of 1898 would seem to indicate that the tenor of Populism in Kansas, at least rhetorically, was on the whole still decidedly progressive.

The period 1897-98 was a time of critical decision for Populists. It was clear that fusion was to be a permanent arrangement. Many Populist leaders managed to make their peace with that situation; the futility of a go-it-alone approach was all too obvious. There were those, too, like Annie Diggs, who halfway convinced themselves that the Democratic party had undergone a significant conversion since the advent of Bryanism.[45] Others, for a variety of reasons, simply could not reconcile themselves to that alliance.

A few of the more radical leaders at this point severed their connections with the party and joined the socialist movement that was just getting under way in Kansas. The Socialist Labor party of Kansas was organized at Pittsburg, Kansas, on November 14, 1897. In September, 1897, G. C. Clemens, clerk of the state supreme court at the time, began the work of organizing the Kansas Union of Social Democrats, which was launched early in 1898.[46]

In his personal journal, Clemens stated his rationale for leaving the party. He was convinced that Populists had been sold out by silver advocates and "led" into an "ambuscade" with malice aforethought. Since the defeat of 1896, these same leaders had "never ceased to conspire to destroy the People's party and to make it a mere feeder for the Democratic party." But that was not for him. "To-day, the Republican and the Democratic party are alike controlled by those who tenaciously and selfishly cling to the old social system which is passing away before their eyes." The Socialist party, he wrote, was the only party that would "stand for the new social order which capitalism itself has made indispensible if the world is to go on." It was "a sign of latter-day capitalism's imbecility" to behold "how the old party leaders flounder when the people demand some means of escape from the tyranny of the trusts." It was clear to him that "Socialists alone, of all mankind, have a political philosophy which can explain modern economic phenomena and suggest a rational cure for modern economic ills." Socialists recognized "that trusts are not evil in themselves. They are among the most important labor-saving machines ever invented by the cunning brain of men. In themselves they are good. They cannot be destroyed, for heaven has sent them to provide the way for compelling a reluctant world to be happy." Controlled by "selfish and greedy" owners they could indeed do great harm. "But let society own the machine and it becomes a blessing and not a curse. Let society operate the trusts, and the wails of a suffering people will give way to songs of joy."[47]

As G. C. Clemens wrote these words, Kansas was entering a new period of ferment and awakened social consciousness. By February, 1898, the circulation of the socialist Girard weekly *Appeal to Reason* had risen to a reported 40,000 copies.[48] A few months later, midway through the campaign of 1898, Charles M. Sheldon's social gospel novel, *In His Steps,* was selling at the rate of more than a thousand copies a day.[49] At the same time, the Topeka *Advocate and News* announced that it was "avowedly a Socialistic paper." As such, so it maintained, it was merely following in the steps of the late Dr. Stephen McLallin.[50] The same paper was convinced that the reception given to Eugene V. Debs when he spoke to a gathering in Topeka early in February, 1898, "illustrated sharply the recent growth of socialistic tendencies." Just a few years back the socialists "would have been allowed to hold meetings only under police surveillance; last week Topeka's chief of police donated $5 towards defraying the expenses of Mr. Debs' address."[51]

The trend was of course not universally proclaimed. Many Populists, men who were neither enthusiastic about the prospects of a Socialist party nor a Fusion party, were momentarily without any political home. William Peffer, for one, argued that Populism's undoing resulted from an affliction of "anaemia" which resulted from taking in "too much Democracy."[52] In June, 1898, Peffer consented to head the Prohibition ticket in Kansas;[53] by 1900 he had returned to the Republican fold.[54] Undoubtedly there were numerous other former Republicans among the Populists who simply could not reconcile themselves to close cooperation with the Democratic party; loyalties and antipathies born of as great an ordeal as the Civil War were not easily erased, as the record of the reform movement had demonstrated on numerous occasions. Many of these individuals soon made their way back to their original political home.

William Peffer would have much preferred a new party if that were possible; that was Percy Daniels' preference as well. In April, 1898, the ex-lieutenant governor published an open letter stating his resignation in Populist defeat and his refusal to work with a Fusion party. The Populist party, he wrote, had had "a grand opportunity, but it is gone. It has been frittered away in petty quarrels and recriminations; in senseless jealousies, and in the success of wire pullers in fastening on the new party the methods and practices of the parties we have abandoned in search of something better."

Daniels' reform zeal was undiminished though. After noting some facts and figures demonstrating the alarming rate at which the distribution of the nation's wealth was widening the gulf between the rich and the poor, he stated: "What idle balderdash—what kindergarden nonsense for any one to talk of free silver as a remedy for such a wrong; or any financial legislation except such as will appropriate some of these fabulous piles of treasure for the employment of the idle, and thereby raising the wages of all who labor." But how was this to be accomplished, he asked? Lincoln Republicans had championed "noble principles," but "the party that promulgated and sustained them is dead and the cadaver stinketh." And those who wear its "purple" lacked sense enough to realize that they have not "inherited its virtues." Jeffersonian Democracy had been "a grand creed"; but the party that had given life to its principles had "been among the mummies of political history for years . . . ." He who "wears its toga," said Daniels, "has been feted and duped by the Borgias, dosed by the Bourbons and drugged by the beasts and money changers of Tammany till he is too dumb to distinguish money except by the jingle." And what of the Populist party and its mantle, asked Daniels? Well, "the child was precocious"; however, it "got bow-legged and wobbled," and tripped "on his mantle" and "fell down stairs." In falling, he acquired "some bad rents in his mantle of promise; and his guardians, with a variety of patches, have tried to conceal even from themselves its true condition."

As Daniels saw it, Populism's "great weakness" had been its "failure" to advance measures to accomplish its proclaimed purposes. He then made his usual plea for a graduated tax and called for the creation of a new reform party.[55]

There was of course no chance that the various reform elements would respond to the call; their incompatibility had been abundantly demonstrated. In an interview reported in September, 1898, ex-Governor Lewelling acknowledged the party's plight but expressed his belief that success would eventually come to the reform movement. It takes time, he said, to introduce "great changes." The various reform factions among Populists, Socialists, and others, were not now sufficiently united for successful national action. But that would "come some day. It may not be as Populists, the name may be changed; but it will come and the principles involved will be identically the same."[56]

The defeat of the fusion forces in the 1898 campaign accelerated the dismantlement of an already debilitated reform machine. Much soul-searching took place. John Breidenthal, who obviously entertained thoughts of salvaging the leadership for himself from the wreck, reasoned that the defeat indicated the need for getting back to "first principles." He pointed to the "large vote" cast for

Mayor Samuel M. "Golden Rule" Jones in the Ohio gubernatorial contest as an independent candidate on a "public ownership platform" as clear indication that "the people are ready for the change from corporate to public ownership of public utilities." He was convinced that the "party which will not only declare in favor of this policy, but [which] will show its good faith by making a vigorous campaign on the issue, will ... secure the support of the laboring classes of all the large cities." Said Breidenthal, "The idea of public against corporate ownership of public utilities and natural monopolies has been a fundamental principle of the Populist party, but of late years it has ceased to agitate for this principle, and just in proportion to its lack of agitation has it failed to meet with success at the polls."[57]

John Breidenthal was forgetting that Kansas was rather short on large cities. He was also discounting the fact that a general decline in reform fervor had taken place—despite an undeniable awakening in the urban centers, as represented by a small but growing socialist movement. Economic and social issues were now apparently secondary to the majority of her citizens. In May, 1899, the Topeka *Mail and Breeze* asked the Republican members of the 1899 legislature what they thought would be "the most important issue" in the 1900 campaign. The only issue upon which there was substantial agreement was "expansion"—or, as their opponents would have phrased it, imperialism and anti-imperialism. Forty-five of one hundred and two Republican legislators rated expansion as the most imporant issue; significantly, only three members listed "sound money," or free silver, as the primary issue.[58]

A remarkable increase in the number of trusts, nationally, intensified interest in that issue; actually, the trust question was ranked second in importance among the Republican legislators (six ranked that issue first; twelve ranked it second). In November, 1899, ex-Governor Lewelling, state senator at the time, was asked if he believed it were possible to control the trusts by legislation. His reply was representative of one significant segment of Populist opinion on that question. "Probably not," he said. "We can destroy them by taxation, but it is not the trust itself that is

harmful, but the abuse of the power derived from organization."
Lewelling went on to say that it was his candid opinion that "no
political party acting under our present form of government will
ever be able to cope with the trusts. Relief may come through a
change in the methods of trade, but I can conceive of nothing
except some form of co-operation between producers and consumers, which means some sort of socialism, though it will be
called by some other name . . . ."[59]

Perhaps the most talented Kansas Populist critic of the
trusts, at this point, was a young man by the name of Carl Schurz
Vrooman. By 1898 this twenty-six-year-old Harvard- and Oxford-
educated farmer-economist, who was a member of a most prominent family of reformers, had made quite a reputation for himself
in the Populist camp.[60] Governor John Leedy had appointed him
to the board of regents which had brought about the reconstitution
of Kansas State Agricultural College in Manhattan. Vrooman had
had considerable to do there with the fight to introduce into the
curriculum the "new political economy," for that had been his
specialty while a student at Oxford. He was, in fact, an excellent
representative of the group of Populists who had made their peace
with fusion and who were endeavoring to convert the Democratic
party to Populist principles.[61]

Late in 1899 Carl Vrooman gave expression to his politico-
economic thought in a widely circulated pamphlet which he entitled *Taming the Trusts*. Drawing upon the background of
Populist experience and thought and a wide familiarity with noted
economists of the new school of thought, Vrooman's work was, in
a sense, a summation of at least one element of Populist thought,
blended with some original insight that one would expect of a
gifted and highly educated young man.

At one point in his discussion, Vrooman referred to the
work of an economist friend, with whom he agreed, to make a
distinction between "natural" and "unnatural" monopolies. Government ownership, he stated, was not the proper remedy for
"unnatural" monopolies; they should and could be dealt with
through government action that would " 'remove the special privileges, which alone sustain their life.' " The "natural" monopolies

could be dealt with in one way only, " 'they must be democratized, transformed into government monopolies.' " As for the bogy of paternalism, he insisted, as Populists had done before on many occasions, "The people are the government, *and the government is the people in their united or corporate capacity.* Therefore, whatever the government does for the people *they* are really doing for themselves, this makes all such help 'self-help,' not 'paternalism.' "[62]

Vrooman's observations in the pamphlet regarding what he thought was the important distinction between the Populist party and the Democratic party also provided a significant insight into the motives of individuals, like himself, who had elected to pursue Populist ends by means of the fusion course. "The Populist party," he wrote, "did nothing more nor less than take good old Simonpure Democratic principles, as enunciated by Jefferson and Jackson, apply them to present-day conditions, and carry them to their logical conclusions. Populism is nothing more nor less than *Democracy up to date.*" As soon as the Democratic party comes to a "full" understanding of the "problems" of modern society, and begins to devote "all its energy and brains to their solution" along lines that are in harmony with "the fundamental principles" of Jefferson and Jackson, "the Populist party will have accomplished its destiny as a distinct and separate political organization, and willingly will become an aggressive wing of the victorious hosts of the rejuvenated Democracy."[63]

By 1900 it was clear that the trusts, if reformers could make them so, would be a major campaign issue; it remained to be seen whether the Democratic party would consent to being brought "up to date."

Although he professed a desire to retire from politics, John Breidenthal was "persuaded," as he put it, to head the Fusion ticket in 1900.[64] The campaign that followed had many curiosities. G. C. Clemens headed the Socialist ticket, and ex-Governor Lewelling, who, interestingly enough, was at that time a land agent for the Atchison, Topeka, and Santa Fe Railway Company, came out in support of Clemens, after charging Breidenthal with a history of treachery.[65] At a Wichita rally in July, Lewelling introduced Clemens by saying: "Mr. Clemens is an old friend of mine and I am glad to say that I am very much interested in the cause of which he is the principal champion in Kansas. The Socialist principles are much superior in many respects to those of the Populists."[66] After he had made his testimonial, the press pursued the former governor, seeking to confirm rumors that he had abandoned the Fusion party for the Socialist. A few days before he was stricken with a heart attack and died while on a trip to Arkansas City on September 3, 1900, Lewelling stated: "I have always had socialistic tendencies. So have we all. We must all come to it. I am not particularly affiliating with them [Socialists], though I admire many of their tenets."[67]

Another one-time Wichita Populist of note, Mary Elizabeth Lease, entered the picture again during that campaign in a new role. Early in 1896 the tempestuous lady had gone back East to lecture. Apparently she had not meant to make the move permanent, but New York gradually became her home. Her reputation was such in the East that she had an appeal which, without too much exaggeration, might be compared to that of "Buffalo Bill" Cody of an earlier time. By April, 1897, according to her, she was working for Joseph Pulitzer, on special assignment for the New York *World*. She had made several visits to Kansas since her departure, and these Lease visits were a reporter's delight. Visits of March and April, 1897, provided some colorful copy. When asked what she thought of the Kansas situation, she said she feared "there is no hope for Kansas and her farmers. This state is hopelessly in the grasp of the railroads and under the heel of the eastern money lenders." As for her own beliefs, she stated quite emphatically, "I am a full-fledged Socialist! Any person who honestly accepts the teachings of the Divine Master must be a Socialist. In other words, socialism is the practice of christianity." She also revealed that she had taken up theosophy since becoming a New Yorker.[68]

During the 1900 campaign the ever-changeable Mrs. Lease was "sent," as she put it, to Nebraska by Mark Hanna in behalf of the Republican party to fight William Jennings Bryan and her old Democratic enemies. She touched Kansas briefly. In one interview she explained that she was with the Republicans now because "as I take it the issue has resolved itself into the old issue of copperheadism versus Republicanism, and as the daughter of an old Union soldier I feel that my place is with the Republican party." Mrs. Lease also stated that the "anti-expansion or alleged imperialism policy" of the Democratic party represented, to her mind, the "most unpatriotic, un-American, unwise issue" that has ever come before the American public, with the exception of the issue of secession.[69]

G. C. Clemens was no threat to anyone, but he had his answer for the kind of campaign the Democratic and Republican parties were waging that year. In one of his speeches, he told his audience to get out the Omaha platform and they would see where it accused "the two old parties of fighting a perpetual 'sham battle' to drown the cry of misery. Has that charge proved false? It was never truer than in this very campaign. What is all this pretended fight over 'imperialism' and 'militarism' and 'hauling down the flag' and the Constitution following the flag . . .?"[70]

But John Breidenthal's campaign was not a sham; he faced the issues squarely. Privately he even sympathized with the Social Democrats. In one letter, written not long after the election, he wrote that he had learned much from his association with them. The "end they desire to attain is the ideal and in time will become a permanent system in this country . . . ." He wanted no abrupt changes, however, for that would be "disastrous." His object was "to see the machinery set on the right combination and the engines started in the right direction," but he wanted to "progress slowly to the end that each step taken should be one in advance."[71]

Before launching his campaign, Breidenthal stated that the principal issues to be discussed would revolve around the questions of money, transportation, antimonopoly, public ownership, imperialism, and militarism. These issues were discussed, and there was no hedging. On the transportation question, for example, Breidenthal stated that the Populist position had "always been that government ownership [of the railroads] is the only solution of this great problem . . . ." The government, he argued, was the only agency that could or would "establish and maintain just and equitable rates." Populists had been "disposed to try the expedient of regulation," but it was now "apparent" that that was a failure and "government ownership is the remedy." The same conclusion, he said, "applies with equal force to the telegraph, telephone and express business."[72] In a speech at Emporia on September 22, Breidenthal reemphasized his contention that regulation was insufficient in dealing with the trusts. "You might as well try to regulate a coyote or a rattlesnake," he said. "You cannot supervise them and you cannot control them. My remedy is to allow the people to run these businesses themselves, but you say this is socialism. Well, maybe it is."[73]

On the issue of socialism, apparently a number of Populist leaders spoke out unequivocally in that campaign. Annie Diggs, who was then being referred to by the opposition press as the "Lady Boss" of the Fusion forces, stated in an interview that she was a socialist, but not a socialist "of the old world"; not a socialist of the school of Karl Marx or Ferdinand Lassalle. She described herself as "an opportunist socialist" and explained that by this she meant that she "would apply socialistic principles to everyday conditions as fast as the conditions would warrant; taking a little today, adding a little more tomorrow and so on."[74]

Perhaps the most notable feature of the whole campaign was the degree of tolerance that existed relative to such pronouncements. It was here that Populism's influence was most discernible. Less than a decade earlier, this Breidenthal campaign would have been besieged in the most caustic way imaginable; in 1900, the Populist-Democratic case was given a generally fair hearing. If they had accomplished nothing else—and they indeed had accomplished more—Populists had contributed mightily to an expansion of the conventional wisdom such as was conducive to a much more creative social dialogue.

Perhaps John Breidenthal's success in polling forty-seven percent of the vote was just as remarkable. It was a losing percentage, to be sure, but significant, considering the kind of campaign that was waged. Breidenthal even ran two thousand votes ahead of William Jennings Bryan, the Democratic presidential nominee, but it was the end of the line, and all but the most self-seeking or dogmatic could plainly see it as such.[75]

Privately, in a letter to his friend J. C. Rupenthal, Breidenthal claimed to be "neither surprised nor disappointed" in the outcome; merely disgusted to think that "a goodly number of alleged Populists and Democrats could be influenced by the full stomach argument." He said he had "always realized that there was a considerable percentage of Populists who were influenced by temporary condition and who would be disposed to return to the Republican party wherever [whenever] the general conditions were more favorable." It was obvious to him that "Only a limited number of people will take the time to solve to their own satisfaction the public questions that have been before the people for a quarter of a century."

Looking to the future, Breidenthal then commented: "While the work of education will go on indefinitely, I am skeptical as to whether any permanent results will be secured in the near future. People will probably continue the present system until they are powerless to overthrow incorporated wealth, except by revolution." The election, he felt, had "demonstrated two things conclusively—one is that the Populist party has outlived its usefulness as a political organization and another is that the Democratic party cannot be used as an instrumentality through which to accomplish any great reform." The Democratic party had its progressive wing, he admitted; but it would not unite in a new movement. The Social Democratic party would be practically worthless except as a "propaganda organization" because it was intent on "accomplishing everything at once." He then offered this bit of political advice: "While I am a socialist, I am convinced that socialism must be a growth . . . [or an] evolution or a development, that is to say, that we cannot inaugurate a complete socialistic system at once, but that we must gradually become possessed of the different public utilities and natural monopolies." It was his belief that "a party occupying middle ground between the extreme socialist and Bryan Democracy would stand a much better show of success and would present far more practical measures than any other."[76]

By 1900, professions to the contrary, John Breidenthal was more progressive than socialist; after 1900 that was even more the case. Soon after his defeat he announced his retirement from politics. The former bank commissioner then applied his considerable abilities to the work of organizing a banking trust company that was destined to become a profitable enterprise.[77]

As for the Populist party itself—or what was left of it—it struggled on for a few more campaigns. Under the chairmanship of Grant Wood Harrington, as a matter of fact, the fusion wing of the party was even more highly organized than it had been under earlier chairmen, including John Breidenthal; but organization was no substitute for enthusiasm.[78] The Republican legislature of 1901 administered the *coup de grâce* by passing a law denying Kansas parties the right to nominate corresponding or fusion tickets.

Dismantlement of the party continued for some time thereafter. Most of the Populists who were destined to return to the Republican party or the Prohibitionist party probably had already done so by 1900; after that date, Populists either went over to the Democratic party or became Socialists or Independents. The Populist party therefore admirably fulfilled the role of a transitional medium which assisted in the creation of new and more effective political alignments.

The personal story of two brothers, Grant Wood Harrington and Wynne Powers Harrington, reveals much about this final act of Populism in Kansas. Both were relatively young; when they left the Democratic party to join the Populists in 1894, Grant was twenty-nine and Wynne was twenty-four. They had both risen to prominence in the declining years of Populism, and in 1902 Grant was chairman of the Populist-Democratic state central committee, W. P. Harrington was chairman of his district's congressional committee and also of the Gove County Populist organization—this particular story takes on added interest by noting that W. P. Harrington was destined, some twenty years later, to write one of the first scholarly accounts of Kansas Populism in a master's thesis at the University of Kansas.[79]

By 1902 both saw the futility of prolonging the life of the

party, but they disagreed on how their individual efforts in behalf of reform could best be employed in the future. In September of that year W. P. Harrington wrote brother Grant that he had done all he could do as chairman of his county organization "to kill the party and clear the rubbish out of the way" for the Democratic party. W. P. Harrington indicated, however, that he could not himself affiliate with the Democratic party as Grant had elected to do, preferring instead affiliation with the Social Democrats. He added:

> I can see that the Socialist movement is not being taken seriously, but it never will be taken seriously if it has to await the pleasure of those who like yourself . . . have hastened to flop into the Democratic party and are hustling for front seats in the band wagon. It will never be taken seriously till it grows, which is all the more reason why I and others should get to work to make it grow. There is nothing about the Democratic party to make me feel at home there. Sometime, maybe, it may get right but I am not going to waste the best years of my life voting for it in hopes that it will get right in the end. . . . It never will get to sound doctrine till it is forced by the growing Socialist party. I know the Democratic party has it in its power to knock the props out from [under] any third party organization whenever it chooses and the time may come when it will absorb the Socialist party; but when it takes up with Socialist ideas it will have need for the men who have been trained in the advocacy of those ideas and I'll have a chance to get into the party then if I want to.

W. P. Harrington went on to tell his brother that his party's candidate for governor was a "false alarm"; that the "whole campaign" was "a hollow sham and you are going to get licked so badly that you won't know yourselves after election." He ended by advising: "The Good Book says that 'he who would save his life shall lose it' and this text I commend to the careful consideration of those who try to discourage Socialism and tie up with . . . [unreformed Democrats] for 'practical reasons.' "[80]

VINDICATION? THE POPULIST LEADER IN THE PROGRESSIVE ERA

In that unrivaled manner of his, Jerry Simpson once remarked:

> Did you ever see a summer storm in the country?
> First there comes a wind-gust, which raises the dust and
> sets it whirling round and round, carrying with it the
> leaves and husks and bits of stick that come into its path,
> and making a tremendous stir among inanimate things
> generally. Everybody cries out: "Whew, what a storm!"
> But that isn't the storm. After the dust is scattered over all
> the piazzas and roofs, and the sticks and straws and leaves
> and chips of dried husk have been blown into the hedge-
> rows and fence corners out of sight, the thunder rolls and
> the lightning flashes and the rain descends, and barns are
> struck and burned and rivers are swollen and bridges
> swept away. That's the storm; the wind-gust was only a
> preliminary.
> It's the same with a great political movement. The
> little fellows, the human chips and straws, are whirled and
> tossed about in the wind and dust of their own agitation
> and then are laid out of sight in the dark places where no
> man goes. It's the fellows in command of the thunder and
> lightning and rain who come after and do the big work,
> and get the credit of it.[1]

As Simpson told it, the Populists were in "command of the
thunder and lightning and rain," but the observation was not
inappropriate as applied to the relationship between Populism and
progressivism in the broad sense of how they found expression in
and affected American society. The Populist movement was followed by a progressive movement, and the progressives succeeded

in enacting several of the state and national reforms earlier championed by the Populists. It would be foolish, however, to reason that progressivism would not have come about without the previous occurrence of Populism, but it would be even more foolish to assume that the successes of the progressives owed nothing to the Populists.

Populism in Kansas, at any rate, first of all merits an appraisal on its own account. Too often it has been adjudged a failure without serious reflection. How does one measure success or failure? Is this done by weighing the number of legislative accomplishments? If so, what may be said for the Populists? As for labor legislation, they had given Kansas an antiblacklisting law, provided an eight-hour day for all work associated with the state's various governmental units, required the regulation and weighing of coal at the mines, enacted legislation requiring the weekly payment of wages in lawful money, and passed several measures relating to the health and safety of the state's mine workers. For her agricultural interests, they had placed restrictions upon the alien ownership of land, provided for the regulation of warehouses and the inspection, grading, weighing, and handling of grain, placed among the statutes a one-year real-estate redemption law, adopted a measure aimed at prohibiting combinations designed to prevent competition in the buying and selling of livestock, provided for the regulation of stockyards, and established a department for the inspection and weighing of grain, as well as a board of irrigation. As for legislation in the general interest, they had created the office of bank commissioner with power to regulate the activities of the state's banking institutions, created a school-textbook commission, adopted the Australian ballot and had taken steps to minimize corrupt practices in elections, created a court of visitation to regulate railroads operating within the state, and they had written antitrust legislation into the books.

True, several of these measures owed as much to Republicans as Populists, and some of the legislation, the antitrust and alien-land ownership measures for example, also proved ineffective, or, like the court of visitation, were invalidated by the courts. If one minimizes the odds that were stacked against them, the record may seem less than outstanding, but who is to say that even these measures would have been adopted within the same time period had there been no Populist movement? How does one measure the party's impact, moreover, on the administration of state and local government? Unquestionably, the party provided a necessary outlet which enabled an aroused discontent to be channeled in a constructive manner, while at the same time providing a distraught people with hope and a new sense of identity with their government.

When it is recalled that Populists never, at any point, constituted a majority of the Kansas electorate, even their few legislative accomplishments seem remarkable; but this was not the whole of their accomplishment, probably not even their most significant contribution. Populism's greatest bequest, on the national and state levels, was a positive educational experience, which can no more readily be measured nor denied than the influence of a great teacher.

This was the conclusion of many of the Populists themselves. As early as 1895 Annie Diggs made that observation regarding the work of the Populist congressional delegations. She stated that Populism could not have "achieved such widespread and enormous success" in its effort "to educate the people" in any "other capacity." "Had it not been for the ubiquitous Populist in the house and the senate, ready to interject questions, ready to puncture pompous bubbles, ready to tersely and clearly state his common-sense solution of national problems—had it not been for four years of persistent, patient effort of this sort, the country would be in far darker, denser ignorance than it now is." She went on to write that it was "most amazing how dense was the ignorance of congressmen on all theories and all facts pertaining to the newer political economy. But few members of congress had any inkling of economics later than Adam Smith, and their acquaintance with that out-of-date writer was overlapped with . . . traditions and moss-backed fallacies."[2]

In 1901 Annie Diggs insisted that Populism's achievements had been "tremendous and potential." They were "vitalizing influences which ramify throughout the entire national structure."

The party, she added, had "hooted the tariff off the stage"; it had brought the money question to the front; and it had "furnished the country the story of the formation of trusts and combines," helping to focus attention on that vital issue.[3]

Annie Diggs certainly had figured prominently in that undertaking, and she persisted in that effort until her death in 1916. In a 1907 interview she conceded that the Populist party was a thing of the past but stated that she was not sure she was "sorry." "It wasn't the name particularly that I cared about. It was the principles . . . we fought for. 'Clodhoppers' or anything would have served the purpose just as well. But have you noticed . . . the things we asked for and . . . the policies we advocated are not in the least bit dead?"[4] The following year she was interviewed again just before moving from Kansas to New York. She was going East to live with her son and to engage in "the old line of work." The reporter asked if this meant her efforts would again have a political outlet? She replied, rather emphatically: "Indeed no! I am done with party politics forever." She insisted that "Real reform must come now through the education of the people. Partisan organizations are always cowardly. . . . But once a strong public sentiment is created for any reform both the old parties will jump at the chance to work them out in legislation. Well, I am going to New York to help create sentiment that will demand these reforms." The reporter then observed that Populist principles were apparently becoming respectable, to which Annie Diggs responded: "And don't you remember how the press denounced us as traitors and rebel sympathizers and Anarchists? How they twitted us with Judge Doster's expression that 'the right of the user is paramount to the right of the owner?' and declared that we wanted to confiscate everybody's property." Just as quickly she stated that it was "worth all that to know now that we were right and that this good old world regards us in a different light as it comes to understand that many of the issues so crudely advocated were really safe and sane progressive measures."

Asked what had become of her co-workers in the reform cause, Mrs. Diggs remarked that "death had taken many" but some were still active in politics. "So far as I know all of them are just as firm in their Populist convictions as in former days, although they are now members of some other party."[5]

Old age was indeed overtaking the former leaders of Kansas Populism. The major leadership's median age of forty-six in 1890 meant a median age of sixty-six in 1910, the point at which the progressive movement had blossomed throughout the nation. Those who survived into the progressive era and beyond were, on the whole, "firm in their Populist convictions," as Annie Diggs observed, but there was as much diversity in interpretation and application of those convictions as there had been from the beginning.

After his defeat in 1898, Jerry Simpson had published a newspaper for a brief period, appropriately entitled *Jerry Simpson's Bayonet.* This verbal sword was used most effectively by Simpson and his editorial assistants to revenge the scurrilous attack that had been waged against the congressman for eight years; it was also used, but much less effectively, to keep the issue of reform before the people and to prepare the way for Simpson's anticipated return to politics.[6]

But that day never came. Soon after attempting, unsuccessfully, to obtain a senatorial indorsement from the Fusion convention of 1900, Jerry Simpson signed on as a railroad land agent and moved to the territory of New Mexico, where he also renewed his ranching activities. He returned to Kansas in 1905, just a few months before his death in Wichita in October of that year, and momentarily became something of an attraction to the press. One reporter noted that he was the "same old Jerry. The years have mellowed him somewhat, have dimmed the fire, but he is still possessed of that wonderful vein of sardonic humor, and still enjoys keenly the discomfiture of his old-time rivals."[7] Another recorded the following Simpson commentary: "I met some of my old Republican opponents to-day and they said to me: 'Oh, Jerry, you ought to be in Kansas now. Kansas is all Populist now.' Yes, I said to them, you are the conservative business men of the state, and doubtless all wisdom is lodged with you, but you are just learning now what the farmers of the state knew fourteen years ago."[8] Several months later he was quoted as saying: "Talk about the Populist party being dead, when we have converted Roosevelt and Taft! If Roosevelt had made the speeches he is making now four years ago he could not have been elected constable in the most ignorant precinct on Long Island. They are all coming our way. They do not call themselves Populists, but a rose by any other name smells as sweet."[9]

Two months after having uttered these words Jerry Simpson was dead. The young and progressive Victor Murdock, the Republican incumbent of Simpson's Big Seventh congressional seat, who would soon make a name for himself as an Insurgent, delivered Jerry Simpson's funeral oration in Wichita on October 25, 1905.[10] The symbolic relationship between Populism and Republican Insurgency, thus implied, was more than just coincidental.

John Davis had died four years earlier; G. C. Clemens survived Simpson by only one year. Both were active to the end. John Leedy took up mining for a short time in southeastern Kansas, then he moved to Canada where he worked and participated in politics until his death in 1935. Former Congressman William Baker was completely withdrawn from politics after 1897; before his death in 1910, however, he acknowledged the similarities between the doctrines of the Rooseveltian Insurgents and the Populists, although he stated that "Roosevelt is more radical than I." John Grant Otis founded a cooperative colony out in Washington state named Equality and apparently associated with the Socialists until his death in 1916. John F. Willits also joined the Socialist party, waging several campaigns as its nominee for congress in Kansas after 1900. Percy Daniels, with great consistency of ideas, kept up his fight, writing letters and pamphlets and involving himself in newspaper debates almost up to the time of his death in 1916.

For others only a glimpse emerges from existing records: S. M. Scott, the boy wonder of the early organization period, went off to Texas and struck it rich in oil. S. H. Snider found a gold mine in New Mexico. Carl Vrooman subsequently served as assistant secretary of agriculture in President Wilson's administration. Grant Wood Harrington became private secretary to

Democratic Governor George Hodges in 1913 and remained fairly active in Democratic politics until his death in 1952. P. P. Elder also remained active as a Democrat until poor health overtook him in 1908; the old campaigner held on though until 1914. Jerry Botkin, always a crusader, was the Democratic party's unsuccessful candidate for governor in 1908. In 1912 the ex-congressman also waged a personal campaign against Republican Arthur Capper in the latter's bid for the governorship of Kansas. "Overwork in a revival meeting" in 1921 was said to have led to his death in that year. A few, like John Dunsmore, managed to obtain leadership positions within the Republican party on the local level; an even smaller number, like Wesley Bennington, demonstrated more clearly than ever their qualifications for membership in the lunatic fringe. Bennington persisted in his advocacy of lost causes: in 1928 he was the vice-presidential nominee of the National party, which was "devoted to free money and the single tax, with its chief aim to have 'money at cost' issued to the people by the government just as postage stamps are now issued to the people."[11]

Several years before his term had expired in 1903, Senator William A. Harris had appealed for progressive bipartisan support in his bid for reelection; this he failed to obtain.[12] In 1906, however, the ex-senator was the Democratic and reform nominee for governor. Harris was, as ever, a popular figure. He had demonstrated, beyond question, his attachment to progressive principles, and he publicly confessed to considerable "admiration for President Roosevelt," who, according to Harris, had "adopted a great many" of the Democratic party's "best ideas." "In fact," said Harris, "there is a good deal of Democracy permeating through the ranks of the Republican party."[13] Harris came close to winning that election—a mere 2,123 votes was the difference.[14] Afterward, Harris resided in Chicago where he served as president of the American Shorthorn Breeders' Association until his death in 1909. He retained his interest in Kansas politics as before. Not long before his death he was advising fellow Democrats to support Insurgent Republicans who had taken up the cause of reform.[15]

In his campaign for governor, W. A. Harris had had no

more loyal supporter than John Breidenthal, now a successful Kansas City businessman. Certainly, Breidenthal qualified as a progressive. By 1906 the former Populist chairman was calling himself an independent and was an enthusiastic supporter of President Theodore Roosevelt. It seems likely that Breidenthal, still relatively young, would have been drawn back into the political arena had it not been for his untimely death in 1910.[16]

John Breidenthal had viewed the course of events after 1900 as vindication for the Populist struggle of the previous decade. This was probably the feeling of all surviving Populist leaders. For certain it was William A. Peffer's attitude. In 1903 Peffer stated: "Day by day I see our principles growing in both old parties." He commended the leadership of Bryan and Roosevelt, but he believed the president had "shown a better capacity for applying the principles of Populism . . . ."[17] In 1907 he was quoted as saying: "The country now hotly demands legislation it abused me for advocating."[18] With each passing year he was even more pleased with events. When he returned to Topeka from Washington, D.C., in April, 1911, after an absence of nine years, during which time he had been concerned mainly with the preparation of an index for the *Congressional Record,* Peffer stated that he could "derive great entertainment from the present trend of political ideals and policies." Before his death in 1912, the ex-senator proudly classified himself as an "insurgent" and said it was "refreshing to hear the leaders in Congress going over the very things we were discussing years ago."[19]

Predictably, perhaps, Mary Elizabeth Lease hopped aboard the progressive bandwagon in New York as it gained momentum. She had been looking for a Napoleon "to liberate" the "industrial world" ever since 1895.[20] In 1904 she seemed to have found him. In an interview she indicated that she saw Theodore Roosevelt as a "man of destiny, an instrument in God's hands, to send the gift of human liberty to the far off islands of the sea and to give America the proud place of the foremost of the nations that inhabit the face of the earth."[21] Obviously, it was President Roosevelt's aggressive foreign policy that had won Mrs. Lease's admiration; she had long since abandoned any real commitment to social reform.[22] But by 1914 the impulse had become irresistible; she had to speak out. Progressives, she stated, have "adopted our platform, clause by clause, plank by plank." To prove it, "Note the list of reforms which we advocated which are coming into reality. Direct election of senators is assured. Public utilities are gradually being removed from the hands of the few and placed under control of the people who use them. Woman suffrage is now almost a national issue. Prohibition, thank God, is spreading across the country like wildfire." Then, in that unmistakable Lease style, she said: "Brother, the times are propitious. The seed we sowed out in Kansas did not fall on barren ground."[23]

Whether the former Kansas spellbinder took to the hustings again is not clear. She did live on to 1933. During that period of time, with few other former Kansas Populist leaders around to contradict her, she made several rather bold claims concerning her role in the Populist movement.[24]

By surviving until 1933, Mary Elizabeth Lease ranked with Frank Doster; but in practically all other categories the judge left the famous lady way behind. Right up to the very end Frank Doster reveled in playing the role of gadfly. As always, he was the seeker of new ideas; eager to puncture pompous bubbles; intent on solutions he believed would induce to the betterment of humanity.

Judge Doster's opponents (with not a little help from the judge himself) had created such a distorted and unrealistic image of him before he became chief justice that they were unjustifiably shocked and impressed by the sensible manner in which he performed his duties from 1897 to 1903—so much so in fact that there was some Republican support for his reelection in 1902. Not enough for victory, however, and the judge left the court in 1903 to become an assistant attorney for the Missouri Pacific Railroad.[25]

Undoubtedly, Frank Doster moderated his views while on the court, but the change he experienced was not nearly as great as that in the public acceptance or tolerance of the point of view which his position represented. This was best demonstrated in the reception given an address he delivered to the Washburn College graduating class in Topeka in 1901. Among other things, the judge stated that he would concede that "the animating spirit of many of the promoters and managers of the enterprises of the age is selfish, brutal, tyrannical in the extreme, and unchecked, it would speedily involve us in industrial serfdom, but the methods of combination, organization and system which it must of necessity adopt are the methods of social integration which will inevitably widen and strengthen into the legalized state called collectivism." He went on to say that he had "no fear of the permanency of trusts and combinations. The most valuable and comforting lesson that has been taught us was that they were heterogeneous elements which would presently coalesce into the perfect state." The editor of the Topeka *Capital* liked the tone of Doster's address but deplored its "socialistic implications." As the *Capital* saw it, Doster had taken "high ground." In this address, it continued, "There is no appeal to meanness, selfishness, prejudice, passion or any of the lower class of sensibilities."[26] Frank Doster had never employed the "lower class of sensibilities"; the tone was basically the same; the public ear had simply become more attuned to the particular note he had sounded.

Frank Doster affiliated with the Democratic party after he left the state supreme court.[27] Unlike many of his former Populist colleagues, the judge remained for some time quite skeptical about the extent of the G.O.P.'s conversion to reform. In a letter written in 1908, he stated that "the Republican Party has not broken its alliance with the predatory wealth of the country. Its pretensions in that respect are a mere lip proclamation. Among all the influential leaders of the Republican Party, those who have declared their independence of the special interests may be counted on the fingers of one hand." Only "one conspicuous Republican," President Theodore Roosevelt, had "even made the pretense of throwing down the gauntlet to the buccaneers of industrial life . . . ." Beyond that, only "one other man of more than local or secondary prominence and influence has volunteered for a tilt in the tournament with the knights of commercial outlawry—Senator LaFollette." All the others who affected "a desire to be arrayed in their class" were merely "timid" imitators. "With the two exceptions named there is not one of them who for effectiveness of warfare has armed himself with more than a squirt-gun and who is not peering furtively around the corner to assure himself of safety."[28]

By 1910 Doster's views on this subject had changed.

> Take the present day insurgent Republican, or as he likes to style himself, "progressive" Republican. I should think he would be ashamed to look an old-time Populist in the face. Excepting some of the Populist propositions for currency reform, and those are not now matters in issue, and excepting public ownership of the railroads, there isn't a plank in the Populist platforms of the 90s but has been bodily and brazenly appropriated as cardinal tenets of faith by the Kansas insurgent Republicans . . . .

The truth of the matter is, said Doster, "We have been sandbagged" and by "men who for twenty years had been professing lofty scorn of our political possessions."

He hastened to add that he did not want anyone to misinterpret his meaning. "I am not condemning this tardy acceptance of Populistic doctrine by Republican leaders and platform makers. On the contrary, I rejoice in it."

Doster went on to state that he observed "an occasional, though grudging, acknowledgment that the Populist party was a sort of John the Baptist to the new faith, but it is generally coupled with some animadversion tending in the whole to discredit rather than praise." In particular, said Doster, the new champions of reform were saying that Populist leaders had not been sincere and had not made an honest effort to enact these reforms. His answer to that was: "it is a lie, put forth to break the force of the fact that every article in the [Insurgent] Republican creed of today is of Populist origin, and would have been enacted into law but for that campaign of ridicule, vilification and abuse without parallel in the political history of the state, that was waged by many of the very men who now profess belief in the same principles."[29]

Doster overstated his case, but he made a valid and meaningful observation regarding Populism's misfortunes. The ridicule, vilification, and abuse he mentioned did occur, and it was devastating. Why it occurred and why it was effective cannot of course be explained in a few sentences. The answer really includes the whole of this study and more. The primary obstacle to Populist success, however, in Kansas and probably even more so throughout the nation, had been what for lack of better terms must be called a negative climate of opinion. The most antagonistic part of that prevailing attitude would have to be that complex of ideas designated as social Darwinism, which applied the "kiss of death" to this agrarian movement from the beginning by enabling or causing it to be stigmatized as retrogressive.

It was all but axiomatic among the influential, business-minded segment of late nineteenth-century society that nothing progressive could possibly emanate from the laboring classes of the farm or factory. The Populist party leadership in Kansas was severely handicapped by that attitude, despite the rather extraordinary quality and predominantly middle-class origins and associations of that leadership.

But of course Kansas Populism's difficulties cannot all be attributed to this one factor. Although by no means unrelated, there were formidable problems deriving from the character of the leadership and the followship itself. The greatest handicaps afflicting the rank and file stem from its third-party minority status and the spasmodic motivation of economic discontent. As for the leadership, it rated high by most tests of leadership characteristics. Exceptions have been noted, but as a group the Populist leaders in Kansas demonstrated a high degree of sensitivity to the direction of social and industrial tendencies of their society; they were acutely perceptive in gauging the possible courses of community action; and they were unsurpassed in their ability to give dramatic expression to the sentiments or interests of a significant segment of the Kansas populace. Their greatest shortcoming would have to be their inability to reconcile divergent groups in pursuit of common goals. In all fairness, though, it must be said that these leaders were laboring under extraordinarily difficult circumstances.

As political innovators the leaders could make no great claims for themselves. But for them there was innovation aplently in the implementation of the nation's unfulfilled democratic ideals in the new industrial age of the late nineteenth century. These leaders did indeed concern themselves with this problem, and in the dialogue which they conducted, in the program which they advanced, they assisted in launching a progressive quest that continues into the twentieth century.

In the context of their period of origin, it was not Populist principles that were retrogressive—merely the fact that they were championed by and in the name of farmers and laborers. The path to reform could be made much smoother almost overnight if these same principles were embraced by urban, middle-class spokesmen and championed in the name of the middle class. That this change did indeed occur was never more aptly demonstrated within the context of Kansas politics than by this William Allen White editorial that appeared in the December 14, 1906, edition of the Emporia *Gazette*:

> Ten years ago this great organ of reform wrote a piece entitled "What is the Matter with Kansas?" In it great sport was made of a perfectly honest gentleman of unusual legal ability who happened to be running for chief justice of the Supreme Court of this state, because he said in effect that "the rights of the user are paramount to the rights of the owner." Those were paleozoic times; how far the world has moved since then. This paper was wrong in those days and Judge Doster was right; but he was too early in the season and his views got frost bitten. This is a funny world. About all we can do is to move with it.

APPENDIXES

I

Individual Leaders and a Selective List of Sources for Biographical Statistics*

1. Baker, William—*The Advocate,* Topeka, June 25, 1890; Hill P. Wilson, *A Biographical History of Eminent Men of the State of Kansas with Portraits Engraved Expressly for this Work* (Topeka: The Hall Lithographing Company, 1901), 513-15; *Biographical Directory of the American Congresses, 1774-1949* (Washington, D.C.: Government Printing Office, 1950).

2. Bennington, Wesley H.—*New Era,* Topeka, July 21, 1894; *The National Cyclopaedia of American Biography, Being the History of the United States as Illustrated in the Lives of the Founders, Builders, and Defenders of the Republic, and of the Men and Women who are Doing the Work and Moulding the Thought of the Present Time,* Vol. XXI (New York: James T. White and Company, 1931), 402.

3. Biddle, W. H.—*The Advocate,* Topeka, September 13, 1890.

4. Botkin, Jeremiah D.—Wilson, *Eminent Men,* 353-55; *The Advocate,* Topeka, August 22, 1894; Topeka *Daily Capital,* September 2, 1894.

5. Boyle, Louis C.—*Men of Affairs in Greater Kansas City 1912: A Newspaper Reference Work* (Kansas City: The Kansas City Press Club, 1912), 39.

6. Breidenthal, John W.—Undated newspaper clipping, in Kansas Biographical Scrapbook (K.S.H.S.), B, III, 330; Wilson, *Eminent Men,* 625-27.

7. Bush, W. E.—William Montague Bliss, "Kansas—The Sunflower State," *Carter's Monthly,* XII (November, 1897).

8. Clemens, G. C.—*The Commonwealth,* Topeka, April 15, 1885; Charles A. Magaw, *Bulletin of the Shawnee County Historical Society,* Number Fifteen, December 1951, 10-11; Topeka *Daily Capital,* October 8, 1906.

9. Close, Fred J.—Topeka *Daily Capital,* November 30, 1892; *History of the State of Kansas,* Vol. I (Chicago: A. T. Andreas, 1883), 481.

10. Clover, Benjamin H.—*Biographical Record: This Volume Contains Biographical Sketches of Leading Citizens of Cowley County, Kansas* (Chicago: Biographical Publishing Company, 1901), 309-11.

11. Cobun, Marshall W.—Biographical material from an uncatalogued reference contained in K.S.H.S. Library.

12. Cone, Rufus—*History of Wichita and Sedgwick County, Kansas,* Vol. II (Chicago: C. F. Cooper and Company, 1910), 748.

---

* *No biographical information was found for the following individuals: Welburn, J. B.; King, S. S.; Ritchie, J. H.; Artz, H. H.; Allen, S. H.; Tilton, W. A.; Holden, James D.; and Leahy, D. D.*

13. Corning, Cyrus—*History of Shawnee County, Kansas, and Representative Citizens* (Chicago: Richmond and Arnold, 1905), 444-46; *The Republican*, El Dorado, September 19, 1890; *Kansas People*, Lyndon, September 10, 1890.

14. Corning, Eva L.—Biographical Circulars, Vol. I, A-L, K.S.H.S.; *Illustriana Kansas: Biographical Sketches of Kansas Men and Women of Achievement Who Have Been Awarded Life Membership in Kansas Illustriana Society* (Hebron, Nebraska: Illustriana, Inc., 1933), 261.

15. Daniels, Percy—*Portrait and Biographical Record of Southeastern Kansas, Containing Biographical Sketches of Prominent and Representative Citizens of the Counties, Together with Biographies and Portraits of all the Presidents of the United States and Governors of the State of Kansas* (Chicago: Biographical Publishing Company, 1894), 234-37; Wilson, *Eminent Men*, 371-72.

16. Davis, John—Clay Center *Dispatch*, August 22, 1901; John Davis Scrapbooks, K.S.H.S.; *The Daily Times*, February 4, 1888, in Kansas Biographical Scrapbook (K.S.H.S.), D, I, 92, 109; *Biographical Directory of The American Congresses, 1774-1949*.

17. Diggs, Annie L.—George A. Root, typed manuscript, dated February 26, 1944, and entitled "Mrs. Annie LaPorte Diggs," K.S.H.S.; Topeka *Daily Capital*, September 17, 1908; Kansas City *Star*, August 5, 1900.

18. Doster, Frank—Topeka *Daily Capital*, February 26, 1933; Wilson, *Eminent Men*, 581-82; James C. Malin, *A Concern About Humanity*, 132-55.

19. Dunsmore, John—*History of Neo-*sho and Wilson Counties, Kansas* (Fort Scott: Monitor Printing Co., 1902), 438-41.

20. Easter, A. C.—Andreas, *History of the State of Kansas*, Vol. I, 1541.

21. Elder, Peter P.—Wilson, *Eminent Men*, 275-77.

22. Ernst, E. I. Z.—Biographical material contained in the K.S.H.S. Archives.

23. Foote, C. E.—Kansas Historical Collections (K.S.H.S.), VII, 129n.

24. Furbeck, D. I.—Ottawa *Journal and Triumph*, June 21, 1894.

25. Gaines, Henry Newton—William Ansel Mitchell, *Linn County, Kansas: A History* (La Cygne: La Cygne Journal Presswork, 1928), 186-87.

26. Hagaman, James M.—*Biographical History of Cloud County, Kansas* (Logansport: Wilson, Humphrey and Company, 1902-1903?), 218-19; Malin, *A Concern About Humanity*, 89.

27. Harman, Colfax B.—*Lawrence—Today and Yesterday* (Lawrence: Daily Journal World Publication, 1913), 113.

28. Harrington, Grant Wood—Ottawa *Journal and Triumph*, July 19, 1894.

29. Harrington, Wynne Powers—*Kansas State Historical Collections*, XVI, n. 403.

30. Harris, William A.—Wilson, *Eminent Men*, 287-89; *Biographical Directory of the American Congresses, 1774-1949* (Washington, D.C.: Government Printing Office, 1950).

31. Harvey, Alexander Miller—Wilson, *Eminent Men*, 99-101; Bliss, "Kansas—The Sunflower State," *Carter's Monthly*, XII (November, 1897), 565-98.

32. Hebbard, J. C.—James H. Lathrop, *A Memorial of the Late J. C. Heb-*

bard, The Historian and Statistician (Topeka, 1894), 8-19.

33. Hefflebower, David—Topeka *Daily Capital*, September 29, 1912; *The Peoples Herald*, Lyndon, August 20, 1896; Bliss, "Kansas—The Sunflower State," *Carter's Monthly*, XII (November, 1897), 577-78.

34. Henderson, Benjamin S.—*History of Montgomery County, Kansas* (Iola: Press of Iola Register, 1903), 215-16.

35. Householder, M. A.—*Modern Light*, Columbus, October 13, 1892.

36. Hudson, Thomas Jefferson—*Herringshaw's American Statesman* (Chicago: American Publisher's Association, 1906) 278; *Biographical Directory of the American Congresses, 1774-1949* (Washington, D.C.: Government Printing Office, 1950).

37. Ives, John Nutt—Biographical Circulars, Vol. I, A-L, K.S.H.S. Library.

38. Kibbe, William E.—*Portrait and Biographical Record of Leavenworth, Douglas and Franklin Counties, Kansas* (Chicago: Chapman Publishing Company, 1899), 742-43.

39. Lathrop, James Henry—Biographical Circulars, Vol. I, A-L, K.S.H.S. Library.

40. Laybourn, Joseph W.—William E. Connelley, *A Standard History of Kansas and Kansans*, V, 2225-26; *The Peoples Herald*, Lyndon, July 7, 1892.

41. Lease, Mary Elizabeth—Kansas City *Star*, April 1, 1891; James C. Malin, "Mary Elizabeth Clyens Lease," *Dictionary of American Biography*, Vol. XXI (Supplement I), 488-89; Harry Levinson, "Mary Elizabeth Lease: Prairie Radical," *Kansas Magazine*, 1948, 18-24.

42. Leedy, John—Wilson, *Eminent Men*, 45-47.

43. Legate, James F.—Topeka *Daily Capital*, December 18, 1898; Topeka *Mail & Breeze*, December 23, 1899.

44. Lewelling, L. D.—Bliss, "Kansas—The Sunflower State," *Carter's Monthly*, XII (November, 1897), 565-98; W. J. Costigan, *Lorenzo D. Lewelling, in Memorial* (Chicago: Press of Swift & Company, 1902); Wilson, *Eminent Men*, 37-41.

45. Little, John T.—Atchison *Globe*, October 30, 1893; Wilson, *Eminent Men*, 327-29; Kansas City *Star*, December 10, 1926.

46. McCormick, Mrs. Fanny—*The Advocate*, Topeka, August 20, 1890.

47. McCormick, Nelson B.—*Biographical Directory of the American Congresses, 1774-1949* (Washington, D.C.: Government Printing Office, 1950).

48. McLallin, Stephen—Mrs. Annie L. Diggs, *Transactions of the Kansas State Historical Society, 1897-1900*, VI (Topeka: State Printer, 1900), 233-34.

49. Madden, John—Uncatalogued biographical sketch, K.S.H.S. Library.

50. Marshall, William V.—Biographical Circulars, Vol. II, M-Z, K.S.H.S. Library.

51. Maxson, Perry B.—*Transactions of the Kansas State Historical Society, 1907-1908*, Vol. X (Topeka: State Printer, 1908), 267.

52. Morris, W. H.—*The Advocate*, Topeka, August 12, 1896; *A Twentieth Century History and Biographical Record of Crawford County, Kansas* (Chicago: Lewis Publishing Company, 1905), 175.

53. Osborn, Russell Scott—Atchison *Globe*, October 30, 1893; Biograph-

ical Circulars (K.S.H.S.), Vol. II, M-Z.

54. Otis, John Grant—*Kansas People,* Osage City, November 5, 1890; *Biographical Directory of the American Congresses, 1774-1949* (Washington, D.C.: Government Printing Office, 1950).

55. Peffer, William A.—Hortense Marie Harrison, "The Populist Delegation in the Fifty-Second Congress, 1891-1893," master's thesis (The University of Kansas, 1933), 10-12; *Biographical Directory of the American Congresses, 1774-1949* (Washington, D.C.: Government Printing Office, 1950).

56. Prather, Van B.—*History of Wyandotte County, Kansas and Its People* (Chicago: Lewis Publishing Company, 1911), 519-21.

57. Pratt, Morton A.—Wichita *Daily Eagle,* August 8, 1911.

58. Rich, Ben—*In Remembrance* (n.p., n.d.), 45; *The Advocate and News,* Topeka, August 31, 1898.

59. Riddle, Taylor—*Twentieth Biennial Report of the Board of Directors of the Kansas State Historical Society, 1914 to 1916* (Topeka: State Printer, 1916), 68; Autobiographical sketch, dated January 29, 1913, K.S.H.S.

60. Ridgely, E. R.—Pittsburg *Kansan,* June 4, 1896; *A Biographical History of Eminent Men of the State of Kansas,* 379-81; *Biographical Directory of the American Congresses, 1774-1949* (Washington, D.C.: Government Printing Office, 1950).

61. Rightmire, William Franklin—Topeka *Daily Capital,* December 25, 1929; Autobiographical sketch, dated December 16, 1910, K.S.H.S.

62. Sankey, Robert Alexander—*Kansas: A Cyclopaedia of State History Embracing Events, Institutions, Industries, Counties, Cities, Towns,* *Prominent Persons, etc.* (K.S.H.S.), 296-98.

63. Scott, S. M.—*The Advocate,* Topeka, June 20, 1894.

64. Sears, William Henry—Manuscript, Sears Collection, K.S.H.S. Archives.

65. Shinn, Albert C.—*Portrait and Biographical Record of Leavenworth, Douglas and Franklin Counties, Kansas* (Chicago: Chapman Publishing Company, 1899), 664-65.

66. Simpson, Jerry—Harrison, "The Populist Delegation in the Fifty-Second Congress, 1891-1893," 14-18; *Biographical Directory of the American Congresses, 1774-1949* (Washington, D.C.: Government Printing Office, 1950).

67. Snider, S. H.—Atchison *Globe,* October 30, 1893.

68. Snow, Edwin H.—*The United States Biographical Dictionary. Kansas Volume: Containing Accurately Compiled Biographical Sketches, into which is Woven the History of the State and Its Leading Interests* (Chicago: S. Lewis & Company, Publishers, 1879), 374-75.

69. Soloman, Henry C.—Atchison *Globe,* July 16, 1894.

70. Stryker, William—*Reno County Public Schools Biennial Report and Course of Study, 1899-1900* (Hutchinson: School and Fireside Printers, 1900), 46; Topeka *Daily Capital,* February 25, 1918; Autobiographical sketch on Kansas State Historical Society form, dated June 14, 1893, Biographical Circulars, Vol. II, M-Z.

71. Taylor, Edwin—Letter contained in the K.S.H.S. Archives which is listed as a special collection.

72. Vickery, Mrs. Fanny Randolph—A. L. Diggs, "The Women in the Alliance Movement," *Arena,* VI (July, 1892), 169-70.

73. Vincent, C.—Biographical Circular (K.S.H.S.).

74. Vincent, H.—Biographical Circular (K.S.H.S.).

75. Vincent, William D.—Wilson, *Eminent Men*, 449-51; *Biographical Directory of the American Congresses, 1774-1949* (Washington, D.C.: Government Printing Office, 1950).

76. Vrooman, Carl S.—Topeka *Journal*, April 8, 1915.

77. Wait, Mrs. Anna C.—Diggs, "The Women in the Alliance Movement," *Arena*, VI (July, 1892), 178; Topeka *Daily Capital*, March 21, 1901; Manuscript autobiographical sketch, K.S.H.S.

78. Waterbury, Edwin Stevens—Uncatalogued biographical sketch contained in K.S.H.S.

79. Willits, John F.—McLouth *Times* (Souvenir Edition), November 25, 1898, 63-64.

80. Wood, Samuel N.—William E. Connelley, *A Standard History of Kansas and Kansans*, III, 1268-69.

81. Zercher, D. C.—*The Advocate,* Topeka, September 3, 1890.

II

Composite Comparison of the Major Kansas Populist Leadership for the Years 1890 and 1896*

1890 (63 individuals)	1896 (54 individuals)
46 Median Age	47 Median Age
1870 Median Year to Kansas Ohio, New York, Pennsylvania, and Virginia most common native states	1871 Median Year to Kansas Same breakdown here
65% Non-farmers	71% Non-farmers
35% Farmers and/or stock raisers, or associated with farming in some capacity	29% Farmers and/or stock raisers, or associated with farming in some capacity
26 Former Third-Party Men	24 Former Third-Party Men
1 Former Democrat	10 Former Democrats
9 Former Republicans	2 Former Republicans
20 College Graduates	26 College Graduates

III

Members of the 1893 House for Whom Information Was Obtained by Individual Reference and the Sources of that Information†

1. Chappel, Thomas—*Who's Who in Topeka* (Topeka: Adams Brothers Publishing Company, 1905), 19. Populist.

---

* *The original charts from which these statistics were compiled are housed in the Regional History Division of the Kenneth Spencer Research Library, The University of Kansas.*

† *The K.S.H.S. Library also contains a collection, in four volumes, of press*

2. Chrisman, M. B.—*History of the State of Kansas,* Vol. II, (Chicago: A. T. Andreas, 1883), 1224. Republican.

3. Clarke, J. W. (M?)—*A Biographical History of Central Kansas,* I (New York and Chicago: Lewis Publishing Co., 1902), 8. Populist.

4. Clouter, J. F.—*Weekly State Journal,* Topeka, February 12, 1885. Republican.

5. Drew, A. H.—Hugoton *Hermes,* August, 1961 (75th Anniversary Historical Edition). Populist.

6. Dunsmore, J. M.—*History of Neosho and Wilson Counties, Kansas* (Fort Scott: Monitor Printing Co., 1902), 438-41. Populist.

7. Eastman, D. W.—*The Chronical Monthly Magazine,* I (June, 1894), 12-13. Published in Burlingame, Kansas. Republican.

8. Elting, Richard O.—Connelley, ed., *Kansas and Kansans,* V, 2083-84. Republican.

9. Glenn, William M.—Connelley, ed., *Kansas and Kansans,* IV, 1688. Republican.

10. Graham, James—Topeka *Daily Capital,* February 12, 1909. Populist.

11. Green, Edward F.—*Handbook of the Kansas Legislature,* 1901 (Topeka: Crane and Co., 1900), 116. Populist.

12. Hale, Samuel I.—Connelley, ed., *Kansas and Kansans,* V, 2156-57. Republican.

13. Hoch, E. W.—*The Chronicle Monthly Magazine,* I (June, 1894), 14-19. Republican.

14. Humphrey, J. L.—*History of Labette County, Kansas and Repre-* *sentative Citizens* (Chicago: Biographical Publishing Co., 1901), 797-98. Populist.

15. Kerr, Walter L.—*The History of the Early Settlement of Norton County Kansas* (Kansas Norton Champion, 1894), 163. Populist.

16. Pomeroy, John F.—*Kansas: A Cyclopaedia of State History, Embracing Events, Institutions, Industries, Counties, Cities, Towns, Prominent Persons, etc.,* III (Chicago: Standard Publishing Co., n.d.). Republican.

17. Price, W. W.—Brown County *World,* Hiawatha, March 2, 1894. Republican.

18. Rosenthal, Joseph—Kansas City *Star,* November 22, 1925. Democrat.

19. Shaw, James S.—*Kansas Democrat,* Topeka, February 14, 1893. Republican.

20. Swan, William B.—*First Biennial Report of the State Board of Health of the State of Kansas from Jan. 1, 1901, to Dec. 31, 1902* (Topeka: W. Y. Morgan, 1902), 8-9. Republican.

21. Treu, Joseph—*Early History of Wabaunsee County, Kansas* (Alma, Kansas: 1901), 287-88. Populist.

22. Troutman, James A.—*Kansas,* Part I (Chicago: Standard Publishing Co., 1912), 718-20. Republican.

23. Willits, Ledru J.—Connelley, ed., *Kansas and Kansans,* IV, 2053. Republican.

24. Woodworth, C. A.—*Directory of State Government, Kansas, 1877-1878* (Kansas Publishing House, 1877). Populist.

clippings relating to the 1893 house; volume three of these has an unidentified newspaper clipping which provides a sketchy and insufficient account of the background of the Republican house members.

IV

Composite Comparison of the Kansas Legislatures of
1891, 1893, 1895, 1897, and 1899*

Legislative Body	Median Age	Occupation	Removed to Kansas	College Graduates
1891 Senate				
Republicans	45	89.0% non-farmers	1868	20.6%
1891 House				
Populists	46	21.0% non-farmers	1878	22.4%
Republicans	45	63.0% non-farmers	1877	23.8%
1893-97 Senate				
Populists	44	20.1% non-farmers	1871	6.6%
Republicans	48	73.3% non-farmers	1872	28.5%
1893 House				
Populists	45	31.2% non-farmers	1878	25.9%
Republicans	46	60.0% non-farmers	1871	34.1%
1895 House				
Populists	40	25.9% non-farmers	1878-79	29.1%
Republicans	45	57.4% non-farmers	1874-75	29.1%
1897-1901 Senate				
Populists	48	37.5% non-farmers	1872	29.4%
Republicans	44	77.7% non-farmers	1872	36.0%
1897 House				
Populists	44	32.2% non-farmers	1877	21.0%
Republicans	48	73.8% non-farmers	1878	48.7%
1899 House				
Populists	43	34.7% non-farmers	1878-79	31.2%
Republicans	44	65.1% non-farmers	1877	39.1%

The original charts from which these statistics were compiled are housed in the Regional History Division of the Kenneth Spencer Research Library, The University of Kansas.

NOTES

Preface

1. "The Populist Heritage and the Intellectual," *American Scholar*, XXIX (Winter, 1959-1960), 58.
2. Actually, the first scholarly account of Populism was Frank L. McVey's "The Populist Movement," in *Economic Studies* (American Economic Association, 1896), I, 133-209, which did not employ the Turner thesis and which viewed the movement as a truly radical departure. Solon J. Buck's *The Agrarian Crusade: A Chronicle of the Farmer in Politics* (New Haven, 1921) and John D. Hicks' *The Populist Revolt: A History of the Farmers' Alliance and the People's Party* (Minneapolis, 1931) are two general studies that represented the frontier interpretation most influentially.
3. See Thomas H. Greer's *American Social Reform Movements: Their Pattern Since 1865* (New York, 1949); Eric F. Goldman's *Rendezvous with Destiny: A History of Modern American Reform* (New York, 1952); and Richard Hofstadter's *The Age of Reform: From Bryan to F.D.R.* (New York, 1955).
4. See especially C. Vann Woodward's "The Populist Heritage and the Intellectual," *American Scholar*, XXIX (Winter, 1959-1960), 55-72, and Norman Pollack's *The Populist Response to Industrial America* (New York, 1962).
5. See especially George E. Mowry's *The California Progressives* (Berkeley, 1951); Alfred D. Chandler's "The Origins of the Progressive Leadership," in Elting Morison, ed., *The Letters of Theodore Roosevelt*, VIII (Cambridge, 1954), 1462-65; and Otis L. Graham's *An Encore for Reform: The Old Progressives and the New Deal* (New York, 1967).
6. Raymond C. Miller, "The Populist Party in Kansas," unpublished doctor's dissertation (University of Chicago, 1928). Walter T. K. Nugent's dissertation was published as *The Tolerant Populists: Kansas, Populism, and Nativism* (Chicago, 1963).

Chapter I

1. *The Advocate*, Topeka, May 14, 1890.
2. Vernon Lewis Parrington, *Main Currents in American Thought* (3 vols., New York, 1958), I, 11.
3. *Ibid.*, 3.
4. Arthur W. Thompson, "The Gilded Age," in Howard W. Quint and others, eds., *Main Problems in American History* (2 vols., Homewood, 1964), II, 53-54. See also Richard Hofstadter, *The American Political Tradition and the Men Who Made It* (New York, 1961), 45-67, and Sidney Fine, *Laissez Faire and the General-Welfare State: A Study of Conflict in American Thought, 1865-1901* (Ann Arbor, 1957), 3-25.
5. Thompson, in Quint and others, eds., *Main Problems*, II, 54.
6. John Tipple, "The Robber Baron in the Gilded Age: Entrepreneur or Iconoclast?" in H. Wayne Morgan, ed., *The Gilded Age: A Reappraisal* (Syracuse, 1963), 19. Thurman W. Arnold, perhaps better than anyone else, has chopped

through the national mythology to demonstrate how and why American attitudes were affected when the modern corporate structure was grafted onto
American society. See *The Folklore of Capitalism* (New Haven, 1937), especially chapter IX on "The Effect of the Antitrust Laws in Encouraging Large
Combinations."

7. Tipple, in Morgan, ed., *The Gilded Age*, 19-20.

8. See Lee Benson, *The Concept of Jacksonian Democracy: New York as a Test
Case* (Atheneum, 1964), especially the chapter entitled "Positive versus Negative Liberalism."

9. Arnold, *Folklore of Capitalism* (New Haven, 1961), 12.

10. Fine, *Laissez Faire and the General-Welfare State*, 4-5.

11. Thomas C. Cochran and William Miller, *The Age of Enterprise: A Social
History of Industrial America*, revised edition (New York, 1961), 91 ff.

12. Charles Francis Adams, "An Erie Raid," *North American Review*, CXII (April,
1871), 241. Edward Chase Kirkland's *Business in the Gilded Age: The Conservatives' Balance Sheet* (Madison, 1952) and *Dream and Thought in the
Business Community, 1860-1900* (Ithaca, 1956) demonstrate the adaptability
and flexibility of the business mind in the period.

13. Cochran and Miller, *Age of Enterprise*, 111.

14. Tipple, in Morgan, ed., *The Gilded Age*, 16-17. It is not my contention that
post-Civil War economic history was the result of a struggle between "mono-
lithic economic groups." Stanley Coben's "Northeastern Business and Radical
Reconstruction: A Re-examination," *Mississippi Valley Historical Review*,
XLVI (June, 1959), 67-90, demonstrates conclusively that "northeastern
businessmen had no unified economic program to promote." This view has
been substantiated further by Robert P. Sharkey's *Money, Class, and Party: An
Economic Study of Civil War and Reconstruction* (The Johns Hopkins Univer-
sity Studies in Historical and Political Science, Series LXXVII, 1959), and
Irwin Unger's *The Greenback Era: A Social and Political History of American
Finance, 1865-1879* (Princeton, 1964).

15. Edward C. Kirkland, "Divide and Ruin," *Mississippi Valley Historical Review*, XLIII (June, 1956), 11.

16. See C. Vann Woodward, *Reunion and Reaction: The Compromise of 1877
and the End of Reconstruction* (Garden City, 1956), especially the chapter
entitled "The Rejuvenation of Whiggery."

17. Tipple, in Morgan, ed., *The Gilded Age*, 17.

18. Vincent P. De Santis, "The Republican Party Revisited, 1877-1897," in *ibid.*,
93-94.

19. *Ibid.*, 94-95.

20. Ralph Henry Gabriel, *The Course of American Democratic Thought: An
Intellectual History Since 1815* (New York, 1940), 146.

21. *Ibid.*, 147.

22. *Ibid.*, 146 ff.

23. *Ibid.*, 145.

24. It may seem a paradox to say that political democracy was expanding since
many observers, Henry Adams for instance, felt democracy was weakening,
contracting, decaying. This obviously was the case socially and economically,
but in form, at least, political democracy was expanding—the addition of new

states, the extension of political rights to Negroes, and the expansion of the franchise to include women on the municipal level and, later in the period, in some states full participation of women, were, however superficial they may have been, examples of expanding political democracy. In addition, the idea of the sovereign people was kept alive in the period to emerge stronger than ever at the close of the century. In a sense, politics of the era reflected well the aspirations of the majority of the populace who were thoroughly permeated with the materialism and rugged individualism of the age.

25. Kirkland, *Dream and Thought in the Business Community*, 14. Irvin G. Wyllie, in *The Self-Made Man in America: The Myths of Rags to Riches* (New Brunswick, 1954), 83, indicates that the exponents of self-help drew their "texts from the Bible, not from the writings of Darwin and Spencer." Sidney Fine contends, "Businessmen . . . did employ social-Darwinist arguments to justify both competition and consolidation and to combat demands for government regulation." See *Laissez Faire and the General-Welfare State,* n. 100.

26. Spencer's ideas were presented in a number of works. *Social Statics* (New York, 1864); *The Man Versus the State,* ed., Truxton Beale (New York, 1916); *The Principles of Sociology* (3 vols., New York, 1876-97); and *The Study of Sociology* (New York, 1874) are the major works. See also Richard Hofstadter, *Social Darwinism in American Thought,* revised edition (Boston, 1964), especially the chapters entitled "The Vogue of Spencer" and "William Graham Sumner: Social Darwinist." Stow Persons' *American Minds: A History of Ideas* (New York, 1958), 225-29, and Fine's *Laissez Faire and the General-Welfare State,* chapters II-IV, are also useful in assessing the ideas and influence of Spencer.

27. Hofstadter, *Social Darwinism,* 31-32.

28. See Crane Brinton, *English Political Thought in the 19th Century* (New York, 1962).

29. Hofstadter, *Social Darwinism,* 31-35; Persons, *American Minds,* 225-26; Parrington, *Main Currents,* III, 198; Eric F. Goldman, *Rendezvous with Destiny: A History of Modern American Reform,* revised edition (New York, 1956), 68-76; Fine, *Laissez Faire and the General-Welfare State,* 32-33.

30. Hofstadter, *Social Darwinism,* 32.

31. Goldman, *Rendezvous with Destiny,* 71-73; Hofstadter, *Social Darwinism,* especially see chapters entitled "Lester Ward: Critic" and "The Dissenters"; Fine, *Laissez Faire and the General-Welfare State,* chapters VI-IX.

32. George Rogers Taylor and Irene D. Neu, *The American Railroad Network, 1861-1890* (Cambridge, 1956), 1; Samuel P. Hays, *The Response to Industrialism: 1885-1914* (Chicago, 1957), 15-17.

33. *Ibid.*

34. U.S. Bureau of the Census, *Historical Statistics of the United States, 1789-1945,* 200, 202.

35. See Edward C. Kirkland's *Men, Cities and Transportation: A Study of New England History 1820-1900* (2 vols., Cambridge, 1948) on the region's transportation problems and the manner in which they were handled. Lee Benson's *Merchants, Farmers, and Railroads: Railroad Regulation and New York Politics, 1850-1887* (Cambridge, 1955) and John F. Stover's *The Railroads of the South, 1865-1900: A Study of Finance and Control* (Chapel Hill, 1955)

both shed light on the special problems arising from railroad transportation. George Rogers Taylor and Irene D. Neu have put together perhaps the most satisfactory account of the physical integration side of the nation's railroads in their *The American Railroad Network, 1861-1890*. Thomas C. Cochran's *Railroad Leaders, 1845-1890: The Business Mind in Action* (Cambridge, 1953), which reviews the careers of sixty-one railroad leaders and supplies almost three hundred pages of biographical data and correspondence, provides invaluable insights into the relationship of the railroads and their spokesmen to American society. Paul W. Gates' *Fifty Million Acres: Conflicts over Kansas Land Policy, 1854-1890* (Ithaca, 1954) is also quite useful in revealing a special phase of the railroad problem in conjunction with land distribution. See especially his discussion of "Railroad Purchase of Indian Reserves." Leslie E. Decker's *Railroads, Lands, and Politics: The Taxation of the Railroad Land Grants, 1864-1897* (Providence, 1964) fulfills a similar need. Two recent studies, Albert Fishlow's *American Railroads and the Transformation of the Ante-Bellum Economy* (Cambridge, 1965) and Robert Fogel's *Railroads and American Growth: Essays in Econometrics* (Baltimore, 1964), although arriving at somewhat conflicting conclusions, are both useful and stimulating econometric analyses.

36. Paul W. Gates, *The Farmer's Age: Agriculture 1815-1860* (New York, 1960), 212, 416; Hays, *Response to Industrialism*, 13-15; Cochran and Miller, *Age of Enterprise*, 211-12.

37. Hays, *Response to Industrialism*, 13-15, 27; Tipple, in Morgan, ed., *The Gilded Age*, 24-25. Undoubtedly, James C. Malin has made the single greatest contribution to explaining the exacting demands required of those who undertook to farm the plains country. See Malin's *Winter Wheat in the Golden Belt of Kansas* (Lawrence, 1944), especially 102-37. Allan G. Bogue's *Money at Interest: The Farm Mortgage on the Middle Border* (Ithaca, 1955), 1-6, provides a useful summary statement on the special pecuniary requirements for farming on the "Middle Border."

38. Hays, *Response to Industrialism*, 15.

39. *Ibid.*, 17-19; Cochran and Miller, *Age of Enterprise*, 47, 67-68; Stover, *American Railroads* (Chicago, 1965), 88.

40. Hays, *Response to Industrialism*, 20.

41. Arthur Bestor, "The Ferment of Reform," in Richard W. Leopold and Arthur S. Link, eds., *Problems in American History* (Englewood Cliffs, 1958), 266.

42. Hofstadter, *Social Darwinism*, 47.

43. The writer has in mind particularly the development of substantive due process in application to property rights. See Alfred H. Kelly and Winfred A. Harbison, *The American Constitution: Its Origin and Development* (New York, 1963), especially chapter nineteen. See also Fine's *Laissez Faire and the General-Welfare State*, especially the chapter entitled "Laissez Faire Becomes the Law of the Land."

44. Wilfred E. Binkley, *American Political Parties: Their Natural History*, revised edition (New York, 1958), 278-320; Matthew Josephson, *The Politicos, 1865-1896* (New York, 1938).

45. Paul W. Gates has written that "few would dispute today that it was 'insatiable land-hunger,' rather than any idealistic notion of making Kansas a free

or a slave state, that drew the bulk of the 100,000 people who rushed across the Missouri line in the period from 1854 to 1860." *Fifty Million Acres*, 1. See also pages 1-4, and 109, for Gates' comments on the nature of Kansas settlement. Roy Franklin Nichols' *The Disruption of American Democracy* (New York, 1962), especially the chapter entitled "Territorial Nightmares," is also useful for this period of Kansas settlement.

46. A. Bower Sageser, "The Rails Go Westward," in John D. Bright, ed., *Kansas: The First Century* (4 vols., New York, 1956), I, 223.

47. *Ibid.*, 228.

48. U.S. Department of Commerce, *Sixteenth Census of the United States, 1940, Population, Kansas* (Washington, Government Printing Office, 1941); and John D. Bright, "At the Turn of the Century," in Bright, ed., *Kansas*, I, 533.

49. The decade of the 1850s saw sixty-one percent of the working-force engaged in farming in some capacity; the 1860s, fifty-nine percent; the 1870s, eighty-one percent; and the 1880s fifty-five percent. U.S. Department of Commerce, *Fifteenth Census of the U.S., 1930, Population, Kansas*, I, 339.

50. William Frank Zornow, "The Basis of Agrarian Unrest in Kansas, 1870-1890," in Bright, ed., *Kansas*, I, 463.

51. James C. Carey, "People, Problems, Prohibition, Politicos and Politics—1870-1890," in Bright, ed., *Kansas*, I, *passim*.

52. Burton E. Lyman, "Voting Behavior of Kansas Counties, 1862-1936: As Measured by Pluralities for Governor and Secretary of State," unpublished master's thesis (University of Kansas, 1937), 142-43.

53. The actual percentages were these: 1864, 78.6; 1868, 68.8; 1872, 66.6; 1876, 63.1; 1880, 60.4; 1884, 58.1; 1888, 55.3. Svend Peterson, *A Statistical History of the American Presidential Elections* (New York, 1963), 40-56.

54. James C. Carey, "People, Problems, Prohibition, Politicos and Politics—1870-1890," in Bright, ed., *Kansas*, I, 392; and William Frank Zornow, *Kansas: A History of the Jayhawk State* (Norman, 1957), *passim*.

55. E. L. Godkin, "Aristocratic Opinions of Democracy," *North American Review*, C (July, 1865), 209-10.

56. Carey, "People and Politics," in Bright, ed., *Kansas*, I, 371.

57. *Ibid.*, 372-74. For a treatment of the fraudulent activities in Barber County see Myron C. Scott's "A Congressman and His Constituents, Jerry Simpson and the Big Seventh," unpublished master's thesis (Fort Hays Kansas State College, 1959), 28-29.

58. Paul Gates, in *Fifty Million Acres*, has covered the story of the scramble for lands by settlers and railroad officials as well as anyone.

59. Zornow, *Kansas*, 119-30. See also Ernest B. Bader, "Kansas: The First Decade of Statehood, 1861-1871," in Bright, ed., *Kansas*, I, 210-11, and Carey, "People and Politics," in *ibid.*, 394. See Gates, *Fifty Million Acres*, 143-46, for one treatment of Senator Pomeroy's activities. In a recent article, James C. Malin challenges the "purity of the 'Purifiers'" who defeated Pomeroy, and suggests that the senator was the victim of his own kind of devious tactics. See "Some Reconsiderations of the Defeat of Senator Pomeroy of Kansas, 1873," *Mid-America: An Historical Review*, XLVIII (January, 1966), 47-57.

60. Carey, "People and Politics," in Bright, ed., *Kansas*, I, 395.

61. Raymond C. Miller, "The Populist Party in Kansas," unpublished doctor's dissertation (University of Chicago, 1928), 4-5.
62. Pittsburg *Kansan,* November 6, 1889. The editor of this paper subsequently became a Populist, and the *Kansan* became the leading Populist paper in Crawford County.
63. See Henry Nash Smith's *Virgin Land: The American West as Symbol and Myth* (Cambridge, 1950), especially chapter sixteen, for an excellent treatment of the role played by myths in the settlement of the West.
64. Zornow, "The Basis of Agrarian Unrest in Kansas," in Bright, ed., *Kansas,* I, 473-75.
65. Some important exceptions were these: in 1874 the Republican party demanded in its platform legislation regulating railroad rates within the state (Topeka *Commonwealth,* August 30, 1874); in 1882 the Democratic party platform led the way in a call for direct election of president and vice-president and U.S. senators; the Democrats of the state also proposed in that year that elections of all federal officers be placed under the control of the national government (Topeka *Daily Capital,* September 1, 1882).
66. Among these proposals were a call for an income tax, a postal money-deposit system, laws protecting the health and safety of miners and factory workers, government ownership of railroads and telegraphs, direct election of United States senators, national laws for the arbitration of labor-management disputes, woman suffrage, and support for greenbacks as full legal tender (State party platforms for the 1872-1888 period may be found in Topeka *Commonwealth,* June 13, 1872; August 28, 1872; September 6, 1872; September 12, 1872; August 7 and 30, 1874; May 20, 1876; July 30, 1876; August 16, 1876; Topeka *Daily Capital,* September 24, 1877; July 7, 1878; August 28, 1878; September 6, 1878; July 30, 1880; August 9 and 24, 1882; September 1, 1882; July 18, 1884; June 15, 1886; August 12, 1887; July 7 and 28, 1888; and August 30, 1888).
67. James C. Malin, *A Concern About Humanity: Notes on Reform, 1872-1912 at the National and Kansas Levels of Thought* (Lawrence, 1964), see especially 19 ff.
68. In 1878 the Republican party denounced "the issue of an irredeemable 'absolute money,' legal-tender scrip, as a species of repudiation," but it endorsed the "withdrawal of the National Bank notes, substituting therefor greenback currency issued directly by the Government, as the sole paper currency of the country." The 1878 Republican platform endorsed, in addition, "a double-coin standard of values" as "preferable to a single standard . . . ." Neither of these proposals appeared again from 1878 to 1888. The 1882 Republican platform called for laws to "prevent unjust discrimination by railroad companies . . . ." The Republican platform of 1884 demanded that the board of railroad commissioners, established by the 1883 legislature, be given the powers necessary to accomplish its purpose. The 1888 platform denounced "all great trusts as oppressive to the people," and called for "stringent laws to protect . . . workingmen against contract, pauper or Chinese immigrants . . . ." The Republican platform that year also advocated a reduction in the legal rate of interest on money to six percent and a reduction in the maximum contract rate to ten percent (Topeka *Daily Capital,* August 28, 1878; August

9, 1882; July 18, 1884; July 28, 1888). Platform statements hardly guarantee the enactment of appropriate legislation even when endorsed by a party as dominant as was the Republican party in Kansas. All the parties contending in the 1878 campaign proclaimed their sympathy for regulation of railroad rates but the issue remained to be debated in the Populist decade. The 1884 call for strengthening the powers of the board of railroad commissioners by the Republican party was likewise not attended to and the issue carried over into the 1890s. The 1889 Republican legislature did make the change in interest rates the party had supported in 1888.

69. Zornow, "The Basis of Agrarian Unrest in Kansas," in Bright, ed., *Kansas,* I, 474.
70. James E. Boyle, *The Financial History of Kansas* (Economic and Political Science Series [Madison, 1908]), V, 57, 71, 76.
71. Miller, "The Populist Party in Kansas," 18-19.
72. Zornow, "The Basis of Agrarian Unrest in Kansas," in Bright, ed., *Kansas,* I, 456; Zornow, *Kansas,* 143.
73. Miller, "The Populist Party in Kansas," 27; Malin, *Winter Wheat,* 102-37; Zornow, "The Basis of Agrarian Unrest in Kansas," in Bright, ed., *Kansas,* I, 474.
74. U.S. Department of Commerce, *Eleventh Census of the United States, Report on the Public Debt,* 77.
75. Miller, "The Populist Party in Kansas," 27.
76. Zornow, "The Basis of Agrarian Unrest in Kansas," in Bright, ed., *Kansas,* I, 464.
77. The trend of settlement had been largely from northeast to southwest. See James C. Malin, "The Turnover of Farm Population in Kansas," *Kansas Historical Quarterly,* IV, 339.
78. Miller, "The Populist Party in Kansas," 29.
79. Raymond Miller concluded that the "Interest rate on this debt, and on chattel mortgages which were even more common, was excessive. The state law set 12% as the maximum interest, and in 1889 reduced it to 10%, but the law was more honored in the breach than in the observance. To the face interest charge must be added agents' commissions, bonus, costs, and the like, all of which were deducted from the amount received by the debtor" (*ibid.,* 33). Allan Bogue's *Money at Interest* traces the activities of *two* large and *reputable* loan companies doing business in the area. His study proves that these two companies conducted their business in an ethical manner. At the same time, Bogue points out that actual profits were hard to determine (p. 19), that loan rates were higher in the new counties (pp. 114-24), that "local agents functioned with too little supervision and gouged commissions from the settlers, which they did not report to the companies" (p. 275). Bogue also notes, "Charlatan companies were allowed to survive and by their competition force sounder companies into reckless practices" (p. 276).
80. Miller, "The Populist Party in Kansas," 35.
81. For a discussion of this question see Leslie E. Decker's *Railroads, Lands, and Politics.* Decker's study illustrates that the railroads had "important advantages" in their struggle with the settlers, but he also points out that this conflict "cannot be correctly counted as a struggle between the forces of private

monopoly, exploitation, and injustice on the one side and the forces of public welfare, conservation, and fair play on the other" (p. 250).

82. Zornow, "The Basis of Agrarian Unrest in Kansas," in Bright, ed., *Kansas*, I, 458. Sol Miller, a prominent Republican leader throughout the period in question, wrote in 1896: "It was for a long time too plain that Republican Legislatures of Kansas simply obeyed the orders of the railroad companies. The Railroad and other committees were made up largely of railroad attorneys. Nothing could be done without the consent of the railroad companies. The Railroad Commissioner law, that is supposed to be for the purpose of maintaining justice between the people and railroads, was really got up by the attorneys of railroad companies, in order to ward off the enactment of laws regulating freight rates" (From an article entitled "Republican Shortcomings," *The Weekly Kansas Chief,* Troy, December 31, 1896).

83. Zornow, "The Basis of Agrarian Unrest in Kansas," in Bright, ed., *Kansas,* I, 465-71.

Chapter II

1. Hill P. Wilson, *A Biographical History of Eminent Men of the State of Kansas with Portraits Engraved Expressly for this Work* (Topeka, 1901), 449-51.

2. W. D. Vincent, *Government Loans to the People,* no publisher, place, or date given, People's Party Pamphlets (6 vols., Kansas State Historical Society), I. Cited hereafter as K.S.H.S.

3. Jennie Small Owen (annalist), *The Annals of Kansas 1886-1925* (2 vols., Topeka, no date), I, 6-8.

4. Topeka *Daily Capital,* September 16, 1886.

5. Article by William D. Vincent, Clay Center *Dispatch,* August 22, 1901; John Davis Scrapbooks (13 vols., A-M [J missing], K.S.H.S.). The Nebraska State Historical Society contains a portion of John Davis' library. Three boxes of pamphlets, speeches, and miscellaneous items, thirty-one volumes in all, constitute the John Davis collection there. No manuscript material is included, few marginal notes appear, and the K.S.H.S. does have copies of almost all the items that are contained in this collection.

6. Address by John Davis at the Lyon County Fair on September 19, 1873, Kansas Biographical Scrapbook (K.S.H.S.), K, 27, 48, 85.

7. Clay Center *Dispatch,* August 22, 1901.

8. *Kansas Farmer,* Topeka, February 16, 1887.

9. *Ibid.,* March 17, 1887.

10. *Ibid.,* April 21, 1887.

11. Hortense Marie Harrison, "The Populist Delegation in the Fifty-Second Congress, 1891-1893," master's thesis (University of Kansas, 1933), 10-12.

12. *Ibid.*

13. *Ibid.*

14. *Kansas Farmer,* Topeka, June 21, 1882. The novel ran serially between March 1, 1882, and July 5, 1882.

15. *Ibid.,* July 5, 1882.

16. Regarding the anarchist question, in September he wrote that "the people sometimes need to be aroused, but peaceable means must be employed. Anarchists are our enemies, and we must suppress them by legal methods"

(*ibid.*, September 22, 1887). In October he stressed that the paper was "not an organ of any party, sect or order" (*ibid.*, October 27, 1887). In November he defended the tariff in several issues against attacks by its opponents. He made it clear, however, that he favored a reduction of the tariff where that reduction would assist the nation's consumers in obtaining the necessities of life at a lower price (*ibid.*, November 3 and 10, 1887). In December he attacked trusts and advocated the issuance of money by the general government and called for a separation of the government from all banking institutions (*ibid.*, December 1, 1887).

17. *Ibid.*, April 30, 1890.

18. Charles A. Magaw, *Bulletin of the Shawnee County Historical Society*, Number Fifteen (December, 1951), 10-11.

19. *Ibid.*, and Topeka *Daily Capital*, October 8, 1906.

20. Magaw, *Bulletin*, Number Fifteen (December, 1951), 10-11.

21. Topeka *Commonwealth*, April 15, 1885.

22. Magaw, *Bulletin*, Number Fifteen (December, 1951), 10-11.

23. G. C. Clemens, *The Labor Problem, Stated for the Busy and the Tired* (Enterprise, 1887), 4, People's Party Pamphlets (K.S.H.S.), I.

24. *Ibid.*, 5.

25. *Ibid.*, 8.

26. Wilson, *Eminent Men*, 371-72.

27. *Ibid.*, and *Portrait and Biographical Record of Southeastern Kansas, Containing Biographical Sketches of Prominent and Representative Citizens of the Counties, Together with Biographies and Portraits of all the Presidents of the United States and Governors of the State of Kansas* (Chicago, 1894), 234-37.

28. Letter dated July 18, 1888, published in the Girard *Press*, August 1, 1888.

29. Daniels to Ingalls, August 2, 1888, in Percy Daniels, *Swollen Fortunes and the Problem of the Unemployed* (no publisher, no place, 1908), 36-38, People's Party Pamphlets (K.S.H.S.), VI.

30. Ingalls to Daniels, August 7, 1888, *ibid.*

31. Daniels to Ingalls, August 12, 1888, *ibid.*

32. Letter published in the Girard *Press*, August 1, 1888.

33. Percy Daniels, *A Crisis for the Husbandman* (Girard, 1889), 4.

34. *Portrait and Biographical Record of Southeastern Kansas*, 236-37.

35. McLouth *Times* (Souvenir Edition), November 25, 1898, 63-64.

36. *The Advocate*, Meriden, November 22, 1889.

37. Biographical Circulars (K.S.H.S.), M-Z, II.

38. *The Advocate*, Meriden, November 22, 1889.

39. *Ibid.*, February 27, 1890.

40. W. V. Marshall, *The Industrial Handbook: Embracing a Concise Statement of the Nature, Cause and Effects of Existing Industrial Ills; with a Practical Method of Relief* (Winfield, 1890), 5-12, People's Party Pamphlets (K.S.H.S.), II. See also W. V. Marshall, *Cumulative Taxation* (Winfield, 1890), People's Party Pamphlets (K.S.H.S.), II.

41. *The Advocate*, Topeka, March 20, 1890.

42. In particular see J. B. Welburn's *Heaven on Earth; Described and How Secured* (Atchison, 1889). Welburn believed that the institution of private

property should and would eventually be abandoned, although he opposed the use of force to accomplish that end (p. 12).

43. *Kansas Farmer*, Topeka, June 18, 1890.

44. James D. Holden, *Free Freight and Government Railways; A Proposition to Restore to Society Essential Rights of Which it has been Wrongfully Divested; and to make Men Generally the Beneficiaries of Government, Instead of Its Victims* (no date, no publisher), 2, People's Party Pamphlets (K.S.H.S.), I.

45. *Ibid.*, 19.

46. *The Advocate*, Topeka, January 30, 1890.

Chapter III

1. Solon J. Buck's *The Granger Movement: A Study of Agricultural Organization and Its Political, Economic, and Social Manifestations, 1870-1880* (Cambridge, 1913) and *The Agrarian Crusade* (New Haven, 1920) provide the most thorough account of this phase of agrarian activities.

2. Elizabeth N. Barr, "The Populist Uprising," in W. E. Connelley, ed., *History of Kansas, State and People* (5 vols., 1928), II, 1137-47.

3. John D. Hicks, *The Populist Revolt: A History of the Farmers' Alliance and the People's Party* (Bison edition, Lincoln, 1961), 96-127.

4. See *ibid.*, 97-98, and 104-13, for a discussion of the origins of the Northern and Southern Alliances.

5. Exception was made for country ministers, country teachers, and the editors of farm journals (*ibid.*, 112).

6. *Ibid.*

7. *Ibid.*, 103, 112-13.

8. *The Lyons Republican*, August 9, 1888.

9. Topeka *Capital-Commonwealth*, February 7, 1889.

10. See W. F. Rightmire, "The Alliance Movement in Kansas—Origin of the People's Party," *Transactions of the Kansas State Historical Society, 1905-1906*, IX, 1-8. Rightmire stated that this State Reform Association was formed in Wichita on December 19-20, 1888, to replace the Union Labor party state committee and the National Order of Videttes, the latter of which was a secret organization of third-party men about which there is little real information and much speculation. See James C. Malin's *A Concern About Humanity: Notes on Reform, 1872-1912 at the National and Kansas Levels of Thought* (Lawrence, 1964), 159-65, for a discussion of the National Order of Videttes.

11. Newton *Weekly Journal*, August 23, 1889, and *Kansas Commoner*, Newton, August 16, 1889.

12. *The News*, Cambridge, February 8, 1889.

13. The platforms are reprinted in Hicks, *The Populist Revolt*, 427-30.

14. *Ibid.*, 124.

15. *Kansas Farmer*, Topeka, July 16, 1889.

16. Wichita *Daily Eagle*, May 3, 1889.

17. *Ibid.*, August 23, 1889.

18. Annie L. Diggs, *Transactions of the Kansas State Historical Society, 1897-1900*, VI, 233-34.

19. *The Advocate*, Meriden, September 21, 1889.

20. *Ibid.*, October 5, 1889.
21. Rightmire, "The Alliance Movement in Kansas," *Transactions of the Kansas State Historical Society*, IX, 1-8.
22. *Kansas Farmer*, Topeka, December 25, 1889.
23. *Ibid.*, February 14, 1889.
24. Topeka *Daily Capital*, November 5, 10, 1889.
25. *Ibid.*, December 8, 1889.
26. Dr. McLallin had played an active part in the August 14, 1889, Newton meeting, and was appointed by that convention as the Alliance's press representative. See the *Kansas Commoner*, Newton, August 16, 1889.
27. *Kansas Farmer*, Topeka, February 26, 1890.
28. The 1888 Union-Labor platform is contained in the Topeka *Daily Capital*, August 30, 1888. John J. Ingalls was, of course, a most extraordinary Kansas politician. See William E. Connelley, *Ingalls of Kansas: A Character Study* (Topeka, 1909), and Burton John Williams, "John James Ingalls: A Personal Portrait of a Public Figure" (unpublished Ph.D. dissertation, University of Kansas, 1965).
29. On this matter see Rightmire's "The Alliance Movement in Kansas," *Transactions of the Kansas State Historical Society*, IX, 1-8.
30. See Dr. McLallin's discussion of the origins of the Kansas People's party in an editorial contained in *The Advocate*, Topeka, August 22, 1894.
31. Only five of the sixty-eight subsequently emerged as significant Populist leaders. See *ibid.*, April 2, 1890.
32. *Ibid.*, August 22, 1894.
33. Rightmire, "The Alliance Movement in Kansas," *Transactions of the Kansas State Historical Society*, IX, 1-8.
34. *The Advocate*, Topeka, August 22, 1894.
35. *Ibid.*, May 14, 28, and June 4, 11, 1890.
36. *Ibid.*, April 30, 1890.
37. Wichita (Weekly) *Eagle*, January 13, 1891.
38. *Kansas Farmer*, Topeka, April 30, 1890.
39. *Ibid.*, May 14, 1890.
40. *The Advocate*, Topeka, May 21, 1890.
41. *Biographical Record: This Volume Contains Biographical Sketches of Leading Citizens of Cowley County, Kansas* (Chicago, 1901), 309-11.
42. *The Advocate*, Topeka, May 14, June 18, 25, July 23, 1890, and August 22, 1894.
43. Unfortunately, either a detailed description of this first convention does not exist or it eluded my search.
44. Topeka *Daily Capital*, August 14, 1890; *The Advocate*, Topeka, August 27, 1890; and Rightmire, "The Alliance Movement in Kansas," *Transactions of the Kansas State Historical Society*, IX, 1-8.
45. W. F. Rightmire, Autobiographical Sketch dated December 16, 1910, K.S.H.S. Library.
46. *Ibid.*; Topeka *Daily Capital*, December 25, 1929.
47. Topeka *Daily Capital*, August 14, 1890; *The Advocate*, Topeka, August 27, 1890.

48. *The Proceedings of the Twenty-Ninth Republican State Convention of Kansas* (Topeka, 1890), 64-66.
49. *The Advocate,* Topeka, January 9, 1890.

Chapter IV

1. Paul W. Glad's *McKinley, Bryan, and the People* (Philadelphia, 1964), 13-31, contains a useful discussion of these two patterns of thought. Richard Hofstadter's *Age of Reform,* however, more than any other work, has utilized the agrarian myth in interpreting the Populist movement. Assuming that the Populists were dominated by the agrarian mystique, Hofstadter contended that "In Populist thought the farmer is not a speculating businessman, victimized by the risk economy of which he is a part, but rather a wounded yeoman, preyed upon by those who are alien to the life of folkish virtue" (p. 73). This appraisal does not hold true as applied to the leadership of the Populist party in Kansas; it was the opponents of the Populists who employed the agrarian myth, not the Populists. Paul Glad has noted this, and makes a valid point when he writes, "The true realists of 1896 were those who sought to rid themselves of preconceptions, who tried to examine the realities themselves, and who formulated programs without resort to traditional images" (*McKinley, Bryan, and the People,* 50).
2. See Appendix I for a listing of the various source materials that were consulted in preparing this analysis. See also Appendix II for a composite comparison of the major Kansas Populist leadership for the years 1890 and 1896.
3. The Harvard, Stanford, and Oxford alumni were, respectively, John Grant Otis, W. P. Harrington, and Carl Vrooman.
4. Oskaloosa *Times,* July 9, 1891.
5. *Kansas Commoner,* Wichita, April 28, 1892. Mrs. Lease at one point made the following statement about religion: "I do not belong to any church. I cut loose and left the church behind me long ago. I was reared a Catholic, but I do not think I could be called orthodox, even in my youth. I account to myself for my conduct, and to God" (Kansas City *Star,* April 1, 1891).
6. *Voice of True Reform* (Topeka, 1891), 42.
7. J. M. Dunsmore, "Epistle to be Read at His Funeral as His Last Message of Love," special collection, K.S.H.S. Archives.
8. Speech in U.S. senate, May 12, 1892, Kansas Collected Speeches and Pamphlets (K.S.H.S.), XV, 9.
9. For Jerry Botkin's statement see the Topeka *Daily Capital,* September 2, 1894. For an especially good insight into Mrs. Diggs' views, see her penciled note to G. C. Clemens on the inside cover of a social gospel treatise written by George D. Herron entitled *The New Redemption* (New York, 1893), which is contained in the K.S.H.S.
10. *The Advocate,* Topeka, December 30, 1891. For an especially precise statement in opposition to social Darwinism see Governor L. D. Lewelling's "Speech at Huron Place," July 26, 1894, typed manuscript, K.S.H.S. Archives.
11. W. D. Vincent, "Government Loans to the People," People's Party Pamphlets (K.S.H.S.), I.
12. Unsigned letter to the editor, *The Advocate,* Topeka, September 26, 1894.

Numerous references could be made to statements by Populist leaders on paternalism. Some especially good examples are those of William Alfred Peffer, *Kansas Farmer*, Topeka, January 1, 1890, and "The Mission of the Populist Party," *The North American Review*, CLVII (December, 1893), 666; Frank Doster, "What is Government For?" *The Agora*, II (October, 1892), 120-26; and R. A. Sanky in the *Kansas Commoner*, Wichita, March 1, 1894.

13. Unsigned letter to editor, *The Advocate*, Topeka, September 2, 1891.

14. Kansas City *Journal*, November 20, 1902, quoting a Kansas City *Star* interview of 1897.

15. *Ibid.*

16. *The Advocate*, Topeka, September 5, 1894.

17. From an address before the Shawnee County Farmers' Institute delivered in Topeka in February, 1890. *Kansas Farmer*, Topeka, March 5, 1890.

18. Chester McArthur Destler, *American Radicalism 1865-1901: Essays and Documents* (New York, 1963), 20.

19. See Arthur S. Link's *Woodrow Wilson and the Progressive Era, 1910-1917* (New York, 1963), 18-22, for a discussion and contrast of Theodore Roosevelt's New Nationalism and Woodrow Wilson's New Freedom.

20. *The Advocate*, Topeka, February 27, 1890.

21. Link, *Woodrow Wilson and the Progressive Era*, 20-22.

Chapter V

1. Barr, "The Populist Uprising," in Connelley, ed., *Kansas and Kansans*, II, 1148-49.

2. Mrs. Lease apparently signed herself Mary E. Lease. This led her Republican opponents to supply the name Ellen, since it rhymed with "Yellin." Mary Ellen stuck so well that some historians yet today mistakenly use it. One prominent example is Eric F. Goldman in his *Rendezvous with Destiny*.

3. Harry Levinson, "Mary Elizabeth Lease: Prairie Radical," *Kansas Magazine*, 1948, 18-24; James C. Malin, "Mary Elizabeth Clyens Lease," *Dictionary of American Biography*, XXI (Supplement I), 488-89; William G. Clugston, *Rascals in Democracy* (New York, 1941), an interesting but highly inaccurate account of Mrs. Lease, 91-95; Wichita *Eagle*, June 14, 1925. For information concerning Lease's activities in behalf of the Union-Labor party in 1888 see *Kansas Commoner*, Newton, October 5, 1888.

4. William Allen White, *Autobiography* (New York, 1946), 218-19. One's impression of Mrs. Lease was decidedly affected by political persuasion; White's account was no exception. Compare it with the following: "Mrs. Lease is a tall woman—fully five feet ten inches, and rather slender. Her face is strong, good, not pretty, and very feminine. There is no mark of masculinity about her. She is woman all over. Her hair is a dark brown and evenly parted in the center and smoothed down at the sides with neat care. Her nose, chin and cheek bones announce themselves strongly. However, they give no sense of harshness to her face." Kansas City *Star*, April 1, 1891.

5. Kansas City *Star*, April 1, 1891.

6. *Ibid.*, October 25, 1914.

7. *The Monitor*, Wellington, October 3, 1890.

8. Kansas City *Star*, April 1, 1891. Apparently Mrs. Lease had made the above remarks about Senator John J. Ingalls several weeks earlier in a speech she delivered in Albaugh's opera house in Washington, D.C. Senator Ingalls had of course already been defeated at that point. It was this situation that created a rather humorous incident: Mrs. Lease and a woman friend, while visiting on capitol hill, encountered the lame-duck senator on his way to a committee meeting. Mrs. Lease's friend spotted him first and hurried on ahead to ask if he would like to meet one of his constituents—Mrs. Mary E. Lease. On hearing that name, Senator Ingalls replied quite definitely: "I do not care to meet that woman; only Indians and women will scalp a man after he is dead." See a letter by Charlotte Smith, *The Advocate*, Topeka, April 15, 1891.

9. Mrs. Lease later denied having originated the statement, but she said she let it stand because she thought "it was a right good bit of advice." See Topeka *State Journal*, May 25, 1896; Kansas City *Star*, October 26, 1914.

10. Unidentified newspaper clipping contained in Kansas Biographical Scrapbook (K.S.H.S.), D, II, 26-29.

11. Kansas City *Star*, August 5, 1900; Topeka *Daily Capital*, September 17, 1908. Mrs. Diggs was apparently influenced by Mrs. Helen E. Sterritt, owner of the music store and also an energetic and strong-minded individual, who subsequently went to Chicago herself to participate actively in journalism. See Topeka *Daily Capital*, September 17, 1908.

12. See the *Daily Journal*, Lawrence, March 2, and November 3, 1882.

13. Kansas City *Star*, August 5, 1900.

14. *Ibid.*

15. *Ibid.*

16. Her speech at Osborne on October 25, 1890, was representative: she began by repeating the words "Financial conspiracies," "Great revolutions." She then paused for a moment to assess the effect of her pronouncement. She then explained: the Topeka *Capital* labeled her an "Anarchist" and she had quoted those "dangerous words to see if the people were afraid of her." The words were not her own, she said; they belonged to Senator Plumb (Kansas' junior Republican senator), who had said on the floor of congress, " 'Financial conspiracies breed great revolutions.' " "We have had our financial conspiracies for many years," she said, "and today we see an example of the revolution." Following an interruption of great applause and cheers, she proceeded with her account of what ailed society, using Senator Plumb as an authority. She then turned her attention to the labor problem, asking "Why there are so many poor men out of employment, even in the sound of the factory whistle; why women and children are forced into the workshop to earn their daily bread, so that even Sitting Bull says he 'Don't see how white men can treat their squaws so.' " She then drew a vivid picture of luxury and squalor, progress and poverty in Washington, D.C., as she had witnessed it only a few blocks from the White House. She quoted Senator Ingalls as having said, in 1878, "The poor are growing poorer and the rich richer, and by the end of this century the middle class will have entirely disappeared." She then spent some time on the question: "Why has he done nothing to prevent this?" See *County News*, Osborne, October 30, 1890.

17. *Biographical Record, Cowley County*, 309-11.

18. John Davis, "The New Slavery," Select Pamphlets (K.S.H.S.).
19. *Kansas People*, Osage City, November 5, 1890.
20. Otis to Clover, *The Advocate*, Topeka, January 9, 1890. Otis later made two attempts at establishing cooperative settlements: one in 1897 in Colorado at Piñon, and another in 1898 in the state of Washington at a place called Equality. See Kansas Biographical Scrapbook (K.S.H.S.), D, II, 13-14, and Topeka *Daily Capital*, December 14, 1900.
21. *Peoples Herald*, Lyndon, September 29, 1890.
22. Wilson, *Eminent Men of Kansas*, 513-15; Lincoln *County Sentinel*, February 10, 1910; *The Advocate*, Topeka, June 25, 1890.
23. Holton *Weekly Recorder*, July 25, 1890.
24. Victor Murdock, *Folks* (New York, 1921), 55-56.
25. Harrison, "The Populist Delegation in the Fifty-Second Congress, 1891-1893," 14-18; Myron C. Scott, "A Congressman and His Constituents, Jerry Simpson and the Big Seventh" (unpublished master's thesis, Fort Hays Kansas State College, 1959), *passim*.
26. Wichita *Eagle*, July 19, 1934; see also the three short letters by Jerry Simpson in the K.S.H.S Archives. Homer E. Socolofsky's *Arthur Capper: Publisher, Politician, Philanthropist* (Lawrence, 1962), p. 37, contains some lively anecdotal material on Simpson's spelling.
27. White, *Autobiography*, 217-18.
28. While a member of congress, Simpson and five others introduced George's book into the *Congressional Record* so they could make copies of it available to constituents throughout the country. There was also a report that Henry George himself was willing to campaign for Simpson in 1894. See *The Advocate*, Topeka, June 13, 1894.
29. Hamlin Garland, "The Alliance Wedge in Congress," *The Arena*, V (March, 1891), 451.
30. See the Wichita *Weekly Eagle*, October 17, 1890, for an especially bitter attack against Simpson on religious grounds.
31. *Alliance Bulletin*, Harper, September 26, 1890.
32. It has been stated that Jerry Simpson dubbed Hallowell "Prince Hal" (for example, John Hicks' *The Populist Revolt*). Actually, Republicans had developed the "illusion" of Hallowell's royalty at least as early as 1888. See Wichita *Eagle*, October 14, 1888, and September 23, 1890.
33. Topeka *Daily Capital*, October 26, 1890.
34. Grant Wood Harrington, "As Jerry Told It," typed manuscript dated June 30, 1938, K.S.H.S. Archives. G. W. Harrington was one of the leaders of Kansas Populism, serving as party chairman in 1901-02. This story he relates was reportedly told to him some ten years after the event.
35. Jerry Simpson credited Victor Murdock of the Wichita *Eagle* with having "hung the name onto" him (G. W. Harrington, "As Jerry Told It"). Actually, there is some doubt as to who originally applied the label. It was either Murdock of the *Eagle* or Ralph Easley of the Hutchinson *News*. M. C. Scott has researched this matter thoroughly in his master's thesis on Simpson, and concludes that the *News* rather than Murdock was responsible. Both Easley and Murdock claimed the honor. For their respective claims see the Hutchinson *News*, July 25, 1891, and the Wichita *Eagle*, July 24, 1891.

In a speech delivered in New Hampshire in April, 1891, the then Congressman Simpson made the following remark: "A red-headed editor out in Kansas [Murdock] told his readers that I went sockless. That's a lie, but there are lots of farmers in Kansas to-day who are stockingless and almost clothingless, they and their wives and children. They don't go that way because they want to, I assure you. They would be pleased to wear white shirts and silk socks and broadcloth, and if they ever get one-half of the privileges from this government that the capitalists have got they will be able to. . . . Those men are going to be heard in the next few years and don't you forget it." See the clipping from the *Mirror and Farmer,* Manchester, April 2, 1891, People's Party Clippings (K.S.H.S.), I, 30-34.

36. The editor was O. E. Learnard of the Lawrence *Journal,* quoted in the Topeka *Advocate,* November 19, 1890.

37. See the issues of the Topeka *Daily Capital* for September to November, especially October 1, 3, 10, and 18, 1890.

38. *Ibid.,* October 11, 1890.

39. One Populist noted, "In the south, people are told that this movement is of northern origin, a Republican device to disrupt the Democratic party of the south, strike down white rule, and establish black supremacy instead, while in the north, politicians tell us the movement is a southern institution, devised by southern Democrats . . . and designed to destroy the Republican party of the north . . . and thereby abrogate all the results of the war." Letter to editor, *The Advocate,* Topeka, February 25, 1891.

40. Topeka *Daily Capital,* November 6, 1890.

41. Governor Humphrey polled 39.0 percent of the votes and his margin of victory was 6,845 votes. Willits polled 36.8 percent of the vote, while ex-Governor Charles Robinson, the Democratic nominee, polled 24.2 percent. Robinson's candidacy definitely hurt Willits' chances. Robinson, in addition to having been Kansas' first governor as a Republican, had run as the Greenback-Labor candidate for governor in 1882. For the voting statistics see Clarence J. Hein and Charles A. Sullivant, *Kansas Votes: Gubernatorial Elections, 1859-1956* (Lawrence, 1958), 26-27.

42. *The Advocate,* Topeka, September 29, 1897.

43. Topeka *Daily Capital,* November 11, 1890.

44. Forty-six was the median age. The oldest Populist was seventy-two and the youngest thirty-two; thirty-seven (including delegates) were fifty or more, fifty-five were forty-nine or less. Actually, eighty-four of eighty-eight (96.5 percent), for whom information was available, were associated with farming in some capacity, although 26.1 percent of those engaged in farming had been connected with some other occupation or profession before they became farmers. Sixty-six of ninety-five (69.5 percent) were born in Ohio, Indiana, New York, Illinois, Virginia, or Kentucky. The breakdown on the foreign born was as follows: Ireland, four; England, three; Wales, two; Switzerland, one; and Canada, one. Forty-one of eighty-seven (47.1 percent) had affiliated with the Republican party until 1890; seventeen of eighty-seven had affiliated with the Democratic party until 1890. Actually, twenty-nine of eighty-seven (33.4 percent) had been active in third-party politics, and the most common political route traveled had carried them from the Republican

party to the Greenback party and then to the Union-Labor party. Educational background material was available for fifty-eight; of these, thirteen (22.4 percent) had graduated from college; another eight (13.7 percent) had attended college; sixteen (27.5 percent) had an academy education, and twenty-one (36.2 percent) had only a common-school education. Compiled from W. W. Admire, *Legislative Handbook* (Topeka, 1891).

45. Again, forty-five was the median age for thirty-two Republican representatives (includes delegates); the oldest was sixty-six and the youngest twenty-nine. Twelve were fifty or older and twenty were forty-nine or younger. Actually, twenty-three of thirty-four (67.6 percent) were born in Pennsylvania, Ohio, Indiana, or New York. Occupational information was available on nineteen house Republicans, and twelve of these (63.1 percent) could be classified as business or professional men; seven (36.8 percent) were farmers or stock raisers. Also five of the twenty-one for whom information was available had graduated from college; another had attended college; nine (42.2 percent) had an academy education, and six (28.5 percent) had only a common-school education.

46. Forty-five was the median age of thirty-six Republican senators; ten were fifty or older. Occupational information was available for thirty-five, and thirty-one (88.5 percent) were business or professional men (seventeen lawyers, seven business proprietors, and five bankers). While only six of these men had served in the previous senate, seventeen of thirty-eight (48.5 percent) had previous legislative experience.

47. A. J. R. Smith in the *Populist,* Topeka, December 3, 1892.

48. Smith stated, "It was agreed unanimously that our proper course, under the circumstances, was to stand by Peffer until he proved himself false to the principles of the party, a consummation we then expected." See the *Populist,* Topeka, December 3, 1892. The Topeka *Advocate* (February 12 and 18, 1891) was also quite unenthusiastic about the selection of Peffer.

49. St. Louis *Globe-Democrat,* quoted in *The Advocate,* Topeka, February 18, 1891.

Chapter VI

1. *The Advocate,* Topeka, November 19, 1890.

2. *Senate Journal, 1891,* 573, 775, and 836; *House Journal, 1891,* 1138.

3. The 1890 Republican platform is contained in *Proceedings of the Twenty-Ninth Republican State Convention of Kansas,* 49-59.

4. *Senate Journal, 1891,* 806. See also *The Advocate,* Topeka, March 25, 1891, for a discussion of this railroad bill. Populist spokesmen maintained that this measure was "an adaptation of the Iowa schedule of freights and fares which exceeded the rates of Iowa by nearly twenty per cent but even then still provided a thirteen per cent reduction in Kansas rates."

5. *The Advocate,* Topeka, March 25, 1891; *Senate Journal, 1891,* 531.

6. See the statement by the committee chairman on page 531, *Senate Journal, 1891.*

7. *Ibid.,* 389, 457, 486, and 574-76.

8. Women already had the right to vote in local elections.

9. *House Journal, 1891,* 247-48.

10. *Ibid.,* 490-91.

11. *Ibid.,* 527.

12. February 18, 1891.

13. Elder had written in 1867, at the time woman suffrage was being debated along with Negro suffrage in Kansas, that his "whole impressions and opinions are most emphatically against it on grounds of propriety." He added, "nearly every voter in Franklin County [was] for Negro suffrage had not the Legislature so unwisely and foolishly submitted Female Suffrage with it." See letter from Elder to Sam Wood, dated April 27, 1867, Woman Suffrage Collection, K.S.H.S. Archives.

14. Wilson, *Eminent Men of Kansas,* 275-77.

15. *House Journal, 1891,* 526-27.

16. *The Advocate,* Topeka, February 25, 1891.

17. The house vote was as follows: sixty-six Populists for, sixteen against, and seventeen abstaining; three Republicans for, thirteen against, and eight abstaining; three Democrats voted against the bill, and two abstained. See *House Journal, 1891,* 527.

18. *Ibid.,* 714; *The Advocate,* Topeka, March 11, 1891.

19. Hicks, *The Populist Revolt,* 178-81.

20. The Kansas Populist state central committee made an official statement indorsing a national political organization on December 17, 1890, which was published in the Topeka *Advocate* on that date.

21. W. F. Rightmire, "The Alliance Movement in Kansas," *T.K.S.H.S.,* IX, 1-8.

22. Hicks, *The Populist Revolt,* 207-08.

23. The Kansas delegates to Ocala who supported the call for the Cincinnati conference were S. W. Chase (Populist State Chairman), John Davis, General John H. Rice, C. Vincent (editor of the *Economic Quarterly*), Dr. Stephen McLallin, Ben Clover, J. V. Randolph, J. F. Willits, Jerry Simpson, Frank Williams, P. B. Maxson, Thomas H. Butler, W. H. Biddle, Van B. Prather, R. B. Frye, and H. Vincent (editor of the Winfield *Nonconformist*). See *The Advocate,* Topeka, December 24, 1890.

24. *The Advocate,* Topeka, December 25, 1890; Hicks, *The Populist Revolt,* 209.

25. Rightmire, "The Alliance Movement in Kansas," *T.K.S.H.S.,* IX, 1-8, and Hicks, *The Populist Revolt,* 208-09. Rightmire stated that the "Kansas delegates, to preserve harmony in the Alliance, suppressed and withdrew the call, and as a reward were given two of the national offices." Except for his choice of words to say "suppressed and withdrew" instead of postponed, Rightmire's account rings true, although as indicated above corroborating evidence was not uncovered.

26. About 250 "self-appointed delegates" were said to have been present for the meeting, which ran from January 13 to January 17. Among those in attendance were Ben Clover, Mary E. Lease, General John H. Rice (temporary chairman), John Willits, Sam N. Wood, Annie L. Diggs, Carl Vrooman, Wesley Bennington, Mrs. M. H. McLallin, D. C. Zercher, Van B. Prather, James Lathrop, W. F. Rightmire, T. W. Gilruth, S. H. Snider (Union-Labor candidate for congress in the seventh district in 1888), W. N. Allen, and Noah Allen. See the *Declaration of Principles, Platform, Constitution and By-Laws*

of the National Citizens' Industrial Alliance and Proceedings of the National Assembly (Topeka, 1891), and Rightmire, "The Farmers Alliance in Kansas," *T.K.S.H.S.,* IX, 1-8. It is interesting to note that Ben Clover and John Willits were active in this organization; since Clover was no longer president of the state Alliance, and both Clover and Willits had moved on up to national Alliance activities, it may be an indication that the state Alliance had practically outlived its usefulness in Kansas. It would also lend support to the belief that state Alliance leaders had earlier worked closely with the Reform Association. Frank McGrath of Beloit had been elected president of the Alliance in October, 1890, and McGrath did not indorse the call for the Cincinnati conference at Ocala. See *The Advocate,* Topeka, December 24, 1890.

27. Thomas W. Gilruth was elected president; Noah Allen (Wichita), vice-president; W. N. Allen, treasurer; and S. H. Snider, national lecturer.

28. Rightmire, "The Alliance Movement in Kansas," *T.K.S.H.S.,* IX, 1-8.

29. Hicks, *The Populist Revolt,* 210.

30. Rightmire was unquestionably intimately involved in the activities that culminated in the Cincinnati conference. He stated that he secured "by correspondence the call issued at Ocala, Fla., in the previous December, with all the signatures attached . . . ." After "securing the signatures of the officers and many of the members of the Kansas house of representatives to this call, . . . [I] attached thereto the signatures that had been attached to the Ocala . . . call, and gave it to the . . . press . . . ." As far as can be ascertained, Rightmire also arranged to change the time of the meeting until May because the original date conflicted with the Kansas legislative session. See *The Advocate,* Topeka, May 6, 1891, for confirmation on the role of Rightmire.

31. Without undertaking a systematic search of local newspapers throughout the state it would be impossible to say with certainty exactly how the Cincinnati delegations were determined, but a number of the Kansas participants were duly elected delegates from their particular orders.

32. *Nonconformist,* Winfield, May 24, 1891, and Topeka *Advocate,* May 27, 1891. See also Hicks' *The Populist Revolt,* 212-13, and Rightmire, "The Alliance Movement in Kansas," *T.K.S.H.S.,* IX, 1-8.

33. Hicks, *The Populist Revolt,* 213-14; Rightmire, "The Alliance Movement in Kansas," *T.K.S.H.S.,* IX, 1-8.

34. Rightmire stated that, if it looked as though those who opposed the formation of a third party were going to have the upper hand, third-party advocates were prepared to gain control of the platform committee and "delay the report until the delegates had returned home in disgust; then to recommend that all action be postponed until the . . . meeting at St. Louis on February 22, 1892." See Rightmire, "The Alliance Movement in Kansas," *T.K.S.H.S.,* IX, 1-8.

35. *Ibid.*

36. The Union-Labor party's candidate for vice-president in 1888, an old Greenbacker by the name of Cunningham, served as temporary chairman. See *The Advocate,* May 27, 1891.

37. On this matter, Rightmire stated: "Upon the temporary organization of the conference, the members of this caucus were given control of the committee on platform. A committee on permanent organization was appointed, every

member of which was an old-time Greenbacker." See Rightmire, "The Alliance Movement in Kansas," *T.K.S.H.S.*, IX, 1-8.

38. Donnelly had attempted, unsuccessfully, to get the convention to commit itself to third-party action during this afternoon session; his effort created quite a furor, highlighted by an animated and stinging protest from General James B. Weaver. See Hicks, *The Populist Revolt*, 213.

39. Rightmire, "The Alliance Movement in Kansas," *T.K.S.H.S.*, IX, 1-8. Rightmire maintained that he and the three gentlemen named above prevailed upon the secretary of the committee and persuaded him to add the crucial clause.

40. The conference selected H. E. Taubeneck of Illinois for its national chairman. Kansas' representatives on the committee were P. P. Elder, Levi Dumbauld (State Chairman), and R. S. Osborn. See *The Advocate*, Topeka, May 27, 1891.

41. *Ibid.*

42. *Ibid.*, September 16, 1891. Platform contained in Hicks' *The Populist Revolt*, 433-35.

43. There was a note of ambiguity in the action of the convention, however, which enabled both its radical and cautious participants to go away pleased. Those who had counseled delay could point to the language of the platform which had declared merely that "we believe that the time has arrived for a crystallization of the political reform forces of the country and the formation of what should be known as the People's Party of the United States of America." The radicals could point to the obvious fact that a National People's party executive committee already existed. Certainly, Kansas leaders regarded this Cincinnati conference as having established a national party. See for example the discussion of Annie Diggs in *The Advocate*, Topeka, June 10, 1891. See also *ibid.*, September 16, 1891.

44. According to St. John, "the only thing that distinguished it from the old party conventions was its visionary Sub-treasury scheme, which has no foundation either in justice or common sense . . . . The idea of making the government a public pawnbroker is idiocy." See the Wichita *Weekly Beacon*, May 29, 1891.

45. *The Advocate*, Topeka, June 10, 1891.

46. Thomas E. Watson, "The Negro Question in the South," *The Arena*, VI (October, 1892), 541-42.

47. Senn was a fifty-year-old native of Switzerland who came to Kansas in 1858 by way of Wisconsin. He had fought in the Civil War for the North and had voted Republican until the early eighties. In 1887, he had been a delegate to the national Union-Labor convention in Cincinnati. See *Admire's Political and Legislative Handbook for Kansas in 1891*.

48. *The Advocate*, Topeka, December 10, 1890.

49. This is true only as a generality; there was a tendency in certain areas for those Alliance members who opposed third-party action to disassociate themselves from the Alliance, leaving the order even more in the hands of the opposite persuasion.

50. *The Advocate*, Topeka, December 24, 1890.

51. *Ibid.*, February 18, 1891.

52. *Ibid.*, April 22, 1891.

53. Dumbauld, a state representative from Lyon County, replaced S. W. Chase as chairman early in February, 1891. See *ibid.*, February 18, 1891.

54. *Ibid.*, April 22, 1891. See also *ibid.*, June 24, 1891, on the McGrath controversy.

55. At the meeting there was no clash between McGrath and anti-McGrath forces. W. H. Biddle of Butler County, who was active in the leadership of the Citizens' Alliance also, was elected president. McGrath did not drop out of the Alliance entirely; in December he was appointed by the executive committee of the state Alliance as a delegate to the St. Louis conference. Six months after the St. Louis conference he returned to the Republican party. See *ibid.*, October 28 and December 16, 1891, and August 10, 1892.

56. Malin, *A Concern About Humanity*, 195.

57. *The Advocate*, Topeka, January 30, 1890; *Kansas Farmer*, Topeka, September 10 and October 22, 1890.

58. See especially the issues of April 9, 1890, and June 15, 1892.

59. Letter to editor, *The Advocate*, September 23, 1891.

60. Malin, *A Concern About Humanity*, 37 and 203; *Kansas Farmer*, Topeka, September 10, 1890.

61. See for example Jerry Simpson's "The Political Rebellion in Kansas," *The Farmers' Alliance History and Agricultural Digest* (Washington, D.C., 1891); B. H. Clover, "Sectionalism," *ibid.*; James D. Holden, *Metallic Money and Hard Times: Why They are Inseparable* (Emporia, 1891); S. N. Wood, "Wood's Manifesto: An Address to the People of Kansas," delivered at Herington, Kansas, April 20, 1891 (Topeka, 1891); Rev. Dr. James H. Lathrop, *Voice of True Reform* (Topeka, 1891).

62. *The Advocate*, Topeka, May 27, 1891.

63. Article by John Grant Otis, *The People's Herald*, Lyndon (Osage County), June 25, 1891.

64. Quoted in *The Advocate*, Topeka, April 15, 1891.

65. Two examples are those of *The People's Herald*, Lyndon, April 23, 1891, and *The Advocate*, Topeka, April 15, 1891.

66. Wilson, *Eminent Men of Kansas*, 581-82; Topeka *Daily Capital*, February 26, 1933; Malin, *A Concern About Humanity*, 132-52. See also Michael J. Brodhead's recently completed study entitled "Judge Frank Doster: Kansas Populist and Reform Ideologue" (unpublished doctoral dissertation, University of Minnesota, 1967).

67. The four writers mentioned by Doster were William Graham Sumner, Edward Atkinson, David A. Wells, and Francis A. Walker.

68. *Central Advocate*, Marion, May 29, 1891. See also James C. Malin's discussion of Doster and this speech in *A Concern About Humanity*, 132-52.

69. Malin, *A Concern About Humanity*, 146-49.

70. See the Topeka *Daily Capital*, April 1, 1891, for John J. Ingalls' stand and a compilation of Republican press reaction. See the Wichita *Weekly Eagle*, January 23, 1891, also, and the letter of Ingalls presented at a meeting of Republican editors of the seventh congressional district published in the Topeka *Advocate*, June 3, 1891.

71. *The Weekly Troy Chief*, February 26, 1891. Sol Miller edited this paper which

was recognized as the mouthpiece of Cy Leland, the leading Republican "boss" in Kansas.

72. Quoted in *The Advocate*, Topeka, June 3, 1891.

73. *Ibid.*

74. Quoted in S. S. King, *Bondholders and Bread Winners* (n.p., 1892), People's Party Pamphlets (K.S.H.S.), IV.

75. In Kansas, throughout the 1890s, and before, there was an election each and every year; in the odd years a portion of the local offices were contested.

76. S. M. Scott, assistant state lecturer of the Alliance, was given the special task of promoting the subtreasury plan (Kansas City *Star*, July 22, 1891). See Scott's work entitled *The Sub-Treasury Plan and the Land and Loan System* (Topeka, 1891). A number of other Populist leaders joined Scott in promoting the plan. It should be noted, however, that there was opposition, even within the Alliance, to pushing the subtreasury plan to the front. William A. Harris, who subsequently was elected to congress and later still to the U.S. senate, opposed the plan in 1891 on the grounds that it violated the Populist principle of "Equal rights to all and special privileges to none" (*Kansas Farmer*, Topeka, August 5, 1891). A. C. Shinn, Populist nominee for lieutenant governor in 1890, joined Harris in speaking out against it and wrote a letter to the Topeka *Advocate*, August 19, 1891, entitled: "Protest against Giving the Sub-Treasury Scheme the Right of Way." Another Populist leader, H. F. True, delivered a speech at Valley Falls, Kansas, toward the end of August, 1891, opposing the plan on the ground that it would cost the party the support of labor (Topeka *Advocate*, September 9, 1891).

77. According to the Topeka *Advocate*, November 18, 1891, Democrats and Republicans worked together in some manner in thirty-eight counties. See also *ibid.*, December 2, 1891, on this subject.

78. *Ibid.*, December 9, 1891.

79. *Ibid.*, December 2, 1891. As James C. Malin has noted, "A part of the success of the Republican party in the off-year elections . . . [1891] is to be explained by the return of Farmers' Alliance men to the old party rather than submitting to be led into the People's party." See *A Concern About Humanity*, 194.

Chapter VII

1. St. Louis platform contained in Hicks, *The Populist Revolt*, 435-39.

2. Quoted in *ibid.*, 228.

3. *Ibid.*, 225-29.

4. *The Advocate*, Topeka, February 17, 1892.

5. Letter to editor dated March 17, 1892, *ibid.*, March 23, 1892.

6. *Ibid.*, July 15, 1891.

7. Letter to editor, *ibid.*, April 20, 1892.

8. No corroborating evidence was found to support the Overmeyer disclosure; however, the story was not denied, which is one indication of its validity. See Overmeyer's open letter dated July 16, 1892, *Kansas Democrat*, Topeka, July 18, 1892.

9. Otis had been elected in 1890 without Democratic opposition. He therefore owed something to the party indirectly, but Otis was not the kind of man to

compromise his principles—defeat rather than victory by fraternizing with Democrats was always the better choice for him.

10. Harris was a fifty-year-old native of Virginia. He was a graduate of Columbian College, Washington, D.C., in 1859 and of the Virginia Military Institute in 1861. He was trained as a civil engineer, and after serving in the Confederate Army in a staff position, he removed to Kansas to assist in the construction of the Union Pacific Railroad. He had also served as agent in the distribution of the Delaware Indian Reservation. After 1876 he had devoted his time to stock raising on his farm in Linwood. Once the Alliance was organized he became active in it and served as chairman of the delegation from the state Alliance to the St. Louis conference of February, 1892. See Wilson, *Eminent Men of Kansas,* 287-89, and *The Advocate,* Topeka, December 16, 1891.

11. Fred Close was a forty-three-year-old native of Pennsylvania who had resided in Kansas since 1866. He had lost one arm in the Civil War and had worked in Kansas as a druggist and farmer. He was a Republican until the mid-eighties, and had held the position of clerk of the district court from 1878 to 1884. He had left the Republican party to work for the Greenback-Labor and Union-Labor parties before joining the Populists in 1890. Following his defeat in 1892, he became Governor Lewelling's private secretary. See Topeka *Daily Capital,* November 30, 1892, and *History of the State of Kansas* (Chicago, 1883), I, 481.

12. King was the author of a popular pamphlet entitled *Bondholders and Bread Winners,* published early in 1892.

13. Clover became involved with a woman in Washington, and his wife charged that she was the kind who "would wear red slippers"; the "red slippers" charge, plus his slovenly performance in congress (he slept through sessions or appeared infrequently), was the undoing of the Cowley County farmer. McLallin wrote, on learning that Clover's wife was seeking a divorce on the grounds of extreme cruelty, that "there may be something in it, but the idea of Benjamin being extremely cruel or extremely anything, except sleepy, is preposterous." Not long after this debacle Clover returned to the Republican party, and in 1899 he committed suicide. See *The Advocate,* Topeka, December 7, 1892, and *Biographical Record of Cowley County,* 309-11.

14. A native of Indiana, Hudson was forty-eight years old and a graduate of Wabash College. He had been elected three times as mayor of Fredonia, Kansas, once to the state legislature, and was twice a delegate to the Democratic national convention (1884 and 1888) before joining the Populists in 1890. See Herringshaw's *American Statesmen* (Chicago, 1906), 278.

15. Cabe and Sullivant, *Kansas Votes: National Elections,* 211.

16. *The Advocate,* Topeka, June 22, 1892, and Ottawa *Journal,* March 22, 1894. It has been often emphasized that Lewelling was a nonentity before this speech; it is true only in a strictly relative sense. He was not much known beyond the boundaries of Wichita (except for his home state of Iowa where he was well known) and Sedgwick County, true, but he was well known within his own domain and had appeared on the rostrum on numerous occasions with the big names of Kansas Populism. See for example the Wichita *Daily Beacon,* October 24, 1890; Wichita *Weekly Beacon,* October 31, 1890; Wichita *Kansas Commoner,* October 30, 1890, and February 18, 1892.

17. W. J. Costigan, *In Memorial of Lorenzo D. Lewelling* (Chicago, 1902), 15-18; Topeka *State Journal*, November 11, 1892; Wichita *Daily Beacon*, June 15, 1892; *The Advocate*, Topeka, June 22, 1892.
18. *The Advocate*, Topeka, June 8, 1892.
19. *Ibid.*, April 13, 1892.
20. *Ibid.*, June 22, 1892.
21. *Ibid.;* see also August 24 and October 26, 1892; and *Kansas Democrat*, Topeka, June 16, 17, 22, and 30, 1892. Overmeyer stated that he was to have the nomination for congressman at large. "Yet upon the eve of their convention," he wrote, "they [Populist leaders] insisted that I should change my politics and they utterly ignored the Midland Hotel agreement. I in turn declared myself a democrat, and declared that I would not be a candidate except upon condition of such recognition of the democratic party as was contemplated by the Midland agreement. I thereupon declined to allow my name to go before the convention." See *Kansas Democrat*, Topeka, July 18, 1892.
22. Little was elected on the Greenback ticket as prosecuting attorney of Johnson County in 1882 and 1884. He replaced John Ives, the only successful man on the ticket in 1890; Ives, as attorney general, had been a member of the board of railroad assessors that had reduced the railroad assessment and therefore had lost the support of his party.
23. Biographical Circulars (K.S.H.S.), M-Z, II; William Ansel Mitchell, *Linn County, Kansas: A History* (La Cygne, 1928), 186-87; Atchison *Globe*, October 30, 1893; *History of Wyandotte County* (Chicago, 1911), 519-21; *The Advocate*, Topeka, September 13, 1890. It is interesting to note that eight out of fifteen of the Populist nominees in 1892 (including congressional candidates) were mentioned in the Topeka *Advocate* for the place they eventually received on the ticket.
24. Harris was in England at the time of his nomination. He had quite a reputation as a cattle breeder in Kansas, and had gone abroad, apparently, for the purpose of obtaining special breeding stock. See *The Advocate*, Topeka, July 20, 1892.
25. Letter to editor by T. J. Smith, McPherson, dated June 28, 1892, *ibid.*, July 8, 1892.
26. People's Party Clippings (K.S.H.S.), I, 38-39.
27. It was said that the Topolobampo lands comprised "millions of acres of the richest agricultural, timber and mineral lands in Mexico, but it was far removed from lines of communication and difficult of access." See Wilson, *Eminent Men of Kansas*, 625-27.
28. *Ibid.*
29. In 1896 Smith wrote that he would have won in 1892 had it not been for the fact that Cy Leland "sulked." See *Weekly Kansas Chief*, Troy, October 22, 1896, and Malin, *A Concern About Humanity*, 38-39.
30. For the Republican platform see the Topeka *Daily Capital*, July 3, 1892.
31. *Kansas Democrat*, Topeka, July 7 and August 6, 1892. See also *The Advocate*, Topeka, February 1, 1893.
32. Davis and Baker had stalwart Democratic opponents who accounted for 1.4 percent and 3.3 percent of the vote in their districts. See Cabe and Sullivant, *Kansas Votes: National Elections*.

33. *The Advocate,* Topeka, August 24, 1892.
34. *Ibid.,* November 3, 1892. Carroll's name stayed on the ballot, but the effectiveness of his withdrawal was shown by the fact that he polled only 161 votes in a district where the Democratic nominee in 1890 polled 13,250 votes. Close had refused to step down even though Populists of the Brown-Doniphan district nominated him for the state senate in hopes of encouraging his withdrawal. This unsystematic process of fusion resulted in poor strategy: in 1890 the Populists had run a poor third to the Democrats of the first district; the Democrats of the second district had run a poor third to the Populists. By running a Populist in the first and a Democrat in the second their ticket was weakened. See Cabe and Sullivant, *Kansas Votes: National Elections,* 122 and 124.
35. Hicks, *The Populist Revolt,* 231-33; platform contained in *ibid.,* 439-44.
36. Among other offices, Gresham had served as postmaster general (1883-84) and as secretary of the treasury (1884) under President Arthur. In 1892 he was serving as federal circuit judge with court in Chicago. He subsequently served as President Cleveland's secretary of state (1893).
37. *The Advocate,* Topeka, July 8, 1892.
38. Hicks, *The Populist Revolt,* 234.
39. *Ibid.,* 234-37. The Kansas delegation named W. D. Vincent, S. H. Snyder, and J. W. Laybourn as its representatives on the national committee; all three were well-known and long-time third-party men. See the Topeka *Advocate,* July 8, 1892.
40. *The Advocate,* Topeka, July 22, 1892.
41. Letter to editor from Lindsborg, Kansas, dated August 2, 1892, *ibid.,* August 17, 1892.
42. Letter to editor, dated August 6, 1892, *Kansas Democrat,* August 6, 1892.
43. The Lawrence *Daily Journal* and the Topeka *Daily Capital* were two of the leading Republican newspapers and two prime examples of Republican strategy in the campaign.
44. See the issues of the *Weekly Kansas Chief,* Troy, from July to November, especially that of September 22, 1892. Miller was still referring to the governor as "Lorraine" in November, 1894. See *ibid.,* November 8, 1894.
45. Topeka *Daily Capital,* October 9, 1892. See also the issues of October 28, 30, and November 8, 1892. Hudson's attack was not just the argument of the old guard. See the speech of E. W. Hoch in his campaign for a seat in the house, reported in *The Advocate,* Topeka, September 21, 1892. Hoch was one of the "young crowd," and he took the position that the People's party was "a socialistic party" and "a professional calamity party."
46. *The Advocate,* Topeka, September 28, 1892.
47. Floyd B. Streeter, *The Kaw* (New York, 1949), 311.
48. Breidenthal demanded an immediate trial and was acquitted. Populists got their revenge a few months later when Governor Lewelling made Breidenthal state bank commissioner. See *The Advocate,* Topeka, October 12, 1892.
49. The Lawrence *Daily Journal,* October 20, 1892, quoted Simpson but gave no source.
50. Editor Hudson maintained a constant personal campaign against Simpson. Apparently, in Hudson's mind Simpson was Populism personified. Incidentally,

the *Capital* used the term "Sockless Socrates" in its issue of June 21, 1891. There has been some debate as to who was to have the honor of originating that variation on the sockless theme. W. A. White has been awarded the credit but did not personally claim the honor. J. K. Hudson's claim is hereby registered.

Simpson was almost invariably caricatured as a sockless tramp. Apparently this had an effect upon his manner of dress, which was, of course, originally not out of the ordinary; so much so that in his effort to compensate he opened himself up to attack as a "dude." The Topeka *Daily Capital*'s Washington correspondent published this report on May 15, 1892: "Jerry Simpson's new spring outfit makes the Washington dudes green with envy. He came out last Sunday with kid gloves, a dazzling necktie, striped trousers and a very pretty walking stick. Jerry is known in Washington as one of the neatest and best dressers in Congress."

51. *Ibid.*, October 28, 1892.
52. Topeka *Advocate*, November 9, 1892.
53. Cabe and Sullivant, *Kansas Votes: National Elections*, 124-25.
54. *Ibid.*, 120-27, and Hein and Sullivant, *Kansas Votes: Gubernatorial Elections*, 26-29. H. L. Moore won over the Republican incumbent Funston only after he had successfully contested the election.
55. *House Journal, 1893*, 3-5.

Chapter VIII

1. Lewelling was born into a Quaker family. His father, a noted antislavery lecturer, died when Lorenzo was two, and his mother was killed in a fire when he was nine, leaving the boy in the care of an older sister. After serving briefly with an Iowa regiment in the Civil War (his family had demanded and obtained his release since he was under age), Lewelling had been a bridge-construction worker in Tennessee, a teacher in a Negro school in Missouri in the employ of the Freedman's Aid Society, a student and graduate of Eastman's Business College in Poughkeepsie, New York, a towpath boy on the Erie Canal, a carpenter in Toledo, a railroad section hand, a student-instructor and graduate of Whittier College in his home town, all before he was twenty-three years old. From 1868 to 1880, with the exception of two years (1870-72) when he managed a farm and edited a small weekly paper in Salem, Lewelling had worked in Iowa's reformatory system, serving as superintendent of Iowa Women's Reform School most of that time. From 1880 to 1882, he had edited the Des Moines *Capital*, an "antiring" Republican paper founded by himself; and, at the time he came to Kansas, he was serving as president of the board of directors of the State Normal School. See Wilson, *Eminent Men of Kansas*, 37-41; Dawn Daniels, "Lorenzo D. Lewelling—A Leader of the Kansas Populists," unpublished master's thesis, Northwestern University, 1931; William M. Bliss, "Kansas—The Sunflower State," *Carter's Monthly*, XII (November, 1897), 565-98; *The Advocate*, Topeka, August 10, 1892.
2. Kansas State Governor Messages (K.S.H.S.), II. The address is quoted by Barr, in *Kansas and Kansans*, II, 1168-69, and then by Hicks in *The Populist Revolt*, 275, in a loosely edited form.

3. See the issues of January 10 and March 14, 1893.

4. Topeka *State Journal*, February 18, 1893.

5. See Governor Lewelling's statement in the Topeka *Advocate*, January 25, 1893.

6. A. W. Stubbs, a Republican from Haskell County, was awarded the certificate from district 121 as a result of a transposition of votes. The state board of canvassers was aware of this but refused to correct the county clerk's error. Republicans organized without Stubbs and awarded the seat to the actual winner, Democrat Joseph Rosenthal, on the opening day. Rosenthal joined the Republican house on January 11, as did the other two Democrats. See *House Journal, 1893,* 7.

7. A tie vote was certified between O. M. Rice (Populist) and T. C. Ballinger (Republican) in Coffey County. According to law it then became the duty of the Republican-dominated state board of canvassers, upon notice to the candidates, to cast lots to determine who would be awarded the certificate. Populists maintained that "without notice to Mr. Rice, or any one representing him the state board of canvassers went into secret session and came out in a few minutes, claiming to have performed their duty, and claiming that Mr. Ballinger . . . had drawn the lucky number." On further investigation of the Coffey County election results, Populists claimed to have proved "that there was no tie, as the Populist had a majority of the votes, and the officer made a fraudulent return."

Altogether, Populists challenged ten Republican-held seats—that of Ballinger, plus several on the ground that illegal votes, miscount of ballots, and bribery had contributed to their certification; in one case it was claimed that the Republican representative was a resident of Oklahoma, and in one or two other cases it was maintained that the certified Republican representatives had been postmasters at the time of their election. Populists, of course, were not successful in unseating a single one of these men. Republicans, on the other hand, eventually unseated four Populists—two in a recount; two more who were declared ineligible because they allegedly held the office of postmaster at the time they claimed their certificates of election. See *The Advocate,* Topeka, January 18, 1893; *House Journal, 1893,* 69, 82, 125, 127, and 175.

8. See the statement by George Douglass and E. W. Hoch in the *House Journal, 1893* (Republican), 60-63, for a concise and convincing statement of the Republican position.

9. *Ibid.,* 20-22, 60-63; *House Journal, 1893* (Populist), 7-8.

10. Topeka *Daily Capital*, January 11, 12, 1893; *House Journal, 1893* (Republican), 23-27.

11. *House Journal, 1893* (Republican), 27-28; *The Advocate,* Topeka, January 25, 1893.

12. *The Advocate,* Topeka, January 12 and 25, February 1, 7, and 15, 1893; Topeka *State Journal*, January 10, 11, 20, 26, and 27; Topeka *Daily Capital*, January 11, 12, 18, 27, 31; *Kansas Democrat*, Topeka, January 26 and 31.

13. On the first vote in the senate there was no majority for Martin, and seven Populists in the house refused to vote for the Democrat. Actually Populists had enough votes to elect a Populist. There were fifty-seven duly elected Populist representatives present and twenty-four Populist senators. These eighty-one votes would have been a majority of the 160 members present at the joint

session. Populists were unable to agree on one man, however, and there was the added possibility that a Democratic majority in the U.S. senate would refuse a seat to a Populist about whose election there was the slightest doubt. See *The Advocate*, Topeka, February 1, 1893; *House Journal, 1893* (Republican), 112-16.

14. *House Journal, 1893* (Republican), 112-16.

15. See the letters of John Dunsmore and George Douglass addressed to each other on January 30 and 31, in *ibid.*, 132-35.

16. *Ibid.*, 213-33.

17. *Ibid.*, 224-30.

18. *Ibid.*, 232-41; *The Advocate*, Topeka, January 15 and 22, 1893; Topeka *Daily Capital*, February 15, 16, and 17, 1893.

19. *House Journal, 1893* (Republican), 241-51; Topeka *Daily Capital*, February 16, 1893. It is quite possible that Governor Lewelling had no intention of using the militia to clear the hall, and that he gave the colonel the order because the latter had rather foolishly publicized his intentions.

20. Kansas City *Mail*, February 16, 1893; Wichita *Daily Eagle*, February 16, 1893; Marion *Times*, February 16, 1893; and Kansas City *Gazette*, February 16, 1893.

21. Apparently George R. Peck, attorney for the Santa Fe Railroad and a prominent Republican leader, acted as the go-between. The Kansas State Historical Society Archives has both copies of the original agreement. The copy retained by George Douglass appears to be the first copy. It is said that Douglass' copy is in the handwriting of Peck, but it appears to be the handwriting of Governor Lewelling. Lewelling's copy is quite probably the handwriting of Peck. Perhaps this is why Lewelling did not release it until May, 1900. See *House Journal, 1893* (Republican), 248-50, for Lewelling's proposition to the Douglass house, and for the Republican proposal it prompted.

22. The complete record of the decision (Gunn Habeas Corpus case), including testimony, argument, the majority opinion of Chief Justice Horton, and the dissenting opinion of Populist Justice Allen, is contained in *ibid.*, 764-914.

23. In addition to the Australian ballot law, the senate sponsored a law providing a one-year time period for the redemption of real estate, and another requiring the "weekly payment of wages in lawful money of the United States." The act against corrupt practices in elections was the pet reform of Speaker George Douglass. This measure had been defeated by the Republican senate in 1891, and Douglass had publicly criticized senate Republicans for defeating a bill that had received every vote but one in the house. Another house measure provided for the regulation of "the weighing of coal at the mine." See *The Advocate*, Topeka, April 8, 1891, quoting the Wichita *Daily Eagle* on the Douglass election measure. See also *House Journal, 1893*, 762; *Senate Journal, 1893*, 853.

24. *House Journal, 1893*, 492, 964-74; *Senate Journal, 1893*, 677, 598-685.

25. Apparently because of the legislative war no biographical record was compiled on the 1893 legislature. The senate, which served from 1893 to 1897, was included in the sketches of the 1895 legislature, but the house of 1893 was missed. Information on sixty-eight of 125 of the house members is available since this number served in an earlier or later legislature, and by individual

reference biographical material was obtained on twenty-four of the remaining fifty-seven members. See Appendix III for a listing of the sources consulted in that endeavor.

26. Forty-four was a median age based on thirty-three of fifty-eight determinations. Actually, eighteen of thirty-five were natives of the states named above, and five of thirty-five (14.2 percent) were born on foreign soil. Twenty-four of thirty-five (68.8 percent) were farmers or stock raisers; only five of thirty-five were strictly business or professional men.

27. Eight lawyers, six merchants, five bankers, three physicians, two real estate men, one manufacturer, one surveyor, and one editor-publisher (twenty-eight of forty-six or 60 percent) made up the group of business or professional men. Fourteen farmers or stock raisers (fourteen of forty-six or 30.4 percent) were included in the Republican ranks. Thirty of forty-seven (63.8 percent) were natives of the states named, and four of forty-seven were foreign born.

28. Seven of the fifteen Republican senators were lawyers, one was in the electric railway and light business, one was a mill-owner, one was a physician, two were editor-publishers, and three were farmers and/or stock raisers. Only one Populist senator out of fifteen for whom the information was available was a college graduate, whereas four Republicans were college graduates. Five of twenty-four Populists and seven of fifteen Republicans had had previous legislative experience. Former party affiliations among Populist senators were approximately the same as among the Populists of the 1893 house. Compiled mainly from *Hand Book of the Kansas Legislature of 1895* (Topeka, 1895).

29. *The Modern Light* (Columbus) was the major Populist paper in Cherokee County, and it was a good example of the turmoil in Populist ranks caused by the Artz controversy. The paper published the charges on January 26, 1893, quoting the Leavenworth *Times* which, in turn, had quoted the Colorado Springs *Telegraph*. The Populist paper called for an investigation, and stated that "the People's party cannot afford to start out with this kind of reform." Apparently the charges were true (perhaps with mitigating circumstances) or the Lewelling administration would have denied them in vigorous fashion.

30. Formally Artz had resigned, but at the request of the governor. See the Topeka *Advocate*, February 28, 1894.

31. Letter from Legate to the editor of the *Capital*, dated March 4, 1893, and published in the Topeka *Advocate*, March 15, 1893. James F. Legate was widely known in Kansas politics long before the Populist era as "Slippery Jim," the man who "arranged the deals and handled the money" in the Republican party (Topeka *Daily Capital*, August 3, 1902). Legate said he used the money attempting to get a number of Republican and Democratic representatives to go into the Dunsmore house, and according to his account he failed in this because the railroad companies had their own fund to see that these men stayed "fixed." See *The Advocate*, March 29, 1893.

32. *The Advocate*, Topeka, March 22, 29, 1893; May 17, 1893; September 19, 1894. See also a letter by Fred J. Close to Professor William Stryker, dated August 24, 1894, Governor Lewelling's Letters (K.S.H.S. Archives).

33. Corning's paper was first called *The People*, and he moved it from Paola, Kansas, to Topeka and began publication on March 25, 1893. It became the *New Era* when he consolidated it with the paper of that name published by

two sons formerly in Council Grove. First issue as the *New Era* was on June 10, 1893. The paper continued until shortly after the Populist administration was defeated in 1894. A. J. R. Smith's *The Populist* began publication earlier, first edition May 7, 1892, and terminated at about the same time as the *New Era*.

34. *Kansas Commoner,* Wichita, September 28, 1893.

35. *New Era,* Topeka, March 25, and April 8, 1893. E. Z. Ernst, the originator of the Labor Exchange, quickly denied any connection with Corning.

36. *Ibid.,* April 8, 1893.

37. *Ibid.,* May 20, 1893.

38. *Ibid.,* October 21, 1893.

39. *The Populist,* Topeka, April 22, 29, and May 19, 1893.

40. Kansas City *Star,* quoted in the *New Era,* Topeka, June 7, 1893.

41. *The Advocate,* Topeka, April 4, 1894; see also May 23, 1894.

42. Topeka *Daily Capital,* November 11, 1893. Much of the above material relating to Mrs. Lease was previously published in an article entitled "Intolerant Populist? The Disaffection of Mary Elizabeth Lease," *The Kansas Historical Quarterly,* XXXIV (Summer, 1968), 189-200.

43. Wichita *Beacon,* November 14, 1893.

44. See letters of April 15, May 25, and December 28, 1893, from Governor Lewelling to M. E. Lease, Governor Lewelling's Letters (K.S.H.S.). Apparently fellow board member M. A. Householder (state senator from Columbus) had more influence in determining appointments. See a letter from Lewelling to Dr. J. D. Van Nuys, April 22, 1893, *ibid.*

45. *The Advocate,* Topeka, July 27, 1892. The editor published a statement by Mrs. Lease and a letter from the New York adjutant general's office, dated July 21, 1892, that confirmed the death of her father as she claimed.

46. *Ibid.* In 1904 Mrs. Lease remarked: "My father and brothers died on the field of battle defending the flag and the Union that the Democratic party, represented by [William Jennings] Bryan and [Adlai E.] Stevenson, sought to destroy." Newspaper clipping dated September 27, 1904, in Kansas Biographical Scrapbook (K.S.H.S.), L, I, 130-31. See also the Leavenworth *Times,* September 22, 1900.

47. Kansas City *Star,* January 2, 1894.

48. *The Herald,* Pleasanton, January 12, 26, 1894; *The Advocate,* Topeka, January 3, and March 14, 1894; *New Era,* Topeka, January 6, 1894.

49. *The Herald,* Pleasanton, January 26, 1894.

50. Kansas City *Star,* January 27, 1894.

51. *The Advocate,* Topeka, January 31, 1894.

52. Manuscript Biography of M. E. Lease by James Arnold, K.S.H.S. Archives. In the appended note Mrs. Lease asked Mr. McCray to send her "Herald or tell me when to get it." This would seem to indicate she desired a copy of *The Herald* which contained her letter attacking the administration. Since it was published in Pleasanton on January 26, 1894, this would indicate that this sketch was written immediately before or after that date. Mrs. Lease was clearly James Arnold; internal evidence demonstrates this convincingly. In addition, the signature of Mrs. Lease from a letter to Judge H. Kelley contained

in the Historical Society and the handwriting on the manuscript biography are the same.

53. *Transactions of the Kansas State Historical Society, 1905-1906* (Topeka, 1906), IX, n. 414; Topeka *Daily Capital*, June 2, 1889.

54. For D. O. McCray's finished product, which ignored everything Mrs. Lease had provided, see "The Farmers' Alliance and the Populist Party," in *Transactions of the Kansas State Historical Society, 1905-1906*, 425-26.

55. Manuscript Biography of M. E. Lease, K.S.H.S.

56. Mary E. Lease *v.* J. W. Freeborn, *The Advocate*, Topeka, February 14, 1894. Governor Lewelling was aware that he could not remove Governor Humphrey's holdovers on the board of charities without cause (see Lewelling to A. P. Elder, April 11, 1893, Letters, K.S.H.S.), but he believed he could remove his own appointees at will; a Republican court did not agree.

57. A strong commitment to woman suffrage and prohibition, two causes she felt were threatened by fusion with Democrats, could explain Mrs. Lease's action in the controversy were it not for the fact that she abandoned the cause of equal suffrage during the summer of 1894, and by 1896 she renounced prohibition (Topeka *Daily Capital*, September 15, 1894; Topeka *State Journal*, May 25, 1896). Her actions were unbelievably erratic. Early in the campaign of 1894 she even attempted to win back the good graces of the Populist organization; in doing so she put herself in a hopelessly contradictory position. She announced that she was going to enter the campaign to defend Governor Lewelling. She said that "the governor is innocent of every charge brought against him by the character assassins who are hounding him. I cannot stand silently by and see this campaign of slander proceed against one whom I know to be innocent" (Topeka *Daily Capital*, September 14, 1894). For a discussion of Mrs. Lease's political thought see Malin, *A Concern About Humanity*, 84-87.

58. See especially Edward Wallis Hoch's article in *The Agora* (April, 1893), 280-83, and *The Last War* (Topeka, 1893); C. S. Gleed, *The Agora* (April, 1893), 292; J. G. Water's speech in the Topeka *Daily Capital*, November 5, 1893. In his *Agora* article E. W. Hoch wrote: "If the Governor had an adviser who believes either in God or in our form of government, his name should be given to an anxious public. I do not know him. All, so far as I know, were either Socialists or anarchists, with the possible exception of Judge Webb . . . ."

59. See especially the Topeka *Advocate*, April 19, November 22, 1893; *The Kansan*, Pittsburg, March 30, November 9, 30, 1893. The editor of the Pittsburg *Kansan* recommended Lawrence Groulund's *The Co-operative Commonwealth* in his effort to promote a better understanding of socialism. G. C. Clemens and a number of other Populist leaders were in touch with Groulund (see a letter from Groulund to Clemens dated November 13, 1893, K.S.H.S. Archives), and the noted socialist leader was in Topeka for several weeks in December, 1893, to establish a "headquarters" there and to lecture on socialism. See *The Advocate*, Topeka, December 20, 1893.

60. *The Advocate*, Topeka, November 22, 1893.

61. Topeka *Daily Capital*, November 5, 1893.

62. Hoch, *The Last War*, 1.

63. Troutman was one of the leading conservative members of the Douglass house.

64. Speech entitled "The First (And Last) People's Party Government on Earth,"

delivered on January 29, 1894, as part of *The Kansas Day Club Addresses* (Hutchinson, 1901).

65. Topeka *State Journal*, December 4, 1893.

66. For a compilation of Kansas and national press reaction to the Lewelling circular, see the Topeka *Daily Capital*, December 10, 13, 1893.

67. For a special insight into the conduct of Governor Lewelling see his official correspondence during the miners' strike in southeast Kansas, especially his letter to Percy Daniels (in Girard), July 17; to a Captain O. S. Casad (in Pittsburg), July 18; to Sheriff Arnold (in Weir City), July 24; to L. Walters (in Weir City), July 24; and to Frank P. McLennan, July 26, 1893. In the last letter, Lewelling stated: "I admit, without equivocation, that the sympathy of the present administration is with the striking miners. I believe they are being wronged by the mine owners in the present controversy . . . but while this is true the interests of the state, of this very administration and the interests of all workingmen in general require that the strikers shall remain within the requirements of the law." See also Lieutenant Governor Daniels' report on the strike in A. G. Lucas' manuscript "Biography of Maj. Gen. Percy Daniels" (K.S.H.S. Archives), 36.

68. Governor Lewelling answered an appeal for aid to the western counties by writing: "I . . . agree with you that 'Sympathy with suffering humanity is the fundamental principle with all genuine Populists.' After all we are compelled to be practical and adopt methods which are business like, which is another name for heartlessness, in dealing with each other." See Lewelling to G. G. Allen (Meade, Kansas), July 15, 1890, Letters, K.S.H.S. Archives.

Chapter IX

1. From a speech by Charles E. Harbaugh delivered on January 29, 1894, as part of *The Kansas Day Club Addresses*, 123.

2. Leland, like many a political boss of his time, was a shadowy figure, about whom there is much speculation but little documentation. He was, however, a native of Wisconsin, where he was born in 1841. After moving out to Troy, Kansas, in 1858, he had been quite successful in the mercantile business. The November 23, 1893, *Weekly Troy Chief* noted that Leland was rather affluent. It reported: "He has two general stores, deals in grain, lumber and coal, runs an elevator, operates a pork packing establishment, carries on a meat market, and keeps an eye on the operation of a number of farms. Besides the farms under cultivation, he has two or three stock farms, where besides feeding cattle and raising mules, he breeds first-class horses . . . ." The only elective office that Leland had ever held was that of county commissioner; his talents were applied through the mechanism of the local, state, and national Republican organizations. For an interesting but slightly exaggerated account of Cy Leland's role in the 1894 campaign, see Walter T. K. Nugent's "How the Populists Lost in 1894," *Kansas Historical Quarterly*, XXXI (Autumn, 1965), 245-55.

3. Topeka *Daily Capital*, June 8, 1894; Nugent, "How the Populists Lost in 1894," *Kansas Historical Quarterly*, XXXI (Autumn, 1965), 250-51.

4. Ottawa *Journal and Triumph*, June 21, 1894.

5. *Ibid.;* Topeka *Daily Capital,* June 13, 1894.
6. Ottawa *Journal and Triumph,* June 21, 1894; Topeka *Daily Capital,* June 13, 14, 1894.
7. Ottawa *Journal and Triumph,* June 21, 1894. F. G. Adams of the State Historical Society was convinced that this prayer was of some historic consequence, for he requested a copy from the minister who was identified only as Reverend Goodner. The minister reconstructed the prayer from memory and sent a copy to Adams in a letter dated June 22, 1894. The segment that brought the response from the convention, as he reconstructed it, reads like this: "The morals of our people waning, the pulpit and the press prostituted to the base ends of plutocratic greed; free speech and free assembly denied, a slavery coming upon us, unsurpassed by America's former chattel system, and all this sought to be made perpetual!! In view of this, we, in unspeakable grief, lift our hearts to Thee O God of Ages!! With a deep sense of the grievous wrongs done us, by him, we, nevertheless, ask thine infinite mercy upon the chief executive of this nation—when he shall repent of his sins, and turn away from his monstrous evils. May he, his cabinet, and a boodling congress, be led by such means as Thou, the Infinite alone canst ordain, to fear further encroachment upon the rights of an outraged people!!" The remainder of the prayer called for support of woman suffrage and the victory of the party at the polls. Reverend Goodner to F. G. Adams, June 22, 1894, special collection, K.S.H.S. Archives.
8. Nugent, "How the Populists Lost in 1894," *Kansas Historical Quarterly,* XXXI (Autumn, 1965), 250-51.
9. Breidenthal and Lewelling were severely handicapped in any effort to pack the committee, since there was a desire to call the convention under the "Omaha Ordinance for the Purification of Politics," according to which all officeholders were forbidden to participate in any convention of the party. See the manifesto of the Shawnee County People's party committee to that effect, published in *The Advocate,* Topeka, March 28, 1894. Also, since extreme antifusionists had charged that Lewelling and Breidenthal were preparing "to surrender the principles of the reform cause in this state to the British financial Hessians, the Democrats of Kansas," it was necessary for the Populist organization to avoid all appearances of a desire to influence the convention's decisions. See the "secret circular" issued by Noah Allen and W. F. Rightmire in behalf of the National Citizen's Alliance, in the *Kansas Commoner,* Wichita, June 7, 1894.
10. Ottawa *Journal and Triumph,* June 21, 1894. The reporter representing this paper compiled a record of the convention which was complete enough to have been an official record. Except where otherwise indicated, the author has relied upon this report for material concerning convention happenings.
11. *New Era,* Topeka, June 16, 1894.
12. Lest there be any misunderstanding, it must be noted that this element of nativism was restricted almost without exception to this extreme antifusion group. It would be wholly erroneous to assume that Populism was generally nativistic. As a party, the nativism within Populism was negligible compared to that in the Republican party. Walter Nugent noted in his study of Kansas Populism that "the Republican party was the home of immigration restriction on racist grounds . . . , whether in the East or in Kansas." See *The Tolerant*

Populists: Kansas, Populism and Nativism (Chicago, 1963), 101. Numerous references to Republican nativism could be cited to document this statement; indeed, just a casual examination of the Topeka *Daily Capital* throughout the 1890s will demonstrate it without question. See also *The Kansas Day Club Addresses* for a compilation of Republican leadership statements, a number of which are replete with nativism. It is perhaps significant that those few Populists who did have a nativistic strain were generally anti-Democratic; most of them, as a matter of fact, came to the Populist party from the Republican party. It should also be noted that the convention adopted a resolution denouncing the anti-Catholic and nativistic American Protective Association.

13. *Kansas Commoner*, Wichita, June 7, 1894, and the Topeka *Advocate*, June 6, 1894.

14. Populist Party Clippings (K.S.H.S.), I, 118-19.

15. *The Advocate*, Topeka, July 1, 1894; W. P. Harrington, "Populist Party in Kansas," *Collections of the Kansas Historical Society*, XVI, 434-35.

16. Typed manuscript, "Speech at Huron Place," K.S.H.S. Archives; Topeka *Daily Capital*, July 27, 1894. This speech in manuscript form is thirty-one typed pages in length, and is obviously a very rough draft.

17. *The Advocate*, Topeka, September 19, 1894; see also an article by G. C. Clemens entitled "The Philosophy of the Omaha Platform: Not Paternalism but Fraternalism," *ibid.*, September 5, 1894.

18. Topeka *Daily Capital*, August 3, 1894; *The Advocate*, Topeka, August 8, 1894. Clover's reward, according to the Topeka *Advocate* (May 22, 1895), was that of farmer for the boy's reform school in Topeka at $29.75 a week.

19. Letter to John W. Breidenthal, dated August 28, 1894, Topeka *Daily Capital*, September 2, 1894.

20. *Ibid.*, August 21, 1894. Republican gubernatorial candidate Morrill employed essentially the same argument in his campaign; see his speech at Fredonia, reported in the Topeka *Daily Capital*, September 6, 1894.

21. *New Era*, Topeka, June 16, 30, 1894.

22. See especially *ibid.*, July 21, 1894.

23. *The Advocate*, Topeka, August 29, 1894.

24. *Kansas Commoner*, Wichita, October 25, 1894; *The Advocate*, Topeka, October 24, 1894; *The Weekly World*, Girard, October 25, 1894. Other than Corning, Wesley Henry Bennington, named for associate justice of the supreme court, was the only one on the ticket whose name was known to Populist politics either before or after the election. Bennington was then president of the Commonweal Army of Kansas. See Topeka *New Era*, July 21, 1894.

25. *Kansas Commoner*, Wichita, October 25, 1894.

26. Ben Henderson argued the cause of the Corning ticket, which raises the question of whether both Henderson and Corning were Cy Leland's agents. Walter Nugent believes that to be the case but, as he has written, "No one will ever know to what extent the destruction of fusion by means of those useful tools—Cy Corning, Ben Henderson, and the woman's suffrage issue—was a matter of conscious planning by Leland. It is entirely possible that the whole plan was laid before the Republican convention which met in early June, before the Populist convention, many months before the election." The course pursued by Corning's *New Era*, in itself, is practically enough evidence to prove his

implication, but until more conclusive evidence is uncovered indicating that Henderson made his fight for woman suffrage at the instigation of Leland (which appears unlikely), this writer must see Henderson as an unstable, anti-Democrat prohibitionist who played into Cy Leland's hand. See Nugent, "How the Populists Lost in 1894," *Kansas Historical Quarterly*, XXXI (Autumn, 1965), 255.

27. Perhaps the most exploited charge was the Republican story that fiendish Populist doctors had performed brutal and mutilating operations on the patients of the institution for the feebleminded.

28. In the third congressional district the incumbent Populist, T. J. Hudson, decided not to run again because of personal financial difficulties, and J. D. Botkin was a late replacement. See *The Advocate*, Topeka, September 19, 1894.

29. The woman-suffrage vote as reported in *ibid.*, December 19, 1894.

30. Hein and Sullivant, *Kansas Votes: Gubernatorial Elections*, 27, 31; Cabe and Sullivant, *Kansas Votes: National Elections*, 128-31.

31. Woman suffrage was probably more effective in driving Democratic votes away from the Populist ticket than was the breakdown of fusion itself. The Democratic candidate, Overmeyer, received only 26,709 votes. Compare this with the 71,357 votes for the Democratic candidate in 1890 and 107,528 in 1888. See *The Advocate*, Topeka, December 19, 1894; Hein and Sullivant, *Kansas Votes*, 25, 27.

32. *New Era*, Topeka, November 10, 1894.

33. *Ibid.*, February 3, 1895.

34. The Kansas State Historical Society has a copy of the formal program Republicans printed for the affair.

Chapter X

1. Kansas State Governor Messages (K.S.H.S.), II.

2. Full text of the message is contained in *The Advocate*, Topeka, January 16, 1895.

3. For an excellent example see the speech of Charles A. Sheldon (secretary of the Republican League and a banker from Burlingame), January 29, 1895, contained in *The Kansas Day Club Addresses*.

4. B. B. M'Call, "Why I Am Not a Populist," January 29, 1895, *ibid.*

5. Twenty-five of eighty-seven (28.7 percent) were identified as farmers or stock raisers; nine more (16.3 percent) were engaged in farming in association with banking, real estate, merchandizing, engineering, and surveying. Actually, fifty-three out of eighty-nine (58.2 percent) were born in the states named. Two were natives of Kansas; eleven (12 percent) were born on foreign soil. Information compiled from George W. Crane's *Advance Sheets of the Hand Book of the Kansas Legislature* (Topeka, 1895).

6. Based on twenty-eight cases where age information was provided, seven (24.1 percent) Populist representatives were fifty or older. The youngest was thirty-one and the oldest sixty-two. Twenty-five of thirty-one (80.6 percent) Populist representatives were born in the states indicated above. None were native Kansans; three (9.6 percent) were born on foreign soil. Five of thirty-two

Populists were Union veterans. Religious affiliations were available for Populists and Republicans but were so mixed as to seem irrelevant. It is perhaps worth noting, however, that sixty-three of eighty-nine (70.7 percent) Republicans expressed their church affiliation, while only thirteen of thirty-two Populists (40.6 percent) so committed themselves.

7. Among the Republicans of the house there were twenty-eight lawyers (three of whom were also engaged as a banker, loan agent, and a railroad advertising agent), thirteen merchants, two bankers, one merchant-banker, one realtor-banker-farmer, three realtor-farmers, one real estate broker, one manufacturer, one "railroad builder" and mine owner, one merchant-farmer, one mill owner, one contractor, two physicians, three editor-publishers, two farmer-ministers, one clerical worker, one surveyor, one surveyor-farmer, one farmer who was also a civil engineer, one carpenter, and one blacksmith. Their number was completed by twenty-five farmers and/or stock raisers. Among the Populists were nineteen farmers and/or stock raisers, two teacher-farmers, one lawyer-farmer, one farmer who was also a mill operator, one editor-farmer, one banker-farmer, one physician, and one miner.

8. See the analysis of the senate on page 137.

9. Two measures passed by the legislature authorized Arlington and Sylvia townships in Reno County to issue bonds for the construction of flour mills; both were vetoed by Governor Morrill. In his veto of one of these the governor stated: "It seems to be the intention of the bill to enable a municipal township to go into the milling business. Counties, townships and other political subdivisions of the state were not organized, nor was it ever intended they should be organized for such purposes. I regard such legislation as vicious and a step in the wrong direction. If a township or city is to go into the milling business, I see no reason why municipal organizations cannot engage in divers kinds of enterprises coming into direct competition with individual enterprises and all tending in the direction of the state owning and controlling all manner of private business. It is contrary to the very spirit of our constitutions and a direct step toward paternalism and against good government." The governor's veto message prompted *The Advocate* (March 13, 1895) to state, "Had the citizens of these townships asked the privilege to issue their bonds to be presented as a bonus to some milling corporation as an inducement to erect a flouring mill to be operated for the private gain of said corporation, it is not likely their bill would have been vetoed. That would not be paternalism in the eyes of Governor Morrill; but when they ask the privilege of issuing their own bonds for their own benefit and to relieve themselves from the extortions of an arbitrary and avaricious milling trust, such paternalism . . . is not to be thought of." This issue does indeed point up a valid and basic difference between many Populists and Republicans—and Democrats too, for that matter. An obvious contradiction, which Governor Morrill did not attempt to reconcile, was the continuing sanction of the legislature and the executive for the purchase of gas, water, and electric plants by municipalities from private companies.

10. R. H. Semple, "The Legislature of 1895," *The Agora,* IV (April, 1895), 261-67.

11. *Senate Journal, 1895,* 489-90, 605-06. Senate bills 41, 47, 95, and 285.

12. *House Journal, 1895,* 1661.
13. *Ibid.* See house bills 335, 541, 768, and 862 on pages 1609, 1628, 1649, and 1659. The platforms of both parties had indorsed the irrigation measure. See Topeka *Daily Capital,* July 15, 1894, and Populist Party Clippings (K.S.H.S.), I, 84-86.
14. Harold U. Faulkner, *Politics, Reform and Expansion* (New York, 1959), 141-51.
15. Speech in the house delivered August 18, 1893, Kansas Collected Speeches, IX (K.S.H.S.). Senator Peffer and Congressman Thomas J. Hudson also went on record with similar efforts.
16. Faulkner, *Politics, Reform and Expansion,* 151.
17. November 22, 1893.
18. In a recent article, Robert F. Durden has written that "to most Populists of the period socialism was the real, late-coming 'cow-bird' that tried to capture the nest." Interpreting Henry D. Lloyd to have meant that free silver was not an initial part of the Populist program, Durden then proceeds to his satisfaction to demonstrate that free silver was not the "cow-bird" of the reform movement. Leaving aside the fact that the article was made possible by a clever interpretation of Lloyd's famous statement, Mr. Durden's article fails to deal adequately with the Populist position on the money question. As late as 1896, Senator Peffer defined that position adequately when he declared: "the money that the People's party demand is gold, silver, and paper. Populists believe in the unlimited and free coinage of both the metals, and if there is not enough of coin money in the country, supplement it with paper money. The difference between the Populists and the Democrats and the Republicans is this: That we do not believe in private notes of any kind to circulate as money; we do not believe in the Government of the United States or the Congress . . . delegating its authority 'to coin money and to regulate the value thereof' to any class of people under heaven. We believe it is a function of government, and a sovereign function, to prepare and to issue its own money—its own gold money, its own silver money, its own paper money . . . ." (*Congressional Record,* 54th Cong., 1st. sess., p. 2479). Mr. Durden's article, "The 'Cow-bird' Grounded: The Populist Nomination of Bryan and Tom Watson in 1896," *The Mississippi Valley Historical Review: A Journal of American History,* L (December, 1963), 397-423, may have some general validity as applied to southern Populism, from which his material is largely drawn, but it must be seriously qualified when applied to Kansas Populism.
19. *The Advocate,* Topeka, February 14, 1894.
20. The Populist platform of 1894 is contained in Populist Party Clippings (K.S.H.S.), I, 84-86.
21. Topeka *Daily Capital,* July 15, 1894.
22. Taubeneck's proposals were noted in *The Advocate,* Topeka, December 12, 1894.
23. Letter to editor, *ibid.*
24. *Ibid.*
25. *Ibid.,* February 6, March 6, and March 27, 1895.
26. One significant Kansas publication was that of J. M. Waterman entitled *Silver*

Threads Among the Gold: A Plea for the Free Coinage of Silver (Delphos, 1895), People Party Pamphlets (K.S.H.S.), II.

27. June 18, 1895.

28. July 9, 1895.

29. J. F. Willits was president of the state Alliance again in 1895, J. B. French was secretary, and John Otis was lecturer. See *The Advocate,* Topeka, February 6, 1895.

30. *Ibid.,* October 2, 1895.

31. *Ibid.,* October 9, 1895, and February 5, 1895.

32. *Ibid.,* December 18, 1895, and January 1, 1896.

33. Letter to editor, *ibid.,* February 5, 1896.

34. *Ibid.,* April 29, 1896.

35. Before undertaking this state study the writer researched and studied the Populist movement in Osage County. This county was selected because it was strongly Populist and Progressive, and, because of its coal-mining industry, the existence of a significant labor element afforded an opportunity to arrive at some conclusions regarding the cooperation between the farmer and the laborer. Most of the material for the study was drawn from *The Peoples Herald* (a Populist weekly published in Lyndon) and the *Kansas People* (a Republican weekly published in Osage City).

36. For material concerning the background of the leadership of the party in Osage County and their approach to reform, see *The Peoples Herald,* Lyndon, especially the issues of September 12, October 31, 1890; December 15, 1892; and October 10, 31, 1895; *Kansas People,* Osage City, November 5, 1890.

37. Norman Pollack has stated that labor was the conservative, "retarding influence" of the farmer-labor coalition. The voting patterns of Osage County, at least, would support that contention. See Pollack, *Populist Response to Industrial America,* 61.

38. Utilizing the census of 1895 the writer discovered that there were around 824 of 1180 heads of families residing in the city who were classified as laborers (mostly miners), 50 as farmers, and 306 as business or professional. The occupational breakdown for the city's four wards was: first ward, 273 laborers, 206 business and professional, and 25 farmers; second ward, 341 laborers, 94 business and professional, and 18 farmers; third ward, 98 laborers, 3 business or professional, and 3 farmers; fourth ward, 112 laborers, 3 business or professional, and 4 farmers. See Kansas State Census, 1895, Osage Co., CCLXXII (K.S.H.S.).

The votes for governor in the city by ward for the elections of 1890, 1892, 1894, and 1896 were as follows (*The Peoples Herald,* Lyndon, November 12, 1890; November 17, 1892; November 15, 1894; November 13, 1896):

	1890			1892			1894			1896		
	R	P.P.	D	R	P.P.	D	R	P.P.	D	R	P.P.	D
1st	49/	134/	42	128/	229/	2	141/	134/	27	135/	171	—
2nd	65/	69/	15	112/	75/	5	107/	78/	8	127/	70	—
3rd	91/	57/	14	111/	76/	11	115/	77/	17	98/	99	—
4th	74/	25/	21	100/	61/	1	106/	30/	15	91/	49	—

The analysis of Osage City voting is complicated by several factors: the city contained a significant foreign-born element (510 heads of families out of 1180) and 91 Negro families resided in the city. It is likely that a number of the former had no vote (an average for the number of votes cast at any one election would be about 650), and that most of the latter remained with the Republican party.

The writer also applied a similar treatment to the town of Burlingame which supported the Republican ticket in every election throughout the decade. Burlingame was second in size but first in affluence. The census revealed that there were 208 heads of families who were classified as business or professional by occupation, 48 as farmers, and 164 as laborers. The Republican margin of victory in the elections roughly approximated the ratio of three to two. Since the town cast its vote as a unit, the writer has no way of determining how these groups voted, but based on the findings in Osage City, it seems likely that the Republican ticket was supported by a substantial percentage of the labor vote.

39. *The Peoples Herald,* Lyndon, February 14, 1895.

40. *Ibid.,* March 21, 1895.

41. *Ibid.,* March 28, 1895.

42. *Ibid.,* April 25 and May 30, 1895.

43. *Ibid.,* May 30, 1895.

44. *Ibid.,* August 29, 1895.

45. *Ibid.,* October 24, 1895.

46. See *ibid.* for September 12 and October 31, 1890, for the presentation of the party's candidates to the voters in that first campaign.

47. For the record, this trend continued in Osage County. While the party's leaders kept the emphasis on the "solid-citizen" types, pushed fusion, and increasingly focused the party's efforts on the towns rather than the countryside, the Farmers' Alliance, which remained in the hands of an element of the original leadership, attacked the party's new spokesmen for having sold out party principles and leading the party to defeat behind William J. Bryan.

48. *The Peoples Herald,* Lyndon, November 7, 1895.

49. *The Advocate,* Topeka, April 29, 1896.

50. *The Peoples Herald,* Lyndon, July 2, 1896. Norman Pollack has concluded that "Populism was not deceived on silver; it remained radical to the end." As applied to the leadership of the Kansas Populists this conclusion has general validity, although there was a minority segment which looked to silver as a panacea. The issue appears to have had a more deceptive appeal for the rank-and-file Populist. See Pollack, *The Populist Response to Industrial America,* 143.

Chapter XI

1. John D. Hicks, *The Populist Revolt,* 349-67. The literature of the 1896 campaign is extensive; among the works that aid considerably in understanding that crucial election are: Paul Glad, *McKinley, Bryan and the People,* and *The Trumpet Soundeth, William Jennings Bryan and His Democracy, 1896-1912* (Lincoln, 1960); H. Wayne Morgan, *William McKinley and His America*

(Syracuse, 1963); James A. Barnes, "Myths of the Bryan Campaign," *Mississippi Valley Historical Review*, XXXIV (December, 1947), 367-404; and William Diamond, "Urban and Rural Voting in 1896," *American Historical Review*, XLVI (January, 1941), 281-305. Two recent studies, Stanley L. Jones' *The Presidential Election of 1896* (Madison, 1964) and Robert F. Durden's *The Climax of Populism: The Election of 1896* (Lexington, 1965), both contribute invaluably to this discussion.

2. Girard *World* (Weekly), July 16, 1896.
3. *The Advocate*, Topeka, July 22, 1896, compiled a list of newspapers supporting Bryan's indorsement. For *The Advocate's* reaction to the Bryan nomination see the July 15, 1896, edition.
4. Newspaper clipping, dated July 22, 1896, from St. Louis, contained in the Kansas Biographical Scrapbook (K.S.H.S.), B, III, 302.
5. Quoted in Hicks, *The Populist Revolt*, 365.
6. *Ibid.*, 357-67.
7. *The Advocate*, Topeka, July 29, 1896.
8. The central committee statement was dated October 31, 1896, and published in *ibid.*, October 28, 1896.
9. W. J. Costigan led an unsuccessful fight within the convention to prevent Breidenthal's reelection as state chairman. It was charged that among other things Breidenthal had "spent money amounting to thousands of dollars . . . to defeat the nomination of ex-Governor Lewelling at the Abilene convention . . . ." The charge was denied. Lewelling later stated that Breidenthal had also done "his best to defeat" his "renomination" in 1894. See *ibid.*, August 12, 26, and September 9, 1896; Kansas Scrapbook Biography (K.S.H.S.), B, III, 308.
10. *The Advocate*, Topeka, August 12, 1896.
11. The biographical record of John W. Leedy is quite incomplete. See George W. Crane's *Advance Sheets of Hand Book of the Kansas Legislature, 1895*, and Wilson's *Eminent Men*, 45-47. Later, while visiting Kansas in April, 1897, Mary Elizabeth Lease maintained that she, "with a few trusty friends, was instrumental in breaking the Topeka slate ["Harris for Governor and Breidenthal for the Senate"] that had been fixed for the Abilene convention . . . ." She maintained that "by bringing up Lewelling as a candidate for Governor, which I did at every point in the state, I divided the forces and they were compelled to drop Harris and compromise on Leedy." No corroborating evidence was found to support this claim. See the Topeka *Daily Capital*, April 27, 1897.
12. *The Kansas Blue Book* (Topeka, 1897).
13. *The Weekly Kansas Chief*, Troy, July 30, 1896.
14. Malin, *A Concern About Humanity*, 203.
15. *Ibid.*
16. Emporia *Gazette* (Weekly), May 14, 1896.
17. *Ibid.*, August 6, 1896.
18. *Ibid.*, August 13, 1896.
19. *Ibid.*, October 29, 1896.
20. The "What's the Matter with Kansas" editorial appeared in the weekly on October 1, 1896. Too often, this article had been dealt with as an aberration

of sorts; as if White wrote the article in a moment of anger resulting from his having been "ganged" by Populist partisans. This no doubt happened, as White noted in his *Autobiography*, but the philosophy and argument of the article was not as much out of the ordinary as the progressive William Allen White of later years wanted his posterity to believe.

21. G. C. Clemens, *An Appeal to True Populists*, People's Party Pamphlets (K.S.H.S.), VI.

22. Clemens went before the board of certification arguing the case of the Populists against certification of the middle-of-the-road ticket for a place on the ballot. See the statement by Clemens on this matter in *The Advocate*, Topeka, October 28, 1896.

23. It was of course a Republican board of certification that approved the middle-of-the-road electoral ticket. The mid-road faction was represented in argument before that board and later before the state supreme court by Republican counsel—before the state supreme court it was former Chief Justice Horton, a Republican, who argued their case. See *ibid*.

24. "Final Address to Populists," Populist State Central Committee (Anti-Fusion), People's Party Pamphlets (K.S.H.S.), VII.

25. Abe Steinberger was the leader of the mid-roaders. He was president of the Kansas Reform Press Association at the time. This organization met in October, however, and adopted a resolution censoring Steinberger's actions. In the election, the mid-road ticket polled only a fraction of the votes. In Girard, Steinberger's home town, only five votes were cast for the mid-road ticket; only seventy votes were cast in all of Crawford County, in which Girard is located. See *The Advocate*, Topeka, October 28, 1896; Girard *World* (Daily), November 12, 1896.

26. *The Advocate*, Topeka, October 21, 1896; *The Weekly Co-Operator and Topeka Press*, October 2, 1896.

27. *The Advocate*, Topeka, October 14, 1896.

28. Kansas City *Star*, September 10, 1896; Kansas City *Times*, September 11, 1896.

29. G. C. Clemens challenged Willits and Steinberger to deny that in preparation for this tour, "the Republican Mayor of Topeka and another Republican hired the opera house for his first speech." He asked if they would deny in his "presence that they were not to pay a dollar for that special train in which Watson was to have toured Kansas? That no Populist on earth was to pay a dollar? That it was 'tendered' to them by the obliging railroad company which has not been so kind to the wicked 'fusionists' of Abilene?" See *The Advocate*, Topeka, October 28, 1896.

30. Letter to editor Steinberger, Girard *World* (Weekly), October 28, 1896.

31. Emporia *Gazette*, November 5, 1896.

32. January 12, 1897.

33. The explanation for Governor Leedy's vapid oratory may well be explained by the following commentary that appeared in the Topeka *Daily Capital*: "John W. Leedy made a reputation as a stump speaker while a member of the State Senate. He had a gift of gab . . . . He had a style of his own, which was entertaining, and the galleries always were crowded when it became known that he would have something to say. His quick wit offset his rough manners, and the vigor of his attack . . . made his butchery of the English language

less apparent." It was felt that he had been advised to be careful in his use of English, and consequently had developed a fear of criticism on this account. In the *Capital*'s estimation, the last time Leedy had delivered a speech "with fire in it" was at the Abilene convention; since then, throughout the campaign of 1896 and later, his speeches had been edited by Ed Little, who became Governor Leedy's private secretary. See the issue of February 20, 1898.

34. *Ibid.*, January 12, 1897.

35. Statistics compiled largely from *The Kansas Blue Book*. The previous party affiliations of Populists in the senate had not altered significantly. Former Republicans, Democrats, and third-party men were represented by the ratio of five, two, and three respectively.

36. Among the eight Popocrats were two physicians, and one each of the following: banker, merchant, farmer, lawyer, livestock dealer, and real estate and lumber dealer. There were no former third-party men among the Popocrats; all were Democrats, although four had only joined that party in 1890, after leaving the Republican party. As far as could be determined, former Republicans, Democrats, and third-party men were represented among the house Populists by the ratio of five, three, and two respectively. Altogether, there were ninety-six inexperienced legislators in the house. Only thirteen Populists and twelve Republicans had served in a previous legislature. Taking all factions together, there were twenty-nine experienced legislators; only twenty-five of these had served in the preceding house. This ranked the house of 1897 as the least experienced house since that of 1891.

37. *The Advocate,* Topeka, August 5, 1896.

38. *Ibid.*, December 2, 1896.

39. *Ibid.*, and December 9, 1896.

40. Wilson, *Eminent Men,* 203-05.

41. Topeka *Daily Capital,* January 21, 1897. Peffer's services were not entirely unappreciated; as a matter of fact praise was forthcoming from some unexpected sources: the *Capital* (February 12, 1897) quoted an article from the Philadelphia *Press* which said that Senator Peffer had won "the respect of all the members of the Senate." The *Press* noted that he had come "to Washington six years ago, in company with Jerry Simpson, the 'sockless statesman of Medicine Lodge,' and of the two he was considered the greater freak. Six years in the Senate has, however, changed the common opinion with regard to him. Instead of being a blatant demagogue and Populist fire-eater, he has turned out to be a very mild-mannered gentleman indeed, who has, of course, the crazy notions of the Populists, but whose presentation of these notions has been made in the prosiest, least sensational manner imaginable."

42. Coincidentally, the last edition of *The Advocate* published before Peffer assumed editorship (March 10, 1897) announced the death of Dr. Stephen McLallin. McLallin died on March 4. *The Advocate* spoke highly of his work, and well it might, for McLallin and his paper had been for five years the conscience and inspiration of Kansas Populism.

43. *House Journal, 1897,* 1262, 1302; *Senate Journal, 1897,* 1091, 1203.

44. Populist-Democrat-Silver Republican senators opposing the bill were: John Armstrong, engineer-farmer, Great Bend; W. B. Crossan, lawyer and Silver Republican nominated by the Populists, from Paola; Hugh Farrelly, a Demo-

cratic lawyer from Chanute; Frank Field, cattle and grain shipper from Pretty
Prairie; George Hanna, Clay Center creamery merchant; W. A. Harris, engi-
neer-surveyor-farmer from Linwood; W. H. Ryan, merchant and cattle and
grain shipper from Brazilton; E. T. Shaffer, farmer and stock raiser from Ful-
ton; and Henry Zimmer, from Kansas City, whose occupation was market
gardening. See *The Kansas Blue Book, 1897*, and the Topeka *Advocate*,
March 31, 1897.
45. *House Journal, 1897,* 1170-71.
46. *Ibid.*
47. March 3, 1897.
48. *House Journal, 1897,* 33-34.
49. *Ibid.,* 908, 911; *Senate Journal, 1897,* 680; Topeka *Daily Capital*, February 24,
1897. Grant Wood Harrington, who had been Harris' private secretary for a
time, stated in an editorial, "The Harris bill did not contain a maximum rate,
but it gave the commissioners full authority to fix rates and then power to
enforce them." Harrington contended that this bill "was shot to pieces in the
Senate committee on railroads . . . ." See Harrington's editorial, first published
in the Hiawatha *Democrat*, in the Topeka *Daily Capital*, November 3, 1897.
50. Topeka *Daily Capital*, February 25, 1897.
51. *Senate Journal, 1897,* 680.
52. *House Journal, 1897,* 911.
53. Topeka *Daily Capital*, March 10, 1897.
54. Costigan's statement from an undated Topeka *Daily Capital* clipping, Kansas
Biographical Scrapbook (K.S.H.S.), C, IV, 255.
55. See John Dunsmore's letter to W. H. Sears, July 28, 1898, Sears Collection,
K.S.H.S. Archives.
56. Virginia Noah Gibson, "The Effect of the Populist Movement on Kansas State
Agricultural College," unpublished master's thesis, Kansas State College of
Agriculture and Applied Science, 1932, *passim.* See also the lengthy letter by
George T. Fairchild giving a full and objective account of what had transpired
at the college, which is contained in Topeka *Daily Capital*, September 10, 1897.
57. In defense of its actions the board made the following statement regarding
academic freedom: "We hold the principle of freedom of science equal in rank
and importance with the principles of freedom of thought, of speech, of the
press, and of the ballot. We note with deep concern the menace to this and
other forms of true freedom through the steady aggrandizement of power in
the hands of organized wealth. We find alleged economists in cases prosti-
tuting their science to the service of their masters, while men of unquestioned
attainments, who refuse to distort and conceal important truth, and to sell
their manhood for bread, are tried for economic heresy, or dismissed on
spurious pretexts, and practically blacklisted; a subservient press concealing,
condoning, or applauding the act." *Minutes of the Board of Regents*, Kansas
State Agricultural College, Vol. B, 160-63, as quoted in the appendix of *ibid.*
93-102.
58. April 12, 1897.
59. April 13, 1897.
60. Gibson, "The Effect of the Populist Movement on Kansas State Agricultural
College," 83-85.

Chapter XII

1. Letter from W. H. Bennington to J. S. Ensminger, Topeka *Daily Capital*, February 9, 1897. See also J. S. Ensminger's letter to Governor John Leedy, *ibid.*, February 7, 1897.

2. Anticipating an endless barrage of attacks on the governor, the Topeka *Capital* began numbering its disclosures. On February 14, 1897, that paper ran an article entitled "Second Shot at Governor Leedy," in which Populist Railroad Commissioner Joseph G. Lowe took the governor to task for his selection of William Rogers for appointment to the board of regents of the state agricultural college. On February 16 the same paper published a protest from Washington County Populists which accused Rogers of being "loud mouthed, indecent, and vulgar," "obscene in his remarks," "wholly unfit," "addicted to the use of liquors," a "blasphemer and an infidel," and an "outcast socially." The appointment of Rogers was confirmed despite the attack.

3. See Scott, "A Congressman and His Constituents," *passim.*

4. Simpson and McKay both held shares in the Barber County *Index*. Soon after the campaign of 1896, the rivalry between the two culminated in a struggle, initiated by Simpson, to gain control of the paper. The McKay faction won the fight and the war was on in earnest. *Ibid.;* see also Medicine Lodge *Cresset,* March 19, 1897; Barber County *Index,* March 17, 1897.

5. Topeka *Daily Capital,* January 26, 1897.

6. *Ibid.,* April 10, 1897. While visiting Kansas in April and July, 1897, Mary Elizabeth Lease stated on both occasions that she believed the former governor was "the victim of a Breidenthal conspiracy" aimed at destroying "Lewelling's political future." See *ibid.,* April 27, 1897, and July 15, 1897.

7. *Ibid.,* April 11, 1897.

8. *Ibid.,* April 6, 1897.

9. Medicine Lodge *Cresset,* July 30, 1897; Barber County *Index,* May 19, 1897. Despite an intensive search, no material was found to support the accusation that Jerry Simpson engaged in such extensive lobbying activities. Although it is of course possible that Simpson was guilty as charged, it seems more likely that he used his influence to obtain passage of the senate railroad bill in the house, fearing its defeat would mean no railroad legislation. Simply to advise for or against a particular matter would be interpreted as lobbying. On the other hand, the record does reveal that in one appearance before the legislature Simpson advised the legislators to maintain "a place in the skirmish line of all reforms," as well as to "see that the eternal agitation is kept up . . . ." See the Topeka *Daily Capital,* January 30, 1897.

10. The investigating committee's proceedings are reported in the April-May-June 1897 issues of *ibid.*

11. Senator Householder later remarked in a speech delivered in Baxter Springs (quoted in *ibid.,* October 12, 1897), "Thirteen Populist Senators besides Harris voted for the Harris freight rate bill. The others could not be bought." Several Populist senators, L. D. Lewelling, Frank Fields, and George Hanna for example, were subsequently called before their county committees to explain their votes. As a matter of fact, the Populist central committee of Dickinson County called upon Senator George Hanna to submit his resignation. See *The*

Advocate, Topeka, June 9, 1897; Topeka *Daily Capital,* April 7, 1897, and May 16, 1897.

12. Topeka *Daily Capital,* April 21, 1897.
13. *Ibid.,* April 11, 1897.
14. *The Advocate,* Topeka, April 7, November 24, and December 15, 1897.
15. Topeka *Daily Capital,* February 3, 1898.
16. Clipping dated December, 1896, in Kansas Biographical Scrapbook (K.S.H.S.) L, I, 189.
17. *The Advocate and News,* Topeka, February 9, 1898.
18. Governor Leedy came in for a good deal of criticism from temperance elements after he delivered a noncommittal address before the State Temperance Union which met in Topeka on May 18, 1897. See the Topeka *Daily Capital,* May 19, 1897.
19. Taylor Riddle was Frank Doster's brother-in-law. Breidenthal, who was then rather quietly exerting his efforts in opposition to Governor Leedy's renomination, resigned and the central committee selected Riddle. Taylor Riddle was elected to the position in June, 1898. Breidenthal's actions at this point are not clear as revealed in accessible documents. The Leedy administration, however, had sponsored and obtained salary cuts almost across the board. Breidenthal's salary as bank commissioner was dropped from $2500 to $2000; this may have been at the root of the matter. Breidenthal's only comment at the time was: "This knocks me out." G. C. Clemens protested the cut rather vigorously, and apparently a number of the individuals affected felt that favoritism had been shown in the matter. See the Topeka *Daily Capital,* February 19, 21, 23, 1897.
20. *Ibid.,* January 1, 1898.
21. The official correspondence of the Leedy administration is quite skimpy and badly kept; after the outbreak of the Spanish-American War, matters relating to the mobilization, in some fashion or another, practically pushed everything else aside.
22. Newspaper clipping dated February 18, 1898, which is contained in Kansas Biographical Scrapbook (K.S.H.S.), D, II, 20.
23. *Ibid.*
24. Topeka *Daily Capital,* March 30, and July 2, 1898; Kansas Collected Speeches and Pamphlets (K.S.H.S.), XV; Senator Harris to John P. St. John, *State Journal,* Topeka, July 8, 1898.
25. Kansas Collected Speeches and Pamphlets (K.S.H.S.), XV, 1.
26. *Ibid.,* 3. Richard Hofstadter has written that Populists "distinguished between wars for humanity and wars of conquest. The first of these they considered legitimate, but naturally they had difficulty in discriminating between the two . . . ." Hofstadter has also written that the Populists were "profoundly nationalistic and bellicose," and that the jingoism of the 1890s was nowhere "stronger than among the Populists." The literature of Kansas Populism does demonstrate that many Populists did indeed distinguish between "wars for humanity and wars of conquest"; however, the record also demonstrates that most of them had very little difficulty in "discriminating between the two." They recognized imperialism and militarism when they saw it. There were leaders among the Kansas Populists whose attitudes concerning the actions of

Spain in Cuba verged on the jingoistic, but to say that this sentiment was stronger among the Populists than among other elements, Republicans for example, would be an overbold estimate of the situation if not a complete distortion of the facts. See Hofstadter, *Age of Reform* (New York, 1955), 85-88.

27. Topeka *Daily Capital*, February 18, 1898.

28. Apparently Ed Little, Leedy's secretary and a recent recruit from Republican ranks, urged the appointment of Funston. William H. Sears, Senator W. A. Harris' secretary, was slated for the appointment until a "false" newspaper story from Washington, D.C., under the name of Senator W. A. Harris, was published criticizing Governor Leedy's handling of the mobilization. Frederick Funston went on of course to compile an outstanding military record. On this matter see, in particular, a letter by W. A. Sears to Richard J. Oulahan, February 27, 1917, Sears Collection, K.S.H.S. Archives.

29. Topeka *Daily Capital*, April 28, 1898.

30. *Ibid.*, issues of May 1897; in particular that of May 15, 1897.

31. Wright to W. H. Sears, August 11, 1898, Sears Collection, K.S.H.S. Archives. For the record, Isom Wright was a college graduate and former-teacher-turned-farmer from Great Bend.

32. Ex-Senator William Peffer was a prominent example. See Peffer's *Americanism and the Philippines* (Topeka, 1900). Peffer had actually left the Populist party by the summer of 1898 when he became the Prohibition party candidate for governor. E. R. Ridgely was perhaps the outstanding "big policy" advocate among the party's leaders in 1898-1900. See especially his speech in the house on June 15, 1898, Kansas Collected Speeches and Pamphlets (K.S.H.S.), XV, 13; Ridgely to W. H. Sears, October 20, 1899, Sears Collection, K.S.H.S. Archives.

33. Kansas Collected Speeches and Pamphlets (K.S.H.S.), XV, 11, and 16. See also the newspaper clipping dated February 3, 1899, by John Davis, in his Scrapbook (K.S.H.S.), K, 54-55, and the Topeka *Daily Capital*, January 21, 1899, for Senator Harris' position on the Philippines; also a letter from W. A. Harris to Annie Diggs in the Topeka *Daily Capital*, July 2, 1898. See the anti-imperialistic poem by Mrs. Diggs entitled "Little Brown Brothers," which a newspaper of September 9, 1898, said had created "much comment, favorable and unfavorable," in Kansas Biographical Scrapbook (K.S.H.S.), D, III, 14. See also the Leavenworth *Standard*, August 1, 1900, Kansas Biographical Scrapbook (K.S.H.S.), H, II, 102-03, for the views of Senator W. A. Harris. For substantial evidence demonstrating Republican support for an imperialistic and militaristic foreign policy see the speeches of Scott Hopkins, E. W. Hoch, and John Dawson in *The Kansas Day Club Addresses* for January 29, 1900. Dawson's, entitled "The White Man's Burden" (pp. 448-53), is especially revealing.

34. Topeka *Daily Capital*, June 17, 1898.

35. *Ibid.*, June 14, 1898; Kansas Scrapbook Biography (K.S.H.S.), L, III, 303.

36. *People's Party Campaign Handbook* (Hiawatha, 1898). See also Malin, *A Concern About Humanity*, 45-6.

37. Daniels to ex-Senator William A. Peffer, *Independent News*, Girard, April 24, 1898; Topeka *Daily Capital*, September 8, 1898.

38. A comparison of this 1899 house revealed nothing especially different from

NOTES TO PAGES 215-217

that of 1897. Forty-four was the median age for the Republicans; forty-three for the Populists. Thirty-six of eighty-nine (40.4 percent) Republicans were fifty or more years old; only six of twenty-two (22.2 percent) Populists were fifty or older. The oldest Republican in the house was seventy-three and the youngest twenty-one; the oldest Populist was sixty-five and the youngest thirty-two. Populists and Republicans, in greater numbers, claimed states like Ohio, Indiana, Pennsylvania, Illinois, and New York as their place of birth, although the Populists included more natives from Kentucky, Missouri, and Iowa. The median year of entry of the Republicans into the state was 1877; for the Populists it was 1878-79. Most of the Republicans were business or professional men (65 percent), while only twenty-three of eighty-nine were engaged strictly in farming and/or stock raising. The typical Populist was a farmer and/or stock raiser (fourteen of twenty-three), although one out of three was a business or professional man. Four out of every ten Republicans were college graduates; whereas three of every ten Populists were college graduates. There were fewer former third-party men among the Populists of this house: only one of twelve was listed as such; while eight of twelve had been Republicans until 1890 and three of twelve had been Democrats. Compiled primarily from *The Kansas Blue Book* (Topeka, 1899). For a composite comparison of the legislatures of 1891, 1893, 1895, 1897, and 1899, in chart form, see Appendix IV.

39. Hein and Sullivant, *Kansas Votes: Gubernatorial Elections;* and Cabe and Sullivant, *Kansas Votes: National Elections.*

40. *House Journal, 1898-99 (Special Session),* 45, and 175; *Senate Journal, 1898-99 (Special Session),* 125.

41. Malin, *A Concern About Humanity,* 210.

42. See *The Advocate,* Topeka, August 25, 1897, for the text of Peffer's speech. See also his article entitled "The Passing of the People's Party," *The North American Review,* CLXVI (January, 1898), 12-23, for additional proof that Peffer was expounding undiluted Populist doctrine.

43. Letter dated September 6, 1897, *The Advocate,* Topeka, September 15, 1897.

44. Letter dated September 22, 1897, *ibid.,* September 29, 1897.

45. For material relative to Annie Diggs' position see the Topeka *Advocate,* October 6, 1897, and the Topeka *State Journal,* January 6, 1898. Two years later Mrs. Diggs was asked by a reporter if she thought the Democrats were "sincere in their advocacy of so many of the principles originally enunciated by the Populists?" She replied: "Oh, my! no, I don't think a great majority of them are. But the spirit is spreading and they may come around to it after awhile." See the Kansas City *Journal,* August 1, 1900.

46. Malin, *A Concern About Humanity,* 44; *The Advocate and News,* Topeka, January 12, 1898; Clemens' Notebooks, K.S.H.S. Archives. These notebooks were undated and uncatalogued and, apparently, undiscovered before the writer came upon them. One of these contains this remark: "So numerous and so urgent have become the requests from Populist comrades that I shall take the initiative in organizing a socialist party with which true Populists may unite and once more find a congenial political home that I can no longer resist. I must forsake the fusionists or the Socialists—it is no longer possible for them to remain together."

47. Clemens' Notebooks, K.S.H.S. Archives.

48. *The Advocate and News,* Topeka, February 23, 1898.

49. *Ibid.,* October 19, 1898.

50. *Ibid.,* October 12, 1898.

51. Eugene V. Debs spoke in Topeka on February 4, 1898, to a crowd estimated to be 2,000. *Ibid.,* February 9, 1898.

52. *Ibid.,* January 12, 1898; "The Passing of the People's Party," *North American Review,* CLXVI (January, 1898). Peffer's antipathy toward the Democratic party had its roots deep in the sectional conflict, roots that were nurtured by strong prohibitionist feeling and, later, by opposition to the Democratic party's stand on imperialism. He maintained, however, that it was based primarily upon the allegation that the party was a state's rights party and foe of centralized power which was antithetic to the aims of the reform movement.

53. *The Advocate and News,* Topeka, June 15, 1898.

54. Kansas City *Star,* May 3, 1901.

55. Letter to ex-Senator William A. Peffer, *Independent News,* Girard, April 24, 1898.

56. Topeka *Daily Capital,* September 8, 1898.

57. Newspaper clipping dated November 11, 1898, Kansas Biographical Scrapbook (K.S.H.S.), B, II, 305-06. Breidenthal had contributed as much as anyone to the eclipse of the very principle he was now lamenting. Professor James C. Malin has written that Breidenthal "might be characterized as a contradictory multiple personality—a curious blend of idealism and the crude realism of the 1890's." See *A Concern About Humanity,* 212. Certainly his actions are difficult to comprehend. A contemporary opponent of Breidenthal noted what he called the "curious contradiction of the man's nature" in the following commentary: "Believing in the most extreme forms of socialism, Breidenthal has in his official relations stood steadfastly for the property rights and privileges of the individual. He has made a bank commissioner acceptable to the state banks which come under his supervision . . . . The truth is that Mr. Breidenthal has enforced the state supervision of banks, very closely following the rigid regulations of the government. He has made the state banks as nearly like the national banks as the state laws would warrant. And yet in theory he believes the national banks are all wrong, and if he had his way he would wipe them out." The explanation for Breidenthal's actions, according to this observer, was that he was "most radical in his socialistic beliefs and most conservative in his application of them." See the Topeka *Mail and Breeze,* February 10, 1899.

58. Topeka *Mail and Breeze,* May 5, 1899.

59. Topeka *State Journal,* November 15, 1899.

60. See Ross E. Paulson's forthcoming study entitled *Radicalism and Reform: The Vrooman Family and American Social Thought, 1837-1937* (Lexington, 1968?).

61. Topeka *State Journal,* April 8, 1915.

62. Carl S. Vrooman, *Taming the Trusts* (Topeka, 1900), 23-24, 69.

63. *Ibid.,* 75.

64. Breidenthal to J. C. Rupenthal, February 9, 1900, Rupenthal Collection, K.S.H.S. Archives.

65. Lewelling to W. H. Sears, March 27, 1900, Sears Collection, K.S.H.S. Archives. The stationery upon which this letter was written identified Lewelling as manager of the Hurd Land Company in Wichita, which was serving as "immigration agents" for the railroad named above. Sears had written Lewelling seeking support for his bid for the nomination as lieutenant governor. Lewelling declined the support by stating: "I am taking very little interest in politics this year, as I am too much occupied with business." See also a newspaper clipping contained in Kansas Biographical Scrapbook (K.S.H.S.), L, III, 308.

66. Kansas City *Journal,* July 10, 1900; Kansas Biographical Scrapbook (K.S.H.S.), L, II, 40.

67. Kansas Biographical Scrapbook (K.S.H.S.), L, II, 50. Actually Lewelling's turn toward socialism was no sudden departure. As early as October, 1897, the former governor readily admitted that he was a socialist. He had said then, however, that he doubted "the advisability of going as fast as the extreme socialists want to go." "The people are not yet ready to accept socialism. They must be educated. I know that socialism will triumph some time in this country, but it must come by degrees." See the Topeka *Daily Capital,* October 20, 1897.

68. Topeka *Daily Capital,* March 18, April 1, 9, 27, July 15, 1897.

69. Leavenworth *Times,* September 22, 1900; newspaper clipping dated September 27, 1904, in Kansas Biographical Scrapbook (K.S.H.S.), I, 130-31.

70. Clemens' Notebooks, K.S.H.S. Archives.

71. Breidenthal to J. C. Rupenthal, January 3, 1901, Rupenthal Collection, K.S.H.S. Archives.

72. Newspaper clipping, Kansas Biographical Scrapbook (K.S.H.S.), B, III, 309.

73. Topeka *Daily Capital,* September 24, 1900.

74. Newspaper clipping in Kansas Biographical Scrapbook (K.S.H.S.), D, II, 26-29. See also the editorials of the *Farmers Advocate,* Topeka, which was edited by Annie Diggs from September 13, 1901, to about February 21, 1902.

75. Breidenthal's vote was 164,793; Republican W. E. Stanley's vote was 181,897 (51.9 percent). Hein and Sullivant, *Kansas Votes: Gubernatorial Elections;* Cabe and Sullivant, *Kansas Votes: National Elections.*

76. Breidenthal to J. C. Rupenthal, January 3, 1901, Rupenthal Collection, K.S.H.S. Archives. Regarding Breidenthal's remark that the Socialists wanted to accomplish "everything at once," the following commentary by G. C. Clemens is most revealing: "While socialism is the end they keep always in view, Socialists recognize that until that end be attained they must live in the world as it is, changed by such means as they can use to make it more bearable in the meantime. A good Christmas dinner is a delicious thing to look forward to, but the breakfast of this morning must be such as we can get. I shall not refuse to eat ham and eggs to-day to have turkey with dressing sometime next year." Clemens' Notebooks, K.S.H.S. Archives.

77. The Rupenthal Collection in the K.S.H.S. Archives contains a number of letters relative to Breidenthal's business venture.

78. See, for example, the correspondence and material of the party's Legislative Bureau relative to the 1902 campaign, which is contained in the K.S.H.S. Archives.

79. Ottawa *Journal and Triumph,* July 19, 1894. W. P. Harrington's thesis was

published in the *Collections of the Kansas State Historical Society,* XVI, 403-50, as "The Populist Party in Kansas."

80. W. P. Harrington to Grant Wood Harrington, September 24, 1902, Correspondence of the Democratic and People's Party Legislative Bureau, K.S.H.S. Archives.

Chapter XIII

1. Jerry Simpson, "The Plain People," *The Illustrated American* (September 11, 1897), 332.

2. *The Advocate,* Topeka, February 16, 1895.

3. Kansas City *Star,* June 2, 1901. See also the *Farmers Advocate,* Topeka, December 20, 1901.

4. Topeka *Daily Capital,* May 3, 1907. See also Kansas Biographical Scrapbook (K.S.H.S.), D, V, 141. Mrs. Diggs warmed very slowly to President Roosevelt; she seriously questioned his basic instincts. In 1902, she made this revealing appraisal of the president: "More and more as the days go by I am impressed by an apparent hardness of character in Mr. Roosevelt; a lack of fine sensibility, an absence of warm, human sympathy, without which even the sturdiest, bravest man falls short of greatness." See the *Farmers Advocate,* Topeka, January 10, 1902.

5. Topeka *Daily Capital,* January ?, 1906 [1908?], Kansas Biographical Scrapbook (K.S.H.S.), D, V, 138. Mrs. Diggs edited the *Farmers Advocate* from 1901 to 1902; from 1902 to 1904 she toured Europe. In 1912 she published a work entitled *Bedrock: Education and Employment, the Foundation of the Republic* (Detroit, 1912) in which her main concern was the creation of a bureau of employment. A typical passage reads: "The republic is not safe with an *ignorant* citizenship. Likewise, the republic is not safe with an *unemployed* citizenship. It will not do to leave education to the uncertainties or the fluctuations of private enterprise. . . . Likewise, an employed citizenship is so vital to national health and national progress that there should speedily be set in motion the machinery of organization to rescue industrialism from the disastrous fluctuations and dehumanizing uncertainty of our private, personal and unscientific regime." See also Topeka *Daily Capital,* April 13, 1904; *ibid.,* clipping in Kansas Biographical Scrapbook (K.S.H.S.), D, V, 138.

6. Myron C. Scott, "A Congressman and His Constituents," 176-78. In a recent article, actually published after this work was on its way to the editor, Karel Denis Bicha ("Jerry Simpson: Populist Without Principle," *The Journal of American History,* LIV [September, 1967], 291-306) presents a most unfavorable portrait of this Populist congressman. Even though the interpretation were one he had heard on numerous occasions from 1886 to 1900, it seems certain that Jerry Simpson would have been most exasperated to learn that he "became a Populist without principle"; or, better yet, that "he rarely possessed the courage of his convictions." Simpson most likely would not even be willing to grant the interpretation of himself as a pragmatic political type—as this critic of Bicha's interpretation would see his actions—but to say that he was or "became a Populist *without principle*" who "rarely possessed the courage of *his convictions*" is saying something quite different, even if we ignore

the apparent contradiction (italics added). It is an interpretation that the historical record will not support. If Professor Bicha were to remove Simpson's activities from the historical vacuum within which they are considered in this article, his alleged deviation from alleged or assumed Populist dogma or doctrine would fade away. In the final analysis, the Populist leadership and movement was notable for a great variety of thought and personality, and the personality of Jerry Simpson probably revealed this Populist trait more clearly than any other. By all means, Jerry Simpson should not be taken to task for his alleged betrayal of something that never existed—a fixed Populist ideology.

7. Interview in Chanute, Kansas, Kansas City *Star*, May 9, 1905.
8. Kansas City *Times*, May 2, 1905.
9. Kansas City *Star*, August 4, 1905.
10. Topeka *Daily Capital*, October 4, 1905; Kansas Biographical Scrapbook (K.S.H.S.), S, IX, 227.
11. The numerous volumes of the Kansas Biographical Scrapbook contained in the K.S.H.S. Library served as the chief source for this information.
12. Topeka *Daily Capital*, December 13, 1901.
13. *Ibid.*, May 11, 1906.
14. Hein and Sullivant, *Kansas Votes: Gubernatorial Elections*.
15. Kansas City *Star*, August 12, 1909.
16. Topeka *State Journal*, November 2, 1906.
17. Kansas City *Star*, September 6, 1903; Kansas Biographical Scrapbook (K.S.H.S.), P, XI, 106.
18. Topeka *State Journal*, June 27, 1907; Kansas Biographical Scrapbook (K.S.H.S.), P, XII, 197.
19. Topeka *Daily Capital*, April 11, 1911; Kansas Biographical Scrapbook (K.S.H.S.), P, XIV, 26.
20. See her book entitled *The Problem of Civilization Solved*.
21. Newspaper clipping dated September 27, 1904, Kansas Biographical Scrapbook (K.S.H.S.), L, I, 131.
22. In a 1905 article she was quoted as saying that she no longer was interested in woman suffrage. She said, "You know I never went in much for that sort of thing. Women have enough to be thankful for that they are Americans." See the newspaper clipping dated September 6, 1905, Kansas Biographical Scrapbook (K.S.H.S.), L, VI, 197. In 1915 Mrs. Lease stated: "Only a few people in each state have risen to normal civilization. The many are endowed with citizenship which they are not capable of, or which they do not use intelligently." See a letter to editor, August 31, 1915; Topeka *Daily Capital*, September 5, 1915.
23. Kansas City *Star*, October 25, 1914; Kansas Biographical Scrapbook (K.S.H.S.), L, VI, 202.
24. See especially her claim relative to the naming of the People's party, Kansas City *Star*, October 25, 1914. Perhaps she was not too far off in her analysis of the quality of Kansas Populist leaders: she rated Frank Doster as the most outstanding of them all. "He was head and shoulders above the rest of us," she said. "Unfortunately we did not understand him or appreciate him at his full value then." Jerry Simpson "was overrated. There was not a great deal of depth to him. He possessed a combination of Canadian and Irish humor

and it was with this that he moved his audiences, and he understood the tricks of politics and was quick enough to make the most of his opportunities." William A. Peffer "was a good man and an honest man, but utterly lacking in brilliancy and without the first suggestion of magnetism." She had rather special praise for John W. Leedy. His name, recalled, brought forth this response: "Ah, there was a sterling honest man. He was not with us at the start, but . . . he made good. John Leedy was a man who could not be tempted by money or office. He was tried and stood the test." See *ibid.*

25. Topeka *Daily Capital*, November 19, 1902.

26. *Ibid.*, June 13, 1901; see also Kansas City *Journal*, June 14, 1901, and Kansas Biographical Scrapbook (K.S.H.S.), D, II, 232.

27. Doster retained his interest in politics throughout. In 1914 he made an unsuccessful bid to obtain the Democratic nomination for U.S. senator. Still later he served as legal advisor to Democratic Governor Jonathan Davis. See Topeka *Daily Capital*, February 26, 1933; Michael Brodhead, "Judge Frank Doster," unpublished doctoral dissertation (University of Minnesota, 1967).

28. Doster to H. S. Martin (chairman of the Democratic state committee), September 21, 1908, Special Collection, K.S.H.S. Archives.

29. Kansas City *Journal*, September 10, 1910; Republican Party Clippings (K.S.H.S.), VII, 295-96.

BIBLIOGRAPHY

Newspapers

Unquestionably, the most important source for the preparation of this study has been the extensive collection of state and county newspapers housed in the Kansas State Historical Society. These public journals contain a wealth of primary material that reveals the day-by-day historical record of Kansas politics in the 1890s as nothing else can. Numerous newspapers were consulted; some were studied intensively, and others at random. The list that follows includes those that were especially useful in this endeavor.

The Advocate, Meriden, 1889-1890.
The Advocate, Topeka, 1890-1897.
The Advocate and News, Topeka, 1897-1900.
Emporia *Gazette*, 1895-1896.
Farmers Advocate, Topeka, 1901-1904.
Kansas Chief, Troy, 1890-1896.
Kansas City *Star*, 1890-1896.
Kansas Commoner, Wichita, 1890-1894.
Kansas Democrat, Topeka, 1890-1896.
Kansas Farmer, Topeka, 1883-1891.
Kansas People, Osage City, 1888-1890.
Lawrence *Journal*, 1890-1894.
Lawrence *World*, 1890-1894.
Modern Light, Columbus, 1890-1894.
New Era, Topeka, 1893-1895.
Newton *Kansas Commoner*, 1889-1890.
Ottawa *Journal and Triumph*, 1890-1894.
The Peoples Herald, Lyndon, 1890-1900.
Pittsburg *Kansan*, 1889-1894.
The Populist, Topeka, 1892-1895.
Topeka *Daily Capital*, 1889-1900.
Topeka *Mail and Breeze*, 1898-1900.
Topeka *State Journal*, 1890-1895.
Wichita *Daily Eagle*, 1889-1894.

Manuscripts, Scrapbooks, and Collections

Arnold, James (M. E. Lease). Manuscript Biography of M. E. Lease, K.S.H.S. Archives.

Biographical Circulars. K.S.H.S. Library.

G. C. Clemens' Notebooks. K.S.H.S. Archives.

Collection of Newspaper Cartoons Dealing with the Populists. K.S.H.S. Library.

Correspondence of the People's Party and Democratic State Committees. Legislative Bureau, Campaign of 1902, K.S.H.S. Archives.

Davis, John. Personal Library. 32 vols., Nebraska State Historical Society Library.

————. Scrapbooks of Clippings, Mainly About the Populist Party and Davis' Activities. 13 vols., A-M (J missing), 1886-1899, K.S.H.S. Library.

Farmers' Alliance Clippings. K.S.H.S. Library.

Harrington, Grant Wood. Typed manuscript, "As Jerry Told It," June 30, 1938, K.S.H.S. Archives.

Kansas Biographical Scrapbooks. K.S.H.S. Library.

Kansas Collected Speeches and Pamphlets. K.S.H.S. Library, especially vols. IX, XIV, and XXII.

Kansas Governor Messages. K.S.H.S. Library.

Kansas Senate and House Journals, Legislatures of 1891, 1893, 1895, 1897, 1899.

Governor Leedy's Letters. K.S.H.S. Archives.

Lewelling, L. D. Manuscript of a Speech at Huron Place, July 28, 1894, K.S.H.S. Archives.

Peffer, Douglas M., compiler. Cartoons and Scrapbooks Relating to W. A. Peffer and the Populist Party, 1891-1896, 3 vols., K.S.H.S. Library.

People's Party Clippings. K.S.H.S. Library.

J. C. Rupenthal, Jr., Collection. K.S.H.S. Archives.

William Henry Sears Collection. K.S.H.S. Archives.

Sears, William Henry. Scrapbook of Miscellaneous Clippings, K.S.-H.S. Library.

Pamphlets, Broadsides, and Circulars

Anti-Fusion Populist State Central Committee. *Final Address to Populists.* People's Party Pamphlets, K.S.H.S., Vol. VII.

Baker, E. R. *Money Monopoly: A Treatise of Money and Finance.* Winfield: Vincent, 1890.

———. *Subject of Money Considered from the Standpoint of Law, Science, History, Reason, with Numerous Quotations from the Best Authorities in Europe and America.* Winfield: Vincent, 1887.

Campbell, G. *Island Home.* Oswego, 1894. People's Party Pamphlets, K.S.H.S., Vol. VI.

Clemens, G. C. *An Appeal to True Populists.* No imprint. People's Party Pamphlets, K.S.H.S., Vol. VI.

———. *Common-sense View of the Anarchist Case with Some Points Apparently Unnoticed by Others.* 1894. People's Party Pamphlets, K.S.H.S., Vol. I.

———. *Damnable! Police Infamies of a Single Week.* 1887. Broadside contained in the K.S.H.S. Library.

———. *The Labor Problem, Stated for the Busy and the Tired.* Enterprise: Anti-Monopolist Job Office, 1887. People's Party Pamphlets, K.S.H.S., Vol. I.

———. *A Primer of Socialism.* Topeka: Western Socialist News, 1900?

———. *Ultimate Aim of Trades-Unions.* 1889. People's Party Pamphlets, K.S.H.S., Vol. I.

Cobun, M. W. *Treatise on U.S. Money.* Great Bend: Beacon, 1892. People's Party Pamphlets, K.S.H.S., Vol. I.

Corning, Eva. *A Tribute to the Moving Forces of Reform of 1892.* Circular, K.S.H.S.

Culverwell, James. *History of the National Army of Rescue.* Dentonia, 1888. People's Party Pamphlets, K.S.H.S., Vol. I.

Daniels, Percy. *Conquering March of Capital. Man vs. Mammon with Petition to and Action of the Kansas Legislature.* 1897. People's Party Pamphlets, K.S.H.S., Vol. VI.

———. *A Crisis for the Husbandman.* Girard: Herald, 1889. People's Party Pamphlets, K.S.H.S., Vol. III.

———. *Cutting the Gordian Knot.* Pittsburg: Kansan Print, 1896.

———. *Free Coinage of American Labor into Honest Dollars.* 1895. People's Party Pamphlets, K.S.-H.S., Vol. III.

———. *A Lesson of To-Day and a Question of To-Morrow.* Girard:

Western Herald, 1892. Speech delivered by Percy Daniels in Girard, Kansas, on October 1, 1892. People's Party Pamphlets, K.S.H.S., Vol. III.

————. *The Midnight Ride of Paul Revere*. Pittsburg, n.p., 1896.

————. *Sunflower Tangle over Problems of Taxation*. Topeka: Hamilton, 1894. People's Party Pamphlets, K.S.H.S., Vol. III.

————. *Swollen Fortunes and the Problems of the Unemployed*. 1908. People's Party Pamphlets, K.S.H.S., Vol. VI.

Davis, Charles S. *The Relation of Political Parties to Woman Suffrage*. People's Party Pamphlets, K.S.-H.S., Vol. III.

Davis, John. *The Railroad Question*. Hutchinson News, 1890.

————, and Stockwell, L. A. *Public Ownership of Railroads*. Girard: Wayland, 1898.

Donnelly, Ignatius. *The Golden Bottle; or, The Story of Ephraim Benezet of Kansas*. New York and St. Paul: D. D. Merrill Company, 1892.

Dunning, N. A. *An Appeal to Populists and a Defense of Mr. Thos. E. Watson*. 1896, K.S.H.S. folder.

Ernst, E. Z. *Progressive Hand Book of the Labor Exchange*. Olathe, 1894. People's Party Pamphlets, K.S.H.S., Vol. II.

Farrell, W. H. *The Crisis or the Way to Settle the Gold and Silver Question*. Revised edition. Leavenworth: Ketcheson, 1896. People's Party Pamphlets, K.S.H.S., Vol. V.

Fish, G. H. *Hew to the Line, A Master or Slave*. Winfield: Vincent, 1891. People's Party Pamphlets, K.S.H.S., Vol. VI.

Gleed, Charles Sumner. *A Bird's-eye View of the Political Situation in Kansas, with Special Reference to the People's Party*. Topeka: Republican State Headquarters, 1893.

Harman, Colfax B. *Shylock's Judgment*. Valley Falls: Harman, 1893. People's Party Pamphlets, K.S.H.S., Vol. I.

Harrington, Grant W. *People's Party Campaign Handbook, 1898*. People's Party State Central Committee. Hiawatha, 1898.

Hart, H. A., and Rhodybeck, L. K. *Pointers! Being a Brief Digest of Debt, Interest, Usury, Mortgage and Foreclosure, with Comments and Chapter on Equity*. Winfield: Vincent, 1889. People's Party Pamphlets, K.S.-H.S., Vol. I.

Hello Kansas! The Fall of Ingalls, and What Happened . . . by a Tired Man. Topeka: Crane & Company, 1900.

History of the Famous Coffeyville Dynamite Outrage. Winfield: Nonconformist, 1889. People's Party Pamphlets, K.S.H.S., Vol. I.

Hoch, E. W. *The Last War, A Bloodless Battle for Constitutional Government*. Topeka: Republican State Headquarters, 1893.

Holden, J. D. *Free Freight and Government Railways: A Proposition to Restore to Society Essential Rights of Which It Has Been Wrongfully Divested; and to Make Men Generally the Beneficiaries of Government, instead of Its Victim*. 1891. People's Party Pamphlets, K.S.H.S., Vol. I.

————. *Is It Ignorance? Or is It Treachery? Are Our National Rulers the Tools, or, are They the Dupes of the Money Changers? The Law of Legal Tender*. Topeka: Bureau, 1893. People's

Party Pamphlets, K.S.H.S., Vol. I.

———. *Light on the Money Mystery*. Emporia: Reform Publishing Company, 1896. People's Party Pamphlets, K.S.H.S., Vol. V.

———. *Metallic Money and Hard Times. Why They Are Inseparable*. Emporia: Republican Steam Print, 1890. People's Party Pamphlets, K.S.H.S., Vol. VII.

———. *Solving the Money Mystery*. Emporia: Reform, 1896. People's Party Pamphlets, K.S.H.S., Vol. III.

———. *Why Times are Hard, or the Philosophy of Poverty*. Emporia: Reform Publishing Company, 1896. People's Party Pamphlets, K.S.H.S., Vol. V.

Howe, Samuel T. *Facts Concerning the Coinage of Gold and Silver in the United States*. Topeka, 1896.

———. *Record Evidence Showing the Mendacity of Populist Figures*. Republican State Central Committee. Topeka, 1894.

———. *Record of the Republican State Administration as Compared with Its Populist Predecessor*. Topeka, 1896.

Kent, W. H. *A Historical Review of the Causes and Issues that Led to the Overthrow of the Republican Party in Kansas in 1892, Including a History of the Exciting Events of the Legislative Imbroglio and Its Final Settlement, in which Bloodshed and Internecine War were Narrowly Averted*. Topeka: Daily Press, 1893.

King, S. S. *Bond-holders and Bread-winners*. Kansas City, 1892. People's Party Pamphlets, K.S.H.S., Vols. IV and V.

———. *A Few Financial Facts, Being a Series of Kindergarten Lessons on the Silver Question*. Kansas City: Callender, 1895. People's Party Pamphlets, K.S.H.S., Vol. IV.

———. *The Gulf Outlet, Showing the Advantages Coming to the People of the United States in Conducting Their Commerce*. Kansas City: Record, 1896.

———. *The Producer Consumed. Showing the Unfair and Unequal Distribution of Wealth Created in the U.S.* Kansas City: Lane, 1898. People's Party Pamphlets, K.S.H.S., Vol. VI.

———. *A Revelation: The True Story of a Bit of Kansas Politics Showing the Blackmail, Boodle and Betrayal Connected Therewith*. Kansas City: Lane, 1896.

———. *Seed Time and Harvest*. Kansas City, 1894. People's Party Pamphlets, K.S.H.S., Vol. 14.

Lathrop, James H. *A Memorial of the Late J. C. Hebbard, The Historian and Statistician*. Topeka, 1894.

———. *The Phonograph of Human Liberty*. Topeka, 1902.

———. *Voice of True Reform*. Topeka: Lathrop, 1891. People's Party Pamphlets, K.S.H.S., Vol. I.

Lease, Mary Elizabeth, and Brumbaugh, J. M. *Joint Debate on the Land, Finance and Transportation Questions*. Concordia, 1891.

Marshall, William V. *Cumulative Taxation*. Winfield: Vincent, 1890. People's Party Pamphlets, K.S.H.S., Vol. II.

———. *The Industrial Handbook: Embracing a Concise Statement of the Nature, Cause and Effects of Existing Industrial Ills; with a Practical Method of Relief*. Winfield: H. & L. Vincent Printers, 1890. People's Party Pamphlets, K.S.H.S., Vol. II.

Maxson, P. B., and Hebbard, J. C. *Hand-book Devoted Mainly to the Money Question and to Matters Connected with and Growing Out of the Same.* Topeka: Hamilton, 1891.

Middle-of-the-Road Populist State Committee, *Populism.* No imprint. People's Party Pamphlets, K.S.-H.S., Vol. VI.

Peffer, William Alfred. *Agricultural Depression; Causes and Remedies.* Report Submitted to the Senate Committee on Agriculture and Forestry. Washington: Government Printing Office, 1894.

———. *The Farmer's Side: His Troubles and Their Remedy.* New York: D. Appleton and Company, 1892.

———. *Tariff Manual; Being a Nonpartisan Statement of Facts and Figures Showing the Origin, History, Use, Object and Effect of Tariff Legislation in the United States.* Topeka: Hall, 1888.

People's Party, *Equal Rights to All.— Save the Homes of the People by Voting in the Interests of the Laboring Man.* Topeka: Alliance Publishing Company, 1890? Broadside.

People's Party State Central Committee. *Stubborn Facts.* Topeka: Advocate, 1894. People's Party Pamphlets, K.S.H.S., Vol. II.

Pigott, J. P. *What the Leaders Who Have Inaugurated the So-Called Populist Party Propose—Their Idea of Government—Paternalism of the Worst Kind, etc.* No imprint [1894].

Plain Talk About Free Silver, A Dialogue. A Republican answer to *Coin's Financial School.* No imprint. K.S.H.S.

Points for Populists as to Organizing the House of Representatives. People's Party Pamphlets, K.S.H.S., Vol. VI.

Populist Hand-book for Kansas. A Compilation from Official Sources of Some Facts for Use in Succeeding Political Campaigns. Vincent, 1891.

Populist State Central Committee. *People's Party Economy v. Republican Extravagance.* 1897. K.S.H.S.

Practical Hints to Kansas Populists About Methods of Work, by One of the Pops. Wellington: Voice Printery, 1895.

Republican Election Methods in Kansas General Election of 1892, and Legislative Investigations, Session of 1893. Topeka, 1893.

Ritchie, J. H. *Lecture on the Sub-Treasury Plan.* Winfield: Free Press, 1892. People's Party Pamphlets, K.S.H.S., Vol. I.

Sankey, R. A. *The Silver Question.* Wichita: Commoner, 1892. People's Party Pamphlets, K.S.H.S., Vol. V.

Scott, S. M. *Sub-Treasury Plan and Land and Loan System.* Topeka: Hamilton, 1891. People's Party Pamphlets, K.S.H.S., Vol. I.

Sherman, Porter. *Current Politics.* Kansas City, 1888. People's Party Pamphlets, K.S.H.S., Vol. I.

Smith, Carey. *Condition of Our Country, Its Cause and Remedy.* Dodge City: Times, 1888.

Thayer, A. F. *Tariff Truths.* Maple Hill: n.p., 1888. People's Party Pamphlets, K.S.H.S., Vol. I.

Tilton, W. A. *A Just Appraisement for Service: The Remedy for Strikes and Hard Times.* Register Print, 1897.

———. *Sound Money.* Oxford: n.p., n.d. People's Party Pamphlets, K.S.H.S., Vol. I.

————. *The Way Out, A Few Thoughts Relative to the Condition of the Labor and Producing Classes, and Its Connection, (As to Cause and Effect), with Past and Present Legislation; Embodying Suggestive Agencies by which Justice Shall be Accorded to All.* Winfield: H. & L. Vincent Printers, 1890. People's Party Pamphlets, K.S.H.S., Vol. I.

Turner, R. W. *Wheat is Up and Silver Down; Both are a Dollar a Bushel. The Argument of the Bimetallist is Exploded.* 1897. People's Party Pamphlets, K.S.H.S., Vol. V.

Vincent, W. D. *Government Loans to the People.* Clay Center: Argus, 1886. People's Party Pamphlets, K.S.H.S., Vol. I.

Vrooman, Carl S. *Taming the Trusts.* Topeka: Advocate, 1900. People's Party Pamphlets, K.S.H.S., Vol. V.

Waterbury, Edwin S. *The Legislative Conspiracy in Kansas. Court vs. Constitution. Who are the Anarchists?* No imprint.

Waterman, J. M. *Silver Threads Among the Gold. A Plea for Free Coinage of Silver.* Delphos: Republican Job Print, 1895. People's Party Pamphlets, K.S.H.S., Vol. II.

Waterman, Myron A. *Between Millstones.* Lawrence: Jeffersonian Publishing Company, n.d.

Welburn, J. B. *Heaven on Earth; Described and How Secured.* Atchison: Haskell, 1889. People's Party Pamphlets, K.S.H.S., Vol. II.

Wilson, Joseph. *John Davis, The People's Candidate for Congress in the Fifth District: The Next Congressman.* Marysville: The People's Advocate, 1890.

Wood, Samuel N. *Wood's Manifesto: An Address to the People of Kansas.* Topeka: Hamilton, 1891. People's Party Pamphlets, K.S.H.S., Vol. I.

Zercher, Daniel C. *Stubborn Facts in a Nutshell: Manifesto by the State Central Committee of the People's Party.* Topeka: Advocate Publishing Company, 1894. Published in English, German, and Swedish.

Autobiographies, Memoirs, and Reminiscences

McNeal, T. A. *When Kansas was Young.* New York: The Macmillan Company, 1922.

Murdock, Victor. *Folks.* New York: The Macmillan Company, 1921.

Rightmire, W. F. "The Alliance Movement in Kansas—Origin of the People's Party," in the *Transactions of the Kansas State Historical Society,* IX (1906), 1-8.

————. "Organization of the National People's Party," in *Transactions of the Kansas State Historical Society,* XVII (1926-1928).

White, William Allen. *Autobiography.* New York: The Macmillan Company, 1946.

Miscellaneous Books, Pamphlets, Official Proceedings, and Compilations

Adams, Zu. *Catalogue of the Kansas Territorial and State Documents in the Library of the State Historical Society, 1854-1898.* Topeka, 1900.

Andreas, A. T. *History of the State of Kansas.* Chicago: A. T. Andreas, 1883.

Baldwin, Sara Mullin, ed. *Illustriana Kansas: Biographical Sketches of Kansas Men and Women of Achievement Who Have Been Awarded Life Membership in Kansas Illustriana Society.* Hebron Nebraska; Illustriana Incorporated, 1933.

Bentley, O. H., ed. *History of Wichita and Sedgwick County, Kansas.* 2 vols., Chicago: C. F. Cooper and Company, 1910.

Biographical Directory of the American Congresses, 1774-1949. Washington, D.C.: Government Printing Office, 1950.

Biographical Record: This Volume Contains Biographical Sketches of Leading Citizens of Cowley County, Kansas. Chicago: Biographical Publishing Company, 1901.

Breidenthal, John W. *Agitate. Educate. Organize.* A price catalogue of reform literature. Topeka, 1896?

Cabe, June G., and Sullivant, Charles A. *Kansas Votes: National Elections, 1859-1956.* Lawrence: University of Kansas Governmental Research Center, 1957.

Connelley, William E., comp. *History of Kansas, State and People.* 3rd edition, 5 vols., Chicago: American Historical Society, 1928.

Declaration of Principles, Platform, Constitution and By-Laws of the National Citizens' Industrial Alliance and Proceedings of the National Assembly. Topeka: Alliance Tribune Job Print, 1891.

Ernst, E. Z. *The Organizer's Guide.* Olathe: Progressive Thought Company, 1897.

Goodspeed, Weston A., ed. *The Province and the States: A History of the Province of Louisiana Under France and Spain, and of the Territories and States of the United States Formed Therefrom.* 7 vols., Madison: The Western Historical Association, 1904.

The Farmers' Alliance History and Agricultural Digest. Washington, D.C.: Alliance Publishing Company, 1891.

Hein, Clarence J., and Sullivant, Charles A. *Kansas Votes: Gubernatorial Elections, 1859-1956.* Lawrence: University of Kansas Governmental Research Center, 1958.

Herringshaw, Thomas William, ed. *Herringshaw's American Statesman.* Chicago: American Publisher's Association, 1906.

History of Montgomery County, Kansas. Iola: Press of Iola Register, 1903.

History of Wyandotte County, Kansas and Its People. Chicago: Lewis Publishing Company, 1911.

Hollbaugh, E. F. *Biographical History of Cloud County, Kansas.* Logansport, Illinois: Wilson, Humphrey and Company, 1902-1903?

Hudson, James K. *Letters to Governor Lewelling.* Topeka, 1893.

Kansas: A Cyclopedia of State History, Embracing Events, Institutions, Industries, Counties, Cities, Towns, Prominent Persons, etc. Chicago: Lewis Publishing Company, 1906.

King, James L., ed. *History of Shawnee County, Kansas and Representative Citizens.* Chicago: Richmond and Arnold, 1905.

Lawrence—Today and Yesterday. Lawrence: Daily Journal World Publication, 1913.

Men of Affairs in Greater Kansas City 1912: A Newspaper Reference

Work. Kansas City: Kansas City Press Club, 1912.

Mitchell, William Ansel. *Linn County, Kansas: A History.* La Cygne: La Cygne Journal Presswork, 1928.

The National Cyclopaedia of American Biography, Being the History of the United States, as Illustrated in the Lives of the Founders, Builders, and Defenders of the Republic, and of the Men and Women who are Doing the Work and Moulding the Thought of the Present Time. Vol. XXI, New York: J. T. White and Company, 1931.

Owen, Jennie Small, annalist. *The Annals of Kansas, 1886-1925.* 2 vols., Topeka, n.d.

People's Party Club. *Constitution and By-Laws.* 1892. People's Party Pamphlets, K.S.H.S., Vol. VI.

Petersen, Svend. *A Statistical History of the American Presidential Elections.* New York: Frederick Ungar Publishing Company, 1963.

Populist State Central Committee. *People's Railroad Hand-book for Kansas.* 1892. K.S.H.S. Library.

Portrait and Biographical Record of Leavenworth, Douglas and Franklin Counties, Kansas. Chicago: Chapman Publishing Company, 1899.

Portrait and Biographical Record of Southeastern Kansas, Containing

Biographical Sketches of Prominent and Representative Citizens of the Counties, Together with Biographies and Portraits of all the Presidents of the United States and the Governors of the State of Kansas. Chicago: Biographical Publishing Company, 1894.

Proceedings of the Alliance Women's Association of Barton County, Kansas. Great Bend: Beacon Job Print, 1891. People's Party Pamphlets, K.S.H.S., Vol. V.

Reno County Public Schools Biennial Report and Course of Study, 1899-1900. Hutchinson: School and Fireside Printers, 1900.

A Twentieth Century History and Biographical Record of Crawford County, Kansas. Chicago: Lewis Publishing Company, 1905.

The United States Biographical Dictionary. Kansas Volume: Containing Accurately Compiled Biographical Sketches, into which is Woven the History of the State and Its Leading Interests. Chicago: S. Lewis and Company, 1879.

Wilson, Hill P. *A Biographical History of Eminent Men of the State of Kansas with Portraits Engraved Expressly for this Work.* Topeka: Hall Lithographing Company, 1901.

Books

Adams, Charles Francis, Jr., and Adams, Henry. *Chapters of Erie.* Ithaca: Cornell University Press, 1956.

Arnold, Thurman W. *The Folklore of Capitalism.* New Haven: Yale University Press, 1961.

Bellamy, Edward. *Looking Backward, 2000-1887.* Boston: Houghton Mifflin, 1890.

Beer, Thomas. *The Mauve Decade: American Life at the End of the 19th Century.* New York: Alfred A. Knopf, Inc., 1926.

Benson, Lee. *The Concept of Jacksonian Democracy.* Princeton: Princeton University Press, 1961.

Bogue, Allan G. *Money at Interest: The Farm Mortgage on the Middle Border.* Ithaca: Cornell University Press, 1955.

Boyle, James E. *Financial History of Kansas. University of Wisconsin Bulletin in Economics and Political Science.* Vol. V, no. 1, Madison, 1909.

Bright, John D., ed. *Kansas: The First Century.* 4 vols., New York: Lewis Historical Publishing Company, Inc., 1956.

Brinkley, Wilfred E. *American Political Parties: Their Natural History.* 3rd edition, New York: Alfred A. Knopf, 1958.

Brinton, Crane. *English Political Thought in the 19th Century.* Cambridge: Harvard University Press, 1949.

Buck, Paul H. *The Road to Reunion, 1865-1900.* Boston: Little, Brown and Company, 1937.

Buck, Solon J. *The Granger Movement: A Study of Agricultural Organization and Its Political, Economic, and Social Manifestations, 1870-1880.* Cambridge: Harvard University Press, 1913.

————. *The Agrarian Crusade: A Chronicle of the Farmer in Politics.* New Haven: Yale University Press, 1921.

Clemens, Gaspar Christopher. *The Dead Line, A Kansas Story of Society, Religion and Politics.* Topeka: Advocate Publishing Company, 1894.

Cochran, Thomas C. *Railroad Leaders 1845-1890: The Business Mind in Action.* Cambridge: Harvard University Press, 1953.

Commager, Henry Steele. *The American Mind: An Interpretation of American Thought and Character Since the 1880's.* New Haven: Yale University Press, 1950.

Connelley, William E. *Ingalls of Kansas: A Character Study.* Topeka: The Author, 1909.

————. *The Life of Preston B. Plumb, 1837-1891.* Chicago: Browne and Howard Company, 1913.

Davis, John. *Napoleon Bonaparte, A Sketch Written for a Purpose.* Boston: Arena, 1896.

Decker, Leslie E. *Railroads, Lands, and Politics: The Taxation of the Railroad Land Grants, 1864-1897.* Providence: Brown University Press, 1964.

Destler, Chester McArthur. *American Radicalism, 1865-1901: Essays and Documents.* New London: Connecticut College, 1946.

————. *Henry Demarest Lloyd and the Empire of Reform.* Philadelphia: University of Pennsylvania Press, 1963.

Diggs, Annie L. *Bedrock: Education and Employment, the Foundation of the Republic.* Detroit: The Social Center Publishing Company, 1912.

Durden, Robert F. *The Climax of Populism: The Election of 1896.* Lexington: University of Kentucky Press, 1965.

Emery, Sarah E. V. *Seven Financial Conspiracies Which Have Enslaved the American People.* Revised edition, Lansing: Smith, 1891.

Faulkner, Harold U. *Politics, Reform and Expansion, 1890-1900.* New York, Evanston and London: Harper and Row, 1963.

Fine, Sidney. *Laissez Faire and the General-Welfare State: A Study of Conflict in American Thought 1865-1901.* Ann Arbor: University of Michigan Press, 1957.

Fishlow, Albert. *American Railroads and the Transformation of the Ante-Bellum Economy.* Cambridge: Harvard University Press, 1965.

Fite, Gilbert C. *The Farmers' Frontier, 1865-1900.* New York: Holt, Rinehart and Winston, 1966.

Fogel, Robert. *Railroads and American Growth: Essays in Econometric History.* Baltimore: Johns Hopkins Press, 1964.

Friedman, Milton. *A Program for Monetary Stability.* New York: Fordham University Press, 1959.

Gabriel, Ralph Henry. *The Course of American Democratic Thought: An Intellectual History Since 1815.* New York: Ronald Press Co., 1940.

Gates, Paul W. *The Farmer's Age: Agriculture 1815-1860.* New York: Holt, Rinehart and Winston, 1960.

———. *Fifty Million Acres: Conflicts over Kansas Land Policy, 1854-1890.* Ithaca: Cornell University Press, 1954.

Ginger, Ray. *Age of Excess: The United States From 1877 to 1914.* New York: Macmillan, 1965.

———. *Altgeld's America: The Lincoln Ideal versus Changing Realities.* New York: Funk and Wagnalls, 1958.

———. *The Bending Cross: A Biography of Eugene Victor Debs.* New Brunswick: Rutgers University, 1949.

Glad, Paul W. *McKinley, Bryan and the People.* Philadelphia and New York: J. B. Lippincott Company, 1964.

———. *The Trumpet Soundeth: William Jennings Bryan and His Democracy, 1896-1912.* Lincoln: University of Nebraska, 1960.

Gleed, J. W. *Is New York More Civilized than Kansas?* New York: Forum Publishing Company, 1894.

Goldman, Eric F. *Rendezvous with Destiny: A History of Modern American Reform.* Revised edition, New York: Vintage Books, 1956.

Graham, Otis L., Jr. *An Encore for Reform: The Old Progressives and the New Deal.* New York: Oxford University Press, 1967.

Greer, Thomas H. *American Social Reform Movements: Their Pattern Since 1865.* New York: Prentice-Hall, 1949.

Griswold, A. Whitney. *Farming and Democracy.* New York: Harcourt, Brace and Company, Inc., 1948.

Harrington, W. P. "The Populist Party in Kansas," *Collections of the Kansas State Historical Society,* Vol. XVI.

Harvey, William Hope. *Coin's Financial School.* Chicago: Coin Publishing Company, 1894.

Haynes, Frederick Emory. *Third Party Movements since the Civil War, with Special Reference to Iowa: A Study in Social Politics.* Iowa City: State Historical Society of Iowa, 1916.

———. *James Baird Weaver.* Iowa City: State Historical Society of Iowa, 1919.

Hays, Samuel P. *The Response to Industrialism: 1885-1914.* Chicago: University of Chicago Press, 1957.

Herron, George D. *The New Redemption.* New York: Thomas Y. Crowell and Company, 1893. A social gospel novel.

Hibben, Paxton. *Peerless Leader, William Jennings Bryan.* New York: Farrar and Rinehart, Inc., 1929.

Hicks, John D. *The Populist Revolt: A*

History of the Farmers' Alliance and the People's Party. Minneapolis: University of Minnesota Press, 1931.

Hofstadter, Richard. *The Age of Reform: From Bryan to F.D.R.* New York: Alfred A. Knopf, 1956.

———. *The American Political Tradition and the Men Who Made It.* New York: Alfred A. Knopf, Inc., 1948.

———. *Social Darwinism in American Thought.* Revised edition, Boston: Beacon Press, 1964.

Johnson, Walter. *William Allen White's America.* New York: H. Holt, 1947.

Jones, Stanley L. *The Presidential Election of 1896.* Madison: University of Wisconsin Press, 1964.

Josephson, Matthew. *The Politicos, 1865-1896.* New York: Harcourt, Brace and Company, 1938.

———. *The Robber Barons: The Great American Capitalists, 1861-1901.* New York: Harcourt, Brace and Company, 1934.

The Kansas Day Club Addresses. Hutchinson: W. Y. Morgan, 1901.

Kelly, Alfred H., and Harbinson, Winfred A. *The American Constitution: Its Origins and Development.* 3rd edition, New York: W. W. Norton and Company, Inc., 1948.

Kirkland, Edward C. *Business in the Gilded Age: The Conservatives' Balance Sheet.* Madison: University of Wisconsin Press, 1952.

———. *Dream and Thought in the Business Community, 1860-1900.* Ithaca: Cornell University Press, 1956.

———. *Industry Comes of Age; Business, Labor and Public Policy, 1860-1897.* Vol. VI, "The Economic History of the United States," New York: Holt, Rinehart and Winston, Inc., 1961.

———. *Men, Cities and Transportation: A Study in New England History 1820-1900.* 2 vols., Cambridge: Harvard University Press, 1948.

Knoles, George H. *Presidential Campaign and Election of 1892.* Stanford University Press, 1942.

Kolko, Gabriel. *Railroads and Regulation, 1877-1916.* Princeton: Princeton University Press, 1965.

Kramer, Dale. *The Wild Jackasses; the American Farmer in Revolt.* New York: Hastings House, 1956.

Lease, Mary E. *The Problem of Civilization Solved.* Chicago: Laird and Lee, Publishers, 1895.

Leech, Margaret. *In the Days of McKinley.* New York: Harper and Brothers, 1959.

Leopold, Richard W., and Link, Arthur S., eds. *Problems in American History.* Englewood Cliffs: Prentice-Hall, Inc., 1957.

Lerner, Max. *America as a Civilization.* New York: Simon and Schuster, 1958.

Levine, Daniel. *Varieties of Reform Thought.* Madison: State Historical Society of Wisconsin, 1964.

Link, Arthur S. *Woodrow Wilson and the Progressive Era, 1910-1917.* New York: Harper and Row, 1963.

Lloyd, Henry D. *Wealth Against Commonwealth.* New York: Harper, 1895.

McCloskey, Robert Green. *American Conservatism in the Age of Enterprise, 1865-1910: A Study of William Graham Sumner, Stephen J. Field and Andrew*

Carnegie. New York: Harper and Row, 1964.

McMurry, Donald LeCrane. *Coxey's Army: A Study of the Industrial Army Movement of 1894.* Boston: Little, Brown and Company, 1929.

McVey, Frank LeRond. *The Populist Movement.* Vol. I, "Economic Studies." London: S. Sonnenschein and Company, 1896.

Malin, James C. *A Concern About Humanity: Notes on Reform, 1872-1912 at the National and Kansas Levels of Thought.* Lawrence: The Author, 1964.

——. *Winter Wheat in the Golden Belt of Kansas: A Study in Adaptation to Subhumid Geographical Environment.* Lawrence: University of Kansas Press, 1944.

Marx, Leo. *The Machine in the Garden: Technology and the Pastoral Ideal in America.* New York: Oxford University Press, 1967.

Merrill, Horace S. *Bourbon Leader: Grover Cleveland and the Democratic Party.* Boston: Little, Brown and Company, 1957.

Moody, John. *The Masters of Capital: A Chronicle of Wall Street.* New Haven: Yale University Press, 1919.

Morgan, H. Wayne, ed. *The Gilded Age: A Reappraisal.* Syracuse: Syracuse University Press, 1963.

——. *William McKinley and His America.* Syracuse: Syracuse University Press, 1963.

Mowry, George E. *The California Progressives.* Berkeley: University of California Press, 1951.

Nichols, Roy Franklin. *The Disruption of American Democracy.* New York: Macmillan Company, 1948.

Noblin, Stuart. *Leonidas LaFayette Polk: Agrarian Crusader.* Chapel Hill: University of North Carolina Press, 1949.

Nugent, Walter T. K. *The Money Question During Reconstruction.* New York: W. W. Norton and Company, 1967.

——. *The Tolerant Populists: Kansas, Populism and Nativism.* Chicago: University of Chicago Press, 1963.

Nye, Russell Blaine. *Midwestern Progressive Politics: A Historical Study of Its Origin and Development, 1870-1950.* East Lansing: Michigan State University Press, 1959.

Paulson, Ross E. *Radicalism and Reform: The Vrooman Family and American Social Thought, 1837-1937.* Lexington: University of Kentucky Press, 1968?

Peffer, William A. *Americanism and the Philippines.* Topeka: Crane and Company, 1900.

——. *Geraldine or What May Happen.* Novel serialized in the *Kansas Farmer,* Topeka, March 1-July 5, 1882.

Persons, Stowe. *American Minds: A History of Ideas.* New York: Holt, Rinehart and Winston, 1958.

Pollack, Norman, ed. *The Populist Mind.* Indianapolis and New York: The Bobbs-Merrill Company, Inc., 1967.

——. *The Populist Response to Industrial America: Midwestern Populist Thought.* Cambridge: Harvard University Press, 1962.

Quint, Howard H., *et al.,* ed. *Main Problems in American History.* 2 vols., Homewood, Illinois: The Dorsey Press, 1964.

Ridge, Martin. *Ignatius Donnelly: The Portrait of a Politician.* Chicago:

University of Chicago Press, 1962.

Saloutos, Theodore, and Hicks, John D. *Agricultural Discontent in the Middle West, 1900-1939.* Madison: University of Wisconsin Press, 1951.

Shannon, Fred A. *The Farmer's Last Frontier: Agriculture, 1860-1897.* Vol. V, "The Economic History of the United States." New York: Farrar and Rinehart, 1945.

Sharkey, Robert P. *Money, Class and Party: An Economic Study of Civil War and Reconstruction.* Baltimore: Johns Hopkins Press, 1959.

Simkins, Francis B. *Pitchfork Ben Tillman, South Carolinian.* Baton Rouge: Louisiana State University Press, 1944.

Smith, Henry Nash. *Virgin Land: The American West as Symbol and Myth.* Cambridge: Harvard University Press, 1950.

Socolofsky, Homer E. *Arthur Capper: Publisher, Politician, and Philanthropist.* Lawrence: University of Kansas Press, 1962.

Stedman, Murray S., Jr., and Stedman, Susan W. *Discontent at the Polls: A Study of Farmer and Labor Parties, 1827-1948.* New York: Columbia University, 1950.

Streeter, Floyd B. *The Kaw.* New York: Farrar and Rinehart, 1941.

Taylor, Carl Cleveland. *The Farmers' Movement, 1620-1920.* New York: American Book Company, 1953.

Taylor, George Rogers, and Neu, Irene D. *The American Railroad Network, 1861-1890.* Cambridge: Harvard University Press, 1956.

Thorelli, Hans Birger. *The Federal Antitrust Policy: Organization of an American Tradition.* Baltimore: Johns Hopkins University, 1955.

Unger, Irwin. *The Greenback Era: A Social and Political History of American Finance, 1865-1879.* Princeton: Princeton University Press, 1964.

Woodward, C. Vann. *Origins of the New South.* New York: Oxford University Press, 1962.

————. *Reunion and Reaction: The Compromise of 1877 and the End of Reconstruction.* Boston: Little, Brown and Company, 1951.

————. *Tom Watson, Agrarian Rebel.* New York: Macmillan Company, 1938.

Zornow, William Frank. *Kansas: A History of the Jayhawk State.* Norman: University of Oklahoma Press, 1957.

Articles

Barnes, James A. "The Gold-Standard Democrats and the Party Conflict," *Mississippi Valley Historical Review,* XVII (December, 1930), 422-50.

————. "Myths of the Bryan Campaign," *Mississippi Valley Historical Review,* XXXIV (December, 1947), 367-404.

Barr, Elizabeth N. "The Populist Uprising," in William Connelley, ed., *A Standard History of Kansas and Kansans,* Vol. II, 1115-95. New York: Lewis Historical Publishing Company, 1918.

Bicha, Karel Denis. "Jerry Simpson: Populist Without Principles," *The Journal of American His-*

tory, LIV (September, 1967), 291-306.

Bliss, William M. "Kansas—The Sunflower State," *Carter's Monthly,* XII (November, 1897), 565-98.

Breidenthal, John. "The Farmer and the Banker," *Quarterly Reports,* Kansas State Board of Agriculture, March, 1898, 42-47.

Clemens, G. C. "Satan, the Boss Knocker," *Kansas Knocker: A Journal for Cranks* (April, 1900), 29-33.

Clover, Benjamin H. "Sectionalism," *Farmers' Alliance History and Agricultural Digest* (1891), 253-56.

Cox, LaWanda F. "Agricultural Wage Earner, 1865-1900," *Agricultural History,* XXII (1948), 95-114.

Davis, C. Wood. "The Farmer, the Investor and the Railway," *Arena,* III (February, 1891), 291-313.

Delap, S. A. "The Populist Party in North Carolina," *Historical Papers,* XIV, 40-74. Durham: Trinity College Historical Society, 1922.

Destler, Chester M. "Consummation of a Labor-Populist Alliance in Illinois, 1894," *Mississippi Valley Historical Review,* XXVII (March, 1941), 589-602.

———. "The Opposition of American Businessmen to Social Control During the 'Gilded Age,' " *Mississippi Valley Historical Review,* XXXIX (March, 1953), 641-72.

Diamond, William. "Urban and Rural Voting in 1896," *American Historical Review,* XLVI (January, 1941), 281-305.

Diggs, Annie L. "The Farmers' Alliance and Some of Its Leaders," *Arena,* V (April, 1892), 590-604.

———. "The Women in the Alliance Movement," *Arena,* VI (July, 1892), 167-69.

Dillon, Sidney. "The West and the Railroads," *North American Review,* CLII (April, 1891), 443-52.

Doster, Frank. "Kansas Puritanism and Prohibition," *Plain Talk,* III (July, 1928), 21-27.

———. "What is Government For?" *Agora,* II (October, 1892), 120-26.

Durden, Robert F. "The 'Cow-Bird' Grounded: The Populist Nomination of Bryan and Tom Watson in 1896," *Mississippi Valley Historical Review,* L (December, 1963), 397-423.

Ellis, Elmer. "The Silver Republican in 1896," *Mississippi Valley Historical Review,* XVIII (1932), 519-34.

Farmer, Hallie. "The Economic Background of Frontier Populism," *Mississippi Valley Historical Review,* X (1924), 406-27.

———. "Economic Background of Southern Populism," *South Atlantic Quarterly,* XXIX (1930), 77-91.

———. "The Railroads and Frontier Populism," *Mississippi Valley Historical Review,* XIII (1926), 387-97.

Ferkiss, Victor C. "Populist Influences on American Fascism," *The Western Political Quarterly,* X (June, 1957), 350-73.

Fuller, L. W. "Colorado's Revolt Against Capitalism," *Mississippi Valley Historical Review,* XXI (December, 1934), 343-60.

Garland, Hamlin. "The Alliance Wedge in Congress," *Arena,* V (March, 1892), 447-67.

Garretson, O. A. "The Lewelling Family," *Iowa Journal of History* and Politics, XXXVII (October, 1929), 548-63.

Gates, Paul W. "The Homestead Law in an Incongruous Land System," American Historical Review, I (July, 1936), 562-81.

Harvey, A. M. "Hamilton and Jefferson and the American Constitution," Collections of the Kansas State Historical Society, 1926-1928, XVII, Topeka, 1928.

Hicks, John D. "Birth of the Populist Party," Minnesota History, IX (September, 1928), 219-47.

———. "Ignatius Donnelly," Mississippi Valley Historical Review, VIII (June, 1921), 80-132.

———. "People's Party in Minnesota," Minnesota History Bulletin, V (November, 1924), 531-60.

———. "Persistence of Populism," Minnesota History, XII (March, 1931), 3-20.

Johnson, Claudius O. "The Story of Silver Politics in Idaho, 1892-1902," Pacific Northwest Quarterly, XXXIII (1942), 283-96.

Klotche, J. Martin. " 'United Front' Populists," Wisconsin Magazine of History, XX (1937), 375-89.

Knauss, James O. "The Farmers' Alliance in Florida," South Atlantic Quarterly, XXV (1926), 300-15.

Lease, Mary E. "Do Kansas Women Want the Right to Vote?" Agora, II (January, 1893), 196-99.

———. "Unfinished Creation," Agora, II (January, 1893), 258-63.

Levinson, Harry. "Petticoat Politician," Kansas Magazine, 1949, 20-23.

Lewelling, L. D. "Address of Gov. Lewelling to the Kansas representatives at the World's Fair in Chicago," Report of the Kansas Board of World's Fair Managers. Topeka: Hamilton Printing Company, 1894.

———. "Problems Before the Western Farmer," North American Review, CLX (January, 1895), 16-20.

McCray, D. O. "The Farmers' Alliance and the Populist Party," in Transactions of the Kansas State Historical Society, 1905-1906, 425-26.

McMurry, D. L. "Industrial Armies and the Commonweal," Mississippi Valley Historical Review, X (December, 1923), 215-52.

Magaw, Charles A. "Gasper C. Clemens," Bulletin of the Shawnee County Historical Society (December, 1951), No. 15, pp. 10-11.

Malin, James C. "At What Age Did Men Become Reformers," Kansas Historical Quarterly, XXIX (Autumn, 1963), 250-61.

———. "Notes on the Literature of Populism," Kansas Historical Quarterly, I (February, 1932), 160-64.

———. "Some Reconsiderations of the Defeat of Senator Pomeroy of Kansas, 1873," Mid-America: An Historical Review, XLVII (January, 1966), 47-57.

Miller, Raymond C. "Background of Populism in Kansas," Mississippi Valley Historical Review, XI (March, 1925), 469-98.

Morris, Ralph C. "The Notion of a Great American Desert East of the Rockies," Mississippi Valley Historical Review, XIII (September, 1926), 190-200.

Nichols, Jeanette. "Bryan's Benefactor: Coin Harvey and His World," The Ohio Historical Quarterly, LXVII (1958), 299-325.

Nixon, Herman Clarence. "The Cleavage within the Alliance Movement," Mississippi Valley His-

torical Review, XV (1928), 22-33.

Nugent, Walter T. K. "Some Parameters of Populism," *Agricultural History,* XL (October, 1966), 255-70.

Peffer, William A. "The Farmers' Alliance," *Cosmopolitan,* X (April, 1891), 694-99.

———. "The Farmers' Defensive Movement," *Forum,* VIII (December, 1889), 464-73.

———. "Government Control of Money," *Farmers' Alliance History and Agricultural Digest,* 1891, pp. 262-71.

———. "The Mission of the Populist Party," *North American Review,* CLVII (December, 1893), 665-78.

———. "The Passing of the People's Party," *North American Review,* CLXVI (January, 1898), 12-23.

Polk, Leonidas L. "The Farmers' Discontent," *North American Review,* CLIII (July, 1891), 5-12.

Pollack, Norman. "Hofstadter on Populism: A Critique of *The Age of Reform,*" *Journal of Southern History,* XXVI (November, 1960), 478-500.

Saloutos, Theodore. "The Agricultural Problem and Nineteenth-Century Industrialism," *Agricultural History,* XXII (November, 1946), 156-74.

———. "The Professors and the Populists," *Agricultural History,* XL (October, 1966), 235-54.

Semple, R. H. "The Legislature of 1895," *Agora,* IV (April, 1895), 261-67.

Shannon, Fred A. "The Homestead Act and the Labor Surplus," *American Historical Review,* XLI (July, 1936), 637-61.

Simpson, Jerry. "The Knocker Who Knocks on the Knocker," *Kansas Knocker: A Journal for Cranks* (July, 1900), 19-21.

———. "The Plain People," *Illustrated American,* September 11, 1897, 332-35.

Svenson, Karl A. "Third Party Legislators," *Journal* [Kansas State Bar Association], XVII (February, 1949), 293-316.

Tracy, Frank B. "Menacing Socialism in the Western States," *Forum,* XV (May, 1893), 332-42.

Vrooman, Carl S. "The Agricultural Revolution," *Century Magazine,* XCIII (November, 1916), 111-23.

Weinstein, Allan. "Was There a 'Crime of 1873'?" *The Journal of American History,* LIV (September, 1967), 307-26.

Wellborn, Fred. "The Influence of the Silver-Republican Senators, 1889-1891," *Mississippi Valley Historical Review,* XIV (March, 1928), 462-80.

White, William Allen. "The End of an Epoch," *Scribner's Magazine,* LXXIX (June, 1926), 561-70.

Wish, Harvey. "John Peter Altgeld and the Background of the Campaign of 1896," *Mississippi Valley Historical Review,* XXIV (March, 1938), 503-18.

Woodward, C. Vann. "The Populist Heritage and the Intellectual," *American Scholar,* XXIX (Winter, 1959-1960), 55-72.

Unpublished Monographs

Barcus, George L. "The People's Party." Master's thesis, University of Kansas, 1902.

Brodhead, Michael J. "The Early Career of E. W. Hoch, 1870-1904."

Master's thesis, University of Kansas, 1962.

———. "Judge Frank Doster: Kansas Populist and Reform Ideologue." Doctoral dissertation, University of Minnesota, 1967.

Bryant, Girard Thompson. "The Populist Movement and the Negro." Master's thesis, University of Kansas, 1938.

Daniels, Dawn. "Lorenzo D. Lewelling —A Leader of the Kansas Populists." Master's thesis, Northwestern University, 1931.

Dew, Lee A. "Populist Fusion Movements as an Instrument of Political Reform, 1890-1900." Master's thesis, Kansas State College of Pittsburg, 1957.

Ecroyd, Donald Howarth. "An Analysis and Evaluation of Populist Political Campaign Speech Making in Kansas, 1890-1894." Doctoral dissertation, University of Iowa, 1949.

Flory, Raymond. "The Political Career of Chester I. Long." Doctoral dissertation, University of Kansas, 1955.

Frank, Keith. "Jerry Simpson: A Populist." Master's thesis, Northwestern University, 1939.

Gibson, Virginia Noah. "The Effect of the Populist Movement on Kansas State Agricultural College." Master's thesis, Kansas State College of Agriculture and Applied Science, 1932.

Harrington, W. P. "The Coxey Movement." Undergraduate thesis read before the Seminary of Political Science, Stanford University, 1895.

———. "The Populist Party in Kansas." Master's thesis, University of Kansas, 1924.

Harrison, Hortense Marie. "The Populist Delegation in the Fifty-Second Congress, 1891-1893."

Master's thesis, University of Kansas, 1933.

Lucas, A. G. Manuscript Biography of "Percy Daniels." K.S.H.S. Archives.

Lyman, Burton E. "Voting Behavior of Kansas Communities 1862-1936 as Measured by Pluralities for Governor and Secretary of State." Master's thesis, University of Kansas, 1937.

Miller, Glenn H. "Financing the Boom in Kansas, with Special Reference to Municipal Indebtedness and the Real Estate Mortgages." Master's thesis, University of Kansas, 1954.

Miller, Raymond C. "The Economic Basis of Populism in Kansas." Master's thesis, University of Chicago, 1923.

———. "The Populist Party in Kansas." Doctoral dissertation, University of Chicago, 1928.

Preshaw, Ada. "The Populist Movement in Kansas." Master's thesis, Columbia University, 1926.

Root, George A. "Mrs. Annie La Porte Diggs." Typed manuscript, K.S.H.S. Library.

Svenson, Karl A. "The Effect of Popular Discontent on Political Parties in Kansas." Doctoral dissertation, Iowa State University, 1948.

Walbourn, Edwin J., Jr. "Rump Legislature of Kansas, 1893: An Evaluation." Master's thesis, Kansas State College of Pittsburg, 1950.

Warner, Martha A. "Kansas Populism: A Sociological Analysis." Master's thesis, Kansas State College of Pittsburg, 1956.

Williams, Burton John. "John James Ingalls: A Personal Portrait of a Public Figure." Doctoral dissertation, University of Kansas, 1965.

INDEX

Lewelling, L. D., his address at the 1892 Populist state convention, 117; victory of, 128; his background and his inaugural address, 129-31; the "Tramp Circular," 148-49; address at Huron Place, 164; vote of in 1894, 168; speaks out against bribery charges, 208; statement of, regarding trusts, 221-22; supports the candidacy of Clemens on the Socialist ticket, 223-24; concerning his nomination in 1892, 275n; biographical sketch, 278n; mentioned, 125, 134, 135, 138, 141, 144, 152, 163, 186, 188, 190, 197, 205, 207, 210, 215, 220, 277n, 280n, 283n, 284n, 292n, 296n, 301

Lincoln, Abraham, 105

Little, John T., 119, 167, 276n

Lloyd, Henry D., mentioned, 10, 177

Looking Backward, 2000-1887, 81

M'Call, B. B., speech of, 172, 175

McCormick, Mrs. Fanny, 60

McCray, David Owen, 145, 208

McGrath, Frank, state Alliance leader resists third-party activity, 102-3; mentioned, 271n, 273n

McKay, George Washington, 207

McKinley, William, mentioned, 185, 190, 196

McLallin, Dr. Stephen, leads the way in the call for third-party action, 53; quoted relative to the origin of the People's party, 55; an outspoken critic of social Darwinism, 67; persuades Annie Diggs to join his editorial staff, 79; comment on Corning, 141; name appears in Lease note, 145; on socialism, 147; fights the move to make silver the issue, 176; retires as editor, 179; mentioned, 54, 93, 104, 114, 118, 177, 218, 270n, 275n, 294n

McLallin, Mrs. M. H., 270n

Malin, James C., comment of relative to the meaning of the 1890 election, 103; on the appeal of the silver issue in Kansas, 190

Marshall, William V., champions competition and opposes the cooperative movement, 46-47; mentioned, 71-72

Martin, John, encourages Democrats to support the Populist ticket, 122; mentioned, 119, 125, 133

Martin, Governor John A., remark of, 35; mentioned, 107

Marx, Karl, mentioned in speech, 108; mentioned in statement by Annie Diggs, 226

Maxson, P. B., 270n

Midland Hotel Conference, 115

Mill, John Stuart, mentioned in speech, 108

Miller, G. E., 158

Miller, Raymond, comment of relative to Kansas mortgages, 28

Miller, Sol, comment of, 110; his reaction to the 1896 Populist national convention, 189-90; on the influence of railroads in Kansas, 260n; mentioned, 122, 126, 277n

Mitchell, Charles F., 182

Moore, H. L., 116, 122, 127

Morrill Act, 14

Morrill, E. N., strikes a keynote for his administration, 170; mentioned, 122, 151, 152, 168, 190, 210

Morris, I. M., 51

Morris, W. H., 189

Murdock, Marshall, blasts the Kansas legislature, 52

Murdock, Victor, on why Simpson came out West, 83; mentioned, 236

National Citizens' Industrial Alliance, organization of, 97

New Freedom, mentioned in relationship to a Populist factional position, 71, 72

New Nationalism, mentioned in relationship to a Populist factional position, 71

New York *Sun,* comments of, 110-11

North American Review, reference to, 5, 8

Norton, Colonel, mentioned, 98

Ocala, Alliance meeting of, 96
Origin of Species, 9
Osage City (Kansas), voting patterns of, 290n
Osage County (Kansas), analysis of the voting patterns therein, 180-83
Osborn, Russell Scott, comment of, 141; mentioned, 60, 119, 131-32, 163, 167, 272n
Otis, John Grant, comment on religion, 66; biographical sketch and his campaign for congress in 1890, 80-81; quoted with respect to the meaning of Populism, 105; mentioned, 104, 115, 128, 159, 162, 236, 274-75n, 290n
Overmeyer, David, reveals an alleged fusion deal, 115; mentioned, 119, 276n

Parrington, Vernon L., interpretation of, 2
Peck, George R., 143, 280n
Peffer, William Alfred, his background and his position on the eve of the revolt, 37-39; advises against hasty political moves, 52; begins publication of "The Way Out," 54; open letter by, 55; opposes Senator Ingalls, 57; on the Gospel of Wealth, 67; candidate for the U.S. senate, 87; elected U.S. senator, 90; remarks to the Cincinnati conference, 99; the issue of his reelection, 199-200; heads Prohibition ticket in Kansas, 219; his response to progressivism, 238; his reaction to some prominent issues in Kansas politics, 261n; explains the Populist position on money, 289n; mentioned, 53, 54, 104, 179, 183, 209-10, 216, 294n, 298n, 300n
Peoples Herald, The, 182, 183
Pittsburg *Kansan*, poem quoted from, 25
Plumb, Preston B., exposes a weak link in the reform chain, 106; mentioned, 54, 104, 133
Polk, L. L., 123

Pomeroy, Samuel C., career terminated, 24
Populism, the problem of spasmodic motivation, 31-32; force and direction of, 32; the issue of cooperation versus competition, 71-72; a fundamental position of, stated by W. D. Vincent, 68; what it signified in the minds of its followers in 1891, as expressed by J. G. Otis, 105; the essence of, as stated by J. M. Dunsmore, 216; denouement of, 215; historical interpretation of, 264n, 285n, 286-287n, 289n, 291n, 297n, 302n
Populist party, organization of, in Kansas, 56; the platform of 1890, 60-61; a caricature of its leaders, 63; a composite of state leaders, 63-65; its victories in the 1890 campaign, 87-88; the 1890 effort outside Kansas, 95; the Cincinnati conference, 97-99, 272n; the St. Louis conference (1892), 113-14; the 1892 state convention, 116-21; the Omaha convention (1892), 123-24; the 1894 state convention, 152-63; the vote in the state election of 1894, 168; the 1896 state convention, 187; the Sewall-Watson arrangement in Kansas, 187; the fusion effort of 1896, 188-89; the state convention of 1898, 214-15; the state campaign of 1900, 225-27; achievements of the party in Kansas, 232-34; assessment of the leadership, 242-43
Power, C. A., 96
Prather, Van B., 119, 270n
Prohibition, role of, in Kansas politics, 100-1; as an issue in Lewelling's administration, 139; special relationship to woman suffrage, 153, 157, 162, 190; Leedy's position on, 210

Railroads, impact of expansion, 12-13; federal assistance to, 14; some Kansas statistics, 18-19; appeal of in early Kansas history, 18, 20; financing of in Kansas, 27-28
Randolph, J. V., 270n